The Science of
Attorney Advocacy

The LAW AND PUBLIC POLICY: PSYCHOLOGY AND THE SOCIAL SCIENCES series includes books in three domains:

Legal Studies—writings by legal scholars about issues of relevance to psychology and the other·social sciences, or that employ social science information to advance the legal analysis;

Social Science Studies—writings by scientists from psychology and the other social sciences about issues of relevance to law and public policy; and

Forensic Studies—writings by psychologists and other mental health scientists and professionals about issues relevant to forensic mental health science and practice.

The series is guided by its editor, Bruce D. Sales, PhD, JD, ScD (hc), Indiana University; and coeditors, Bruce J. Winick, JD, University of Miami; Daniel A. Krauss, JD, PhD, ABPP, Claremont McKenna College; and Valerie P. Hans, PhD, Cornell University Law School.

* * *

The Science of Attorney Advocacy

HOW COURTROOM BEHAVIOR
AFFECTS JURY DECISION MAKING

Jessica D. Findley
Bruce D. Sales

AMERICAN PSYCHOLOGICAL ASSOCIATION
WASHINGTON, DC

Published by
American Psychological Association
750 First Street, NE
Washington, DC 20002
www.apa.org

To order
APA Order Department
P.O. Box 92984
Washington, DC 20090-2984
Tel: (800) 374-2721; Direct: (202) 336-5510
Fax: (202) 336-5502; TDD/TTY: (202) 336-6123
Online: www.apa.org/pubs/books
E-mail: order@apa.org

In the U.K., Europe, Africa, and the Middle East, copies may be ordered from
American Psychological Association
3 Henrietta Street
Covent Garden, London
WC2E 8LU England

Typeset in Goudy by Circle Graphics, Inc., Columbia, MD

Printer: United Book Press, Baltimore, MD
Cover Designer: Berg Design, Albany, NY

The opinions and statements published are the responsibility of the authors, and such opinions and statements do not necessarily represent the policies of the American Psychological Association.

Library of Congress Cataloging-in-Publication Data

Findley, Jessica D.
  The science of attorney advocacy : how courtroom behavior affects jury decision making / Jessica D. Findley and Bruce D. Sales. — 1st ed.
     p. cm. — (Law and public policy)
  Includes bibliographical references and index.
  ISBN-13: 978-1-4338-1098-5 (alk. paper)
  ISBN-10: 1-4338-1098-0 (alk. paper)
  1. Jurors—United States—Decision making. 2. Jurors—United States—Psychology.
3. Trial practice—United States. I. Sales, Bruce Dennis. II. Title.

  KF8972.F56 2012
  347.73'752—dc23
                                            2011030196

British Library Cataloguing-in-Publication Data

A CIP record is available from the British Library.

Printed in the United States of America
First Edition

DOI: 10.1037/13495-000

To my parents
—*Jessica D. Findley*

To Betsy
—*Bruce D. Sales*

CONTENTS

ACKNOWLEDGMENTS

We thank Judith Becker and Matthias Mehl for their careful read of and helpful suggestions on an earlier version of this manuscript.

The Science of
Attorney Advocacy

1

INTRODUCTION

Texas multimillionaire and oil heir T. Cullen Davis and his estranged wife, Priscilla, were in the process of a bitter, public divorce trial in August 1976. Reports indicated that Davis was livid on August 2 when the judge awarded Priscilla $5,000 per month in spousal maintenance (Gribben, n.d.; Rosenthal & Cochran, 1977). The night of the divorce proceeding, Priscilla and her boyfriend, Stan Farr, went out to celebrate the victory, leaving her 12-year-old daughter, Andrea, home alone in the $6 million Fort Worth mansion, where Priscilla was living ("The Law: Murder," 1977).

When Priscilla and Farr arrived home, she discovered the alarm had been deactivated and a bloody handprint was on the wall leading down to the basement (Gribben, n.d.; Rosenthal & Cochran, 1977). As Priscilla called for Farr, an intruder dressed in black with a woman's black wig on his head emerged from the laundry room and said "hi" before shooting Priscilla in the chest. Farr and the intruder struggled, and Farr was shot four times. Priscilla fled, screaming "Cullen shot me!" (Cochran, 1977a). The shooter caught up with Priscilla when she fell outside and was trying to drag her back into the mansion when another couple approached the mansion. The intruder then shot the young man, allowing Priscilla and the other woman enough time to escape, one to flag down a passing car and one to run to a neighbor's house and call the police (Rosenthal & Cochran, 1977).

When the police arrived, Farr was dead in the kitchen (Rosenthal & Cochran, 1977), and Andrea, also dead, was found in the basement with a gunshot wound to her chest (Gorney, 1978). The other people who were injured survived, but they were about to be subjected to the lengthy and difficult trial of T. Cullen Davis for the murder of his estranged wife's 12-year-old daughter. (No trial was ever held for the murder of Farr because of concerns that a Texas jury would not convict because of "Texas Victorianism," or as one prosecutor indicated, "Killing a wife's lover is no big deal here." [Steele & Kasindorf, 1977, p. 30]).

Davis arguably hired the best defense money could buy (e.g., Rosenthal & Cochran, 1977). Richard "Racehorse" Haynes served as Davis's lead defense counsel, and at the time, Haynes had the reputation of being one of the best criminal lawyers in America (Rosenthal & Cochran, 1977). Haynes quickly began implementing strategies that undoubtedly helped him earn his accolades as a top defense lawyer. First, he successfully achieved a change of venue to Amarillo, Texas, which had a reputation as a conservative community that frowned upon women who cheated on their husbands (Gorney, 1978; Gribben, n.d.). The new venue was likely to work against the prosecution, whose main witness was Priscilla—a busty, platinum blonde who frequently wore revealing outfits and a necklace that spelled out "Rich Bitch" in diamonds (Rosenthal & Cochran, 1977).

Next, Haynes went to work establishing his case that Davis had an alibi for the time of the murder (Gorney, 1978). As part of his strategy to boost the believability of the alibi, Haynes planned to provide alternative scenarios that someone else committed the crime. Haynes later explained his strategy to the American Bar Association (ABA): "Say you sue me because you say my dog bit you. Well, now this is my defense: my dog doesn't bite. And second, in the alternative, my dog was tied up that night. And third, I don't believe you really got bit. And fourth, I don't have a dog" (Curriden, 2009).

Haynes waited until his cross-examination of Priscilla to fully explore alternative scenarios for the murders that contradicted the prosecution's theory that Davis committed the crime. Chief prosecutor Joe Shannon described the strategy as, "It's a defense of ABC—Anybody But Cullen" (Rosenthal & Cochran, 1977). During the 13-day cross-examination of Priscilla, Haynes explored the possibilities that (a) Priscilla had masterminded the murders to get Davis's money (Rosenthal & Cochran, 1977), (b) Farr was the primary target of the murders (Cochran, 1977b), (c) Priscilla wanted Farr dead in order to end her relationship with him (Gorney, 1978), and (d) unknown drug dealers may have been involved in the murders (Steele & Kasindorf, 1977).

In addition, Haynes supplemented his strategy by attacking the prosecution's chief witness. He described Priscilla as a "Machiavellian influence" and a "Dr. Jeckyll and Mr. Hyde," who associated with "scuzzies, scallawage, rogues, and brigands" (Gorney, 1978). In support of his portrayal of Priscilla, Haynes used a photograph of a former drug-dealing boyfriend and Priscilla in which the boyfriend only wore a sock on his genitals, elicited information from her about several former lovers (Cochran, 1977b), presented testimony that she participated in orgies (Gorney, 1978), accused her of being addicted to Percodan and marijuana (Rosenthal & Cochran, 1977), and alleged that she corrupted the morals of the young people in her care on a trip to College Station, Texas, during which sex and drug use occurred (Gorney, 1978).

Haynes's strategy to discredit Priscilla appeared to have worked. When her testimony was over and she left the courtroom, some of the women in the audience hissed at her (Hollandsworth, 2001). One reporter claimed that Haynes had successfully painted Priscilla as the "biggest slut in the state" (Gribben, n.d.). Another report claimed that "when Haynes finished with her, the jury had practically forgotten that her own daughter had been murdered" (Hollandsworth, 2001, p. 30). Haynes's success at putting Priscilla on trial instead of Davis was further documented by reports that a courtroom observer said, "I can tell she's guilty, just by looking" (Clemons, 1979, p. 70). However, the ultimate support for the success of Haynes' trial strategy was the verdict: not guilty (Rosenthal & Cochran, 1977).

THE IMPORTANCE OF TRIAL ADVOCACY

Attorney representation is basic to the concept of a fair trial. The Sixth Amendment to the United States Constitution states: "In all criminal prosecutions, the accused shall enjoy the right . . . to have the Assistance of Counsel for his defence." This right was expanded to state courts through the Fourteenth Amendment. In *Powell v. Alabama* (1932), a case that overturned the convictions of African American defendants for capital offenses because they did not have a lawyer's assistance in their defense, Justice Sutherland explained the importance of legal representation:

> The right to be heard would be, in many cases, of little avail if it did not comprehend the right to be heard by counsel. Even the intelligent and educated layman has small and sometimes no skill in the science of law. If charged with crime, he is incapable, generally, of determining for himself whether the indictment is good or bad. He is unfamiliar with the rules of evidence. Left without the aid of counsel he may be put on trial without a proper charge, and convicted upon incompetent evidence, or evidence irrelevant to the issue or otherwise inadmissible. He lacks both

the skill and knowledge adequately to prepare his defense, even though he have a perfect one. He requires the guiding hand of counsel at every step in the proceedings against him. Without it, though he be not guilty, he faces the danger of conviction because he does not know how to establish his innocence. (pp. 68–69)

There is no right to an attorney in most civil trials; for an exception see laws relating to involuntary civil commitment where an actual loss of liberty can occur. This poses a considerable risk to one's personal and financial interests because arguably legal representation is vital for civil litigation. In response, many attorneys will take certain civil cases on a contingent fee basis (Lind et al., 1990), while nonprofit legal aid organizations will represent some clients whose incomes fall below a certain threshold and whose case is not prohibited by the rules of their organization (Houseman & Perle, 2003).

In American courts, legal representation is defined by the adversarial system of justice, which is founded on the idea that truth will emerge victorious from pitting each side's arguments and evidence against the other. The courtroom becomes a metaphorical arena, in which the attorneys must act as gladiators, prepared to battle for their clients. Instead of using weapons, however, the lawyers' arsenal comprises their intellect—their ability to outwit and outstrategize the opposing attorney to win the trier of fact's (i.e., the jury, or the judge in a bench trial) favor.

The perception of lawyers as aggressive warriors for their clients also stems from their ethical guidelines, which require them to zealously advocate for their clients: "The duty of a lawyer, both to his client and to the legal system, is to represent his client zealously within the bounds of the law" (ABA, 1980, Canon 7). "A lawyer must . . . act with commitment and dedication to the interests of the client and with zeal in advocacy upon the client's behalf" (ABA, 2009, Rule 1.3, comment).

As the T. Cullen Davis trial illustrates, lawyers do not dispassionately apply the law to the facts like a judge or jury should or try to balance the various interests of all involved like a legislator should (Markovits, 2003). Instead, they are responsible for molding the facts and the law in a way that is likely to benefit their clients, sometimes in a way that appears unsavory to a layperson or scientist (Markovits, 2003). For example, Racehorse Haynes was known for strenuously advocating for his clients by confusing issues with many alternative scenarios, even though this strategy meant badgering and discrediting opposing witnesses. One prosecutor complained: "Haynes's technique is to go on and on. He gets time on his side and gets the jury thinking about everything but the facts in the case" (Axthelm, 1978, p. 83). In response to the criticism, Haynes retorted:

I've been accused a thousand times of using red herrings and wasting time, but I owe it to my client to make sure that law-enforcement people have dotted all their i's and crossed their t's. I like that red-her-ring talk anyway. Many times, that's what the prosecutor says when he really means, "Oh damn it, this guy just showed that his client didn't do it." (Axthelm, 1978, p. 83)

Not all trial advocates approach their role in same way as Haynes. For example, in Harper Lee's Pulitzer Prize winning novel *To Kill a Mockingbird*, attorney Atticus Finch relied on logic and the evidence to defend his client. Finch was representing a black man who had been charged with raping and beating a white woman. In his closing argument, Finch logically argues that it was impossible for the defendant, who did not have use of his left hand because it had been mangled in an accident, to have assaulted the woman because the evidence indicated that the perpetrator was left-handed. Finch argued that the woman's father, who was left-handed, was likely to have been the one who manufactured the assault:

> Her father saw it, and the defendant has testified as to his remarks. What did her father do? We don't know, but there is circumstantial evidence to indicate that Mayella Ewell was beaten savagely by someone who led almost exclusively with his left. We do know in part what Mr. Ewell did: he did what any God-fearing, persevering, respectable white man would do under the circumstances—he swore out a warrant, no doubt signing it with his left hand, and Tom Robinson now sits before you, having taken the oath with the only good hand he possesses—his right hand. (Lee, 1960, pp. 272–273)

Although Haynes and the fictional Atticus Finch used different approaches to advocate on behalf of their clients, finding successful advocacy approaches and techniques is essential for the practicing bar. Indeed, its importance is exemplified by the writings of legal practitioners and academics who offer recommendations to attorneys for maximizing success in court. In addition, their commentary has been put into trial practice handbooks and is frequently taught in law schools as part of the trial advocacy curriculum (e.g., Mauet, 2005). These strategies are often derived from past personal experience or from studying strategies employed by other successful attorneys. Occasionally, the trial manuals even claim insight into "courtroom psychology," but typically the trial commentators are relying on "pop" psychology (i.e., popular assumptions or intuition about how people respond socially and behaviorally in areas such as communication, comprehension, and persuasion), seldom using social and behavioral scientific research as the basis for their proposed strategies.

It is troubling that the strategies many attorneys are being taught and rely on to advocate for their clients may be unsubstantiated or even contradicted by social scientific research. In the event of a trial, at a minimum, one is likely to risk financial losses, but in the event of criminal charges, one could potentially lose his or her liberty. When attorneys use advocacy techniques that are based on untested assumptions and intuitions about human behavior, their clients' interests may be jeopardized.

THE GOALS OF THIS VOLUME

Given the importance of trial advocacy in our legal system, and the importance of differentiating intuition and speculation from scientific proof of efficacy, the primary goal of this volume is to consider critically the scientific support for the advocacy recommendations by trial commentators and identify the limitations in their recommendations. Where there is research directly on point (i.e., conducted in a trial or simulated trial setting), we cite it. We also incorporate research that, although not conducted to assess attorney persuasiveness, is nonetheless informative for understanding their strategies and actions. We also define key concepts using legal definitions when the trial commentators provide them, resorting to common English-language definitions when no legal one is available. English-language definitions are a logical default when the law and trial commentator do not provide an alternative. Lawyers are most likely to use the common language definitions for words because they often have no scientific training. We then operationalized whatever definition was applied, using scientific definitions for our critical analysis of the relevant scientific literature. Finally, we discuss scientific theories that may help address these attorney behaviors. Based on our critical review of the relevant scientific literature, our secondary goal is to suggest research-based advocacy techniques that are likely to persuade the jury and that we hope will encourage a new generation of research in this important area.

Although the judge would serve as the trier of fact where there is no jury, our recommendations focus on juror and jury influence for two reasons. First, the trial commentators primarily strategize about jury trials and not bench trials. Second, even though judges and jurors are subject to cognitive biases, there is not enough research to presume that jurors and judges will respond in substantially similar ways to attorney advocacy. Indeed there is good reason to presume that they would not. Judges have special expertise, not represented among most jurors: three years of legal training, years of trial practice prior to ascending to the bench, and familiarity with the trial commentators' recommendations for attorney advocacy. Although judges, like all humans, experience cognitive biases they likely would be more critical consumers of attorney trial strategies and techniques than jurors. Until empirical research on judges' versus jurors' reactions to attorneys proves otherwise, scholarly rigor dictates that we not assume that our analysis will apply equally to both groups.

The chapters are organized to thoroughly review advocacy recommendations. First, each chapter summarizes the trial commentators' recommendations
with regard to a specific area of advocacy. As a convention throughout the
book, we use the phrase "trial commentators" to refer to lawyers and law
professors who write about how practicing attorneys should conduct their
in-court advocacy. We use the terms "lawyers" and "attorneys" interchangeably
to refer to practicing attorneys who are the intended audience for the trial
commentators' advice. Next, each chapter critically evaluates the legal recommendations in light of the relevant social and behavioral scientific research
literature and draws conclusions about the likely success of using the strategies
during trial given the current state of the scientific knowledge.

Using this template, Chapter 2 reviews research addressing trial commentators' claims about how the attorneys' courtroom demeanor affects
attorney persuasiveness. The chapter is organized according to the scientific
literature's identification of likability, honesty, and confidence as the underlying characteristics of demeanor that are perceived by others.

Given the importance of attorney communication, Chapters 3, 4, and 5
separate out the recommendations of trial commentators with regard to
verbal and nonverbal communications. Chapter 3 focuses on attorneys' verbal
communications, critically considering trial commentators' recommended
techniques for improving comprehension and persuasiveness of the attorneys'
verbal message. Chapters 4 and 5 deal with the nonverbal aspects of communication. Researchers typically define nonverbal communication as "individual
differences in sending (i.e., encoding) and/or receiving (i.e., decoding) abilities"
(Burgoon & Bacue, 2003, p. 181), which includes the following:

1. kinesics, which are visual body movements or body language
   (e.g., gestures, facial expressions, and gaze);
2. paralinguistics, paralanguage or vocalics, which is the use of vocal
   cues other than the specific words (e.g., pitch, loudness, tempo);
3. physical appearance, which includes manipulated features of
   appearance (e.g., clothing, hairstyle, and adornments such as
   jewelry) and features (e.g., height) that are not manipulable;
4. haptics, which refers to one's use of touch to communicate;
5. proxemics, which refers to one's use of interpersonal distance
   and spacing;
6. chronemics, which includes the use of time as part of the message
   (e.g., waiting time, lead time, and amount of time spent with
   someone); and
7. Artifacts, which are objects and environmental features that
   may be manipulated to carry messages from their users (Burgoon,
   1985).

Researchers do not always agree about how to categorize some of the various aspects of nonverbal communications. For example, some scholars include intonation as a nonverbal, prosodic aspect of linguistics (e.g., Cruse, 1990), whereas other scholars categorize intonation primarily as an element of paralinguistics (e.g., Pennycook, 1985). Likewise, a narrow definition of paralinguistics may focus on vocal aspects of language; on the other hand, a broad definition of paralanguage extends the term to include kinesics and proxemics (e.g., Pennycook, 1985).

Given the disagreement about how to categorize nonverbal communication, we have chosen to focus on two overarching categories: paralinguistics, which is discussed in Chapter 4; and kinesics, which is discussed in Chapter 5. Like some scholars, we exercise flexibility with the classifications of nonverbal behavior and subsumed some of the other classes of nonverbal language under these categories for convenience in responding to trial commentators' claims. For instance, trial commentators note that attorneys should be loud because of the distance they must stand from the jury. Therefore, we subsumed distance under the paralinguistics chapter where we discuss loudness, instead of including a separate category of proxemics. We have subsumed additional nonverbal classes such as physical appearance and artifacts under kinesics because many of the trial commentators' strategies relate to physically manipulating these features.

Chapter 6 focuses on developing the attorney–client relationship for increasing effectiveness at trial. This chapter investigates trial commentators' beliefs concerning a close attorney–client relationship and why they believe it is useful not only for obtaining information to use at trial but also for persuading the jury about the credibility of the client.

Chapter 7 explores trial commentators' beliefs about the importance of storytelling at trial. In addition to other legal assertions about how narratives can be persuasive at trial, a major focus of this chapter is the role of the attorney's theory and theme as part of the storytelling strategy.

Chapter 8 concludes the exploration into the advocacy recommendations offered by trial commentators by considering the methodological limitations in the extant research, discussing ways of targeting future research to improve the effectiveness of attorney advocacy, and exploring the importance of using theory to focus future research. The chapter also discusses the need for developing attorney–researcher partnerships to advance this area of potential research.

In conclusion, this book is primarily intended to familiarize researchers in psychology, communications, linguistics, and other social sciences with the trial strategies being espoused by trial commentators; critically consider the existing scientific research relevant to trial advocacy; and provide valuable information about the effectiveness of current recommendations by trial commentators. Trial commentators and practicing attorneys should find our integration of prior trial commentators' advice of interest and value. In addition, trial commentators and practicing attorneys should find interesting how their assumptions and recommendations about what makes good lawyers and lawyering in court fare under critical scientific scrutiny. Ultimately, our hope is that this knowledge will stimulate more collaborations between social scientists and attorneys and promote substantial programmatic research into this area, which will lead to more effective legal advocates who can meet their ethical, professional, and legal obligations.

2

ATTORNEY DEMEANOR

Many lawyer-written trial advocacy books highlight the importance of attorney demeanor (i.e., behavior and conduct) in achieving a successful case outcome. These books identify the following behavioral characteristics as key to winning favor with the jury: likability, honesty, and credibility. This chapter discusses each of these characteristics. We first present the claims in the legal literature about attorney demeanor. We then review the science that directly or indirectly addresses those claims, and conclude with a discussion of the accuracy of attorney claims, the quality of the science that addresses those claims, and the implications for attorney demeanor and advocacy.

ATTORNEY DEMEANOR IN THE LEGAL LITERATURE

Likability

Most trial commentators agree that attorneys whom jurors find likable will have a significant advantage over those attorneys whom jurors do not like. Unfortunately, trial commentators do not explicitly define likability. Thus, we must assume that they intended the common meaning of the term. That is, *likability* refers to the extent to which the lawyer is perceived by the jurors as possessing favorable qualities (i.e., pleasing, agreeable, appealing, attractive, sympathetic; *American Heritage Dictionary of the English Language*, 2000; *Merriam-Webster's Collegiate Dictionary*, 2009; *Compact Oxford English Dictionary of Current English*, 2005).

Lawyers associate being perceived as likable by jurors as increasing the jurors' trust in them (Perrin, Caldwell, & Chase, 2003) and belief in their credibility (Kosieradzki, 2001) and as increasing their ability to persuade jurors (Fontham, 2002). The underlying logic for these attorneys is that jurors favor people they like and thus are more likely to see the lawyers' court presentations as effective (Easton, 1998). Some trial commentators go even further, arguing that juries give verdicts to people that they like (Berg, 2003/2006; Mauet, 1992, 2005) on the logic that "if the jurors like an attorney, they will often bend themselves into pretzels to find in his or her client's favor" (Singer, 2000, p. 80).

Trial commentators suggest several strategies for cultivating likability. One is to appear similar to the members of the jury, based on the belief that people tend to trust and like people who are more similar to them (Perrin et al., 2003). Some trial commentators suggest offering selective, personal disclosures when speaking to the jury as a way to make this similarity connection (Perrin et al., 2003). However, there are two problems with this approach. First, the similarity-connection proponents do not specifically discuss in what ways lawyers should try to appear similar. Second, some trial commentators highlight the importance of lawyers being themselves (Bocchino, 2001; Easton, 1998). For example, Bocchino (2001) believed that lawyers must have an accurate self-image and be realistic about their abilities and how they are viewed by others. For Bocchino, if an attorney uses tactics or techniques outside the attorney's "natural range" (p. 7), he or she will "ring false" (p. 7) to the jurors, thereby hurting the attorney's likability in the eyes of the jury.

On the assumption that good manners will be pleasing, agreeable, appealing, and attractive to jurors, a second strategy to convince jurors that an attorney is likable is to use good manners with the jury. The quality of good manners is typically referred to in the legal literature as "being courteous" (Easton, 1998; Lubet, 2000; Mauet, 1992; Murray, 1995). Some trial commentators encourage trial lawyers to (a) be polite (e.g., saying "please" and "thank you"; Fontham, 2002, p. 74; Ball, 1993, 1997; Perrin et al., 2003); (b) build lawyer–jury rapport by treating the trial participants and the court personnel with respect (Perrin et al., 2003); (c) be "friendly, helpful, and caring" (Ball, 1993, p. 8; 1997, p. 10); and (d) be on their best behavior, even when not in trial because the jury may see their behavior outside of trial and make judgments about the lawyer that carry over to the trial (Singer, 2000). More specifically, these and other trial commentators encourage trial lawyers to introduce themselves and cocounsel at the beginning of the voir dire (Singer, 2000), appropriately address the court (Murray, 1995), apologize when in the wrong (Perrin et al., 2003), and be respectful of opposing counsel and his or her witnesses (Lubet, 2000; Rumsey, 1986).

Similarly, some trial commentators advise lawyers against displaying behaviors that would be considered bad manners, including avoiding personal attacks against opposing witnesses, lawyers, and parties because people who make these attacks "look cheap," because jurors find this behavior condescending (i.e., the behavior implies that the jury will use prejudice rather than the merits of the case to reach its decision), and because personal attacks dilute the effectiveness of "truly devastating" evidence (Rumsey, 1986, p. 79). They also recommend that lawyers avoid behaviors that would lead jurors to believe that they are sarcastic or patronizing (Jeans, 1993); egotistical (Easton, 1998); "control freak[s]" because jurors will "dig in their heels in natural rebellion"; self-aggrandizing because jurors "resent showoffs" (Singer, 2000, p. 80); or rude or disrespectful to the opposing counsel, witnesses, and the judge (Lubet, 2000; see also Jossen, 1986; Rumsey, 1986). Trial commentators note that acting rudely is counterproductive because "jurors, like most people, do not like shows of hostility or anger" (Jossen, 1986, p. 70; Berg, 2003/2006) and this behavior will alienate the judge and jurors (Haydock & Sonsteng, 1991).

Although showing good manners is stressed in the trial advocacy literature, it will require insight into situational factors in the trial. For example, being overly friendly with the opposing side is not advised, as jurors will conclude that "the trial is simply a game" (Easton, 1998, p. 58). In addition, trial advocates are cautioned to be assertive, insistent, or even aggressive in some situations (Jeans, 1993). For example, while trial lawyers are advised to always be respectful, sometimes trial lawyers must let the jurors know that they do not respect what the opposing counsel or experts are trying to do in the courtroom (Easton, 1998). In addition, there will be times when a witness or opposing counsel should lose the right to the attorney's respect, and in these situations the jury will expect the attorney to treat that person accordingly (Perrin et al., 2003).

A third recommended strategy for building likability is for lawyers to show themselves as real people: "any trial attorney can captivate the jurors' hearts and minds if . . . he or she allows the jurors to see the full, unguarded person inside the professional" (Association of Trial Lawyers of America, 2003). By demonstrating vulnerability, the trial attorney will project himself or herself as a person who is willing to "forgo self-protection" to protect the client (Association of Trial Lawyers of America, 2003).

Honesty

The legal literature suggests that if jurors perceive attorneys to possess the quality of honesty, then those attorneys will have more success in persuading the jury. As with likability, no legal definition has been provided for honesty, so once again we are left with the assumption that the common definition of this term was intended. *Honesty* is commonly defined as truthfulness; integrity, or adherence to a strict moral or ethical code; fairness, or avoiding self-interest and following appropriate procedures; and sincerity, or avoiding duplicity (*American Heritage Dictionary of the English Language*, 2000; *Merriam-Webster's Collegiate Dictionary*, 2009; *Compact Oxford English Dictionary of Current English*, 2005). Trial advocacy commentators appear to equate sincerity with being true to oneself (Ball, 1993, 1997; Easton, 1998; Fontham, 2002; Hanley, 1986).

Strategies recommended by trial commentators to help lawyers achieve the appearance of honesty include the following:

1. always telling the truth because the judge and jury rely on the attorney's word (Easton, 1998);
2. not overstating their case (Easton, 1998; Mauet, 1992, 2005; Lubet, 2000);
3. not promising evidence that they do not have (Lubet, 2000; Mauet, 1992, 2005);
4. not breaking promises made in trial (Perrin et al., 2003);
5. not making unsupported arguments (Lubet, 2000; Mauet, 1992, 2005; Perrin et al., 2003);
6. not trying to sneak excluded evidence in through subterfuge (Lubet, 2000; Perrin et al., 2003);
7. conceding unimportant points or issues (Easton, 1998; Perrin et al., 2003);
8. avoiding displays of insincere emotions as an attempt to fool the jury (Easton, 1998; Perrin et al., 2003);
9. avoiding "thinly veiled attempts to ingratiate [oneself] or to manipulate jurors' personal opinions," as it will alienate jurors, reduce the attorney's credibility (Kosieradzki, 2001, p. 67), or appear insincere to jurors (Haydock & Sonsteng, 1991);
10. disclosing personal information about themselves and weaknesses in their cases, as this will make jurors more willing to see attorneys as "human" (Berg, 2003/2006) and more likely to open up during the voir dire questioning (Mauet, 2005; Perrin et al., 2003);
11. avoiding appeals to jurors' emotions too early in the trial, as it may backfire (sympathy is an "uncomfortable emotion that

makes people feel powerless and vulnerable"), it is unlikely to motivate jurors, and they may believe the attorney is being manipulative (Kosieradzki, 2001, p. 66);

12. inserting drama (i.e., elements of a performance that are unspecified) into the trial presentation (Burns, 1999), as it will aid jurors in finding the truth because it helps activate the jury's capacity to hear whether the case "rings true " (Burns, 1999, p. 137);

13. showing a genuine belief in the client and client's case (Easton, 1998; Fontham, 2002) because doing otherwise will lead the judge and jury to conclude that they should not care (Haydock & Sonsteng, 1991); and

14. using "passion" to show jurors that the lawyer cares about his or her client and the client's case and is not performing out of professional obligation (Ball, 1993, p. 23; 1997, p. 24).

Although, for the most part, the trial commentators did not specifically tie the above strategies to the definitional components of honesty, they appear to be logically associated with some of the components and with noticeable overlaps between components. Consider the following possible listing of the strategies organized by the definitional components:

Truthfulness:

1. always telling the truth (Easton, 1998);

2. not overstating one's case (Easton, 1998; Lubet, 2000; Mauet, 1992, 2005);

3. not promising evidence that the lawyer does not have (Lubet, 2000; Mauet, 1992, 2005);

4. not breaking promises made in trial (Perrin et al., 2003);

5. not making unsupported arguments (Lubet, 2000; Mauet, 1992, 2005; Perrin et al., 2003);

6. not trying to sneak excluded evidence in through subterfuge (Lubet, 2000; Perrin et al., 2003);

7. avoiding displays of insincere emotions as an attempt to fool the jury (Easton, 1998; Perrin et al., 2003);

8. avoiding "thinly veiled attempts to ingratiate [oneself] or to manipulate jurors' personal opinions" (Kosieradzki, 2001, p. 67);

9. avoiding appeals to jurors' emotions too early in the trial, as it may backfire (sympathy is an "uncomfortable emotion that makes people feel powerless and vulnerable"), it is unlikely to motivate jurors, and they may believe their attorney is being manipulative (Kosieradzki, 2001, p. 66); and

10. inserting drama (i.e., interest or intensity) into the trial presentation (Burns, 1999), as it will aid jurors in finding the truth because it helps activate the jury's capacity to hear whether the case "rings true" (Burns, 1999, p. 137).

Integrity (i.e., adherence to a strict moral or ethical code):

1. always telling the truth (Easton, 1998),
2. not overstating one's case (Easton, 1998; Lubet, 2000; Mauet, 1992, 2005),
3. not promising evidence that the lawyer does not have (Lubet, 2000; Mauet, 1992, 2005),
4. not breaking promises made in trial (Perrin et al., 2003),
5. not making unsupported arguments (Lubet, 2000; Mauet, 1992, 2005; Perrin et al., 2003),
6. not trying to sneak excluded evidence in through subterfuge (Lubet, 2000; Perrin et al., 2003),
7. avoiding displays of insincere emotions as an attempt to fool the jury (Easton, 1998; Perrin et al., 2003), and
8. avoiding "thinly veiled attempts to ingratiate [oneself] or to manipulate jurors' personal opinions" (Kosieradzki, 2001, p. 67).

Fairness (i.e., avoiding self-interest and following appropriate procedures):

1. always telling the truth (Easton, 1998);
2. not overstating one's case (Easton, 1998; Lubet, 2000; Mauet, 1992, 2005);
3. not promising evidence that the lawyer does not have (Lubet, 2000; Mauet, 1992, 2005);
4. not breaking promises made in trial (Perrin et al., 2003);
5. not making unsupported arguments (Lubet, 2000; Mauet, 1992, 2005; Perrin et al., 2003);
6. not trying to sneak excluded evidence in through subterfuge (Lubet, 2000; Perrin et al., 2003);
7. conceding unimportant points or issues (Easton, 1998; Perrin et al., 2003);
8. avoiding displays of insincere emotions as an attempt to fool the jury (Easton, 1998; Perrin et al., 2003); and
9. avoiding "thinly veiled attempts to ingratiate [oneself] or to manipulate jurors' personal opinions," as it will alienate them, reduce the attorney's credibility (Kosieradzki, 2001, p. 67), or appear insincere to jurors (Haydock & Sonsteng, 1991).

Sincerity (i.e., avoiding duplicity; being true to oneself):

1. always telling the truth (Easton, 1998);
2. not overstating one's case (Easton, 1998; Lubet, 2000; Mauet, 1992, 2005);
3. not promising evidence that the lawyer does not have (Lubet, 2000; Mauet, 1992, 2005);
4. not breaking promises made in trial (Perrin et al., 2003);
5. not making unsupported arguments (Lubet, 2000; Mauet, 1992, 2005; Perrin et al., 2003);
6. not trying to sneak excluded evidence in through subterfuge (Lubet, 2000; Perrin et al., 2003);
7. avoiding displays of insincere emotions as an attempt to fool the jury (Easton, 1998; Perrin et al., 2003);
8. avoiding "thinly veiled attempts to ingratiate [oneself] or to manipulate jurors' personal opinions," as it will alienate them, reduce the attorney's credibility (Kosieradzki, 2001, p. 67), or appear insincere to jurors (Haydock & Sonsteng, 1991);
9. disclosing personal information about themselves and weaknesses in their case, as this will make jurors more willing to see the attorney as "human" (Berg, 2003/2006) and more likely to open up during the voir dire questioning (Mauet, 2005; Perrin et al., 2003);
10. avoiding appealing to jurors' emotions too early in the trial, as it may backfire (sympathy is an "uncomfortable emotion that makes people feel powerless and vulnerable"), it is unlikely to motivate jurors, and they may believe their attorney is being manipulative (Kosieradzki, 2001, p. 66);
11. showing a genuine belief in the client and client's case (Easton, 1998; Fontham, 2002;) because doing otherwise will lead the judge and jury to conclude that they should not care (Haydock & Sonsteng, 1991); and
12. using "passion" to show jurors that the lawyer cares about his or her client and the client's case and is not performing out of professional obligation (Ball, 1993, p. 23; 1997, p. 24).

The possibility for overlap between the recommended and the definitional components of honesty was implied by a trial commentator's suggestion that demonstrating a sincere belief in the case helps the trial attorney demonstrate integrity, making the trial attorney and his or her case more credible (Hill, 1986). Note that our listing by definitional component is speculative because trial commentators fail to be specific about which strategies fit with which definitional components and because we have not yet considered whether there is relevant empirical data on the factor structure for these components.

Credibility

Credibility typically refers to believability (*American Heritage Dictionary of the English Language*, 2000; *Compact Oxford English Dictionary of Current English*, 2005; *Merriam-Webster's Collegiate Dictionary*, 2009). As previously noted, likability and honesty can generate beliefs in the attorneys' credibility, thereby creating an overlap between the three constructs. For example, dynamism (i.e., the lawyer's enthusiasm about the case), and honesty more generally, are sometimes added to the components for credibility (Perrin et al., 2003). However trial commentators also suggest differences between them, noting that credibility also requires knowledge or competence (e.g., Easton, 1998). Because we have discussed the roles of likability and honesty in attorney demeanor, this section will focus on competence. According to trial commentators, components of competence include education, credentials, experience, and the perception that the lawyer is well prepared (Easton, 1998; Lubet, 2000; Mauet, 1992, 2005; Singer, 2000), organized (Easton, 1998; Lubet, 2000; Mauet, 1992, 2005), efficient (Fontham, 2002), and intelligent (Perrin et al., 2003).

Trial commentators note numerous strategies for building jurors' perception of competence/credibility:

1. be well prepared, including being knowledgeable about the facts of the case, claims, defenses, and exhibits; and grasping the procedural rules governing the trial (Easton, 1998; Lubet, 2000; Mauet, 1992, 2005; Perrin et al., 2003);
2. dress and behave conservatively (Perrin et al., 2003);
3. demonstrate confidence (Jeans, 1993; Jossen, 1986; Lubet, 2000; Mauet, 1992, 2005; Perrin et al., 2003)—*confidence*, in the common use of the word, means a firm belief in one's powers, abilities, or capacities (*American Heritage Dictionary of the English Language*, 2000; *Merriam-Webster's Collegiate Dictionary*, 2009; *Compact Oxford English Dictionary of Current English*, 2005)— trial attorneys appear confident if they take control (Berg, 2003/2006; Haydock & Sonsteng, 1991), act comfortably (Haydock & Sonsteng, 1991), show empathy and interest (Berg, 2003/2006), and are courageous (Easton, 1998); however, displaying cockiness might lead the trial lawyer to ignore potential weaknesses in his or her own case (Jeans, 1993);
4. adopt an authoritative manner (Fontham, 2002);

5. never show surprise, as "professionals in control are never surprised, but enthusiastically involved" (Ball, 1993, p. 9); and

6. keep away from humor because juries are less likely to find in favor of the client "if they are laughing" (Toch, 1961, pp. 62–63); note that Toch specifically referred to the plaintiff as the client in making this recommendation, but he provides no information if avoiding humor should be limited to only one side.

SCIENCE RELEVANT TO TRIAL COMMENTATORS' CLAIMS

Although trial commentators argue that attorney demeanor (i.e., lawyers' ways of behaving and conducting themselves) is critical to achieving a successful case outcome, with demeanor being composed of an attorney's likability, honesty, and credibility, we cannot know whether these arguments are valid without considering scientific research relevant to their assertions. This section critically considers the trial commentators' assertions from such a scientific perspective.

Likability

Although trial commentators do not explicitly define likability, one can assume that they are referring to the common meaning of the term. Therefore, likability would refer to the extent to which the lawyer is perceived by the jurors as possessing favorable qualities (i.e., pleasing, agreeable, appealing, attractive, sympathetic; *American Heritage Dictionary of the English Language*, 2000; *Compact Oxford English Dictionary of Current English*, 2005; *Merriam-Webster's Collegiate Dictionary*, 2009).

Even though trial commentators seem to assume a common definition of likability, there is scientific literature defining likability and detailing some of the qualities that are associated with liking. According to the scientific literature, source likability can be viewed as an attitude (i.e., positive affective evaluations in memory that are linked to particular objects). In other words, source likability can be conceived of as an association in memory between the source and the receiver's positive evaluation of the source (Roskos-Ewoldsen & Fazio, 1992). The personality characteristics that were the most associated with likableness, pleasantness, or enjoyableness were truthful, caring, loyal, honest, friendly, amusing, affectionate, trustworthy, lovable, loving, kind, genuine, entertaining, honorable, and great (Dumas, Johnson, & Lynch, 2002). Some of the characteristics associated with likableness fall under the honesty and credibility constructs trial commentators reference in their discussion of strategies.

Almost all trial commentators stress the importance of being liked by jurors for the attorney to be a successful advocate in court. As just indicated, trial commentators speculate that increasing liking by jurors will increase the attorney's success by influencing the perceived effectiveness of the presentation (Easton, 1998) and make jurors more willing to grant a favorable verdict (Berg, 2003/2006; Mauet, 1992; Singer, 2000).

Does Likability Relate to Success in Advocacy?

Trial commentators' belief that liking increases persuasive success appears to be generally on the mark. According to the scientific literature on persuasion, liking can be a source of influence. People are usually more willing to comply with the requests of friends or other liked individuals (Cialdini, 1987). In addition, the more favorably people evaluate the communicator, the more they modify their attitudes in support of the communicator (Cialdini, 1993). Transfer-of-affect has also been shown to occur, where people make other positive or negative associations based on liking or disliking (Cialdini, 1993). For example, one study compared the responses of men who rated a new car advertisement that included a seductive young woman model with those of men who viewed the same advertisement without the model. Men whose advertisement featured the model rated the car as faster, more appealing, more expensive looking, and better designed than the other men, and they refused to believe that the presence of the young woman had influenced their judgments (Cialdini, 1993; Smith & Engel, 1968). The implication of this study is that men liked the women models and then transferred these positive feelings onto their feelings for the car. These findings suggest that likable attorneys will experience a similar phenomenon, where jurors will transfer their positive feelings toward the attorneys onto the attorneys' clients and arguments.

Some research suggests that when participants' liking of a source is highly accessible in memory and recall, they will exhibit more attitude change in the direction of the source's message than those participants with less accessible evaluations of the source (Roskos-Ewoldsen & Fazio, 1992). Two social psychological theories of persuasion provide insight into how this processing of information and influence can occur. The elaboration likelihood model (ELM; Petty & Cacioppo, 1986) or the heuristic–systematic model of persuasion (HSM; Eagly & Chaiken, 1984) have been proposed to explain how people process persuasive messages. Although differences exists between the two models (see Chaiken, 1987, for an explanation of differences), both are similar in proposing that people process a message centrally or systematically (i.e., through careful and thoughtful scrutiny of the message) or peripherally or heuristically (i.e., through implementation of simple decision rules). According to this framework, source likability may influence persuasion once the cue likability is activated from memory in three ways.

First, liking may bias the processing of the message when the message is processed centrally or systematically. In other words, a receiver may be more likely to consider the source when processing the message arguments and perceive the arguments to be better or stronger if they like the source of the argument. A second possibility is that if the message is being processed peripherally or heuristically, increasing the accessibility of likability could increase the probability that the message recipient will use a likability heuristic in his or her decision making. A third mechanism through which persuasion is potentially affected by accessibility of likability is by increasing the motivation to process the message centrally. Message recipients with low or high motivation are unlikely to be affected by accessibility. Specifically, recipients with low motivation about the communicated issue will likely use peripheral processing of the message while message recipients with high motivation will likely use central processing because they are motivated to think about the issue. However, message recipients with moderate motivation to actively think about a message may be more inclined to centrally process it when they like the source, which could lead to more persuasion if the message contains strong arguments (Roskos-Ewoldsen & Fazio, 1992).

The accessibility of source likability would be most likely to affect persuasion through the first and the third mechanisms because jurors will likely find the topic relevant, a factor that encourages central or systematic processing (discussed in more detail below). Therefore, attorneys whose likability is highly accessible to jurors may be able to influence them to view the arguments more favorably than they would otherwise or to influence them to process the arguments centrally, which would increase the attorneys' persuasiveness if the message contains strong arguments. However, the accessibility of the source's likability must be sufficiently strong to influence persuasion through one of the three mechanisms. In addition, it is difficult to speculate whether an attorney would be so likable as to develop the strong association necessary in the minds of the jurors to influence persuasion via these means.

Even though research does support the general finding that liked communicators are more persuasive than disliked communicators (O'Keefe, 2000; e.g., Eagly & Chaiken, 1975; Giffin & Ehrlich, 1963; Sampson & Insko, 1964), trial attorneys would be wrong to assume that being likable will always win the jury's favor (Brodsky & Cannon, 2006). In fact, "disliked communicators have been found to be more effective persuaders than liked communicators in some studies, even when the communicators are comparable in other characteristics" (e.g., credibility; O'Keefe, 2002, p. 128). For example, one study compared a negative communicator with a positive communicator in their ability to induce participants to eat fried grasshoppers. Although both sources were roughly equal in persuading participants to eat the fried grasshoppers, the disliked communicator was more effective in changing attitudes among participants who did eat the bugs (Zimbardo, Weisenberg, Firestone, & Levy, 1965; see O'Keefe, 2002).

Cognitive dissonance offers an explanation to account for why people would be persuaded by someone they do not like. When people hold two cognitions (i.e., ideas, attitudes, beliefs, or opinions) that are psychologically inconsistent, they experience a state of tension known as cognitive dissonance. To relieve the mental discomfort dissonance produces, people try to find a way to justify the inconsistency (Tavris & Aronson, 2007). In other words, people who find themselves persuaded by an unlikable person will experience dissonance because their feelings about the person and the fact they are doing something for someone they do not like are inconsistent cognitions. To feel good about this discrepancy, they will try to see their decisions in a favorable light by talking themselves into thinking that there was a good reason to go along with the persuasion in the first place. Once this occurs, they are likely to feel more strongly about their decision than those who were persuaded by someone they already liked. Having to justify their actions, they convince themselves that the communicator deserved the positive response. Scientific studies have not investigated the effects of cognitive dissonance in a setting that is comparable to a courtroom (e.g., the jury deciding a case based on the arguments of two attorneys, one likable and one unlikable), but one possible implication of cognitive dissonance for trial advocacy is that likability may not ultimately be as effective as trial commentators claim. It is conceivable that a disliked attorney with good arguments will be more effective than a comparable, liked attorney because of the effects of cognitive dissonance.

In addition, factors other than liking may have a more influential role in the success of a persuasive attempt. When credibility is high but the sender is not liked, credibility seems to be more important in persuasion (O'Keefe, 2002). Another factor, the topic's relevance, is likely to affect the extent to which being liked helps with persuasion. As a topic becomes more personally relevant to the receiver, research suggests that "the ordinary advantage of liked communicators over disliked communicators diminishes" (O'Keefe, 2002, p. 149; e.g., Chaiken, 1980, Experiment 1; Petty, Cacioppo, & Schumann, 1983). The evidence is consistent with the ELM (Petty & Cacioppo, 1986) and the HSM (Eagly & Chaiken, 1984), which take similar approaches to viewing the impact of high involvement in persuasion. According to the ELM, when the message is personally relevant, a central route to persuasion is likely to be used. This approach is characterized by careful and thoughtful scrutiny of the message contents and minimal reliance on peripheral cues such as likability. When personal relevance is low, receivers are more likely to engage a peripheral route to persuasion by relying on simple acceptance or rejection cues such as liking (Cacioppo & Petty, 1987). Relevance plays a similar role in the systematic model of persuasion. According to that model, when receivers perceive the message as personally important or when they believe that their decisions will affect themselves or others, they are likely to engage in detailed processing of the message content in reaching their decision. When the message is of low relevance, receivers are likely to employ a heuristic approach, which requires relatively little effort in judging message validity and relies instead on simple decision rules or cognitive heuristics in decision making (Chaiken, 1980). Given the importance of jury verdicts, this research suggests that most jurors will be unlikely to use a simple decision rule such as likability when reaching their decision and will be more inclined to carefully scrutinize the attorney's arguments before reaching a verdict.

Does Likability Increase Trust and Perceived Credibility?

Trial commentators hold other assumptions and intuitions about how appearing likable will help attorneys be effective advocates for their clients. One belief is that jurors will find attorneys more trustworthy (Perrin et al., 2003) and more credible (Kosieradzki, 2001) if they like them. Increasing liking is commonly associated with increasing judgments of the communicator's trustworthiness in the persuasion literature (O'Keefe, 2002). Perceptions of expertise could also increase under some circumstances. For example, if the communicator is similar to the receiver in education, training, or experience, the receiver may perceive the communicator to be more expert than the receiver would if he or she did not understand the communicator's background (O'Keefe, 2002). However, according to the persuasion literature, some indirect evidence suggests that the receiver's liking for the communicator can influence judgments of the communicator's trustworthiness but not the expertise of the communicator (O'Keefe, 2002). Factor-analytic investigations of credibility judgments indicate that various general evaluation items often load on the same factor as do trustworthiness scales. For example, items such as friendly–unfriendly, pleasant–unpleasant, nice–not nice, and valuable–worthless have been reported as loading on a common factor with trustworthiness items such as honest–dishonest, trustworthy–untrustworthy, unselfish-selfish, and just-unjust (O'Keefe, 2002; e.g., Applbaum & Anatol, 1972; Bowers & Phillips, 1967; Falcione, 1974; McCroskey, 1966). These findings suggest that liking and trustworthiness judgments are more likely to be associated than liking and expertise judgments (O'Keefe, 2002). The influence of the communicator's trust and credibility on the receiver's judgments is discussed later in this chapter.

Are the Trial Commentators' Strategies for Achieving Likability Scientifically Verified?

Increase Perceived Similarity of the Lawyer to Jurors. Trial commentators suggest several strategies for cultivating likability. One recommended strategy in the legal literature for cultivating likability is for attorneys to try to appear similar to jurors based on the belief that people tend to trust and like those who are more similar to them (Perrin et al., 2003). The trial commentators' assumption that similar communicators are more likable, and therefore more persuasive, is generally correct. People do tend to be more influenced by those who are similar to them than by those who are different (Brock, 1965). Most likely, perceived similarities indirectly influence the effectiveness of the persuasive attempt by affecting the receiver's perceptions of characteristics such as likability and credibility that are generally associated with success in persuasion (O'Keefe, 2002; see Hass, 1981; Simons, Berkowitz, & Moyer, 1970). However, the relationship between similarity/dissimilarity and persuasion is complex. Research does not clearly explain which possible similarities are considered important in persuasion and indicates that dissimilar others may be more effective persuaders than similar others at times (O'Keefe, 2002).

Trial commentators generally assume that greater similarity will lead to greater effectiveness with persuasion. For the most part, people like things that are familiar to them (Zajonc, 1968; see Cialdini, 1993), which could explain why people tend to like those similar to them. People also assume groups of friends share the same personality traits (N. Miller, Campbell, Twedt, & O'Connell, 1966; see Cialdini, 1993), further supporting the belief that similarity breeds likability. In addition, it is common for individuals to decide on appropriate behaviors for themselves in a given situation by searching for information as to how similar others have behaved or are behaving (Cialdini, 1987, p. 173; e.g., Latané & Darley, 1970; Schachter & Singer, 1962).

Research findings show that perceived similarities in attitudes (i.e., similar evaluations of attitude objects; Berscheid, 1985; Byrne, 1969, 1971) and background (e.g., Stotland & Patchen, 1961) can positively influence liking. Attitudinal similarities may be perceived through direct expression, third party indication, or presence of other types of observed similarities (O'Keefe, 2002). For example, dress and personal style may communicate similarities to observers. In a study conducted in 1970, the experimenters, wearing either hippie or traditional fashions, asked other college students on campus to lend them a dime. The request was granted more (two thirds of the instances) when the experimenter dressed the same as the student. Dissimilarly dressed experimenters were given the dime less than half the time (Emswiller, Deaux, & Willits, 1971; see Cialdini, 1993). Another study found that marchers in an antiwar demonstration were more likely to sign the petition of a similarly dressed requester and to do so without bothering to read it first (Suedfeld, Bochner, & Matas, 1971; see Cialdini, 1993). Even trivial similarities (Brewer, 1979; Tajfel, 1981) and perceived attitude similarities that are not especially relevant to the topic of the influence attempt have been shown to increase liking (O'Keefe, 2002). In a review of the sales records of insurance companies, customers were more likely to buy insurance when a salesperson was like them in age, height, religion, education, income, politics, and cigarette-smoking habits (Evans, 1963; see Cialdini, 1993).

However, as indicated earlier, persuasive effects of perceived similarities are not straightforward (Simons et al., 1970). Similarities have been shown to: (a) enhance persuasive effectiveness (e.g., Brock, 1965; Woodside & Davenport, 1974), (b) dull persuasive effectiveness under other circumstances (e.g., Goethals & Nelson, 1973; Infante, 1978; King & Sereno, 1973; Leavitt & Kaigler-Evans, 1975; Mills & Kimble, 1973), and (c) have no effect on persuasive effectiveness (e.g., Klock & Traylore, 1983; Wagner, 1984).

Presumably, a similar source will be more likable and more persuasive than a dissimilar source when all other things are equal and facts are not in issue (Norman, 1976). What if all things are not equal and facts are relevant? Consider that "a dissimilar source may enjoy greater persuasiveness if seen as someone with different but credible experiences relevant to the topic" (Rogers, 2007, p. 232). For example, if the topic is the best way to remove a brain tumor, a brain surgeon is likely to be more persuasive than a butcher, even if those receiving the message have more in common with the butcher.

Disliked communicators can at least sometimes be significantly more effective persuaders than liked communicators (O'Keefe, 2002). One study found that agreement from dissimilar others was more compelling than agreement from similar others when the issue was a statement of fact (a verifiable position). Under this condition, agreement from dissimilar others increased the confidence with which people held beliefs (Goethals & Nelson, 1973; see Stiff, 1994). This finding is consistent with our prior discussion of cognitive dissonance. Agreement from similar others may also lead people to question whether their assessment of the issue is "subject to personal biases and predispositions they share with the similar other" (Stiff, 1994, p. 103).

The relevancy of the message is a factor that can also affect whether similarities will help or hurt the persuasive attempt. As personal relevance to the receiver increases, the superior persuasiveness of liked over disliked communicators diminishes. For example, receivers may look at group membership similarities to make "inferences about likely attitudinal similarities between the receiver and communicator" or, more generally, to gauge likability or credibility (O'Keefe, 2002, p. 204). When topics are not especially relevant to the receiver, the group similarities may serve as peripheral cues that trigger corresponding heuristics, thereby enhancing the persuasiveness of the message from similar communicators. On the other hand, receivers are less likely to rely on heuristics to make their decisions when the topics are of greater personal relevance. When topics are personally relevant, group membership similarity is more likely to encourage closer scrutiny of messages from similar communicators, which could enhance or inhibit persuasion depending on the quality of the message's arguments (O'Keefe, 2002; e.g., Fleming

& Petty, 2000; Mackie, Gastardo-Conaco, & Skelly, 1992; Mackie & Queller, 2000; Mackie, Worth, & Asuncion, 1990). This could explain why a review of peer-based health interventions found that the programs were not dependably more successful than programs without such peer bases (O'Keefe, 2002; Posavac, Kattapong, & Dew, 1999). As mentioned previously, since trial issues are critical to jurors' responsibilities, they are unlikely to rely on a simple heuristic such as "the more similar, the more likable, and the more believable" and instead focus on message content for their decision making.

As previously noted in the section entitled Attorney Demeanor in the Legal Literature of this chapter, trial commentators do not specifically discuss in what ways lawyers should try to appear similar to jurors to successfully persuade them. Research is also inconclusive about which areas of similarity are likely to be persuasive. Part of the problem is that the term *similarity* is vague and can mean many things to different people (Rogers, 2007). People may be similar or dissimilar to another in age, sex, occupation, political affiliation, attitudes, personality, group membership, race or ethnicity, geographical birthplace, wealth or social class, hobby interests, neighborhood affiliations, religion, citizenship, physique, education, speech dialect, interpersonal style, and clothing preferences, among others. Because "an infinite number of possible dimensions" exists for similarity (Simons et al., 1970, p. 3), the existing research contains inconsistencies (Atkinson, Winzelberg, & Holland, 1985; Swartz, 1984), making generalizations from it difficult if not impossible.

Another potential problem noted in the Attorney Demeanor in the Legal Literature section is that some trial commentators believe that jurors will find attorneys whom they perceive as being phony to be unappealing, which seems to contradict the recommendation that lawyers should try to purposefully (and perhaps insincerely) increase their similarity to jurors. Research is silent on whether the naturalness of the communicator aids in persuasion. Despite the lack of information directly on point, research examining the strength of persuasiveness for likability compared with credibility offers some interesting insights on the issue. As noted above, credibility appears to have stronger effects on persuasion than does likeability (O'Keefe, 2002). Other research found that persuasive success was influenced more by communicators' expertise than by communicators' attitudinal similarity (Wagner, 1984; Woodside & Davenport, 1974). These results primarily concerned the expertise component of credibility, which does not appear to be clearly related to naturalness as the trustworthiness component of credibility would be. However, these findings do indicate that liking may not be the most important concern in persuasion (O'Keefe, 2002).

Moreover, instead of focusing on a single similarity effect, it is more appropriate to acknowledge that a multitude of variables influence liking, depending on content and context (Huston & Levinger, 1978). When similarity serves as a persuasive cue, it is more likely to directly affect source trustworthiness; attitudes may be indirectly affected to a lesser degree (Stiff, 1994). Ultimately, whether the communicator's similarities/dissimilarities will influence likability seems to depend largely on whether the receiver perceives those similarities/dissimilarities to be relevant to the persuasive attempt (e.g., Swartz, 1984: Receivers' judgments of source's expertise were found to be unrelated to judgments of perceived similarity; O'Keefe, 2002). Given the various factors that influence liking and ultimately persuasion, attorneys are probably better off focusing on developing strong arguments for their case rather than superficially manipulating similarities with jurors in an effort to engender liking with the hope of increasing persuasion. However, when the opposing arguments and facts are close on the merits, likability may have a significant effect. Unfortunately, research has not addressed this point.

Be Courteous (Use Good Manners). Being courteous, or using good manners, is another strategy trial commentators encourage to build lawyer–jury rapport. Many substrategies for being courteous are suggested in the legal literature. Some of those substrategies include being polite, being well behaved, using introductions, properly addressing the court, apologizing when appropriate, and avoiding personal attacks and disrespectful behaviors. Probably because many of these substrategies are highly specific, very little research appears to exist that explicitly deals with the commentators' assertions. However, the available scientific research is informative for many of these topics.

One point where there is some research available is politeness strategies. "Politeness is manifested by the use of polite phrases such as *please* and *thank you* as well as formal names and titles of address" (Steffen & Eagly, 1985, p. 192). One study found that participants considered polite styles fairly likely to be used and to result in compliance and especially likely to produce liking from the receiver. Impolite styles were considered highly unlikely to result in liking (Steffen & Eagly, 1985). However, status may play a role in the effectiveness of politeness strategies. The study found that high-status communicators were considered more likely to use direct and impolite styles and more likely to gain compliance and liking from those styles than low-status communicators (Steffen & Eagly, 1985).

Much in the same way as kids might try to avoid the bully on the playground, trial commentators appear largely to believe jurors will be likewise repulsed by attorneys who exhibit negative behaviors toward others in the courtroom. In fact, when the communicators violate appropriate rules of social exchange (e.g., politeness [Holtgraves, 1997] and fairness [Schreier, Groeben, & Blickle, 1995]), they have been found less likable (Downs, Kaid, & Ragan, 1990; see Whaley & Smith, 2000). For example, rebuttal analogies in persuasion have been found to work against the communicator. Rebuttal analogies function as both argument and social attack because they tend to be criticisms of ideas and also seem to make some kind of character judgment about the people who stated the ideas (e.g., "that's like discussing terms for divorce during a wedding ceremony"; Whaley & Smith, 2000, p. 68). Receivers rate communicators using rebuttal analogy as relatively impolite (Whaley, 1997).

The results of another study indicated that people who used rebuttal analogies were rated as less likable than those who did not use the analogies. The study also found that the participants exposed to rebuttal analogies generated more negative thoughts about the message (i.e., counterarguing) and fewer positive thoughts about the message and that they recalled less arguments than nonanalogy participants. Interestingly, the study did not find that receivers generated negative thoughts about the analogy user, even though they did rate the communicator as less likable than the nonanalogy communicators (Whaley & Smith, 2000).

In contrast, source derogation has sometimes been found to be an effective tool for persuasion (e.g., Belch 1981; Olson, Toy, & Dover, 1978, 1982). Source derogations are thoughts that discount the message due to source reliability (Wright, 1975). Following the ELM, source derogation, like other source characteristics, may affect persuasion by (a) acting as a peripheral cue under conditions of low elaboration likelihood (e.g., recipient not interested in topic); (b) biasing thinking about information in conditions of high elaboration likelihood; and (c) acting as a persuasive argument under high elaboration likelihood conditions. Further research found that messages delivered by sources who are vulnerable to being discredited may invite more scrutiny by others to guard against their own or others' unfair reactions (Petty, Fleming, & White, 1999). In conclusion, even though it appears that attorneys who are impolite may be perceived as less likable by jurors in many situations, more research is necessary to know how jurors are likely to perceive attorneys' negative behaviors.

Trial commentators encourage attorneys to apologize when they are in the wrong as a way to improve their likability. Although no research on point deals with how apologies may affect liking, research generally supports trial commentator's assertion. Empirical studies have demonstrated that an apology can have aggression-inhibiting effects. When the wrongdoer apologized, receivers held more favorable impressions of her and felt more pleasant and refrained from severe aggression toward her compared with when the communicator did not apologize (Ohbuchi, Kameda, & Agarie, 1989). Unfortunately, this study and more recent literature, which focus on client apology in the trial context (e.g, Bornstein, Rung, & Miller, 2002; Jehle, Miller, & Kemmelmeier, 2009), do not address attorney apology.

Trial commentators also encourage attorneys to avoid appearing boastful or conceited. Research has found that people with high self-esteem claim more positive characteristics than those low in self-esteem, especially emphasizing their ability and high level of competence; those low in self-esteem focus on their positive social qualities (Schütz & Tice, 1997; see Vohs & Heatherton,

2001). In general, however, attorneys with high self-esteem may be just as likable as those with low self-esteem. According to research, people with high and low self-esteem appear equally likable under neutral conditions (Vohs & Heatherton, 2001; e.g., Brockner & Lloyd, 1986; Friedman, 1976; Heatherton & Vohs, 2000). On the other hand, trial commentators' concern that attorneys keep their egos in check is justified by research findings that suggest that when people with high self-esteem are disliked, it is generally after they have experienced threats to self. For example, several studies have found that those with high self-esteem became more aggressive following a threat (Heatherton & Vohs, 2000; e.g., Baumeister, Smart, & Boden, 1996; Bushman & Baumeister, 1998). Likewise, other studies found that after a threat, "high self-esteem participants were viewed as antagonistic, which led them to be perceived as unfriendly and unlikable" (Heatheron & Vohs, 2000, p. 732). In addition, in situations in which participants are motivated to make a positive impression on an audience, those high in self-esteem become egotistical and boastful (Schlenker, Weigold, & Hallam, 1990). These research findings suggest that the evaluative pressures of trial may contribute to a negative impression with the jury if attorneys are driven to maintain their high self-esteem.

Given the lack of available research directly on litigation or on simulated trials, it is difficult to draw any solid conclusions about how being courteous is related to likability and persuasiveness. Generally, it does appear that positive interactions (e.g., praise) and politeness can increase liking. Although conflicting views are espoused by trial commentators about the appropriateness of using negative behaviors in trial because such behaviors are argued to be either useful or harmful depending on the circumstances, it is difficult to gauge the impact of negative interactions with the current state of research. Therefore, attorneys should utilize these strategies cautiously.

Be a Real Person. Finally, trial commentators recommend that attorneys appear "real." No research is available on whether appearing real, open, genuine, unguarded, or vulnerable can increase likability in a communicator. However, these components may be associated with honesty or trustworthiness, which, as noted above, have factors that often overlap with liking factors. Honesty and trustworthiness are discussed in more detail in the next section.

Honesty

Honesty is another quality that trial commentators associate with persuasiveness. Although trial commentators do not explicitly define honesty, the common meaning of the term is consistent with scientists' definition: trustworthiness or lack of bias (Walster, Aronson, & Abrahams, 1966). Dimensions associated with trustworthiness include honest–dishonest, trustworthy–untrustworthy, open-minded–closed-minded, just–unjust, fair–unfair, and unselfish–selfish (O'Keefe, 2002; e.g., Applbaum & Anatol, 1972; Baudhuin & Davis, 1972; Berlo, Lemert, & Mertz, 1969; Falcione, 1974; Schweitzer & Ginsburg, 1966; Tuppen, 1974; Whitehead, 1968). These items appear roughly akin to an "assessment of whether the communicator will be inclined to *tell* the truth as he or she sees it" (O'Keefe, 2002, p.183).

Does Honesty Relate to Success in Advocacy?

There is support for trial commentators' position that honesty helps with some aspects of persuasion. Under the ELM, receivers respond to persuasive messages by producing specific cognitions. For example, source cues may lead receivers to perceive the communicator as being objective, biased, or reluctant. When the communicator is perceived as being objective, with no apparent self-interest in the topic and no reason to favor one side over the other, receivers consider him or her trustworthy. Likewise, a communicator who appears reluctant (i.e., advocating a position against his or her own self-interest) is perceived to be trustworthy because his or her information invites less suspicion. On the other hand, when the communicator appears to be biased, receivers are likely to perceive him or her as a source of less trustworthy information because the person appears to be self-serving. Research has found that "both objective and reluctant testimony produced more favorable and fewer unfavorable thoughts than biased testimony" (Benoit & Benoit, 2008, p. 35; Benoit & Kennedy, 1999).

Are Trial Commentators' Strategies for Achieving Honesty Scientifically Verified?

Always Tell the Truth. Trial commentators instruct trial lawyers to appear trustworthy by always telling the truth to the judge and jury. In adhering to their ethical rules, lawyers will likely want to follow this strategy, if only to avoid legal ramifications such as being held in contempt of court. However, an interesting question that arises in evaluating this strategy is whether the judge and jury will be able to accurately determine when a lawyer is lying.

There is social science available on deception. Deceptive communication uses deliberate message distortions as a persuasive strategy for influencing the beliefs, attitudes, and behaviors of others (G. R. Miller, 1983; G. R. Miller & Stiff, 1993). According to research, people are generally unable to accurately detect deception in others (G. R. Miller & Stiff, 1993; see Kalbfleisch, 1985; Kraut & Poe, 1980). In fact, "people typically have difficulty detecting deception at better than chance levels" (Stiff et al., 1989, p. 555; see also Kalbfleisch, 1985; Kraut & Poe, 1980). Most likely, people are inaccurate judges of deceivers because they rely heavily on nonverbal cues when judging message veracity, even though most nonverbal cues are unreliable indicators of deception (G. R. Miller & Stiff, 1993). One study coded for 10 nonverbal cues (blinks, smiles, adaptors, hand gestures, foot gestures, posture shifts, speech errors, pauses, response duration, and response latency) to determine which were indicators of deception. Participants appeared to rely heavily on smiles, posture shifts, pauses, and response duration, and moderately relied on blink rate and hand gestures to make truth/deception judgments, although none of these visual and vocal cues was actually related to message veracity. Only one verbal cue, verbal content (plausibility, consistency, concreteness, and clarity), was correlated with judgments of message veracity (Stiff & Miller, 1986; see G. R. Miller & Stiff, 1993).

These findings are consistent with other study findings in which the nonverbal cues that related to actual truth and deception differed from the cues people actually used to judge deception (G. R. Miller & Stiff, 1993). Studies that held the mode of message presentation constant and varied verbal, vocal, and visual qualities of a source's message found that observers' judgments in these situations were heavily influenced by the visual cue manipulation even though the cues were not helping receivers make accurate veracity judgments. Participants exposed to visual cues associated with deception (e.g., extended adaptors—amount of time during the response that hand is moving while touching the body, indirect eye gaze, frequent posture shifts) rated the source as significantly more deceptive than observers exposed to the visual cue associated with truthfulness (e.g., limited adaptors—direct eye gaze, infrequent posture shifts), but vocal and verbal cue manipulations had little effect on the accuracy of their veracity judgments. In addition, participants who reviewed the written message alone were significantly more accurate judges of deception than those who were exposed to a live message presentation (Stiff et al., 1989; see G. R. Miller & Stiff, 1993). Although situational characteristics like familiarity might affect the relative strength of their influence, people's veracity judgments are heavily influenced by irrelevant cues (G. R. Miller & Stiff, 1993). The most recent empirical studies and reviews of this literature continue to support the earlier conclusion that people are poor deception detectors. As noted by C. F. Bond & DePaulo (2008a): "virtually all *individuals* are barely able to detect lies, and that real differences in detection ability are minuscule" (pp. 485–486; also see, C. F. Bond, 2008; C. F. Bond & DePaulo, 2006, 2008b; C. F. Bond & Uysal, 2007; and G. D. Bond, 2008; but see Ekman, O'Sullivan, & Frank, 1999). Therefore, jurors are unlikely to accurately assess attorney honesty.

Avoid Overstating the Case. Trial commentators instruct trial lawyers not to overstate their case in court as a method for maintaining jurors' trust. Social science has yet to address the effects of overstating, overstepping, inflating, exaggerating, or amplifying evidence in court or in other contexts.

Avoid Promising Evidence That is Unavailable (Avoid Breaking Promises). Attorneys are warned against promising to provide evidence that they cannot or will not introduce into evidence, as well as not to break promises made in court (e.g., telling the jury that they will hear from witness X, and then not calling witness X to the stand). Although no science directly addresses promises in a courtroom situation, research on promises made in employment situations is instructive. In employment relationships, scientists use the phrase *psychological contract* to express promissory beliefs (Robinson & Rousseau, 1994; Rousseau, 1998, 2001). In other words, the basis for psychological contracts is explicit and implicit promises that create reciprocal obligations between the employee and the employer (Montes & Zweig, 2009; e.g., Morrison & Robinson, 1997; Robinson & Rousseau, 1994; Rousseau, 1995, 1998, 2001). These promises are believed to "build trust and positive feelings that serve as the foundation for a strong relationship," among other things (Montes & Zweig, 2009, p. 1244; see Rousseau, 2001; Rubin & Brown, 1975; Shore & Tetrick, 1994).

Scholars in this field argue that because of the relationship established between employees and employers, when employees perceived that the actual delivered inducements are inconsistent with the promise (i.e., a breach of the psychological contract), they will experience stronger reactions than when they perceived a simple discrepancy between what they expected and what they actually experienced on the job (e.g., Montes & Zweig, 2009; Morrison & Robinson, 1997). The harm to the employee–employer relationship appears to occur via a violation of the employee's trust (Montes & Zweig, 2009; Robinson, 1996; Robinson & Rousseau, 1994). In fact, meta-analytic findings indicate that employees who perceived a breach in the psychological contract will feel less trust in the organization, which can lead to negative affective, attitudinal, and behavioral reactions to the organization (Montes & Zweig, 2009; Zhao, Wayne, Glibkowski, & Bravo, 2007). This research suggests that attorneys who violate their promises to the jury may risk hurting their trust with the jury.

Despite these findings, other research suggests that promises may not be as important as what is actually delivered. Research shows that employees' perception of what the employer promised is more important than whether employers actually made those promises. In addition, research indicates that perceptions of psychological breaches and negative reactions can arise regardless of whether promises are actually made. In addition, delivered inducements (e.g., support with personal problems, skill development, or regular bonuses that the company gives the employee) appear to heavily influence perceptions of breach more than discrepancies between what employees believed they were promised and what they receive (Montes & Zweig, 2009). Although further research is necessary to understand the relationship between promises, perceptions of psychological breach, and their influence on receivers' emotions, the implication of these findings for attorneys in court is that both promises by the lawyer about what he or she will deliver and what the lawyer actually delivers in the way of trial evidence are important in jurors' perception of honesty.

Avoid Making Unsupported Arguments. To avoid hurting their appearance of trustworthiness, trial commentators recommend that attorneys not make unsupported arguments. Although the available science does not explicitly address whether making weak arguments hurts one's appearance of honesty, lawyers may want to develop strong arguments for other reasons. When personal involvement is high for jurors, as is likely for jurors during trial, receivers are more likely to rely on systematic (e.g., Chaiken, 1980) or central processing (e.g., Petty, Cacioppo, & Goldman, 1981; Petty et al., 1983) as opposed to resorting to heuristic or peripheral processing, which means that they will carefully scrutinize the evidence. Therefore, the strength of the attorneys' arguments is likely to play a key role in jurors' decision making.

Avoid Trying to Sneak Evidence in Through Subterfuge. Although trial commentators warn attorneys that they can hurt their appearance of honesty by trying to sneak evidence in through subterfuge (e.g., by bringing up information in his or her opening statement that the attorney knows will never be properly admitted during the trial), no scientific evidence is specifically on point.

Concede Unimportant Points. The lawyers' strategy of conceding unimportant points may assist them in appearing to be honest. According to the persuasion literature, acting against one's self-interest is a factor that can increase trustworthiness (Walster, Aronson, & Abrahams, 1966). Arguing against one's self-interest is likely to aid with perceived trustworthiness by making the communicator appear more objective because he or she would have little to gain from adopting that position. As noted earlier, people generally seem somewhat less trustworthy when they have incentives for making statements or when they stand to gain personally from persuading others of their position.

Another potential reason why expectancy disconfirmation may aid in persuasive success is that it may help the attorney appear impartial. People allow themselves to be "more swayed by experts who seem to be impartial than by those who have something to gain by convincing [them]" (Cialdini, 1993, p. 232; see Eagly, Wood, & Chaiken, 1978), with research confirming these results internationally (McGinnies & Ward, 1980). Message receivers base their premessage expectations on available information about the source's personal preferences and the situational pressures, which are called *minitheories*. The communicator confirms or disconfirms these minitheories in the minds of the receivers by the position he or she takes in the message (Eagly, Wood, & Chaiken, 1981; see Stiff, 1994). Receivers are likely to perceive speakers who confirm their premessage expectations as biased because it appears that the speaker's message is based on his or her personal preferences, background, or situational pressures. The communicator bias compromises the validity of the message as an accurate representation of the issue being discussed, thereby diminishing the message's persuasive impact. When a source disconfirms premessage expectations, message recipients must generate a new minitheory to explain why the speaker advocated the position he or she did. This new minitheory generally indicates that especially compelling evidence influenced the communicator to overcome his or her expected bias. Therefore, the receiver perceives that the source is unbiased, which enhances the persuasive effect of the message (Eagly et al., 1978, 1981).

This explanation is supported by a study that looked at how receivers interpreted the trustworthiness of a source who had a proenvironment message that was attributed to a probusiness or a proenvironment background (Eagly et al., 1978). The speaker's background created knowledge bias (i.e., the perception that the source would possess either probusiness or proenvironment information) for the receivers. When receivers were exposed to the proenvironment message attributed to a probusiness source, their premessage expectancies were not confirmed. The audience is likely to determine that a speaker who does not confirm the audience's premessage expectancies is less biased and more persuasive (Stiff, 1994). Apparently, the audience concluded that factual evidence must have been overwhelming to cause the message source to advocate an unexpected position. When premessage expectancies were confirmed, message recipients attributed the position advocated to the source's background characteristics or to situational constraints. These attributes led to the perception of source bias, and the message had limited persuasive effect (Eagly et al., 1978). Expectancy disconfirmation also explains why "advertising studies have found that advertisements that acknowledge ways in which competing products are just as good as the advertised product (or acknowledge weaknesses of the advertised product) are commonly perceived as more credible than when the ad claims superiority on every product feature that is mentioned" (O'Keefe, 2002, p. 189; e.g., Alden & Crowley, 1995; Kamins & Marks, 1988; Pechmann, 1992; for a review, see O'Keefe, 1999). Consumers likely expect product or brand advertisements to exclaim their merits in every area. When the advertisements do not, the consumers' expectancy is not confirmed, and they explain the discrepancy by believing that the advertiser is being more honest (O'Keefe, 2002).

In sum, the scientific research is generally supportive of attorneys' belief that arguing counter to their interests will increase their trustworthiness in the minds of jurors, which can positively influence the persuasiveness of their message. It is possible that attorneys who concede unimportant points will violate jurors' expectancies of attorneys and, thus, increase jurors' perceptions of their trustworthiness. The difficulty of this task for attorneys is to create the impression of violating jurors' expectancies without actually violating ethical codes or hurting their case. For example, although a criminal defense attorney who admitted that her client committed a crime would violate jurors' expectancies and increase the jurors' perceptions of her honesty, she would also risk losing her license unless the admission was coupled with an insanity defense argument. This is why trial commentators limit the strategy to conceding unimportant issues. However, the research on this effect is limited to situations where the expectancy violation is fairly obvious. There is also a strong possibility that jurors will tune out the unimportant issues that arise at trial, decreasing the likelihood that minor expectancy violations would affect jurors' perceptions of attorneys' truthfulness. To properly evaluate the effectiveness of this strategy, further research is needed on how obvious one must be in acting against his or her interests to influence judgments of honesty.

Avoid Insincere Emotions. To increase persuasiveness, trial commentators recommend avoiding insincere emotions (Easton, 1998; Perrin et al., 2003). Promoting the appearance of sincerity is also a common practice in advertising. Advertisers will often present themselves to recipients of their messages as lacking ulterior motives. They may try to appear that they are simply providing information, entertaining, being inquisitive, or expressing their true feelings. For example, a professional actor may finish a commercial sales pitch and then enjoy consuming the product he has been advertising, apparently unaware of the cameras still on him (Goffman, 1974; Simons, 2001). Although this strategy is used to persuade consumers, little research is available about the success of this strategy in accomplishing its goal. Likewise, research is necessary to understand whether the appearance of sincerity will assist trial lawyers in court.

Avoid Manipulating the Jury Through Praising. Praise and other forms of positive estimation have been found to stimulate liking (Cialdini, 1987; e.g., Byrne & Rhamey, 1965). For the most part, people tend to believe praise and to like those who offer it, even if it is probably untrue (Byrne, Rasche, & Kelley, 1974; Cialdini, 1993). One study found that a graduate student was more persuasive when he praised the faculty and student body at his new school (Wood & Kallgren, 1988). In another study, men received comments about themselves from another person who needed a favor from them. Some of the men were given only positive comments, some were given only negative comments, and others received both good and bad comments. The evaluator who provided only praise was liked best, even though the men fully realized that the flatterer stood to gain from their liking him. In addition, the praise did not have to be accurate to be effective. Both untrue and true positive comments produced as much liking for the flatterer (Drachman, deCarufel, & Insko, 1978; see Cialdini, 1987, 1991). However, limitations exist for how far one is willing to accept praise; praise is not effective at inducing liking if one is sure of the flatterer's manipulative intent (Brodsky & Cannon, 2006; Jones & Wortman, 1973; see Cialdini, 1993). In addition, one recent study showed that only women are affected by the ingratiation; women participants found a moderately ingratiating attorney to be the most likable (Brodsky & Cannon, 2006).

Disclose Personal Information. Trial commentators encourage attorneys to disclose personal information about themselves to help put jurors at ease with their honesty. Research suggests that disclosing personal information to jurors may increase persuasiveness. Some research indicates that "establishing their basic truthfulness on minor issues helps [people] appear more believable when stressing the important aspects of their argument" (Cialdini, 1993, p. 220; Settle & Gorden, 1974). The persuasion literature also concludes that a similar strategy called "humble irony" (e.g., "I can admit it freely now. All my life I've been a patsy"; Cialdini, 1993, para. 1) is an effective persuasive tool because the recipient is disarmed by the impression of a warm and personable person who shares the audience's vulnerability (Simons, 2001; see Burke, 1961/1937).

Perhaps another benefit of disclosing personal information to jurors is that it can help establish a sense of intimacy with them. In romantic relationships, increasing intimacy can lead romantic partners to develop a simple decision rule for judging one another's behavior. This rule is called the *truth bias heuristic*, which is the tendency of someone to judge romantic partners as truthful (i.e., "My partner has been truthful in the past, therefore, he or she is being truthful now" [Stiff, Kim, & Ramesh, 1992, p. 328]). Over time, jurors may develop a similar heuristic for the attorney based on a sense of intimacy achieved through the attorney's personal disclosures. It is interesting to note that despite the use of this heuristic, people are no more accurate at detecting deception in their partners than they are at detecting deception in a stranger (Comadena, 1982; Miller et al., 1981). The truth bias heuristic is likely to continue from situation to situation, unless the partner becomes suspicious for any reason. Arousing suspicion is believed to reduce reliance on the truth bias heuristic and result in more active scrutiny of a source's message (Stiff et al., 1992). Therefore, attorneys should be cautious about raising suspicions after deliberating eliciting intimacy in jurors.

Avoid Appealing to Jurors' Sympathies Early on. Although trial commentators caution that eliciting sympathy from the jury too early may make jurors uncomfortable, no scientific literature is available that addresses how jurors or other people will respond to feelings of sympathy at any given point in time.

Insert Drama. Trial commentators favor "drama" as a way of helping jurors determine the truth in the case. No explicit definition of drama was listed in the legal literature, but it appears to reflect the concept of increasing interest or intensity in the communication, which approximates the use of the term *vividness* in the psychological literature. Although no studies have looked directly at the effect of vividness on assessments of truthfulness, some studies have found that vivid information has more impact than does nonvivid information (Nisbett & Ross, 1980; Taylor & Thompson, 1982). Other researchers have found that although participants judged vivid messages to be more persuasive than nonvivid messages, vivid and nonvivid messages did not differ on measures of actual attitude change (O'Keefe, 2002; see Collins, Taylor, Wood, & Thompson, 1988).

Several studies have addressed the impact of vividness or salience on perceptions of likability, attractiveness, and expertise. Presumably, increasing the salience or vividness of extrinsic cues such as communicator likability and expertise should increase their persuasive impact (Chaiken, 1987). One study presented participants persuasive messages attributed to either a likable or unlikable source that were videotaped, audiotaped, or written. The researchers believed that the communicator's nonverbal cues in the videotaped and audiotaped conditions would attract the participant's attention, and therefore, increase the likelihood of triggering the liking-agreement heuristic when the participants were exposed to videotaped or audiotaped formats as opposed to the written format. In fact, participants in the video and audiotaped conditions agreed significantly more with the likable source's message, while the likability manipulation did not affect participants in the written condition. The findings in this study support the implication that people may think more about communicators in broadcast formats (Chaiken & Eagly, 1983; see Chaiken, 1987).

Other research has indicated that people are more likely to retrieve and use the liking-agreement rule when the vividness of a communicator's physical attractiveness is enhanced. In one study, participants processed the persuasive message more systematically when the communicator's physical appearance was not vivid. In other words, when the communicator's appearance was not vivid, participants agreed more with high-quality messages, and they thought more about the message. Participants relied more on heuristic processing when the communicator's appearance was vivid. The post-message opinions of participants in the vivid condition were not influenced by the quality of the argument and were more highly correlated with their perceptions of the communicator rather than with their thoughts about the message (Pallak, 1983; see Chaiken, 1987).

The implication of this research is that "any factor in a persuasion setting that increases either the salience or vividness of extrinsic persuasion cues may enhance persuasive impact, presumably increasing the likelihood that simple decision rules associated with such cues will be activated and used by message recipients" (Chaiken, 1987, pp. 22–23). For example, there is mock jury research that shows that jurors may use simple cues like physical attractiveness in reaching their decisions. In addition, jurors are more likely to award better-looking defendants favorable verdicts under certain conditions (Zebrowitz & McDonald, 1991).

Some note that the range of variables in persuasion settings that may enhance the salience or vividness of extrinsic persuasion cues may be broad (Chaiken, 1987). For example, emotionally toned messages may draw attention to a communicator's attractiveness and facilitate the persuasive impact of this extrinsic cue more than rationally toned messages (Pallak, Murroni, &

Koch, 1983). Increasing the salience or vividness of persuasion cues may not strongly affect attitude change because they are cues that are typically processed in heuristic fashion and thus may increase the likelihood that people will apply simple decision rules in judging the probable validity of the persuasive messages (e.g., Collins et al., 1988). However, people may still be motivated to process the message carefully, such as in a trial situation, and in those cases, people are unlikely to rely on simple cues.

More research in trial settings is critical to further explore this issue because most mock jury research provides a very poor test of the use of central, careful processing of trial information. Potential limitations of mock jury research include vignettes instead of full trial information, photographs instead of actual defendants, and lack of admission of additional factors that jurors would likely to be exposed to in an actual trial and that could influence their verdict (e.g., testimony by real witnesses). Our concern is not with the intrinsic value of simulations but with the way they have been constructed so far. When simulations become so estranged from the reality of real trials, it is impossible to know whether they have any external validity. Even studies that use actual courtroom proceedings are limited. For example, the Zebrowitz and McDonald (1991) study noted above involved small claims court. The generalizability of findings from small claims court to trial courts of general jurisdiction is questionable. In small claims court (a) judges are the trier of fact as opposed to jurors, (b) parties usually represent themselves and do not use attorneys, (c) the risks of losing are low (e.g., under $2,500), and (d) efficiency is a priority and little evidentiary support is necessary. Such in situ studies are unlikely to provide an accurate test of juror decision making in trials outside of small claims court.

Show Genuine Interest in Client and Be Passionate. Trial commentators believe that a trial attorney should show genuine interest in his or her client and should be passionate as a way to demonstrate to the judge and the jury that he or she cares. No scientific information is directly on point about whether interest and passion demonstrate caring. However, passion may contribute to the vividness or salience of information, which is discussed above.

Credibility

While a definition of credibility is absent from the legal literature, social science suffers from an abundance of credibility definitions. Researchers have been inconsistent in defining the variable. Essentially, credibility is a perception engendered by the message source that is held by message recipients (Benoit & Benoit, 2008; Cronkhite & Liska, 1980; Hovland, Janis, & Kelley, 1953) concerning the believability of the communicator (Druckman, 2001; O'Keefe, 2002).

Part of the difficulty in defining credibility is the number of components that have been associated with the term. In general, scientists have associated the construct with perceptions of competence, intelligence, character, sincerity, believability, trustworthiness, dynamism, importance, prestige, status, reputation, and so on. However, the credibility literature is currently focused on source expertise and source trustworthiness (Hovland et al., 1953), even though a third factor, dynamism, is sometimes considered (Berlo et al., 1970; but see Brodsky, Griffin, & Cramer, 2010, who in developing a scale to identify the credibility of expert witnesses identified the following components—confidence, likability, trustworthiness, and knowledge, when testing college undergraduates). The focus of this section is the expertise dimension of credibility because the trustworthiness dimension was addressed in the Honesty section above, while dynamism is likely similar to vividness, which we also discussed above.

The expertise dimension is also sometimes called *competence, expertness, authoritativeness,* or *qualification* (O'Keefe, 2002). Many studies have used factor analysis to study this dimension (e.g., Applbaum & Anatol, 1972; Baudhuin & Davis, 1972; Berlo et al., 1970; Bowers & Phillips, 1967; Falcione, 1974; Markham, 1968; McCroskey, 1966; Schweitzer & Ginsburg, 1966). Scales associated with expertise are directed at assessing whether the communicator is in a position to know what is right or correct: experienced–inexperienced, informed–uninformed, trained–untrained, qualified–unqualified, skilled–unskilled, intelligent–unintelligent, and expert–not expert (O'Keefe, 2002). Factor analysis indicates high internal reliability for measures of perceived expertise that are composed of several of these items (O'Keefe, 2002; e.g., Beatty & Behnke, 1980; Bell, Zahn, & Hopper, 1984; McCroskey, 1966).

Does Credibility Relate to Success in Advocacy?

An important factor in persuasion is source credibility (e.g., Benoit, 1991; Hass 1981). Expertise can provide a simple cue to receivers to allow them to reach a judgment on an issue without having to exert effort to evaluate all the evidence provided (Petty et al., 1981). Studies have found that experts are generally considered more persuasive than nonexpert sources (Aronson, Turner, & Carlsmith, 1963), and high-credibility communicators have been shown to achieve greater attitude change than low-credibility sources (Hovland & Weiss, 1951). In addition, people tend to produce less unfavorable thoughts when they believe the source is credible.

The relevance of the message to the receiver appears to be of importance in determining the impact of the expertise on persuasion. People are more likely to rely on simple cues when they lack the ability to think through a message such as when the message is difficult to comprehend (Petty, Cacioppo, Stratman, & Priester, 2005; e.g., Kiesler & Mathog, 1968; Moore, Hausknecht,

& Thamodaran, 1986; Ratneshwar & Chaiken, 1991) or when people have little or no prior information about the attitude object (Petty et al., 2005; e.g., Cacioppo, Marshall-Goodell, Tassinary, & Petty, 1992; Wood, Kallgren, & Priesler, 1985). Increasing source expertise increased agreement regardless of argument quality in situations where the message was low in personal relevance, probably because people are more likely to exert less effort in reaching their decisions. In contrast, source expertise had no significant impact on attitudes when the message was of high relevance to receivers. When the message is relevant to the person, he or she is more motivated to process the message by carefully considering the information provided, regardless of the source (Petty et al., 1981).

The effects of source credibility are complex (O'Keefe, 2002). Low-credibility communicators have been found to be significantly more effective than high-credibility communicators in some circumstances (O'Keefe, 2002; e.g., Bock & Saine, 1975; Chebat, Filiatrault, Laroche, & Watson, 1988; Dholakia, 1987; Harmon & Coney, 1982; Sternthal, Dholakia, & Leavitt, 1978). Low-credibility sources have a persuasive advantage over high-credibility sources when they are advocating a position toward which the receiver is already favorable (i.e., a proattitudinal message). When the message advocates a position that the receiver initially opposes (i.e., a counterattitudinal message), the high-credibility communicators will tend to be more effective than the low-credibility communicators (O'Keefe, 2002; e.g., Bergin, 1962; Bochner & Insko, 1966; Chebat et al. 1988; Harmon & Coney, 1982; McGinnies, 1973; Sternthal et al., 1978, Study 2). Likewise, sources of moderate credibility can be more effective than high-credibility sources when the audience agrees with the message (Sternthal et al., 1978).

The ELM offers an explanation for why low-credibility sources may be more persuasive than high-credibility sources when the message is close to the receiver's original position. Receivers may assume that the high-credibility source will advocate the position adequately and exert less effort to process the message. On the other hand, the receiver will be more likely to invest the energy in favorable elaboration when the low-credibility source represents a receiver's favored position. Therefore, the communicator's credibility becomes less important when the receiver agrees with the source because the receiver thinks of supporting arguments on his or her own to boost the communicator's position, resulting in the receiver being more persuaded by the low-credibility source. Therefore, low-credibility sources can achieve greater success when they convey a proattitudinal message or the receiver is highly invested in understanding the message (O'Keefe, 2002).

Finally, research has found that the effects of credibility on persuasive outcomes appear to be stronger than the effects of liking (e.g., Lupia & McCubbins, 1998; Simons et al., 1970), attractiveness, or similarity (Wilson

& Sherrell, 1993). For example, one study looked at the persuasive effectiveness of a cold and stingy communicator and a warm and generous communicator arguing for either a relatively small or relatively large award (Wachtler & Counselman, 1981). The most effective pairings were a stingy communicator arguing for a large award and the generous communicator arguing for a small award, most probably because these combinations represented an unexpected position (i.e., the stingy source arguing for a large award and the generous source arguing for a small award) and, thus, were probably perceived as relatively high in credibility (see above for more detailed explanation). However, the cold and stingy communicator was sometimes a more effective persuader, even though the warm and generous source was better liked than the cold and stingy one. In addition, the stingy communicator arguing for the large award was significantly more effective than the generous source advocating the large award (O'Keefe, 2002).

Moreover, although there may be circumstances in which a low-credibility source is more persuasive, research supports trial commentators' belief that credibility is an important factor in trial advocacy.

Are Trial Commentators' Strategies for Achieving Credibility Scientifically Verified?

Trial commentators offer a number of strategies that they expect will increase the perception of attorneys' credibility. Scientific studies can address the likely success of those strategies at trial.

Be Well Prepared. To increase persuasiveness, trial commentators encourage attorneys to present themselves as expert by being knowledgeable about their case and law. Factor analysis (discussed previously) indicates that knowledge elements (i.e., information about the communicator's training, experience, and occupation) are associated with credibility, while other research shows that these elements significantly influence receiver judgments of expertise (O'Keefe, 2002; e.g., Hurwitz, Miron, & Johnson, 1992; Ostermeier, 1967; Swenson, Nash, & Roos, 1984). Unfortunately, however, little systematic research has assessed how this information about the communicator affects credibility judgments (O'Keefe, 2002). Some studies have investigated how citing to the source of evidence (e.g., relevant facts, opinions, and information) helps the communicator's perceived expertise (for reviews and further discussion, see O'Keefe, 1998). Specifically, citing to high-credibility sources for the evidence appears to enhance the communicator's appearance of expertise and trustworthiness, but sometimes these effects are small (O'Keefe, 2002; e.g., Fleshler, Ilardo, & Demoretcky, 1974; McCroskey, 1967, 1969, 1970; Ostermeier, 1967; Whitehead, 1971). Citations to low-credibility sources or citations to poor or irrelevant evidence is not likely to enhance communicator credibility (Luchok & McCroskey, 1978; Warren, 1969).

Dress and Behave Conservatively. Trial commentators believe that dressing and behaving conservatively is important for appearing credible to the jury. Their belief about dress is supported in the persuasion literature. One study found that a man may appear more authoritative by changing his clothes. The study involved a 31-year-old man jaywalking across a street. Half the time, the man was dressed in a crisp business suit, while the other half of the time the man was dressed in a work shirt and pants. The study found that three and a half times as many pedestrians followed the man against the traffic light when he was wearing the suit as opposed to the casual clothes (Lefkowitz, Blake, & Mouton, 1955; see Cialdini, 1993). Another study investigated the difference in how people responded to a young man dressed in civilian clothes (i.e., casual clothes) compared to when he was dressed in a security guard's uniform (i.e., similar to a police uniform). Under both conditions, the young man would ask passersby on the street to comply with some unusual request, such as giving another person change. The study found that people were more likely to obey the requester in the uniform regardless of the type of request (Bickman, 1974; see Cialdini, 1993). Using a firefighter's uniform yielded similar results (Bushman, 1984).

Similar to uniforms, dressing conservatively by wearing a suit or business attire might aid credibility by offering a quick cue for jurors that the attorney is perhaps someone worth listening to or perhaps by increasing the attorney's physical attractiveness, which could influence likability (Chaiken, 1986). Physically attractive communicators have been found to be more persuasive than less attractive communicators in changing attitudes (Chaiken, 1979) and getting what they requested (Benson, Karabenic, & Lerner, 1976). In addition, physical attractiveness has been found to have a halo effect, in that it dominates the way that the person is viewed by others. Physical attractiveness has generalized to other favorable trait perceptions such as talent, kindness, honesty, and intelligence (Cialdini, 1987; e.g., Dion, Berscheid, & Walster, 1972; Rich, 1975; for a review, see Adams, 1977). In addition, those who are more physically attractive tend to be better liked (Berscheid & Walster, 1974). However, studies have found that physical attractiveness is not related to higher rating in expertise and will probably only have weak effects on trust-worthiness (O'Keefe, 2002; e.g., Chaiken, 1979; Horai, Naccari, & Fatoullah, 1974; Snyder & Rothbart, 1971; see also Norman, 1976; Widgery, 1974; cf. Patzer, 1983). In general, source attractiveness appears to have its greatest influence in relatively unimportant situations (Chaiken, 1986).

Given the importance of a trial situation, it is unlikely that the benefits of dress or appearance are going to have great sway with the jurors as to the attorney's expertise or the attorney's case if the attorney does not deliver solid supporting arguments. In addition, no research exists that addresses how behaving conservatively may influence perceptions of expertise or persuasion.

Demonstrate Confidence. Trial commentators emphasize the importance of instilling in jurors the impression that the attorney is confident at trial to further the attorney's appearance of credibility. One study that focused on perceptions of expertise among members of small groups found that perceptions of expertise were related to group members' talkativeness, which was predicted based on confidence and dominance. There was no relationship between confidence and actual expertise (Littlepage, Schmidt, Whisler, & Frost, 1995). Another study that examined expert characteristics and behavior in small groups duplicated the relationship between perceptions of expertise and confidence. Frequent talking was related to both perceptions of expertise and the influence of the expert, and it appears that the expert recognition mediates the relationship between extent of talking and expert influence, with talkative experts appearing more influential than less talkative experts because group members are better able to identify the member with expertise (Littlepage & Mueller, 1997).

In addition to the relationship between perceived confidence and expertise, the link between confidence and influence is a strong one. For example, in pairs where one individual was correct and one was incorrect, the more confident individual's position prevailed in 88% of cases (Johnson & Torcivia, 1967). This finding has been studied extensively in trial scenarios, with research showing a relationship between confidence and perceived accuracy. Witnesses who express the most confidence in their testimony are perceived as being the most accurate by jurors, despite the fact that those witnesses overestimate their own accuracy (Deffenbacher, 1980; Penrod & Cutler, 1995; Sporer et al., 1995). This suggests that confident attorneys will appear more persuasive to jurors.

Trial commentators are rightly concerned that overconfidence (i.e., cockiness) may lead attorneys to ignore weakness in their cases. Although confidence is related to perceived accuracy, it is not always related to actual accuracy. In fact, "the correlation between accuracy of their judgments and the confidence they experience is not consistently high" (Kahneman & Klein, 2009, p. 522; see Arkes, 2001; Griffin & Tversky, 1992), probably because people's memories are biased toward internal consistency of the information rather than its quality (Einhorn & Hogarth, 1978a; Kahneman & Tversky, 1973). For example, an oncologist may be 99% sure that her patient has cancer based on her years of experience in the field and then be proven wrong when medical tests return negative for cancer. In law, police officers and prosecutors may confidently believe a defendant is guilty based on prior experience with similar situations, but then later, the DNA tests prove otherwise. The premortem method (Klein, 2007) has been suggested for reducing overconfidence and improving decisions. Team members begin by describing their plan and then imagine that their plan failed. They then write down all the reasons the project failed in 2 minutes. The idea is that people are better at developing criticisms when they are told that an outcome is certain (Kahneman & Klein, 2009; see also Mitchell, Russo, & Pennington, 1989). To avoid the pitfalls of overconfidence, attorneys may want to take a similar approach on their own or with other lawyers with whom they work.

Adopt an Authoritative Manner. Adopting an authoritative manner is believed to help create the appearance of credibility and assist the attorney with persuading the jury to support his or her case. Social science supports this proposition. When an individual is a legitimate authority, he or she is extremely influential (Aronson, Turner, & Carlsmith, 1963; Cialdini, 1987; Milgram, 1974).

Several classic studies deal with authoritativeness. One is Milgram's study (1963, 1974) on obedience to authority. The question Milgram was interested in answering was to what extent would ordinary people be willing to inflict pain on an entirely innocent other person when it is their job. Milgram told the participants in his study that he was investigating the effects of punishment on learning and memory. The participants were told that their job was to administer increasing levels of shock when the learner erred. In fact, the learner was really a confederate in an adjoining room who would purposely give incorrect responses to the questions, and no shock was actually delivered. Of the participants, 65% delivered the maximum shock possible to the learners, pulling 30 shock switches and ultimately engaging the final switch of 450 volts, even while they could hear the learner shouting in pain. Milgram's proposed explanation for participants' behavior was the presence of men in lab coats who were watching them and urging them to carry out their responsibility, even at the risk to the learner. Because the participants had a sense of duty to authority (i.e., the researchers in lab coats), they complied. In contrast, 100% of participants refused to continue the experiment when the person demanding they continue with the shock delivery was a fellow student (see Cialdini, 1993; English & Sales, 2005).

In another study, a researcher posing as a physician phoned in a request to regular duty nurses telling them to administer 20 mg of Astrogen to a specific patient in the ward. Even though phoned-in prescriptions were against hospital policy, the drug was not authorized, and the prescribed dose was obviously dangerously excessive, 95% of the nurses complied with the request (Hofling, Brotzman, Dalrymple, Graves, & Pierce, 1966; see Cialdini, 1993). Although people are inclined to obey authority figures, this strategy is likely to only work if the attorney can establish the legitimacy of his or her power. In addition, none of the research addresses how people will respond to conflicting authority figures, which is likely to arise at trial if opposing lawyers both establish themselves as authorities.

Never Show Surprise. Although trial commentary urges lawyers against showing surprise, no research addresses this issue.

Keep Away From Humor. The trial literature suggests that humor is inappropriate in a trial. It also appears that communicators who do use humor in persuasion do so at a risk. Humor has had negative effects on perceptions of the communicator, which include decreased liking, lowered perceived trustworthiness, and lowered perceived expertise. Negative effects usually occur when the audience perceives the humor to be excessive or inappropriate (O'Keefe, 2002; see Bryant, Brown, Silberberg, & Elliott, 1981; Munn & Gruner, 1981; Taylor, 1974). However, humor may enhance the audience's liking for the communicator, which may have some impact on perceptions of the communicator's trustworthiness because liking may somewhat influence perceptions of trustworthiness (discussed above), but humor does not appear to affect judgments of expertise (O'Keefe, 2002; see Chang & Gruner, 1981; Gruner, 1967, 1970; Gruner & Lampton, 1972; Tamborini & Zillman, 1981). Therefore, attorneys may be able to safely use small amounts of appropriate humor to enhance their perceived trustworthiness, but not their expertise.

CONCLUSION

Trial commentators argue that attorney persuasiveness is affected by his or her demeanor, which in turn is a simple combination of the effects of likability, credibility, and honesty. The existing research shows that source characteristics such as likability and credibility can influence persuasion. The research also shows that the combination of the source characteristics does not necessarily lead to more effective persuasion. For example, a likable (i.e., warm and generous) and credible source (i.e., advocating a small award) was not found to be as persuasive as a disliked (i.e., stingy) but credible (i.e., advocating a large award) source, even though liked and credible sources typically have an advantage when those characteristics are considered alone. There are overlapping effects between these source characteristics. For example, increasing liking can enhance perceptions of the communicator's trustworthiness. However, some source characteristics appear to outweigh the presence of other source characteristics. For example, as noted in the study discussed above (Wachtler & Counselman, 1981), credibility appears to have a greater influence on persuasion than liking because the stingy, credible source was a more effective advocate then the likable, credible source.

Moreover, although trial commentators believe that by appearing likable, honest, and credible, attorneys will have a significant advantage in trial, these qualities have been shown to serve as simple cues, or heuristics, for decision making and are likely to increase persuasive success only in some circumstances. For example, one may rely on liking as a cue for deciding the legitimacy of an argument: "I like this person; therefore, the person must be right." However, the dual process models of decision making (ELM and HSM) explain that simple decision rules are most likely to be relied on when the receiver is unmotivated or unable to process a message carefully or systematically. Because jurors should take their responsibility in reaching a verdict seriously, it is reasonable to hypothesize that they will be unlikely to use a simple decision rule such as the attorney's likability, honesty, or credibility to reach a decision, and instead will be more likely to rely on the strength of the evidence and arguments for the basis of their decision.

In addition, cognitive dissonance explains that unfavorable characteristics associated with a communicator may actually result in more effective persuasion than a favorable communicator. According to cognitive dissonance, if jurors find themselves being persuaded by a dislikable attorney, then they will convince themselves that there is a good reason for it to justify their inconsistent cognitions, which can lead jurors to hold their decision more strongly than they would if the message came from someone they liked. Thus, disliked attorneys with strong arguments may ultimately have an advantage over a comparable, liked attorney. Low-credibility or moderate-credibility communicators are also more persuasive than high-credibility persuaders when they are advocating a favorable position, perhaps because receivers perceive that they need assistance in developing a strong argument and will expend more effort in elaborating on the argument.

In short, scientific research indicates that the characteristics of the attorney are unlikely to provide a consistent or powerful persuasive advantage at trial. Strong evidence and arguments appear more critical for achieving success (Reskin & Visher, 1986; Visher, 1987). However, for cases where evidentiary strength is not obvious for one party or where jurors are not motivated to be involved in the trial, they are likely to rely on simple heuristics, such as likability, credibility, and honesty to make their evaluations.

3

ATTORNEY VERBAL COMMUNICATIONS

It is self-evident that communication is foundational for successfully persuading jurors. Trial commentators offer advice on three types of communication in the courtroom: *verbal* (i.e., the specific words used to communicate), *paralinguistic* (i.e., the way speech is articulated to convey information), and *kinesic* (i.e., body movements that affect communication). This chapter focuses on verbal communications, Chapter 4 deals with attorney paralinguistics, and Chapter 5 deals with attorney kinesics.

ATTORNEY VERBAL COMMUNICATIONS IN THE LEGAL LITERATURE

Trial commentators appear to favor simple language for courtroom communications. For example, some believe that lawyers should communicate in such a way that 10-year-olds would be able to understand (O'Quinn, 2001). The legal literature on this point notes that sentences should be constrained to 25 words or less during the bulk of the trial and 15 words or less during cross-examination, while sentences should progress "linearly" (i.e., in a straight line) so that people are not confused (Ball, 1993, p. 13).

Another strategy proposed for communicating clearly to jurors is to use short words with few syllables. For example, Murray (1995) argued that the best trial lawyers are "consummately articulate with words no more than five letters and two syllables" (p. 5). Words with four to five syllables should be used "sparingly" (Perrin, Caldwell, & Chase, 2003, p. 25).

Word choices should be intelligible to every juror, with jurors able to grasp "not only the meaning but also the connotation" of the words (Eldridge, 1986, p. 15). Words should be well established in the language (Perlman, 1994), with the lawyer's language "respect[ing] the nature and locale of the case" (Turbak, 1998, p. 69); "words must fit the common denominator of the jury," meaning that words should be familiar to and understood by all members on the jury (Eldridge, 1986, p. 15). Unfamiliar language is thought to impede the message that the lawyer is trying to communicate (Mauet, 1992, 2005), distract jurors (Ball, 1993, 1997; Mauet, 1992), cause jurors to perceive the lawyer as being different from them, and lead them to disconnect from the lawyer (Haydock & Sonsteng, 1991; Mauet, 1992).

One specific piece of unfamiliar language that the legal literature notes as especially important to avoid is "lawyerese" or "legalese" (i.e., technical words specifically used in law). Similarly, policy or other technical jargon should be eliminated when presenting cases (Easton, 1998; Eldridge, 1986; Mauet, 1992, 2005; Perlman, 1994; Toch, 1961). Peppering sentences with jargon essentially makes sentences more complex by replacing simple concepts with unfamiliar or complex words or phrases (Ball, 1993, 1997; Fine, 1998; Fontham, 2002; Haydock & Sonsteng, 1991; Murray, 1995; Perrin et al., 2003). Some trial advocacy strategists believe that using legalese will reflect poorly on the lawyer, leading the jury to see the lawyer as a "hired gun" (Haydock & Sonsteng, 1991, p. 50). However, if the lawyer cannot avoid using legalese, then the lawyer must explain what it means every time it is used because the jury members may not remember what the legal jargon means (Ball, 1993, 1997).

Even though the importance of using simple language is highlighted in the legal literature, some trial commentators caution against taking this goal too far. Lawyers are advised not to talk down to the witnesses or jurors (Haydock & Sonsteng, 1991; Lubet, 2000; Murray, 1995) or underestimate jurors' intelligence because using "baby talk" may infuriate or bore jurors (Singer, 2000, p. 76).

Another goal noted in the legal literature for communicating with the jury is to appropriately convey the specific ideas and images pertinent to the lawyer's case (Haydock & Sonsteng, 1991). Although lawyers are advised not to focus on the specific words delivered but rather on the ideas and images, trial commentators appear to agree that successfully achieving this goal requires carefully selecting words that convey the ideas and images (Ball,

1993, 1997; Haydock & Sonsteng, 1991). For example, trial commentators encourage attorneys to use a thesaurus to better choose words and phrases because proper choices are thought to increase juror understanding and how jurors think about the case (Ball, 1993, 1997). Framing the client in a way that "humanizes" him or her is another example of how lawyers encourage specific uses of words to convey ideas in furtherance of their case. For example, words and phrases such as "friend," "good and decent men and women," "hardworking employees," or "dedicated parents" instead of the usual "plaintiff" or "client" are thought to convey to the jury that the client is someone that the lawyer has a real connection with (Association of Trial Lawyers of America, 2003).

The use of *impact words* is one tool that trial commentators appear to agree helps in emphasizing the specific ideas and images of the lawyer's case (Ball, 1993, 1997; Berg, 2003/2006; Haydock & Sonsteng, 1991, p. 44; O'Quinn, 2001). According to the legal literature, impact words are descriptive words that are used to emphasize specific facts of a case or create more vivid images of an event (Haydock & Sonsteng, 1991). The idea behind impact words is that some words or phrases "naturally bring images of force, impact, and action to listeners' minds" (Perlman, 1994, p. 7). Impact words are thought to be more easily remembered by jurors (Haydock & Sonsteng, 1991) and to help them better visualize the importance of the case (O'Quinn, 2001). Trial commentators believe that impact words should be selected for accuracy (Haydock & Sonsteng, 1991) and forcefulness (Berg, 2003/2006) and placed near the end of the sentence because they convey the attorney's main concern. Furthermore, because of a belief that jurors will stop listening once the main concern is expressed, placing the impact word at the end of the sentence is thought to increase the likelihood that the jurors will pay attention to everything the attorney has said (Ball, 1993, 1997).

Moreover, word choice is considered important by trial commentators for "painting" pictures for the jury (Ball, 1993, 1997; Fine, 1998, p. 37). Using more details in jury communications is thought to increase the accuracy of the image portrayed and to ensure that the trial attorney's desired image of the case is the one that the jurors are picturing in their minds (Haydock & Sonsteng, 1991). To this end, trial commentators encourage using figurative language in the form of examples, analogies, metaphors, and symbols to convey ideas and images (Ball, 1993, 1997; Berg, 2003/2006; Wells, 1988). The emotional component found in figurative language is thought to affect impression formation (Wells, 1988). Figurative speech is also encouraged as a way to bring jurors' own personal associations into play, creating images for the jury and keeping the jurors more alert during the trial process (Ball, 1993, 1997). For example, some metaphors are believed to have an "archetypal connection with the human condition" and, therefore, resonate with the jurors

(Wells, 1988, p. 99), while analogies are believed to "capture [one's] case in a way that will stick with jurors" (Berg, 2003/2006, p. 136). Another reason trial commentators advocate for the use of figurative speech is that analogies and metaphors are thought to contain compact lines of reasoning that efficiently present the trial attorney's case in a clear, compelling way (Wells, 1988).

Finally, the legal literature on trial advocacy contains a list of words that should be avoided during the trial process. Trial attorneys are encouraged to eliminate filler words such as "okay" during their trial communications (Ball, 1993, 1997; Packel & Spina, 1984) and avoid negative descriptions that may inadvertently be applied to jurors. For example, women should not be called "girls" and young African American men should not be called "boys" (Ball, 1993, p. 15; 1997, p. 17). In addition, trial attorneys are advised to avoid contractions unless the vowel sound in the contracted word is different from the vowel sound in the word's uncontracted form (e.g., *don't* vs. *didn't*) because a distraction can obscure the *-n't* and jurors might mishear the meaning of the word (Ball, 1993, 1997).

SCIENCE RELEVANT TO TRIAL COMMENTATORS' CLAIMS

Language can be viewed as a system of signs for conveying meaning (Cruse, 1990). The literature acknowledges that there are several types of signs (e.g., written, linguistic, paralinguistic, kinesic) that people use in communication. It is important to note that there is some disagreement in the literature about terms (e.g., speech vs. linguistics vs. verbal communications) and their definitions. In this chapter, the term *verbal communications* includes the specific "words used and their grammatical arrangements" (Cruse, 1990, p. 141). In addition, under this definition we include sounds (e.g., "um," "hmm") because the trial literature categorizes these sounds as *filler words*. However, usually these noises would be considered part of paralinguistics, which we discuss in Chapter 4. This section critically considers the trial commentators' assertions on verbal communications from a scientific perspective.

Many authors have emphasized the connection between speech communication and the law (Goldswig & Cody, 1990; see Bunn, 1964; Drew, 1985; Rice, 1961; Weiss, 1959), a conclusion that makes intuitive sense given the structure of trials. For example, attorneys must use their verbal communication skills to select a jury, present opening statements, question witnesses, make objections, present closing arguments, and ultimately persuade jurors about the validity of their position. In addition, other authors emphasize the importance of learning rhetoric and argumentation as part of the curriculum for prospective attorneys (Goldswig & Cody, 1990; see Koegel, 1951; Matlon, 1982). Despite the apparent agreement about the importance of verbal skills in trial advocacy, there is still a surprising lack of research on communication in trial settings (e.g., Drew, 1985; Goldswig & Cody, 1990). However, research on persuasion, psycholinguistics, and other fields is instructive for understanding which aspects of attorneys' verbal communications are likely to be effective in trial.

Use Simple Language

Some characteristics associated with legal language include legal terminology (i.e., legalese), lengthy and complex sentences, unusual sentence structure, negation, wordiness, and conjoined words and phrases. Legal stylistic preferences are likely to alienate the public and negatively affect comprehension (Tiersma, 1999). Given the cumbersome characteristics of legal language, trial commentators are correct to favor simple communications in the courtroom.

The impact of legal language is especially evident in the arena of jury instructions. Jury instructions reflect many common characteristics of legal language (e.g., bad grammar, abstract legal concepts, confusing syntax; Elwork, Sales, & Alfini, 1977; Sales, Elwork, & Alfini, 1977; Severance, Greene, & Loftus, 1984; Severance & Loftus, 1982). There is extensive literature demonstrating that jury pattern instructions, written primarily to ensure uniformity and legal accuracy (Tiersma, 2001), are largely incomprehensible. For example, when researchers asked prospective jurors to paraphrase several civil pattern instructions they heard on audiotape, participants accurately paraphrased only 54% of the essential parts (Charrow & Charrow, 1979). Likewise, other research found a comprehension rate of 51% for a series of original pattern instructions (Elwork et al., 1977). Some studies have found even less promising comprehension rates for certain pattern instructions (e.g., Haney & Lynch, 1994; Strawn & Buchanan, 1976).

The comprehensibility of jury instructions can be improved dramatically by rewriting the instructions according to psycholinguistic principles. Many of these principles are discussed in more detail in the following sections, but they include eliminating the use of legal jargon, using familiar words, using concrete words, avoiding homonyms, and decreasing sentence complexity (Lieberman & Sales, 1997). After rewriting instructions according to psycholinguistic principles, jury comprehension reached 80% in one study (Elwork, Alfini, & Sales, 1982). Other studies were also able to achieve improvements in comprehension by rewriting civil jury instructions (e.g., Charrow & Charrow, 1979; Severance et al., 1984; Severance & Loftus, 1982) and death penalty jury instructions (Frank & Applegate, 1998) by using psycholinguistic principles (see English & Sales, 2007; Lieberman & Sales, 1997).

Based on the research on jury instructions, it appears that trial commentators are correct to be concerned with simplifying legal language. The question that now arises is whether their recommended strategies for simplifying language will achieve the desired goal of effective communications with jurors.

Communicate at the Level of a 10-Year-Old

Trial commentators favor communicating at the level of a 10-year-old when speaking to jurors to ensure that the message is understood. No research appears to directly address this assertion by trial commentators, but research on language development in children, adolescents, and adults is informative.

Language development appears to be continuous throughout one's life span, occurring rapidly in infants and young children and slowing down dramatically after preschool (Nippold, 2006). By age 6, most children have a vocabulary (also known as a *lexicon* in the linguistic literature) of approximately 18,000 words, and their vocabulary continues to increase once they are able to read proficiently, usually around age 9 or 10. By early adulthood, people will generally understand and use at least 60,000 different words (Nippold, 2006). Whereas younger children typically understand concrete objects and common action verbs, adults understand a large number of difficult words (e.g., abstract nouns, metalinguistic and metacognitive verbs, adverbs of magnitude, adjectives of emotion, adverbial conjunctions, and academic terms; Nippold, 1998, 2006). Concrete and abstract words are discussed in more detail below.

The ability to grasp figurative expressions, such as metaphors, develops with age. As children grow older, they are better able to "comprehend metaphors that contain complex vocabulary, that speak to human emotions, and that require a greater degree of world experience" (Nippold, 2006, p. 370; see Nippold, 1998). Syntactic development (i.e., sentence structure) also expands with age. For example, adults produce longer and more complex sentences. A 30-year-old adult will typically use sentences of 10 words during conversation compared with a 6-year-old child, who uses approximately six words per sentence (Nippold, 2006). In addition, the use of sophisticated grammatical constructions (e.g., adverbial clauses) and syntactic structures (e.g., passive voice) increases with age (Nippold, 2006; see e.g., Berman & Verhoeven, 2002). Metaphors and sentences are discussed in more detail in the following sections.

Conversational skills continue to improve during adolescence. For example, adolescents are better able to stay on topic, make relevant comments, transition smoothly between topics, and empathize. They also develop skills to entertain the listener, such as telling jokes, telling anecdotes, and using gestures and facial expressions (Nippold, 1998, 2000, 2006). In addition, compared with children, adolescents and young adults can adjust the tone and content of their discourse and are better aware of other people's thoughts, feelings, and emotions (Nippold, 1998).

Environmental and cultural factors can influence language development (e.g., Grant & Gomez, 2001; Hoff & Tian, 2005). Not surprisingly, according to research on jury instruction comprehensibility, higher education level is associated with greater comprehension of jury instructions (Lieberman & Sales, 1997; see Benson, 1985; Buchanan, Pryor, Taylor, & Strawn, 1978; Charrow & Charrow, 1979; Elwork et al., 1982; Forston, 1970; Kramer & Koening, 1990; Severance et al., 1984; Strawn & Buchanan, 1976). Ironically, jurors serving on lengthy trials, which are likely to be more technical, are less likely to have a college education (Lieberman & Sales, 1997; see Cecil, Lind, & Bermant, 1987). Still, it seems likely that most adults' language development is beyond the level of a 10-year-old. Therefore, while attorneys who speak at the level of a 10-year-old will likely ensure jury comprehension, research suggests that this strategy is probably unnecessary to ensure comprehensibility among most jurors. This strategy also potentially conflicts with trial commentators' instruction that attorneys should not use baby talk to the jury, and there is some support that baby talk can negatively affect communications (see below).

Use Short Sentences

Trial commentators argue that sentence length is important for ensuring that jurors understand the attorney's arguments. Before delving into the scientific research addressing trial commentators' beliefs about sentence length, we review sentence classifications because they will be useful for understanding research in this and the next section. Simple sentences contain one independent clause (i.e., a subject and a main verb that make a complete statement). For example, "She ran a race." Simple sentences may be lengthened with prepositional phrase modifiers (e.g., "After training for several months, she ran a race"), adjectives (e.g., "She ran a difficult race"), compound subjects (e.g., "She and I ran a race"), and multiple verbs (e.g., "She ran a race and looked happy"), among other methods. A compound sentence is two independent clauses that can stand independently as sentences, but are connected with a conjunction (e.g., *and, but, or*) to make one sentence (e.g., "She ran for 10 miles, but she was happy she did it"). A self-embedded sentence contains independent and subordinate clauses (i.e., a subject and main verb that do not make a complete statement), which may be connected with relative pronouns (e.g., "The student who failed the exam is studying") or subordinating conjunctions (e.g., "The student is studying because she failed her exam"). A compound–self-embedded sentence is a combination of a self-embedded sentence and a compound sentence (Sales et al., 1977).

Unusually lengthy sentences and "longwindedness" are key features of legal style (Tiersma, 1999, p. 56). For example, one research study investigated sentence length in the British Courts Act of 1971 (Gustafsson, 1975). Legal sentences in the act ranged from 10 to 179 words long, and the average sentence contained about 48 words. Another study examining the British Road Traffic Act of 1972 found even longer sentences (Hiltunen, 1984; see Tiersma, 1999). In this act, sentence lengths ranged from seven to 740 words; the average sentence length was approximately 79 words (Gustafsson, 1975; see Tiersma, 1999). Similarly, the average sentence in one set of jury instructions was 102 words long (Austin, 1984; see Tiersma, 1999). In contrast, sentence lengths in scientific writing was approximately 28 words, while dramatic texts contained only an average of seven words per sentence (Gustafsson, 1975; see Tiersma, 1999).

Although research supports the finding that shorter sentences are usually easier to remember, one study also found that sentences that were nine, 11, and 13 words long were equally well remembered (but not as easily remembered as five- and seven-word sentences; Sales et al., 1977; see Gerver, 1969; Miller, 1973; Wearing, 1973). Likewise, Charrow and Charrow (1979) failed to find that length of jury instructions had an effect on comprehensibility. For example, when they evaluated variables that made up 44 sentences of jury instructions, ranging in length from seven to 72 words, sentence length accounted for only 1.7% of the variation in performance (Charrow & Charrow, 1979). Therefore, the impact of sentence length on memory and comprehension appears less important than predicted in the trial advocacy literature.

Psycholinguistic research on jury instructions has demonstrated that sentence length is really a symptom of a more serious factor affecting memory and comprehension for sentences: sentence complexity. Even though long sentences can be structured simply (Danet, 1980), longer sentences are often more grammatically and psychologically complex because of the addition of new words, phrases, and clauses (Sales et al., 1977). For example, about 20% of the sentences in the British Courts Act contained only one independent clause, but these sentences composed 41% of sentences in scientific prose, making them the most common type of sentence in that field. On average, the legal language in the British Courts Act contained 2.86 clauses per sentence (Gustafsson, 1975; see Danet, 1980). When sentences are embedded (i.e., subordinate clauses are contained within independent ones), they become longer and more complex. Legal language has significantly deeper embedding than most journalistic, literary, or scientific texts (Tiersma, 1999; see Gustafsson, 1975; Hiltunen, 1984). The effects of sentence complexity on comprehension will be discussed in more detail in the following section.

Trial commentators' concern with sentence length is evident from another recommendation that they give lawyers: Use no more than 15 words in a sentence during cross-examination and no more than 25 words in a sentence during the rest of trial. In light of the unusually long sentences found in jury instructions and statutes, trial commentators may be rightly concerned that the lengthy sentences found in legal text also extend to oral legal communications. Tiersma (1999) noted that lengthy sentences are a prominent feature of legal style and suggested that this is true for both speech and writing. Unfortunately, although several studies address sentence length in jury instructions and statutes, there is a dearth of research about whether lengthy sentences are also a feature of lawyers' verbal communications.

Despite the lack of research directly on point, oral legal communications are believed to be less formal, syntactically complex, and lexically dense than written legal language (Tiersma, 1999). This may be the result of lawyers following trial commentators' advice, but it more likely reflects the differences between how people write and speak. Many studies, although not all, have reported key differences between written and oral language in other areas besides law. Research indicates that spoken discourse is typically shorter in length than written language (O'Donnell, 1974; O'Donnell, Griffin, & Norris, 1967). Spoken language contains shorter sentences, fewer words, and words with fewer syllables (e.g., Gibson, Gruner, Kibler, & Kelly, 1966). For example, one study examining grade-school children found that nominal constructions, adverbial clauses, and sentence combining became more prominent in writing than in speech for higher grades (O'Donnell, Griffin, & Norris, 1967). In the academic arena, writing contained more formal vocabulary, more nominal and passive constructions, fewer first person pronouns, and was more impersonal than speech (Chafe & Danielewicz, 1987; see Tiersma, 2000).

Although this research suggests that attorneys are likely to use shorter sentences in their spoken communications than are found in legal writing, one criticism of research comparing written and spoken language is that studies finding differences between the two modalities compared formal written language and informal speech. Variations in sentence length may not result when there is less distinction in the level of formality between written language and spoken language (Akinnaso, 1982; e.g., Blankenship, 1962; Borchers, 1936). The courtroom environment is likely to be more formal than a casual dinner conversation, yet it still seems unlikely that attorneys would use the unusually long sentences that characterize statutes and jury instructions.

The next area of inquiry is what constitutes appropriate sentence length for trial attorneys to employ. In other words, should attorneys cap their sentences at 15 to 25 words to ensure effective verbal communications? The linguistic literature notes that people vary their sentence length depending on the type of communication—conversational or expository. Conversational discourse is more social and less formal (Crystal, 2002; Nippold, Hesketh, Duthie, & Mansfield, 2005). As discussed in the previous section, a 30-year-old adult will typically use sentences of 10 words during conversation (Nippold, 2006). On the other hand, expository discourse uses language to convey information (Bliss, 2002; Nippold et al., 2005). Expository discourse emphasizes accuracy and detail and requires a greater degree of syntactic competence. Increased sentence lengths are also associated with expository discourse (Nippold, 2006).

One study compared conversational and expository discourse in adults, adolescents, and children. Sentence length was measured with the terminable unit, or T-unit, which contains "one independent (main) clause and any dependent (subordinate)" or nonclausal structures that are attached to it or embedded within it (Nippold, 2005, p. 1051; see Hunt, 1970; O'Donnell, 1974). In other words, under the researchers' definition of the T-unit, simple sentences and self-embedded sentences would be considered one T-unit, but a compound sentence or a compound–self-embedded sentence would be considered two T-units. The study found that for conversational discourse, adults in their 20s averaged 9.86 words per T-unit, and adults in their 40s averaged 9.56 words per T-unit. For conversational discourse, T-units ranged from six to 13.44 words for adults in their 20s and from 6.88 to 15.16 words for adults in their 40s. The number of words per T-unit increased for expository discourse, with adults in their 20s averaging 11.04 words per T-unit and adults in their 40s averaging 11.46 words per T-unit. The length of T-units in expository discourse ranged from 8.21 to 13.24 words for participants in their 20s compared with 10.08 to 15.17 words for participants in their 40s (Nippold et al., 2005).

There are two points worth noting about this study. Because of the way a T-unit is defined, it may not accurately reflect sentence length for compound or compound–self-embedded sentences. These types of sentences could be much longer than the average T-unit indicates (e.g., if the sentence combined two T-units with a conjunction). In addition, the study's sample size for the age groups was small ($n = 20$), so individual differences may have influenced the results.

Despite these concerns, this study and other previously discussed research findings are relevant for drawing conclusions about trial commentators' assertions on appropriate sentence lengths during trial. Attorneys' communications in court are most likely considered expository discourse rather than conversational discourse. Therefore, one can expect that attorneys will need to use longer sentences in their communications with jurors than are usually found in everyday conversations. However, based on the finding that the average T-unit in expository discourse is approximately 11 words long, the recommendation that trial attorneys limit themselves to 15 to 25 words per sentence may be superfluous. Even if trial attorneys' sentences are characterized by lengthy sentences typical of legal language, the longest T-unit in the study contained only 15 words, well under the 25-word limit attorneys recommended for most of the trial. And even though T-units do not necessarily reflect sentence length for compound sentences. For example, combining sentences with a conjunction probably will not affect comprehension so long as the individual sentence units are not overly complex.

In sum, research on sentence length suggests that "length should only be a concern when it affects the grammatical complexity of a sentence" (Sales et al., 1977, p. 47). However, in the legal arena, research centers on written statutes and jury instructions. To know for sure how sentence length in lawyers' verbal courtroom communications affects jury comprehension, more research is necessary. In addition, although trial commentators are highly concerned with individual sentence length, the overall length of the communication itself is not addressed. It is possible that factors affecting the length of the overall communication (e.g., number of sentences, amount of time spent talking) and the amount of information contained in speech could have a more critical influence on comprehension than individual sentence length.

Use Linear Sentences

Legal language frequently diverges from typical sentence structures, and trial commentators appear rightly concerned with this practice. For example, in modern English, when a verb is followed by a prepositional phrase and a noun phrase, the common word order is verb–noun phrase–prepositional phrase (e.g., "a business proposal to develop a new product with another company"), but legal language will often use an unorthodox alternative order of verb–prepositional phrase–noun phrase (e.g., "a business proposal to develop with another company a new product"; Tiersma, 1999). Another unusual construction in legal language is to have adverbials precede participles (e.g., "throughout contained"), when the normal word order would be the participle preceding adverbial (e.g., "contained throughout"). Legal language also diverges from ordinary English by commonly placing nonfinite clauses after the nouns that they modify (e.g., "monies herein deposited"), subordinate clauses next to the words they modify (e.g., "the tenant, if dissatisfied with the repairs made by the landlord, may . . . "), and subordinate clauses in the middle of the auxiliary and main verbs (e.g., "the landlord may, with the approval of the tenant, enter . . . "). All of these practices are likely to reduce comprehension (Tiersma, 1999). For example, researchers were able to improve jury instructions by 24% after removing misplaced phrases that contained complicated embedded phrases (Charrow & Charrow, 1979).

Psycholinguistic research is clear that the presence of subordinate clauses is likely to affect sentence recall and comprehension. In fact, of the sentences discussed in the previous section on sentence length, self-embedded sentences (i.e., those that contain subordinate clauses) are the most difficult sentences to recall and comprehend (Sales et al., 1977; see Fodor & Garrett, 1967; Forster & Ryder, 1971; Freedle & Craun, 1970; Hamilton & Deese, 1971; Holmes, 1973; Miller & Isard, 1964; Wang, 1970). Subordinate clauses contained in self-embedded sentences may be adverbials (i.e., acts like an adverb and modifies a verb), relatives (i.e., acts like an adjective and modifies the noun that precedes it), or complements (i.e., a predicate necessary to complete the sentence). In addition, self-embedded sentences can be right-branching, left-branching, or center-embedded (Sales et al., 1977). In right-branching sentences the uninterrupted main clause appears first; in left-branching sentences the uninterrupted subordinate clause appears first; in center-embedded sentences the main clause is interrupted by a subordinate clause (Sales et al., 1977).

The trial commentary suggests that linear sentences are most successful for avoiding jury confusion. Although trial commentators offer little guidance about what constitutes a linear sentence, trial commentators probably mean sentences that unfold left to right (i.e., "right-branching") in the order of subject–verb–object. Trial commentators appear to be correct that people do seem to have an easier time processing sentences left to right. For example, people were better at completing right-deleted sentences (i.e., the second half of the sentence was deleted) compared with left-deleted sentences (i.e., the first half of the sentence was deleted; Forster, 1966; see Sales et al., 1977). In addition, of the types of self-embedded sentences listed here, right-branching ones are typically the most easily recalled. For example, in a short-term task, right-branching sentences with adverbial clauses and complement clauses were more easily recalled (Holmes, 1973; see Sales et al., 1977). Although center-embedded sentences containing relative clauses were more easily recalled in short sentences, recall became more difficult as the number of subordinate clauses increased (Sales et al., 1977; see Blumenthal, 1966; Hamilton & Deese, 1971; Marks, 1968; Miller & Isard, 1964; Stolz, 1967). Right-branching sentences are also the least likely to be affected by the number of subordinate clauses (Goldman-Eisler & Cohen, 1971; Hamilton & Deese, 1971; Sales et al., 1977).

Passive voice is another type of deviation from linear sentence structure that is worth exploring. In sentences using the passive voice, the grammatical subject is really the psychological object (e.g., "The boy was bitten by the dog"). Research reports conflict about the comprehensibility of passive voice over active voice (e.g., "The dog bit the boy"). Although several studies have suggested that passive voice is more difficult to understand than active voice, some studies have found that passive sentences were recalled better than active sentences or were on par with active sentences (Sales et al., 1977; see Anderson, 1974; Blount & Johnson, 1971; Gough, 1966; Hornby, 1972; Huttenlocher, Eisenberg, & Strauss, 1968; Huttenlocher & Strauss, 1968; Lippman, 1972; Wearing, 1973). Confusion over passive voice seems most likely to occur when the subject and object appear logically interchangeable (Sales et al., 1977; Slobin, 1971). In addition, the passive sentence structure may be beneficial for emphasizing the participation of the logical object in an event (e.g., "The child was murdered by that man") or as a method for simplifying sentences when the subject is irrelevant or when the subject is unknown (Sales et al., 1977; see Carroll, 1958; Enkvist, 1964; Klenbort & Anisfeld, 1974; Olson & Filby, 1972; Slobin, 1971; Tannenbaum & Williams, 1968; Turner & Rommetveit, 1968).

Another factor that can influence sentence comprehension is negation. Negative sentences have usually one or two words acting as negators (e.g., "not," "never," "except," "unless," or prefixes such as "un-") that modify the meaning of the sentence (Sales et al., 1977). Negatives require more time to process and cause more comprehension errors. In addition, as the number of negators increases, processing time and error rate similarly increase. The increased processing time is likely due to the extra step that negators add to the comprehension process by requiring both the identification of the item and the denial of it. In addition, negatives focus on exceptions to which people are not expected to respond, and therefore, negatives are likely to make communications more complicated than they need to be (Sales et al., 1977; see Just & Carpenter, 1971; Just & Clark, 1973). Some researchers have proposed that negations may be useful when an exception needs to be emphasized. In these situations, the negative may serve to clarify the issue (Sales et al., 1977; Greene, 1970; Wason, 1965). For example, a prosecutor may say something such as, "It is not against the law for someone to drink before driving; it is only against the law to drive when alcohol has impaired to the 'slightest degree'" (example based on ARS § 28-1381(A)(1)).

In sum, the research findings suggest that the best way for trial attorneys to ensure comprehensibility of complex ideas is by using right-branching sentences with properly placed phrases. These sentence structures are probably less critical when the ideas are simple and only require short sentences. In addition, although linear structure favors the active voice, trial attorneys may want to use the passive voice when (a) the subject and object are not interchangeable, (b) they want to emphasize the logical object, and (c) using the passive voice will simplify the sentence. The research also suggests that, as a general guideline, trial attorneys should frame sentences affirmatively and avoid multiple negatives, but using a single negative may be an effective strategy for emphasizing or clarifying exceptions.

Use Short Words and Few Syllables

For lawyers' verbal courtroom communications to be effective, jurors must first recognize the attorney's words and then remember the words for later recall, or at least the ideas they conveyed. Presumably, trial commentators favor short words with few syllables to help them achieve these two necessities for effective communications. This section explores the relationship between word length and the number of syllables and determines whether words shorter in length and syllables promote comprehension and recall in juries.

The term *word length* has been used in research studies to refer to the number of letters in the word (e.g., McGinnies, Comer, & Lacey, 1952), the number of syllables in the word (Bachoud-Lévi, Dupoux, Cohen, & Mehler, 1998), or the total number of phonological speech segments (Roelofs, 2002). The lack of clear and consistent operationalization of word length in the research literature makes it difficult to discern whether trial commentators are rightly concerned with both the number of letters and the number of syllables in their word choices. The confusion about how to measure word length probably results from "the fact that the number of syllables is typically correlated with word length" (Stenneken, Conrad, & Jacobs, 2007, p. 66). That is, an increase in the number of syllables in a word is likely to increase the number of letters. However, words having the same number of letters may have different syllable and vocalization lengths. For example, the words *moist* and *fiery* contain five letters, but *moist* has one syllable and *fiery* has three (Eriksen, Pollack, & Montague, 1970; see Stenneken et al., 2007). In addition, researchers studying word length must control for other factors such as word frequency (i.e., how often a word appears in the language, discussed in more detail in the following section) because longer words appear to occur less frequently than shorter words (McGinnies et al., 1952).

Although a number of studies have reported "longer response latencies for stimuli with increasing number of syllables," these effects have not been found consistently (Stenneken et al., 2007, p. 66; see Bachoud-Lévy et al., 1998; Ferrand & New, 2003; Forster & Chambers, 1973; Jared & Seidenberg, 1990; Klapp, 1971; Klapp, Anderson, & Berrian, 1973; Lee, 2001; Santiago, McKay, Palma, & Rho, 2000; Spoehr & Smith, 1975). In addition, researchers continue to debate whether longer response latencies are due to syllable number effects or confounds with word-length effects (Eriksen et al., 1970; Roelofs, 2002; Santiago et al., 2000). One potential issue in evaluating syllable effects is the method used. Many studies rely heavily on visual processing instead of oral processing and measure spoken response latencies (e.g., Jared & Seidenberg, 1990). These methods potentially limit the application of these studies to trial settings, which rely mainly on verbal communications and no immediate spoken response from the jury. In sum, more research is necessary before one can firmly assess the role of syllables in effective communication.

Despite this concern, many studies do contribute valuable information toward addressing the veracity of trial commentators' underlying belief that shorter words are more easily comprehended and recalled by jurors. To begin, research does not support trial commentators' contention that shorter words are better for recognition. The potential advantage of longer words over shorter words in recognition is that a short word such as *bet* is likely to have more lexical competition (e.g., *bit, bat, met*) than a longer word such as "dangerous." That is, it may be more difficult to decipher *bet* than *dangerous* because there are many words that are phonetically similar to *bet* (Pitt & Samuel, 2006). In sum, short words may be more difficult to comprehend because they are more likely to activate and compete with multiple, similar word forms (Vitevitch, Stamer, & Sereno, 2008). Early researchers also reported an advantage of longer words over shorter words when being identified in noise (Vitevitch, Stamer, & Sereno, 2008; see Wiener & Miller, 1946). Similarly, other studies using a phonemic restoration methodology, which required "listeners . . . to discrimi-nate words in which a phoneme ha[d] been replaced by noise from one in which noise was added to the phoneme," have found that discrimination was more dif-ficult as word length increased (Pitt & Samuel, 2006, p. 1121). This finding sug-gests that longer words do generate greater lexical activation (i.e., how well the input information "matches a spoken word relative to all other words in the lex-icon"; Pitt & Samuel, 2006, p. 1120; Samuel, 1981, 1996). Listeners and jurors will likely use the additional phonemic cues in longer words to recognize them.

Neighborhood density studies are useful for understanding the advantages of long words over short words. *Neighborhood density* refers to "the number of words that sound similar to a given word after "the addition, substitution, or dele-tion of one phoneme" (Vitevitch et al., pp. 361–362; see Greenberg & Jenkins, 1967; Landauer & Streeter, 1973; Luce & Pisoni, 1998). Words that have many similar words (i.e., neighbors) have a dense phonological neighborhood. For example, *cat* has many neighbors: *at, bat, mat, rat, scat, pat, sat, vat, cab, cad, calf, cap, can, cot, kit*. Words with few neighbors have sparse neighborhoods. For example, *dog* has few neighbors: *dig, dug, dot, fog* (Chan & Vitevitch, 2009).

People are quicker and more accurate at recognizing both monosyl-labic (Luce & Pisoni, 1998) and bisyllabic (Vitevitch et al., 2008) English words with a sparse neighborhood than with a dense neighborhood. In addi-tion, "slips of the ear," where a listener reported hearing something that was not actually uttered by the speaker, occurred more frequently for words with denser neighborhoods than with comparable words (i.e., "content words with similar word length and familiarity ratings as the slips"; Vitevitch et al., 2008; p. 362) randomly drawn from the lexicon (Vitevitch, 2002). Because longer words tend to have fewer neighbors than shorter words (Vitevitch et al., 2008; see Amano, 1996; Frauenfelder, Baayen, & Hellwig, 1993), it appears that jurors will be more likely to accurately comprehend longer words.

The implication that longer words will be less affected by internal and external "noise" in the communication is further supported by more recent research that elaborates on neighborhood density in spoken word recogni-tion. Using the tools of network science, researchers identified the connec-tions between phonological neighbors of a target word to find the clustering coefficient (i.e., "proportion of phonological neighbors [of a target word] that are also neighbors of each other"; Chan & Vitevitch, 2009, p. 1936). For exam-ple, some neighbors of *cat* would also be neighbors of each other (e.g., *hat, bat, mat, rat, vat, sat, bat, scat*). Words with a lower clustering coefficient, or few inter-connected neighbors, were identified more accurately and responded to more quickly than words with a higher clustering coefficient, or many interconnected neighbors (Chan & Vitevitch, 2009). Given that longer words have fewer neighbors, it seems likely that they would also have lower clustering coefficients and, therefore, be more easily recognized in communication.

The next issue is whether the research supports trial attorneys' underlying belief that short words are better recalled than long words. At first glance, memory studies appear to favor short words over long words. For example, in short-term memory tests, immediate serial recall for lists of short words was better than for lists of long words (Tehan & Tolan, 2007; see Baddeley, Thomson, & Buchanan, 1975). Word-length effects in favor of short words were replicated in long-term free recall and serial recall tasks (Russo & Grammatopoulou, 2003; but see Experiment 2 in Tehan & Tolan, 2007). It is important to note that studies finding word length effects involved pure lists of short and long words. When lists were of mixed long and short words, both long and short words were recalled on par with the recall of short words in a pure word list (Hulme, Surprenant, Bireta, Stuart, & Neath, 2004), suggesting that the word-length effect is more tenuous than previous studies indicated (Hulme et al., 2004; Nairne, 2002).

Researchers have proposed various explanations for the word-length effect. The time-based (Brown & Hulme, 1995) and complexity/discrimination accounts (Caplan & Waters, 1994; Neath & Nairne, 1995) are the two most common explanations (see Tehan & Tolan, 2007). Time-based accounts argue that short-term memory traces decay rapidly at a fixed rate. Reliable recall is no longer supported by the trace after about 2 seconds. To prevent decay, one can refresh the trace by rehearsal. Speed is of the essence in this process because forgetting occurs in real time. Quickly rehearsing the items means that there is a greater chance of refreshing the trace (Tehan & Tolan, 2007). In this process, long words are more difficult to remember because they take longer to rehearse than short words. However, some studies have not supported this explanation (Hulme et al., 2004; Nairne, 2002; Tehan & Tolan, 2007).

Complexity accounts for word-length effects also favor short words over long words. According to this account, the memory for long words is affected by the features to assemble at output. Because "complex (long words) have more features to assemble at output than short words, . . . there is a greater probability of assembly error" (Tehan & Tolan, 2007, p. 36). More recently, researchers have added a discrimination dimension to the complexity argument: People are believed to have a better memory for items that are more distinctive. Short, simple items are presumed to be more distinctive because they have less complex phonological representations than long, complex words. The item distinctiveness advantage, therefore, explains why pure short lists are better recalled than pure long lists. In addition, this account explains that the memory for long words is boosted in mixed lists because they become more distinctive when contrasted with the short items on the list (Hulme et al., 2004; see Tehan & Tolan, 2007).

A third explanation of the word-length effect, the item-order trade-off hypothesis, posits that item and order information can be processed separately (Hendry & Tehan, 2005; Tehan & Tolan, 2007). Short words are easier to process at the item level than long words. Because cognitive resources are focused on processing the item itself and not on encoding the order, one would have a good item memory, but a poor order memory, for the long words. This approach "predicts that on tasks that require item information, long words should be better remembered than short words" (Tehan & Tolan, 2007, p. 37; Hendry & Tehan, 2005). When this prediction was tested empirically, long words were better recognized than short words (Hendry & Tehan, 2005; Tehan & Tolan, 2007). Similarly, in a cued-recall task, recall was better for long words than for short words (Tehan & Tolan, 2007).

Although some of the scientific findings support the trial commentators' presumption that short words are better recalled, no clear conclusions can be drawn to the courtroom at this time. First, studies in this area do not readily translate to the types of communications that typically occur in the courtroom. Findings relied on visual presentation of word lists; in contrast, trial lawyers typically communicate verbally with jurors during the course of the trial. Another concern is that many of the studies investigated short-term memory as opposed to long-term memory. *Short-term memory* refers to the small amount of information that can be kept in the mind at a particular moment, while *long-term memory* is the amount of information saved in the brain for later retrieval (Cowan, 1994). In trials, jurors will likely have to rely on their long-term memory during deliberations. Although the few studies that investigated word-length effects in long-term memory tasks have indicated that the effects in the short term are generalizable to the long term (Russo & Grammatopoulou, 2003; Tehan & Tolan, 2007), research in this area is still relatively new and should not be considered dispositive. In addition, jurors will probably not need to recall lists of words as the participants did in the studies. The extent to which word length would affect memory of the attorney's courtroom communications is unclear if the exact words are not as important as the concepts they mean to convey. Second, the proposed accounts explaining word-length effects differ in their predictions of how long words will affect memory compared with short words. More research is necessary to assess which of the proposed explanations (or any new explanations) for word-length effects is most viable to extend these predictions to trial settings.

Use Familiar Language

Trial commentators' belief that familiar language will help attorneys effectively communicate with jurors appears to be largely on the mark. Comprehension is necessary but not sufficient for achieving persuasion. In the psycholinguistic literature, words that have a higher frequency of occurrence in magazines and newspapers (e.g., *the, she, people*) are called high-frequency words (Sales et al., 1977). Studies have confirmed that people are most familiar with high-frequency words (Sales et al., 1977; see Noble, 1954; O'Neill, 1972; Smith & Dixon, 1971b). In fact, the familiarity of words appears to increase logarithmically as frequency increases (Sales et al., 1977; see Begg & Rowe, 1972; Smith & Dixon, 1971a).

Since high frequency and familiarity appear to be related, research on high-frequency words will most closely address trial commentators' beliefs about using familiar words in their trial communications (but see Gernsbacher, 1984). A voluminous amount of research "has been published on the effect of word frequency in visual and spoken recognition" (Luce & Pisoni, 1998, para. 16; e.g., Glanzer & Bowles, 1976; Glanzer & Ehrenreich, 1979; Gordon, 1983; Howes, 1954, 1957; Howes & Solomon, 1951; Landauer & Freedman, 1968; Morton, 1969; Rubenstein, Garfield, & Millikan, 1970; Rumelhart & Siple, 1974; Savin, 1963; Scarborough, Cortese, & Scarborough, 1977; Solomon & Postman, 1952; Stanners, Jastrzembski, & Westbrook, 1975; Whaley, 1978). The literature demonstrates robust findings of the numerous processing advantages for high-frequency words (Luce & Pisoni, 1998).

Several studies investigated the effects of high-frequency words using a perceptual recognition task, which required participants to "read or repeat material they were exposed to for the first time in the experiment" (Sales et al., 1977, p. 32). Participants were faster and more accurate at hearing, reading, and repeating the high-frequency words (Sales et al., 1977; see e.g., Broadbent, 1967; Champagnol, 1971; Paivio & O'Neill, 1970). In addition, lexical decision tasks that require participants to decide whether they are presented with a real word, a nonsense word, or a nonword have also found that words occurring frequently in the language are classified as words more quickly and accurately than infrequently occurring words (Luce & Pisoni, 1998). For trial lawyers, the finding that high-frequency words are perceived more quickly implies that jurors will probably process communications more easily when common words are used.

Another possible advantage of using high-frequency words in trials is that they may help jurors remember the attorney's communications. Most research has discovered a positive correlation between word frequency and memory (Elwork et al., 1977; Luce & Pisoni, 1998; Sales et al., 1977; see Baddeley & Scott, 1971; Duncan, 1973; Hulme et al., 1997). To test whether familiar (and high-frequency) words were more easily stored and recalled, research relied on recall tasks, which typically required subjects to verbalize and recreate a list of words that was previously presented. These studies confirmed a positive relationship between high-frequency words and short-term and long-term recall (Sales et al., 1977; see e.g., Baddeley & Scott, 1971; Bousfield & Cohen, 1955; Duncan, 1973). One study divided words into high, medium, and low frequencies and tested recall short term (30 seconds) and long term (7 days). Participants retained high-frequency words consistently better (Postman, 1970; see Sales et al., 1977). In addition, memory span ("the greatest list length at which the participant could recall correctly") appears to be affected by word frequency (Hulme et al., 1997, p. 1219).

High-frequency words are also likely to improve comprehension. People begin trying to understand a verbal message by decoding the denotative (i.e., explicit) and connotative (i.e., implied) meanings of words. The ease of the decoding process should influence ease in the comprehension of the message. Assuming that familiar, high-frequency words are easiest to decode, then including these words in messages should increase comprehension. In fact, several studies support this conclusion. For example, one study investigated this hypothesis by pairing participants to have them complete a task. One partner was asked to communicate specific words using clues, while the other partner had to use the clues to define the word. This study found that high-frequency words were more successfully communicated than low-frequency words (Loewenthal, 1969; see Sales et al., 1977). As noted by one researcher after summarizing several studies, word frequency is highly important in reading comprehension because word frequency is highly correlated ($r = .80$) with word meaningfulness (Klare, 1968; see Sales et al., 1977). Extending these conclusions to trial settings, it appears that attorney communications should contain high-frequency words to ensure juror comprehension.

High-frequency words are important for perception, memory, recall, and comprehension and may influence jurors' affective evaluations. Compared with high-frequency words, low-frequency words have a higher association with negative feelings (Sales et al., 1977; see Dixon & Dixon, 1964; Johnson, Thompson, & Frincke, 1960; Zajonc, 1968). This research suggests that attorneys who use the kinds of low-frequency words that permeate legal language risk incurring negative reactions from jurors.

Avoid Legalese

Legal jargon and technical vocabulary are common features of legal English. For example, one study on legal language compared lexical items in 455,052 words selected from transcripts of the Amnesty Hearings of the Truth and Reconciliation Commission (TRC) in South Africa with their usage in the Wellington Corpus of Spoken New Zealand English (NZ), which contains 600,000 words and served as a "natural" spoken language comparison (de Klerk, 2003). Legal technical terms may be well known (e.g., *defendant*), vaguely familiar (e.g., *beyond a reasonable doubt*), or completely baffling (e.g., *estoppel*) to the public. Adding another element to the technical vocabulary are legal homonyms, which seem familiar to the average person but have an unexpected meaning in the law (e.g., aggravation; Tiersma, 1999). For example, the TRC corpus contained 9,806 words that could be characterized as legal jargon. In comparison, the NZ corpus contained only 1,162 words that were specialized vocabulary. In addition, many words in the TRC corpus had different interpretations compared with the NZ corpus. For example, *defence* in the NZ corpus was made in reference to rugby, but the TRC usage had a legal meaning (de Klerk, 2003).

This technical legal language may have perceived benefits for trial lawyers. Many lawyers believe that legal language is a precise mode of communication (Tiersma, 2006). In addition, people use the way they speak to mark themselves as members of a group, so lawyers' unique language can be important for developing a bond with other attorneys (Tiersma, 1999). The specialized language of the law may also give attorneys an advantage over opposing witnesses, for example, by confusing them (de Klerk, 2003). Finally, legal language may help lawyers appear more credible to jurors (Tiersma, 1999).

Despite these potential benefits, trial commentators fear that legal language will impede effective communication with jurors and, therefore, recommend that attorneys avoid legalese, and researchers appear to agree (e.g., Charrow & Charrow, 1979; de Klerk, 2003; Sales et al., 1977; Tiersma, 1999). However, few studies have actually investigated the impact of legal terms on understanding. One survey of American decisional law revealed many cases in which jurors were accused of misconduct for looking up legal words such as *assault, battery,* and *culpable* (Tiersma, 1995, 1999). In addition, when 35 participants were asked to paraphrase a set of 14 jury instructions pertaining to an automobile negligence case, the mean number of correct responses for 36 different technical terms was only 34%. The mean score on correct paraphrases increased to 50% when 17 different lexical items were replaced with easier ones (Charrow & Charrow, 1979).

These findings suggest that using legalese is likely to have a negative impact on jurors' comprehension of attorney communications. Thus, it is important that trial attorneys try to limit their use of legal jargon when speaking in trial. Psycholinguistic scholars recommend that legal terms be replaced by more commonly used words (Sales et al., 1977). In addition, trial commentators' recommendation that trial attorneys explain the meaning of necessary legal jargon is probably beneficial to effective communications with jurors. However, it is still unknown whether this improvement in communication clarity increases persuasiveness and if so, to what extent. After all, some attorneys may not want jurors to understand the law so that they can play on jurors' sympathies (i.e., nonlegal aspects of the case such as the defendant's history of abuse; Elwork et al., 1977; English & Sales, 2005; Feigenson, 1997).

Avoid Baby Talk

Although trial commentators encourage attorneys to simplify their speech to ensure juror understanding, they also express concern that attorneys not take this instruction too far by "baby talking" to the jury. Many studies have documented that adults speak differently to children than to other adults (Caporael, 1981; DePaulo & Coleman, 1981, 1986, 1987; see DePaulo & Bonvillian, 1978; Gleason & Weintraub, 1978; Snow, 1977; Snow & Ferguson, 1977). *Baby talk* is a communication style used by adults, typically when speaking to babies or young children who are learning language (Caporael, 1981; DePaulo & Coleman, 1981, 1986, 1987). Baby talk contains special lexical items, such as "choo-choo," and modifications from adult speech, such as "Mommy loves you" (Caporael, 1981; see Ferguson, 1964, 1977). Other characteristics of baby talk include (a) "high pitch and exaggerated intonation contours" (DePaulo & Coleman, 1987, p. 876; 1986); (b) "shorter sentences that are better formed grammatically" (DePaulo & Coleman, 1986, p. 845; 1987); and (c) slow, clear, and repetitive speech (DePaulo & Coleman, 1986, 1987). People may also engage in secondary or extended uses of baby talk (DePaulo & Coleman, 1987). For example, similarities have been observed between baby talk and speech addressed to "foreigners, retarded people, hospital patients, the elderly . . . pets, plants, and lovers (DePaulo & Coleman, 1981, p. 224; see Caporael, 1981; DePaulo & Coleman, 1986, 1987; Ferguson, 1977, 1981; Grimshaw, 1977; Hirsh-Pasek & Treiman, 1982). One study found that participants were highly accurate at judging when baby talk was directed toward children, but were highly inaccurate at judging when baby talk was actually directed toward elderly persons (Caporael, 1981). In addition, baby talk shares similar characteristics with speech classified as patronizing (e.g., "high-pitched, exaggerated intonation, simplified vocabulary/grammar, and included repetitions"; Ryan, Anas, & Gruneir, 2006, p. 98), which has been studied in communications directed toward older adults (e.g., Hummert, Garstka, Ryan, & Bonnesen, 2004) and persons with disabilities (e.g., Braithwaite & Thompson, 2000). Because of the similarities between baby talk and patronizing speech, the implications for both speech styles are discussed in this section. For convenience, we also discuss nonverbal, paralinguistic aspects of baby talk in this section instead of in Chapter 4.

Baby talk may be perceived either positively or negatively depending on the circumstances. On the one hand, "the literature on speech to children suggests that baby talk is used to express affection and nurturance and would therefore be rated as comforting and pleasant" (Caporael, 1981, p. 880; see Ferguson, 1977). In one study, undergraduate participants evaluated recorded messages of health care facility caregivers' communications to care receivers and other caregivers on a 7-point scale for comfort, irritation, pleasantness, and arousal. The ratings indicated that baby talk seems to be perceived as more comforting while non–baby talk is perceived as more arousing and irritating. This study also noted that condescension may be conveyed in the verbal content of the speech instead of the style (Caporael, 1981).

On the other hand, baby talk addressed to adults could be perceived as negative and deprecatory (Caporael, 1981; see Ferguson, 1977). Baby talk directed at adults is associated with "mockery, irony, and sarcasm" by implying that the listener is babylike (Caporael, 1981, p. 877). For example, political opponents have used baby talk to insult their opponents (DePaulo & Coleman, 1981). Patronizing communications have received negative evaluations in a driving accident situation; a family situation; and health settings such as long-term care, a physician's office, and a hospital (Ryan et al., 2006; see Harwood, Ryan, Giles, & Tysoski, 1977; Hummert et al., 2004; Morgan & Hummert, 2000; Ryan, Hummert, & Boich, 1995). Hummert and Ryan (1996) showed that patronizing talk is also considered impolite.

One study used vignettes to evaluate speakers' speech styles. Three conversational scripts depicted an interaction between one of three female salespersons and a male customer (either a 25-year-old or an 80-year-old) and contained one of three helping styles: underhelping (i.e., dismissive and inattentive), overhelping (i.e., overaccommodating speech and questioned customer's choice), and professional style (i.e., appropriate interest, available, and unintrusive). Participants were then asked to rate the salesperson on dimensions of competence (e.g., incompetent, knowledgeable, intelligent), manner (e.g., rude, helpful, patronizing), and satisfaction (e.g., happy, displeased, frustrated). The salesperson's tone of voice, perceptions of customer's satisfaction with his purchase, and perceptions of the likelihood that the customer would recommend the store to a friend were also evaluated. Because the overhelping salespersons' vocal tone is the most exaggerated, and therefore probably closest to baby talk, the results for the overhelping style should be the most informative for drawing implications about baby talk in the courtroom (Ryan et al., 2006).

The results of this study indicated that the professional salesperson received the highest ratings, whereas the underhelping salesperson received the lowest ratings and the overhelping salesperson received intermediate ratings. Participants rated the professional salesperson's voice as more appropriate and less exaggerated than either the overhelping or underhelping salesperson. However, of the three styles, participants were the least likely to judge the overhelping style to be monotone or flat. The salesperson using the professional style also received the highest ratings on the likelihood of customer satisfaction with the purchase and the likelihood of the store receiving a recommendation from the customer. Compared with the professional helping style, an overhelping salesperson was viewed as less competent and less effective in satisfying the customer. However, the underhelping salesperson consistently received the lowest ratings (Ryan, Anas, & Gruneir, 2006). Although this study is limited in its generalizability to the courtroom, the findings do suggest that a professional style will be received the best by jurors. An overhelping style was perceived significantly less positively than the professional style but not as negatively as the underhelping style. Extrapolating this finding to courtroom situations suggests that baby talk will not be perceived positively, but attorneys who are aloof and uninterested in their case will fare worse.c

More recently, researchers started to evaluate possible responses to patronizing speech (Hummert & Mazloff, 2001; see Harwood & Giles, 1996; Harwood, Giles, Fox, Ryan, & Williams, 1993; Harwood et al., 1997; Ryan,

Kennaley, Pratt, & Shumovich, 2000). Several responses have been documented, which include assertive (i.e., statements of competence), passive (i.e., cooperative, neutral), nonrelevant (i.e., ignoring), and humorous (Hummert & Mazloff, 2001; see Harwood & Giles, 1996; Harwood et al., 1977; Ryan et al., 2000). Since jurors are simply observers in the courtroom and attorney communications to jurors flow in a one-way direction, more research is necessary to determine whether jurors' would share these same responses or whether the trial structure will result in individual differences in juror response.

Some research suggests that whether patronizing speech is perceived as appropriate may depend on the context of the communication. For example, patronizing speech may be perceived to be acceptable in institutional situations and with certain populations (e.g., older persons in a hospital setting; Hummert & Mazloff, 2001; see Caporael, Lukaszewski, & Culbertson, 1993; Hummert, Shaner, Garstka, & Henry, 1998). Listeners may also take into account the speaker's motivations in light of the context (Hummert & Mazloff, 2001; Okamoto & Robinson, 1997). For example, participants in one study more positively evaluated a young woman using patronizing talk when participants believed her thoughts indicated caring intentions than when they believed that she had dominating intentions (Harwood & Giles, 1996; see Hummert & Mazloff, 2001). Even if jurors are offended by baby talk or patronizing speech, it is possible that jurors who perceive that the courtroom is an institution where patronizing speech is acceptable or that the attorney has positive motivations will be more accepting of an attorney's use of these communication styles.

In conclusion, although attorneys do not define baby talk and no direct research has evaluated attorneys' use of this type of speech or patronizing speech in the courtroom, research related to this style of speech appears to indicate that baby talk is unlikely to negatively affect jurors' comprehension of lawyers' courtroom communications. This style of speech is characterized by substantial variation in intonation and could mean that jurors will find it more pleasant to listen to than other speech styles. Although the research suggests that baby talk or patronizing speech by an attorney may negatively influence the jurors' perceptions of the attorney and possibly their experience in the courtroom, other factors are likely to minimize the damage. For one, some research suggests that jurors may be accepting of patronizing speech if (a) they perceive that the speech style is appropriate in the courtroom context or (b) they perceive that the lawyer is well intentioned. In addition, even if baby talk negatively affected jurors' perceptions of the attorney, the impact on the attorney's case is likely to be minimal. Since a central route of processing appears more likely than a peripheral route (see Chapter 2, this volume, for more explanation), jurors can be expected to focus on the facts and arguments instead of communicator characteristics. However, direct research on attorney communication is needed to confirm our conclusion.

Convey Ideas and Images Appropriately

One strategy trial commentators recommend is to convey ideas and images appropriately, a strategy that requires careful attention to words. Although trial commentators fail to elaborate on how to select the words for conveying ideas and images, the psycholinguistic literature supports their contention that certain types of words are more effective for communicating ideas.

Concreteness is one property thought to influence lexical processing that has been intensely studied (McDonald & Shillcock, 2001; e.g., James, 1975; Paivio, 1971; Schwanenflugel & Shoben, 1983). *Concrete* words refer to things that "can be perceived by the senses" (McDonald & Shillcock, 2001, p. 297). For example, material objects can be designated by concrete words (e.g., apple; Walker & Hulme, 1999). On the other hand, *abstract* words have no physical referents and include qualities or actions (e.g., happiness; Walker & Hulme, 1999). Concrete words are considerably more effective than abstract words in communicating ideas (Sales et al., 1977).

Semin and Fiedler's (1988, 1989) linguistic category model identifies four classifications of interpersonal behavior, which move along a continuum of concreteness–abstractness (Fiedler, Semin, & Koppetsch, 1991). *Descriptive* action verbs refer to "specific observable actions defined by at least one physically invariant feature" (e.g., call, touch, or visit; Fiedler et al., 1991, p. 148; Semin & Fiedler, 1988, 1989). The next most concrete verbs, *interpretive* action verbs, such as help and cheat, refer to single behavioral episodes that involve some positive or negative evaluation. Growing more abstract are *state* verbs, such as admire, abhor, or like, that denote "enduring emotional or mental states directed at specific object persons" (Fiedler, et al., 1991, p. 148; Semin & Fiedler, 1988, 1989). Last, *adjectives*, such as honest, helpful, or hostile, are considered the most abstract level of language use. Research shows that increasing the level of the abstractness of the linguistic category reflects personal dispositions rather than situational requirements (Semin & Fiedler, 1988, 1989).

Although it is not entirely clear why concrete words are more effective, the literature contains two explanations of the advantage of concrete words worth noting. One explanation is the dual-coding theory, which posits that both concrete and abstract words can be coded verbally into memory, but concrete words can also be coded visually. Because two sources of associated information are available for concrete words, processing is improved (Paivio, 1971; See Elwork et al., 1977; McDonald & Shillcock, 2001; Sales et al., 1977). The other explanation for the advantage of concrete words over abstract words is importance of context for understanding abstract words (McDonald & Shillcock, 2001; Schwanenflugel & Shoben, 1983). Compared to abstract words, concrete words are believed to have richer semantic representations (Walker & Hulme, 1999) and be independent from their semantic contexts (McDonald & Shillcock, 2001). In contrast, abstract concepts are assumed to have additional information associated with them (McDonald & Shillcock, 2001; Schwanenflugel & Shoben, 1983).

Even without exact reasons, concrete words clearly have stronger effects than abstract words on memory, meaningfulness, and comprehension (Sales et al., 1977). In memory recognition and recall tasks, concrete words were recognized more quickly and with more accuracy than abstract words (Gorman, 1961; James, 1975; McDonald & Shillcock, 2001; Sales et al., 1977; see Schwanenflugel, Harnishfeger, & Stowe, 1988; Walker & Hulme, 1999). Results of other studies also support the conclusion that concrete words are more meaningful than abstract words. For example, research participants provided longer definitions and fewer hesitations in responding to concrete words (Lay & Paivio, 1969; Reynolds & Paivio, 1968), were more accurate at selecting synonyms for concrete words than abstract ones (Bloomer, 1961), better understood concrete words than abstractions (Begg & Paivio, 1969; O'Neill, 1972), and had slower true–false judgments of sentences that contained abstract words (Beighley, 1952; Flesch, 1950; see Sales et al., 1977).

Some variables related to concreteness have also been shown to influence comprehension or recall. For example, imageability (i.e., "how easily a mental image of a word can be formed") appears to influence recall similarly to concreteness, and people have better recall for high-imageability words than for low-imageability words (Miller & Roodenrys, 2009, p. 850; Bourassa & Besner, 1994; Caza & Belleville, 1999; Majerus & Van der Linden, 2003; Tse & Altarriba, 2007). Context availability (i.e., "a subjective measure of the ease with which one can think of a particular circumstance in which a word might appear," McDonald & Shillcock, 2001, p. 297) is highly correlated with concreteness and may provide a partial explanation of why concrete words are more easily recalled than abstract ones (Schwanenflugel & Shoben, 1983).

The strong advantage of concrete words for memory and comprehension, which are necessary elements of persuasion, in the literature indicates that trial attorneys should focus on words that relay concrete ideas. In addition, if an abstract idea must be conveyed to the jury, attorneys will likely be able to increase memory and comprehension for the idea by providing concrete examples (Sales et al., 1977).

The psycholinguistic literature also suggests other things that help convey ideas appropriately that were not included in the legal literature. Psycholinguistic research indicates that trial attorneys should limit their use of homographs (i.e., words that are spelled alike), homophones (i.e., words that are pronounced the same way), and homonyms (i.e., both). Even though homonyms sound the same, they differ in meaning. Confusion is likely to arise with the use of homonyms because the word will evoke several meanings associated with the word (Sales et al., 1977; see Conrad, 1974; Elwork et al., 1977; Macnamara, O'Cleirigh, & Kellaghan, 1972; Winograd & Geis, 1974).

Attorneys can try to avoid misunderstanding by eliminating homonyms from their speech, but this may not be practical because there are many homonyms in the English language (Sales et al., 1977; see Elwork et al., 1977). Another approach to aid comprehension of intended meanings is to use only the most common meaning of the homonym. Trial lawyers are also likely to improve jury understanding by manipulating the context in which the homonym is used (Sales et al., 1977; see e.g., Conrad, 1974; Light & Carter-Sobell, 1970; Marcel & Steel, 1973; Sales et al., 1977). For example, attorneys could manipulate the context of a homonym by

1. defining a synonym ("The goal was laudable or noteworthy"),
2. including examples ("Pasta can include spaghetti, penne, and linguine),
3. comparing and contrasting ("The shirt was not pink but red"),
4. giving a contextual description ("The large, crowded auditorium"), and
5. using antonyms ("She was shy, but he was verbose"; Sales, et al., 1977).

Use a Thesaurus

Trial strategists suggest that attorneys use a thesaurus to help choose words that will increase juror understanding. If attorneys are using a thesaurus to find high-frequency alternatives to their low-frequency selections, then this strategy could be effective. However, some research suggests that trial attorneys should use this strategy cautiously because using synonyms in place of previously used words may actually impair comprehension.

Synonyms may work to impair comprehension in two ways: (a) the receiver may incorrectly believe that the synonym was specifically chosen because of its varied connotation; (b) the receiver may incorrectly believe that synonyms are interchangeable when the nuances in meaning of the word were key for understanding the message (Sales et al., 1977). First, the meaning of many synonyms is not completely interchangeable and the meaning may differ in degree (Sales et al., 1977; see Flesch & Lass, 1963; Perrin, 1965). Even when a communicator selects synonyms to avoid repetition, the receiver may misinterpret the communicator's message if he or she believes that the communicator chose specific words to emphasize differences in meaning. The second possibility is based on the finding that participants who were asked to memorize a list of words often erroneously used synonyms to replace words originally learned (Sales et al., 1977; see e.g., Anisfeld & Knapp, 1968; Cermak, Schnorr, Buschke, & Atkinson, 1970; Stark, 1972). This research suggests that people may not denote nuances in a meaning and may misunderstand the communicator's intended message (Sales et al., 1977). Although these possible errors in communication need to be studied more extensively, trial lawyers can probably avoid any confusion by selecting synonyms from high-frequency words and avoid interchanging synonyms unnecessarily.

Although the legal literature does not specifically address antonyms, using a thesaurus may be beneficial for selecting antonyms that will be most understood by jurors. Antonyms can be negatively modified favorable adjectives (e.g., honest–dishonest; polite–impolite) or contain a different root (e.g., honest–deceitful; polite–rude; Sales et al., 1977). Research on antonyms indicates that people have more difficulty comprehending antonyms that are negatively modified adjectives. For example, Salter and Haycock (1972) found that participants were better at thinking of synonyms to a favorable adjective, followed by antonyms of a different root. In addition, using an antonym of a different root only requires a one-step process for comprehension and eliminates unnecessary processing of a message. For example, negatively modified adjectives or placing *not* before the adjective both require a two-step negation to reverse the meaning (Elwork et al., 1977; Sales et al., 1977; see Sherman, 1973). Therefore, trial attorneys may want to avoid negatively modified adjectives and use a thesaurus to select antonyms with different roots.

Despite the potentially negative effects on comprehension, some research indicates that listeners favor speakers who have language that is lexically diverse (i.e., a rich or broad vocabulary; Hosman, 2002). Lexical diversity is believed to influence complexity in the language, which listeners prefer because of the added interest (Hosman, 2002; see Bradac, Desmond, & Murdock, 1977). Lexical diversity has been found to relate to judgments of a speaker's competence, socioeconomic status, and message effectiveness (Hosman, 2002; e.g., Bradac, Courtright, Schmidt, & Davies, 1976; Bradac, Davies, Courtright, Desmond, & Murdock, 1977; Bradac, Desmond, & Murdock, 1977). In addition, high-status speakers who exhibited low lexical diversity were perceived negatively (Hosman, 2002; see Bradac et al., 1976; Bradac & Wisegarver, 1984). Although no research has been conducted on the relationship between lexical diversity and attitude change, the research does suggest that varying the vocabulary somewhat will be helpful for maintaining jurors' interest and contribute to positive perceptions of the attorney.

In sum, lexical diversity may compromise comprehension, but it can also increase interest and lead to positive judgments of a speaker's credibility. Trial attorneys should recall from Chapter 2, Attorney Demeanor, that source factors such as credibility are less likely to influence jurors' judgments when the issue is important. This likelihood suggests that ensuring comprehension should be a priority over increasing perceptions of source credibility. Ultimately, more research needs to be conducted before firm conclusions can be drawn about whether the benefits of lexical diversity outweigh the risks to comprehension.

Humanize the Client

Trial commentators believe that attorneys should carefully select words to frame clients in a way that humanizes them. The research on framing indicates that word selection can influence people's perceptions of information. For example, participants respond differently when analyzing the same scenario framed in terms of likely deaths versus likely lives saved (Kahneman & Tversky, 1984). Therefore, if an attorney can successfully highlight the client's positive characteristics through careful word choices, then lawyers may be able to manipulate how the attorneys perceive the client, but there are limitations to the effectiveness of this strategy. Chapter 6, Attorney–Client Relationship, reviews the research on humanizing the client and dehumanizing the opponent in more detail and draws implications for the trial context.

Insert Impact Words and Detail

Trial commentators believe that using impact words and detail will be more memorable to jurors and help them visualize the case. The persuasion literature has explored language imagery, vividness, and intensity, which are variables that appear similar to trial commentators' impact words. Because these strategies often incorporate detail as a technique to increase vividness and intensity, detail is merged into this section.

Verbal imagery is the "ability of words to elicit images in listeners" (i.e., "vividness effect"; Hosman, 2002, p. 575). Increasing the imagery or vividness should increase persuasion, be more memorable and accessible, and positively influence attitude change (Hosman, 2002; Nisbett & Ross, 1980). The superior memorability of vivid information has also been found in a legal context. Using a mock jury decision task, researchers found that participants were better able to recall the more vivid evidence 48 hours later. This study manipulated vividness by adding irrelevant detail or embellishment to the description of the event (Reyes, Thompson, & Bower, 1980).

Detailed information is closely related to vividness; thus, researchers commonly adjust the level of detail as a way of adding vividness or intensity to a scenario. Mock juror studies of a defendant's guilt are influenced by the level of detail in witness testimony (Bell & Loftus, 1988). In addition, studies found that witnesses who recall specific details of the crime scene appear more credible than those who do not (Bell & Loftus, 1989; Loftus & Goodman, 1985).

While several studies have found a vividness effect, other studies have not been able to support these findings (Hosman, 2002; see e.g., Burns, Biswas, &

Bubin, 1993; Collins, Taylor, Wood, & Thompson, 1988; Rook, 1986; Rossiter & Percy, 1978). In a literature review, Taylor and Thompson (1982) concluded that there was no conclusive evidence to support the idea that "vividly presented information is more persuasive than nonvividly presented information" (Hosman, 2002, p. 375). Differences in conceptualizing and operationalizing vividness may account for the conflicting research results. For example, concrete and specific language, media (e.g., pictures, video), and direct experience are included under vividness in some studies, while others focus only on concrete language items (Hosman, 2002).

Vividness is also closely related to *language intensity*, and perhaps some overlap exists between the two concepts (Hosman, 2002). Emotionality and specificity are the critical features for conveying language intensity (Hamilton, Hunter, & Burgoon, 1990). *Emotional intensity* is the "degree of affect reflected in the source's language," and *linguistic specificity* is "the extent to which a marker denotes a narrow or broad semantic category" (Hamilton & Hunter, 1998, p. 1998). Examples of intense language include the following: *horrible, excellent, enraged, terrified, astronomical,* and *completely* (Hosman, 2002).

Some research supports trial commentators' belief that more intense words influence perceptions of an event compared with less intense words. For example, in one study participants viewed a film of an automobile accident. The participants who answered the question of how fast the cars were going when they "smashed" into each other reported significantly higher speeds than participants who answered the question of how fast the cars were going when they "hit" each other (Loftus & Palmer, 1974). The participants were also asked later whether they had seen any broken glass. Even though the film showed no broken glass, participants who answered the smashed version of the question were more likely to report that they had seen glass than participants who were asked the hit version. The intensity of the language was used to influence observers' recounting of events instead of to persuade (Loftus & Palmer, 1974; see English & Sales, 2005; Tiersma, 1999).

Hamilton and Hunter (1998) used meta-analytic techniques to summarize the language intensity research in persuasion. They first distinguished two approaches to language intensity research. One approach considers language intensity as a stylistic feature of messages, and the other approach considers intensity to reflect the extremity of a source's position on an issue (Hosman, 2002). Using information processing theory, Hamilton and Hunter generated a causal model that indicated that intensity has both positive and negative effects on perceived source credibility. Their results supported the hypothesis that there are two causal paths between intensity and attitude toward the source. In the first path, language intensity increases the perceived dynamism of the speaker, which helps increase the perceived clarity of the message by making the message more interesting to receivers.

Message clarity was also related to positive perceptions and attitudes toward the source (Hamilton & Hunter, 1998). The second causal path existed between language intensity and perceived source competence, with language intensity influencing the perception of how extreme the source's position was. As the extremity of the position increases, the perception of the source's competence decreased and the source was seen as less trustworthy. Message discrepancy and ego (i.e., personal) involvement of the receiver also influenced attitude change under this second path. Intensity had little effect on messages that were congruent with the receiver's attitude, but when a message was discrepant with the receiver's attitudes, then the intensity effect depended on the receiver's ego involvement. Receivers with high ego involvement held negative attitudes toward the source who used intense language, but the attitudes of receivers with low ego involvement were positively affected by language intensity. In addition, source credibility interacted with language intensity, message discrepancy, and ego involvement (Hamilton & Hunter, 1998; see Hosman, 2002). In situations where a high-credibility source issued a discrepant message to a receiver with high ego involvement, language intensity negatively affected attitude change. Language intensity had a positive effect on attitude change when a high-credibility speaker addressed the discrepant message to a receiver with low ego involvement (Hamilton & Hunter, 1998).

Unfortunately, the quality of research on intensity varies with several factors. For example, the intensity of two message versions can differ in marker power (i.e., how much two messages differ in intensity strength) across studies. Some researchers have also confounded the stylistic intensity with extremity of source position. In addition, some researchers have assumed audience uniformity, but their ability to control individual differences in the perceived intensity of the message is likely to be limited (Hamilton & Hunter, 1998). Thus, further research is needed on intensity.

In conclusion, it appears that vividness and imagery probably influence persuasion, memory, and attitudes. Similarly, increasing language intensity can increase perceptions of message clarity, source characteristics, and attitude change. Despite the potential benefits, attorneys should exercise caution with respect to vividness and intensity strategies at trial. Not only are there limitations in research on imagery, vividness, and intensity, but the research findings on intensity suggest that using intense language under the wrong circumstances could backfire on the attorney. In addition, all of the studies dealing with courtroom scenarios focused on the amount of detail in witnesses' accounts rather than attorney communications. Finally, attorneys should be aware that the legal system may constrain the use of vivid or intense language in the courtroom. For example, if an attorney refers in questioning to the cars "smashing" into one another, the opposing attorney may object on the grounds of argumentativeness, assuming a fact not in evidence, or misstating previous testimony (Tiersma, 1999).

Use Figurative Language

Another strategy trial commentators recommend is using figurative language. Trial commentators encourage figurative language as a way to clearly convey ideas, help form advantageous impressions, encourage the jury to pay attention, and help the jurors remember the lawyer's arguments. Metaphors, similes, analogies, and personifications are common types of figurative language (Sopory & Dillard, 2002a). Metaphor follows the form "A is B," and suggests a transfer of attributes from B ("base") to A ("target"). Likewise, simile, analogy, and personification "involve comparisons of concepts or systems of concepts" (Sopory & Dillard, 2002a, p. 383).

The scientific literature supports trial commentators' belief that figurative language does have persuasive advantages. In a meta-analysis of the empirical literature on metaphor (used as a general term to refer to all types of comparison) and persuasion, Sopory and Dillard (2002b) explored whether messages using metaphors exerted a "greater effect on attitude and communicator credibility than literal messages" (Sopory & Dillard, 2002a, p. 409). The meta-analysis revealed that messages using metaphors did have a small persuasive advantage for attitude change compared with literal-only messages. The meta-analysis also revealed additional information about how to use metaphors advantageously.

According to the meta-analysis, one metaphor "was associated with maximum attitude change," compared with messages that contained one metaphor, two to eight metaphors, or nine or more metaphors (Sopory & Dillard, 2002a, p. 409; 2002b). Greater attitude was acheived by extended metaphors (e.g., a central theme that is used repeatedly and in different forms) than nonextended metaphors (Sopory & Dillard, 2002a, 2002b). Metaphors were more persuasive when the target was highly familiar than when the target had low familiarity. For example, American undergraduate students are likely to have trouble understanding a figurative comparison when they have low knowledge of the target (e.g., "Aid to Colombia is like . . . "). On the other hand, when students had high knowledge of the target (e.g., "Seat belt use is like . . . ") communication was facilitated (Sopory & Dillard, 2002a, p. 410). Novel metaphors proved to be better for acheiving attitude change when compared to nonnovel ones. In other words, the metaphors that are likely to be persuasive are the ones that draw new connections between a similar target and base of metaphor (e.g., "She has a heart of gold" is nonnovel; Sopory & Dillard, 2002a, p. 409, 2002b). The implication of this finding is that if the trial attorney wants to make more than one figurative comparison, then extended metaphors (i.e., several subcomparisons stemming from the same base and target) are likely to be more successful than using multiple, distinct, non-extended metaphors. In addition, although attorneys may have little control over the familiarity of their target in complex litigation, they should still try to select metaphors that are going to be understandable and interesting to the jury.

The meta-analysis also showed that there is a relationship between metaphors and source credibility. Messages with metaphors were associated with greater attitude change for communicators with low credibility than for communicators with high credibility. Although Sopory & Dillard (2002a, 2002b) list several possible explanations for this finding, no definitive proof was provided about which was correct. However, people did not more favorably judge communicators who used metaphors than those who used literal language. In addition, a communicator's use of rebuttal analogies (both a counterargument and a form of social attack) was associated with negative evaluations of him or her, as discussed in Chapter 2 (Sopory & Dillard, 2002a; Whaley, 1997, 1998).

The effectiveness of metaphors may also depend on additional factors (Sopory & Dillard, 2002a, 2002b). For example, one potential factor is *literal-mindedness*, which is "the ability to understand figurative language" (Sopory & Dillard, 2002a, p. 419; Morgan, 1997). Metaphors are more persuasive for people who are low on literal-mindedness because they have less difficulty understanding the figurative language. In addition, under the metaphor extension hypothesis, metaphors that build on and extend an opponent's metaphor may be more effective in a debate than new metaphors or literal retorts (Sopory & Dillard, 2002; see Mio, 1996). Future research will need to further investigate the conditions under which metaphor use is most effective. Moreover, although several theories have been used to explain metaphor comprehension and persuasion, it is unclear exactly how metaphors are comprehended and the process by which a metaphor may have a persuasive advantage over literal language.

Avoid Certain Types of Words

The legal literature on trial advocacy contains a list of words that should be avoided during the trial process. This section will address whether trial commentators' beliefs about the use of filler words, negative stereotypes, and contractions are accurate.

Avoid Filler Words

Trial commentators believe that filler words such as *okay* should be eliminated during trial communications. The use of these types of words is closely related to the linguistic features that are associated with a powerless speech style. For example, a powerless speech style is characterized by the frequent use of intensifiers (e.g., *so, very*), hedges (e.g., *kinda, I think, I guess*), hesitations (e.g., *uh, well, you know*), and polite forms (e.g., *please, thank you*). Gestures and questioning intonations in declarative contexts are also elements of powerless style. In contrast, a powerful style is marked less frequently by the use of these linguistic features (Conley, O'Barr, & Lind, 1979; Erickson, Lind, Johnson, & O'Barr, 1978; Hosman, 2002). Some researchers have explored the use of filler words as part of powerful and powerless language in witnesses' testimony, and these findings are informative for drawing implications to trial advocacy strategies.

In the first study on this issue, participants acted as jurors to evaluate either a male or female witness's testimony demonstrating a powerful or powerless speech style on tape recordings or in reading transcripts. The participants consistently found the powerful speaker to be "more credible, sociable, intelligent, and certain" (Hosman, 2002, p. 379). Participants also recommended a substantially larger damage award for the plaintiff supported by the testimony of a powerful witness (Erickson et al., 1978). Follow-up studies confirmed that the powerful style was associated with more positive characteristics (e.g., more competent and attractive; Hosman, 2002; see e.g., Bradac, Hemphill, & Tardy, 1981; Morrill & Facciola, 1992). A meta-analysis that reviewed 16 studies in the powerful/powerless speech literature confirmed that powerful language is more persuasive and more credible than less powerful language (Burrell & Koper, 1998; Hosman, 2002). Although studies on powerful/powerless language focus on witness's testimony, these findings support trial commentators' assertion that filler words should be avoided during trial. However, it is possible that the different role of witness and attorney may influence the findings.

Avoid Negative Descriptions That Could Apply to Jurors

Trial commentators instruct lawyers to avoid negative descriptions that could apply to jurors. Although trial commentators neglected to explain why, it is likely that they are concerned that jurors to whom the negative description applies may become offended. The social psychology research contains a substantial amount of literature on stereotypes, which suggests several possibilities for how a juror would respond if an attorney introduced a negative stereotype that could apply to the juror.

Although categories, or stereotypes, can have negative ramifications if people ignore within group differences and exaggerate between-group differences, stereotypes can also be beneficial. People often use stereotypes as "energy-saving devices" (Tavris & Aranson, p. 57). The categories help people process new information quickly and provide a means of using old information to make decisions efficiently. In addition, categories are useful for understanding group differences and other people's behavior (Freeman & Ambady, 2011; Tavris & Aronson, 2007). In fact, trial commentators acknowledge that these stereotypes can work to the attorney's advantage.

Recall that trial commentators recommend that attorneys frame clients in a way that humanizes them, a strategy that essentially tries to capitalize on jurors' positive stereotypes.

People begin at a fairly early age to sort other people into categories (Tavris & Aronson, 2007). In many cases, they may not even be consciously aware of these associations (Greenwald, Poehlman, Uhlmann, & Banaji, 2009). People quickly organize others according to their status in the ingroup (i.e., individuals' perceptions of their membership in a particular group) or outgroup (i.e., individuals' perceptions that they are not members of a group). In contrast to outgroup members, people view their ingroup members more positively, treat them more positively, reward them more, are more easily persuaded by them, and expect favorable treatment in return (Brewer & Brown, 1998; Tajfel, Billig, Burdy, & Flament, 1971).

People can be categorized based on race, gender, age, sexual orientation, family, politics, religious orientation, career, hobbies, university affiliation, and sports team affiliation, among other things. Not only can a number of categories apply to any one person, but even arbitrary categorizations can influence people's attitudes and behaviors (Tajfel et. al, 1971; see Chapter 5, this volume, for more discussion of minimal conditions for group formations). Even if lawyers perceive that jurors belong to a particular category, these views do not necessarily apply to how the individual would categorize himself or herself. A person's association with one or more social groups forms the basis for his or her self-identity (Seger, Smith, & Mackie, 2009).

Even if the lawyer does comment in a way that may be negatively interpreted by a juror about his or her self-identity, some research suggests that derogatory comments may not have the same effect on ingroup members as they do on outgroup members. One study on the use of derogatory group labels (i.e., negative category labels; e.g., *fag, nigger, kike*) found that homosexual participants reacted in the same way to category (e.g., *homosexual, gay*) as they did to derogatory labels (e.g., *fag, fairy*) that related to their ingroup. Any ingroup reference, even one that was intended to be derogatory, elicited a positive reaction for these participants. In contrast, heterosexual participants reacted less favorably to associations activated by derogatory labels than those activated by category labels (Carnaghi & Maass, 2007). Although the researchers did not try to identify the exact process by which this effect occurred, they speculated that one reason may be that any cue used to evoke the ingroup self-identity may lead to positive feelings in members of that group. However, this study used a subliminal priming paradigm, which presented a prime subliminally before the target stimulus required a word or nonword decision. Therefore, these results may not be generalizable to contexts where a person overtly listens to a derogatory term or is addressed in a derogatory manner (Carnaghi & Maass, 2007).

Other research appears to indicate that people do have emotional, attitudinal, and behavioral reactions to stereotypes. Intergroup emotions theory explains that "the process of social categorization leads people to experience emotions in response to situations and events that they appraise as affecting their ingroup, even if the individual is not directly or personally involved" (Seger, Smith, & Mackie, 2009, p. 460; see also Mackie, Devos, & Smith, 2000; Smith, 1993; Smith et al., 2007). In the trial context, an implication of this theory could be that if a juror perceives himself or herself as being part of a group, then when his or her social identity is explicitly or implicitly activated by the attorney, the person will experience emotions similar to other group members. Empirical tests support hypotheses related to this theory. People state that their emotions converge toward the typical group profile after they are explicitly asked about the emotions they experience as members of a particular group (Smith et al., 2007). Additional studies demonstrate that even when an explicit request to report group-level emotions was absent, making a social identity more salient through priming produced convergence for emotions. People with strong social identity converged more and showed "more similarity between their group-primed emotions and explicitly reported group-level emotions" (Seger et al., 2009, p. 460).

Emotions can predict individual and group attitudes and behaviors, and "previous research has demonstrated that activating a social identity (e.g., through priming manipulations) influences many types of attitudes and social behaviors" (Seger et. al., 2009, p. 461; see e.g., Baldwin, Carrell, & Lopez, 1990; Carli, 1990; Glasman & Albarracin, 2006; Lee & Ottati, 1995; Liss, Crawford, & Popp, 2004). The presence of widely known negative stereotypes about one's group can create a *stereotype threat*, wherein an individual is concerned about confirming the negative stereotype to others (Steele & Aronson, 1995). Researchers investigating stereotype threat gave African American and white students a 30-minute test composed of items from the verbal Graduate Record Examination. In one condition, participants were told that the test was a genuine test of academic abilities (i.e., diagnostic condition); in the other condition, they were told it was just a laboratory exercise (i.e., nondiagnostic condition). Presumably, negative stereotypes about the inferior academic ability of African Americans would only be relevant to participants who were in the diagnostic condition, a result that was supported by the study (Steele & Aronson, 1995, Experiments 1 and 2). In addition, researchers were able to prime the negative stereotypes associated with African Americans and academic achievement simply by asking students to identify their race on a pretest questionnaire. Students in the race-prime condition did about half as well as the students in the no–race-prime condition (Steele & Aronson, 1995, Experiment 4). Similarly, other studies have found "that patronizing communication and elicitation of negative group stereo-types has been shown to lead to withdrawal from activities, reduced sense of control, and undermined recipient self-esteem" (Ryan et. al., 2006, p. 98; see Braithwaite & Thompson, 2000; Hummert et al., 2004; Kemper & Harden, 1999; Levy & Banaji, 2002). Therefore, a negative stereotype from an attorney may serve as a prime that could impede juror performance. For example, suggesting that women are "girls" may create a stereotype threat that women should defer to men, which could harm a female juror's performance in deliberations (see Spencer, Steele, & Quinn, 1999; after a stereotype about their math ability was made salient, high-achieving females performed significantly worse than did males on a math test).

Conversely, positive stereotypes have been shown to have positive effects through a similar process. For example, when Asian American women's Asian identity was cued, they performed better on a math test (Shih, Pittinsky, & Ambady, 1999). In other words, if attorneys remind jurors of positive stereotypes associated with their ingroup, then their performance could improve to align with the stereotype.

In conclusion, the research on stereotypes in the social psychology literature is inconclusive about how lawyers' use of stereotypes that apply to jurors will influence their reactions. According to the research, some possible reactions from jurors to negative stereotypes are as follows: The negative stereotype (a) may not affect the jurors if they do not identify with the group, (b) may elicit positive associations to the juror's ingroup, or (c) could create a stereotype threat causing the juror to withdraw (Steele & Aronson, 1995). In addition, the research suggests that ingroup affiliations may be somewhat flexible. Although trial commentators did not address how outgroup jurors might perceive the use of a negative stereotype, they also might be affected. For example, one study found that heterosexual participants' attitudes toward gays were less positive after exposure to a derogatory group label (e.g., *fag*) compared with a derogatory nonsocial label (e.g., *asshole*; Carnaghi et al., 2005). More research is needed in this area before clear conclusions can be extrapolated to juror behavior in different types of trials.

Avoid Contractions

According to trial commentators, one way that lawyers can assist jurors' comprehension is to avoid contractions. In the linguistic literature, contractions would be considered a *coarticulation*. When they talk, speakers "overlap vocal tract activities for consonants and vowels temporally and spatially" (Fowler & Galantucci, 2005, p. 635). Individual phonemes are affected by the articulation of the adjacent phonemes (Pisoni & Luce, 1987). In other words, coarticulated consonants and vowels are distorted phonetic segments (e.g., Fowler & Galantucci, 2005).

Coarticulation means that the speaker is not providing certain information in the acoustic signal (Fowler & Galantucci, 2005). The listener is left to reconstruct the language forms from auditory cues or auditory and optical cues (Fowler & Galantucci, 2005; see Massaro, 1998; Sawusch & Ganon, 1995). People are able to compensate for less than ideal speech situations, and "under normal listening conditions, the . . . listener may not have to identify all the phonetic input to recognize the words" because only "a small portion of the acoustic waveform needs to be identified for word recognition" (Pisoni & Luce, 1987, p. 38). Context and other constraints help listeners narrow down the list of possible words (Pisoni & Luce, 1987). However, research findings support an advantage for clear speaking over conversational discourse for many listeners (e.g., hearing impaired, elderly, young children, native language listeners, nonnative listeners). One characteristic of clear speaking is precise and accurate articulation of all phonemes. When clear speech is used, intelligibility typically increases as the quality of the listening environment decreases (Uchanski, 2005). Elements of clear speech will be discussed in more detail in Chapter 4, which considers paralinguistic communications.

In sum, trial commentators' belief that contractions are more difficult for jurors to comprehend has been scientifically verified. Avoiding contractions and carefully enunciating words are likely to assist many jurors in understanding the lawyer's communication. However, the extent to which trial commentators should avoid contractions is unclear because people are able to acclimate to a number of factors affecting speech. For example, recall that in phoneme restoration tasks, listeners are often able to restore phonemes that are replaced by or covered up with noise (e.g., Samuel, 1981). Therefore, more research is necessary to understand the extent to which an attorney's use of contractions will affect jurors' comprehension.

CONCLUSION

Although legal style is characterized by legal terminology, lengthy and complex sentences, unusual sentence structure, negation, wordiness, and conjoined words and phrases, trial commentators recommend that lawyers use simple language in court. The characteristics of legal style, which make legal language cumbersome, and the research on jury instructions suggest that the trial commentators' recommendation is correct. For example, several studies show that jurors understand approximately 50% of instructions, and some studies indicate even poorer comprehension rates. Rewriting instructions according to psycholinguistic principles can dramatically improve these levels. Most psycholinguistic scholars recommend that legal terms be replaced by more commonly used words or, if necessary, explained in more common terms. This conforms with trial commentators' related recommendation that attorneys use language that will be familiar to jurors. High-frequency words are more familiar to people, and these words are more easily and more accurately heard, read, repeated, and classified. In addition, compared with low-frequency words, high-frequency words are more easily recalled in short-term and long-term tasks and are more easily decoded for their meanings. People also report more favorable affective evaluations for high-frequency words than for low-frequency words.

Certain types of words are more effective for communicating ideas and should be more effective in attorney communications. Concrete words have stronger effects than abstract words on memory, meaningfulness, and comprehension. Therefore, attorneys should focus on concrete ideas and use concrete examples if an abstract idea must be conveyed. Limiting the use of homonyms or only using the most common meaning of the homonym will likely contribute to improved communication. Improving the jurors' understanding of a homonym may be accomplished by defining a synonym, including examples, comparing and contrasting, giving a contextual description, and using antonyms. While contractions appear to be more difficult to understand, people are able to acclimate to a number of factors affecting speech. Therefore, although careful pronunciation of words may be beneficial to effective communications in court, it is unclear to what extent it is necessary.

Research limitations make it impossible to draw firm conclusions about trial commentators' contentions with regard to short words and few syllables. Short words are not better for recognition. Short words are likely to have more words that sound similar to them than long words, which suggests that jurors will have more success at accurately understanding long words compared with short words. Neighborhood density is another factor that can influence recognition. Words from more dense neighborhoods are less recognizable and more likely to be mistaken for other similar words. Because long words have fewer neighbors, they are more easily recognized than short words. The effects of word length on memory and recollection are less clear. For pure short- or long-word lists, short words are recalled better, but studies involving mixed long- and short-word lists did not replicate this result.

One strategy suggested by trial commentators for simplifying language is not supported. Trial commentators recommend that attorneys communicate at the level of a 10-year-old to ensure understanding. Although jurors are likely to understand communications directed to this age level, it may not lead to more effective communications because most adults possess a higher-level vocabulary and greater conceptual understanding (e.g., regarding abstract words and figurative expressions) and use more complex sentences and conversational skills than most 10-year-olds. Similarly, research does not necessarily indicate that sentence length will affect comprehensibility. Instead, sentence length is likely symptomatic of sentence complexity, which can seriously affect people's memory and comprehension for sentences. For example, sentence embedding is associated with legal language and will create longer and more complex sentences. However, it appears that lawyers should be concerned about sentence length only if the length affects the grammatical complexity of a sentence.

Using linear sentences also simplifies language. Sentences that unfold left to right in the order of subject-verb-object are easier to understand. Right-branching sentences are typically easier for people to complete and recall and are the least likely to be affected by the number of subordinate clauses. Passive voice deviates from linear sentences and may influence comprehension both positively and negatively. Passive voice may be beneficial for simplifying sentences or emphasizing the object in some situations. Negation can negatively influence comprehension by increasing processing time and comprehension errors, although it may be useful for emphasizing or clarifying exceptions.

A thesaurus may be effective if attorneys use it to select high-frequency alternatives to low-frequency words. Negatively modified adjectives are more difficult for people to comprehend and process than antonyms with different roots, so a thesaurus may help attorneys identify antonyms with different roots. Although a speaker's use of lexically diverse language also may have benefits, attorneys should be careful about using synonyms because they may increase jurors' confusion about the message and jurors may incorrectly believe that the words were chosen to emphasize differences.

Framing information through word selection can engender different responses from participants. Therefore, carefully selecting words that highlight a client's positive characteristics can humanize the client for the jurors and make him or her more sympathetic to the jurors (see Chapter 6 for further discussion on the value of humanizing the client).

Vividness and imagery can influence persuasion, memory, and attitudes. Likewise, increasing the intensity of language may increase perceptions of message clarity, source characteristics, and attitude change. However, limitations in the research on imagery, vividness, and intensity exist, and some research findings on intensity indicate that attorneys should use intense language cautiously because under some circumstances intensity is a disadvantage.

Using figurative language also has persuasive benefits. For example, one metaphor is more advantageous than many, while metaphors that are extended, novel, and have high-familiarity targets are associated with greater attitude change. However, the advantage in using metaphors is greater for communicators with low credibility than for communicators with high credibility. In addition, the research does not find that communicators who use metaphors receive more favorable judgments than those who use literal language. Other factors, such as whether the audience is literal-minded and whether the metaphor builds on the opponents' metaphor, may also influence their effectiveness.

Finally, certain types of speech styles are more effective for communicating ideas and should be more effective in attorney communications. When judging witness testimony, jurors consistently favor a powerful speech style, as compared with powerless speech, because the former omits hedges and hesitations. Although trial commentators do not favor baby talk, the available research suggests that this style of speech is unlikely to negatively influence jurors' comprehension of their message. The substantial variation in intonation during baby talk may even increase the pleasantness of the communication. Even if the baby talk is perceived negatively, it will most likely influence jurors' perceptions of the attorney and not the case because jurors are likely to process information centrally rather than peripherally and therefore not base their decision on source cues (see Chapter 2).

4

ATTORNEY PARALINGUISTIC COMMUNICATIONS

The study of paralinguistics (i.e., the study of speech volume/loudness, tone/intonation, pace/rate, inflection, and accent) has demonstrated that meaning can be conveyed through speech variations beyond the actual words (Banse & Scherer, 1996). This chapter largely focuses on *prosody* or the "non-verbal dimensions of speech which have the syllable as their minimal domain and which can be related to the auditory parameters of loudness, duration and pitch" (Couper-Kuhlen, 1996, p. 369). Voice pitch, loudness, inflections, and hesitations used by the speaker are all elements that can influence the meaning conveyed by a sentence. Variation in speech can also convey a substantial amount of information about the speaker's identity (e.g., Monsen & Engebretson, 1977), region of origin (e.g., Clopper & Pisoni, 2005), health, age, and mood (Nygaard, 2005). In addition, it can provide linguistic information about the message (Cutler, 1994). For example, imagine someone saying, "You passed your math test." This simple sentence can convey a number of meanings. Emotional prosody indicates whether the speaker is happy, sad, or angry, among other states (e.g., "You passed your math test!" in a happy voice; Cohen, Douaire, & Elsabbagh, 2001). Sentential prosody differentiates questions from statements or exclamations (e.g., "You passed your math test?" with a slight vocal rise toward the end of the sentence).

Although it appears that paralinguistics can influence the meaning of communications, the question remains as to whether trial commentators' strategies about paralinguistic cues are likely to achieve attorneys' persuasive goals in the courtroom. This chapter considers this issue by first reviewing the trial commentators' recommendations to attorneys. It then critically considers the science relevant to those recommendations and identifies the implications for attorneys' paralinguistic communications.

ATTORNEY PARALINGUISTIC COMMUNICATIONS IN THE LEGAL LITERATURE

One concern for trial commentators is the atypical distance that witnesses and lawyers speak from. The belief is that this increased distance emphasizes the jury as spectator and increases a sense of detachment among jurors (Burns, 1999). To overcome the distance, trial commentators suggest adjusting vocal volume. Vocal volume is also believed in the legal literature to serve as a way to exude presence or an authoritative air in the courtroom, which allows the trial attorney to appear "more confident, in control, and 'right'" (Fontham, 2002, p. 25). Trial attorneys are advised to speak clearly and loudly so that all jurors are able to hear the communication (Eldridge, 1986). In addition, using a slightly greater alternation in vocal volume when speaking specific words or phrases is thought to emphasize important points for the attorney's case (Ball, 1993, 1997). However, trial commentators discourage a loud and boisterous approach in the courtroom (Haydock & Sonsteng, 1991).

Another element of paralinguistics, vocal tone, is also discussed in the legal literature. One commentator noted that "how things are said is more often more important than what is said" (Berg, 2003/2006, p. 130). For example, proper inflection or tone is thought to hold the jurors' attention (Berg, 2003/2006), while subtle changes in vocal tone or pitch are thought to recapture the jurors' attention or emphasize important words or phrases (Ball, 1993, 1997). Trial commentators advise attorneys to avoid monotone presentations (Haydock & Sonsteng, 1991), as "brains are dulled by sameness but powerfully aroused by change" (Ball, 1997, p. 120). Instead, trial attorneys are encouraged to "speak with conviction" (Berg, 2003/2006, p. 132) and to present their cases "agreeably" and "feelingly" (p. 130). Trial commentators also believe that tone can be used to communicate the attorney's feelings to the jury. For example, one commentator noted that clients' names should be spoken in a tone that shows that the attorney trusts, likes, or sympathizes with them (Ball, 1993).

Some commentary in the legal literature was directed at advising people with high voices about how to better communicate with the jury (Ball, 1993,

1997). People with high voices are encouraged to lower pitch when emphasizing things at least half the time and turn their head directly toward whomever they want to hear them best because "high voices are more directional than low voices" (Ball, 1993, p. 18; 1997, p. 19). If people with high voices must turn away from the jury, they are directed to talk louder (Ball, 1993, 1997).

Pace, another element of paralinguistics, is discussed in the legal literature as a method for conveying information to the jury. According to trial commentators, attorneys should make sure to say only one thing at a time (Ball, 1993, 1997). As with tone, it is recommended that subtle changes in pace be used as a way to recapture jurors' attention or emphasize important words or ideas in the attorney's case (Ball, 1993, 1997). However, the legal literature also notes that saying nothing may also serve as an effective way to highlight a point, gain attention, or create a transition (Haydock & Sonsteng, 1991). "Speechifying" by overemphasizing tone and pace are discouraged; instead communications with jurors should flow as if the attorney were in a normal, personal conversation with friends (Ball, 1993, p. 1; 1997, p. 1).

Two other points noted in the legal literature are worth addressing. First, one trial commentator believes that accents are a tool for creating rapport with the jury but may also hurt effectiveness; however, no reason was listed for this belief (Ball, 1993). Therefore, trial attorneys are encouraged to develop the ability to choose when to employ their accent. Second, because people have a tendency to pick up other's vocal patterns, attorneys are cautioned to avoid picking up the vocal patterns of their opponent in the courtroom (Ball, 1993, 1997).

SCIENCE RELEVANT TO TRIAL COMMENTATORS' CLAIMS

Although there is almost no direct science addressing the paralinguistics of attorney communications, there is science addressing the paralinguistics of communications that is informative. This section compares that science with the recommendations of trial commentators.

Vocal Volume

Trial commentators argue that the atypical distance that lawyers are from jurors when communicating with them can create a sense of detachment for jurors. Therefore, they recommend that attorneys increase their vocal volume to overcome this limitation. Trial commentators believe that lawyers will appear authoritative and confident by using increased volume when speaking. The research supports many of the trial commentators' assertions on this point. Before we begin our analysis of vocal volume, it is important to clarify some terms related to this concept. Loudness is an auditory aspect of sound that is perceived by people; intensity is the acoustic (i.e., the properties of sound independent of perception that can be measured mechanically; Frick, 1985) equivalent of loudness. For our purposes, it is not critical to distinguish between these terms.

Trial commentators' belief that an extended distance can negatively affect persuasive communications appears to be largely accurate. Closeness conveys friendship or interest (e.g., Burgoon, 1991; Heslin & Alper, 1983). Typically, people who are friendly and intimate with each other will stand closer together than people who are strangers (Burgoon & Bacue, 2003; see Aiello, 1987; Hayduk, 1983). In addition, people generally interact at closer distances when they perceive the other person to be "attractive, friendly, and positively reinforcing" (Burgoon & Bacue, 2003; p. 205; see Byrne, Ervin, & Lamberth, 1970; Gifford, 1982). Likewise, closer proximity is associated with increased persuasiveness. Studies have also uncovered that compliance rates increase as the distance between the source and the target of the request decreases (Burgoon & Bacue, 2003; see Segrin, 1993). For example, in studies where confederates requested volunteers for participating in a study (Baron, 1978; Baron & Bell, 1976), signing a petition (Buller, 1987), making change (Ernest & Cooper, 1974), and completing a survey (Glick, DeMorest, & Hotze, 1988), participants were more likely to comply when the confederate was close (e.g., 1 to 2 feet) versus far away (e.g., 4 to 6 feet; Burgoon, Dunbar, & Segrin, 2002).

Although distance is clearly an element that can influence persuasive success, in the restrictive courtroom environment attorneys may not be able to stand a comfortable distance from jurors. Unfortunately, there is no research indicating whether a speaker's loudness will help overcome the negative effects of distance by helping jurors feel more attached to the lawyer or client. However, the distance may necessitate that attorneys speak louder simply so that jurors hear them. Scholars recommend that speakers increase their volume when speaking at a distance of approximately 5 to 8 feet away so that the audience can hear; a louder volume should be used when speaking from a distance of 8 to 20 feet (Hall, 1959; see R. S. Ross, 1986).

Loudness may have additional benefits that trial commentators do not indicate. Trial commentators indicate that loudness influences jurors' perceptions of the attorney as an authoritative and confident presence, and research has shown that vocal cues such as loudness connote confidence and authority (Burgoon, Dunbar, & Segrin, 2002). Loudness is one characteristic associated with dominance, dynamism, competence, and emotional stability (Burgoon, Birk, & Pfau, 1990; e.g., Burgoon, 1978; Mehrabian & Williams, 1969). Other studies did not substantiate these findings, but measurement problems could possibly account for the nonsignificant results (Burgoon et al., 1990). Assuming the accuracy of the initial findings, they suggest that loudness may help lawyers appear more authoritative and confident, but the extent to which this will benefit attorneys is still unanswered by current research.

However, research on increasing vocal volume has demonstrated other benefits. For example, when comparing highly persuasive statements to those that were lowest in persuasiveness, one study found that statements that were louder were rated more persuasive than less loud statements (Packwood, 1974). In addition, increasing the intensity in a voice had positive persuasive effects on others (Freedman, 1972). Other researchers have found that increasing intensity up to moderately high levels related to many positive impressions in the areas of extraversion, sociability, dominance, boldness, stability, and logical abilities (Giles & Street, 1985; see Aronovitch, 1976; Robinson & McArthur, 1982; Scherer, 1979b). Thus, increased vocal volume is associated with several positive benefits, but trial attorneys should also recall that jurors are likely to use a systematic approach to evaluating the attorney's message, so the extent to which these positive associations will aid attorneys is still unknown (see Chapter 2, this volume).

Alternation in Vocal Volume for Emphasis

Alternating vocal volume for specific words is mentioned in the legal literature as a strategy for emphasizing important points. *Stress* refers to the property of syllables that gives them prominence within either a word or a sentence (Frick, 1985). In spoken language, key words are typically stressed, and stressing words can increase their loudness (Cohen & Faulkner, 1986; Ladefoged, Draper, & Whitterridge, 1958). However, other research indicates that the perception of stress is different from the perception of loudness (Lehiste, 1970), and studies have shown that other factors, such as pitch, duration, and vowel quality, are relevant in stress (Frick, 1985; see Fry, 1958; Isenberg & Gay, 1978; Morton & Jassem, 1965).

Stress does appear to have some influence on the comprehension and recall of spoken discourse. For example, stress influenced comprehension and recall in elderly listeners when heavy stress was placed at optimal locations in the spoken discourse. However, stress only had small effects on the facilitation of language for the elderly group, and stress had little or no effect on the performance of the younger participants (Cohen & Faulkner, 1986). Therefore, this study suggests that, to the extent that stress is related to vocal volume, it is the loudness that may be the more effective tool for emphasizing key words or phrases for some jurors. More research is needed to understand the extent to which this conclusion is justified.

Being Overly Loud

Trial commentators discourage attorneys from being too loud. Dominance is associated with loudness (Burgoon & Bacue, 2003), which can be beneficial for persuasion. However, the degree of loudness that is likely to be persuasive is probably limited because it can be perceived as an expression of hostility (Costanzo, Markel, & Costanzo, 1969; Packwood, 1974). For example, previous research found that loud voices are associated with anger and contempt, which are dominant types of expressive behavior (Markel, 1965). In addition, individuals expressing anger tend to speak louder than do more submissive individuals (Burgoon et al., 2002; Kimble & Musgrove, 1988). An implication of this research is that attorneys should strive to ensure that they do not come across as angry or hostile as their volume increases. However, no direct research on attorney courtroom behaviors has tested this proposition.

Vocal Tone

Tone usually refers to the emotion that is conveyed in the voice (Nygaard, 2005), and *intonation* typically refers to how language rises and falls in a given segment of speech (Couper-Kuhlen & Selting, 1996). However, the concept has not been clearly defined, and intonation can include the perceived fundamental frequency (F0) of voice (i.e., the acoustic correlate of the rate of vibration) pattern or other features associated with prosody (Vaissière, 2005). One definition of intonation is close to trial commentators' proposed definition of tone: "a symptom of how we feel about what we say, or how we feel *when* we say" (Bolinger, 1989, p. 1). However, this approach has been criticized because analytic interpretations are based only on the analyst's own intuitions (Couper-Kuhlen & Selting, 1996). Trying to tease out a specific definition of intonation is beyond the scope of this chapter, but one should consider the value of research discussed in this section in light of its potential limitations.

Trial commentators consider intonation to be an important aspect of conveying meaning. In fact, intonation serves many functions, including (a) segmenting continuous speech into syntactic units, (b) segmenting continuous speech into informational units, (c) regulating the speaker–listener interaction, (d) communicating intent, (e) communicating the speaker's attitudes, (f) communicating the speaker's emotions, and (g) communicating characteristics of the speaker (Vaissière, 2005). This section focuses on the nonlinguistic functions of tone and intonation.

Listeners appear to be adept at determining the emotional tone of voice from another's speech. For example, happiness and confidence tend to be signaled by an increased pitch (i.e., how high or low a person's voice speaks), increased loudness, and a fast rate of speech. Contempt, boredom, and grief are conveyed by a low pitch and fast rate. Contempt is characterized by loudness; grief and boredom are soft (Scherer, 1979a; 1981; see also Frick, 1985; Murray & Arnott, 1993; Scherer, Banse, Wallbott, & Goldbeck, 1991). Increased pitch height, pitch range, loudness, and rate are characteristic of arousal (Frick, 1985). Many of these emotions have the same or similar prosodic features, which appears to indicate that people use other cues beyond these simple descriptors, such as pitch or loudness, to discriminate emotions (Frick, 1985). Still, emotional prosody appears to provide crucial information for effective communication.

In addition, some research indicates that intonation can influence views of the communicator's persuasiveness (see Burgoon & Bacue, 2005). For example, one study varied interviewers' "tone of voice" as pleasant, neutral, or hostile. Participants who were considered to be good decoders donated more hours of their time when the requester had a pleasant voice; while poor decoders donated more hours of their time to requestors who had neutral voices (Buller & Burgoon, 1986). This suggests that although emotional tone may influence persuasion, individual differences among receivers may influence the effectiveness of persuasive attempts.

Developing the research on emotional prosody is crucial to understanding the extent to which emotional prosody contributes to communication and persuasion. For example, research has yet to explore how emotion is incorporated into linguistic processing and analysis (Nygaard, 2005). In addition, there are many limitations with the current studies, some of which include (a) inconsistent application of the terms given to emotions in various studies; (b) lack of a coherent model of the emotional process (Murray & Arnott, 1993); (c) lack of access to "real-life records of vocal expressions of specific emotions"; (d) difficulty inducing "strong and highly differentiated emotional states in the laboratory"; (e) using only one actor in a study, which cannot account for individual differences or training in vocal expression; (f) lack of investigation into gender differences between actors; and (g) insufficient detail about the conditions under which the emotions are portrayed (Scherer et al., 1991, p. 124).

Proper Inflection

Trial commentators encourage proper inflection or tone as a strategy for holding jurors' attention. Unfortunately, it is unclear exactly what trial commentators are referring to by *inflection*, which is problematic for a scientific analysis of the issue. In linguistics, inflection reflects a more nuanced meaning than tone, but trial commentators appear to be using the terms as synonyms. In contrast to intonation, which extends over a chunk of speech, inflection refers to smooth changes in pitch, and perhaps loudness, that usually occur on one syllable. Various inflections are associated with different emotions. For example, a "quick, large increase in pitch accompanied by an increase in loudness" is an indication of anger (Frick, 1985, p. 422). On the other hand, happiness is associated with gentle changes in pitch (Fonagy, 1978). Inflections may serve as the length of a prosodic contour (i.e., a pattern of pitch and loudness over time) and have the potential for conveying meaning or expressing emotions (Frick, 1985). Unfortunately, the connection between inflection and holding the audience's attention or influencing persuasion is unclear.

More than likely, trial commentators did not intend the meaning of inflection used in the scientific literature. Applying a broader research review to trial commentators' strategy, studies suggest that people understand emotional speech when the emotion and the content of the words match the emotion in the prosody. Research indicates that speakers are capable of describing feelings using words with emotional connotations (e.g., wedding or funeral) in addition to explicit emotional terms (e.g., sad or happy; Nygaard, 2005; e.g., Vakoch & Wurm, 1997; Wurm & Vakoch, 2000). Also, when listeners were presented with sentence-length utterances that were congruent or incongruent with emotional prosody, the emotional tone of voice influenced the interpretation of the utterance in an emotion-congruent manner. In other words, if the message was accompanied by a sad tone of voice, then listeners were more likely to interpret the sentence to have a sad meaning, and the judgments of the tone of voice changed depending on the sentence content. This finding suggests that linguistic processing is not independent of processing for the emotional tone of voice (Kitayama & Howard, 1994; see also Nygaard, 2005).

Another study investigated whether emotional tone of voice would influence the selection and interpretation of word meaning. Researchers selected lexically ambiguous emotional homophones (i.e., one emotional meaning and one neutral meaning) with distinct spellings (e.g., die/dye). The emotional homophones were intermixed with filler words that had happy, sad, and neutral meanings, and the words were said in either a happy, sad, or neutral tone of voice. When the emotional tone of voice was congruent with the emotional meaning of the homophone, listeners were more likely to select the emotional meaning of the homophone. Listeners were more likely to select the neutral spelling of the homophone when the emotional tone of voice was incongruent with the homophone's meaning (Nygaard, 2005; Nygaard & Lunders, 2002). Therefore, lexical selection appears to be influenced by the tone of voice, and although more research is needed on the issue, it appears that consistency between emotional tone and the information conveyed may help jurors follow and understand attorneys' messages.

Subtle Changes in Tone (Avoiding Monotone)

The use of changes in tone appears to be evaluated more favorably than the use of monotone. For example, compared with a normal voice, monotone pitch was associated with decreased perceptions of credibility (Addington, 1971). In addition, greater pitch variability has been linked to perceived speaker dynamism, potency, extraversion, and benevolence (Burgoon, 1985). Greater pitch variability was also associated with the findings of pleasantness (Burgoon et al., 1990). This finding was supported by research on baby talk, one characteristic of which is exaggerated intonation (discussed in Chapter 3, this volume). Participants rated baby talk on a 7-point scale for comfort, irritation, pleasantness, and arousal. Results indicated that baby talk is perceived as more pleasant and comforting while non–baby talk is perceived as more arousing and irritating (Caporael, 1981). Therefore, trial commentators appear to correctly identify that the use of monotone should be avoided. However, potential advantages are less obvious when comparing a normal and more dynamic style of speaking (e.g., Addington, 1971; Burgoon et al., 1990; Pearce & Brommel, 1972).

Changes in tone can convey different emotions, as noted in the previous section, but changing one's intonation may also be beneficial for other reasons. As trial commentators indicate, changes in tone may be useful for emphasizing important ideas. Researchers explain that language is commonly viewed as a symbolic system, where semantic-referential information is arbitrarily assigned to the symbol. Mental representations connect the information with the symbol to ensure language comprehension. In addition, there appear to be nonarbitrary relationships between auditory and visual sensory attributes. In other words, acoustic properties of speech can directly convey semantic-referential information, and speakers can capitalize on these cross-modal associations by mapping visual information onto acoustic-auditory properties of speech (Shintel & Nusbaum, 2007).

Cross-modal associations have been made between pitch and visuospatial properties, such as vertical location, size, and brightness (Shintel & Nusbaum, 2007; e.g., Marks, 1987). For example, a congruent-frequency sound (i.e., high position–high frequency) facilitated the classification of the vertical position of a visual target. Conversely, an incongruent-frequency sound (i.e., high position–low frequency) impaired classification (Shintel & Nusbaum, 2007; see Bernstein & Edelstein, 1971; Melara & O'Brian, 1987). Similarly, speakers who were describing an object's direction of motion by saying either "it's going up" or "it's going down" spontaneously increased their pitch to describe the direction of motion (Shintel, Nusbaum, & Okrent, 2006). These findings suggest that attorneys can potentially adjust their tone in a way that helps convey ideas effectively.

Correcting High Voices

Trial commentators appear to perceive that people with high voices are not as pleasant to listen to and offer lawyers with high voices several strategies to overcome the limitations of their high voice. Although people may be able to control their pitch to some degree, the source of high voices is small vocal tracts, which is a physical characteristic that limits rehabilitation efforts. Large vocal tracts have lower pitches (Vaissière, 2005).

Despite trial commentators' concerns about high voices, they are not necessarily perceived to be less pleasant. However, inconsistent findings make firm conclusions impossible. For example, some studies report that a higher pitch is associated with impressions of competence, dominance, and assertiveness (Scherer, 1978; Scherer, London, & Wolf, 1973); another reported that higher vocal pitch levels were characteristic of kind, humorous, emotional, and immature women, but high pitch did not influence impressions of males (Aronovitch, 1976) unless the range approached that of female voices (Scherer, 1979b; see Giles & Streeter, 1985, for summary). However, other studies have indicated that increases may lead to negative attributions toward the speaker, such as deceit and nervousness (Apple, Streeter, & Krauss, 1979). Additional associations with a high pitch are subordination, submissiveness, nonthreatening, hesitation, uncertainty, or surprise. In contrast, lower pitch is associated with dominance, aggressiveness, threatening, definitiveness, and more authoritarian (Vaissière, 2005). More recent studies have also indicated that clear speech often has a higher fundamental frequency (i.e., pitch) than conversational speech (Bradlow, Kraus, & Hayes, 2003), although some studies have reported individual differences (Krause & Braida, 2004; Picheny et al., 1986; see Uchanski, 2005). Other studies have found intelligibility uncorrelated with acoustic characteristics (e.g., Bond & Moore, 1994), which may indicate that the effect of pitch on intelligibility is due to an increased vocal effort (Uchanski, 2005). Thus, until more research clarifies the effect of high voices on receivers' evaluations, it makes little sense to address the commentators' recommendations more specifically.

Pace

Although trial commentators discuss pace and, more specifically, some strategies related to pace, they do not actually indicate whether they believe faster speaking or slower speaking is perceived more favorably. Research strongly supports that receivers hold more favorable judgments of fast speech over slow speech. People who speak relatively fast with short silent pauses are viewed more favorably than those speaking at a slower rate (Burgoon et al., 2002; see Burgoon et al., 1990; Miller, Maruyama, Beaber, & Valone, 1976; Siegman, 1987; Woodall & Burgoon, 1983). Most research supports this finding. For example, slower speech is evaluated lower on dimensions of competence and sociability, while competency rates increase linearly with speech rate (Giles & Street, 1985; see Brown, 1980; Street & Brady, 1982; Street, Brady, & Putman, 1983). In addition, other findings indicate that faster speech generates more favorable impressions of social attractiveness than slower speech (Street & Brady, 1982). Faster speech was also perceived as more trustworthy than moderate and slow speech (Giles & Street, 1985; Miller et al., 1976), and faster speaking connotes confidence and authority, which are associated with dominance (Burgoon & Bacue, 2003).

Although research indicates that a faster speech rate can positively influence others' perceptions of the individual, the research is less clear about whether that speaker will be more persuasive. For example, studies report inconsistent results: Fast speech rates enhanced persuasiveness (Mehrabian & Williams, 1969; Miller et al., 1976), moderate rates enhanced persuasiveness (Apple et al., 1979), or no significant relationship was found between speech rate and attitude change (Woodall & Burgoon, 1983). In addition, the studies finding that faster speech was associated with increased persuasion are somewhat limited. For example, several studies found that fast speech rate was effective for persuading and gaining compliance when recipients have good decoding skills. Those classified as poor decoders were more likely to comply with a neutral speaker (Buller & Aune, 1986; Buller & Burgoon, 1986; Buller, LePoire, Aune, & Eloy, 1992; Hall, 1980). Another study found that fast-talking communicators were perceived to be more credible and were more persuasive than slow-talking communicators, but participants may have relied on their credibility judgments of the speaker to determine persuasiveness (Miller et al., 1976; see Chaiken, 1987). Indeed, it is not clear from the research if the fast speech rate increased persuasiveness or if the participants' perceptions of the speakers' credibility influenced the results (Giles & Street, 1985).

Some studies have suggested that slower speech may have an impact on the intelligibility of sentences; however, the findings on this issue are also inconsistent. For example, some studies have reported decreases in words per minute in clear speech, but other studies have found that clear speech forms had comparable speaking rates to conversational speaking rates (Uchanski, 2005; see Bradlow et al., 2003; Krause & Braida, 2002; Picheny, Durlach, & Braida, 1986). Similarly, some studies have indicated a correlation between speaking rate and intelligibility, while other studies produced no correlation (Uchanski, 2005; see Bond & Moore, 1994; Bradlow, Torretta, & Pisoni, 1996; Cox, Alexander, & Gilmore, 1987; Hazon & Markham, 2004). In addition, studies evaluating artificial manipulations of the speaking rate of conversational and clear speech (Uchanski, 2005; see Picheny, Durlach, & Braida, 1989; Uchanski, Choi, Braida, Reed, & Durlach, 1996) have produced equivocal results. These findings suggest that speaking rate may contribute to the intelligibility of clear speech for some listeners, but the current state of research makes this conclusion tentative.

However, several other factors may influence how speech rate affects judgments of the speaker (see Giles & Street, 1985). For example, context may influence whether slower speech is perceived negatively. Apparently, listeners are not as likely to judge slow speakers harshly when there is a favorable reason for the slow speech (e.g., helping the audience understand an unfamiliar topic). In addition, slower speech appears to be more acceptable in a formal setting that requires careful and deliberate responses (e.g., employment interviews; Street et al., 1983). Listeners are also likely to be lenient on slow speakers when the topic is stressful (Siegman, 1978).

In sum, it appears that a faster speaking rate may positively influence jurors' perceptions of credibility, but, as noted in Chapter 2, this is likely to have little impact on jurors' decision making if they process the information systematically instead of peripherally. A slower speaking rate may help some listeners' comprehension in the trial context, which is formal and complicated, and may help attorneys influence jurors toward less harsh judgments.

Saying One Thing at a Time

One recommendation trial commentators make is to say one word at a time. "Words are not really separately formed units but tend to flow from one sound to another, . . . [which] affects both articulation and pronunciation" (R. S. Ross, 1986, p. 72). This process is called *assimilation* (R. S. Ross, 1986). It is similar to coarticulation discussed in Chapter 3, so we just address assimilation briefly in this section.

People commonly vary their pronunciations of words from their accepted form in casual speech. Usually listeners report the intended words of the speaker, which indicates that these reduced word forms do not pose a difficulty for listeners (Bond, 2005). However, sometimes listeners err. Two types of errors can occur: (a) the listener fails to recover the intended utterance and inserts plausible but incorrect consonants that could have legitimately been omitted in a reduced pronunciation, or (b) the listener incorrectly perceives the utterance as if it has been reduced when it has not (Bond, 2005). Since jurors are likely to rely on systematic processing, it is critical that they understand the evidence presented verbally. Although it appears that people have acclimated to a number of speech reductions, the extent of their success in this regard and its generalizability to trials are unclear.

Changes in Pace

Trial commentators indicate that changes in pace can emphasize key points and ideas. Like tone, it appears that mapping visual information onto acoustic-auditory properties of speech aids comprehension. For example, when asked to describe a left versus right direction of motion of a fast- or slow-moving object, speakers spontaneously varied their speaking rate to account for the visual speed of object motion. In addition, listeners were significantly better at interpreting information about an object's speed of motion (i.e., fast vs. slow) from sentences describing only the object's direction, with duration of the utterance and the classification accuracy significantly correlated (Shintel et al., 2006).

One experiment investigated "whether referential information conveyed exclusively through motion information is integrated into a perceptual representation of the referent object" (Shintel & Nusbaum, 2007, p. 684). Participants had to determine whether a picture represented an object that had been mentioned in a previous sentence. Sentences describing an object were spoken at a fast or slow rate, and the content of the sentence did not imply any motion. After the sentence, listeners saw a picture of the sentence subject standing still or in motion. A picture of a moving object implied that the object was moving, but an image of a still object implied the opposite. The researchers anticipated that participants would be quicker at verifying that the object had been mentioned in the sentence when the motion implied in the picture and the motion implied in the speech were consistent (i.e., fast speech rate, moving object) instead of inconsistent (i.e., fast speech rate, still object). The experimental results supported the researchers' predictions.

Although this study only relied on a small number of participants ($N = 34$), the findings suggest that visuospatial referential information can be conveyed through analogous acoustic-auditory properties (Shintel & Nusbaum, 2007). In addition, the results are consistent with other studies that suggest that activating perceptual information is a key component of language comprehension (e.g., Stanfield & Zwaan, 2001). In short, these findings appear to support trial commentators' strategy to use pace and other elements of prosody to convey meaning beyond information about the speaker. However, there is not enough research to assess what changes in pace might affect the attorney's myriad communications, theoretically what causes these effects, and how they affect jury decision making.

Saying Nothing

Most research has found that favorable speaker evaluations and length of internal pauses are inversely related (Giles & Street, 1985; see Lay & Burron, 1968; Newman, 1982; Scherer, 1979b; Siegman & Reynolds, 1982). For example, "the use of short silent pauses generates a positive attraction and perceived persuasiveness . . . the presence of frequent silent pauses, filled pauses, and speech hesitations has a negative impact on listeners' attraction toward speakers" (Burgoon & Bacue, 2003, p. 205; see Burgoon et al., 1990; Miller et al., 1976; Siegman, 1987; Siegman & Pope, 1966; Woodall & Burgoon, 1983). However, other studies suggest that competence is conveyed through short pauses of less than 1 second and trustworthiness is conveyed by moderate pauses of 1 to 3 seconds (Baskett & Freedle, 1974; Burgoon, Guerrero, & Floyd, 2010). In addition, context may influence perceptions of silence. For example, legitimate reasons for silence do not elicit negative responses from observers (Newman, 1982; see Giles & Street, 1985).

Pauses may also help speech be more clear and intelligible, but research on this issue is inconclusive. Clear speech contains more pauses, which frequently occur before words beginning with weak syllables (Unchanski, 2005; see Cutler & Butterfield, 1990). Although no intelligibility evaluation was conducted in the study, the researchers hypothesized that the location of the pauses serves as an acoustic cue to help listeners delineate more difficult word boundaries in spoken English. Other research is mixed in its support that pauses help the intelligibility of speech in general. Artificially inserting pauses into conversational speech did not produce an increase in intelligibility, while other research indicated a correlation between the natural occurrence of pauses in clear/slow speech and intelligibility (Uchanski, 2005; Uchanski et al., 1996). However, the role of pauses in the high intelligibility of clear speech is questionable because there was little difference in pause occurrence in clear and conversational speech (Uchanski, 2005; see Bradlow et al., 2003; Picheny et al., 1986). Although more research is necessary to delineate whether pauses contribute to the intelligibility of communications, increasing intelligibility does not appear to be a consistent benefit of pausing.

Trial commentators' main contention is that pausing may be a successful technique for emphasizing points, gaining attention, or creating a transition. Despite the research indicating that pauses are associated with negative perceptions and do not necessarily influence intelligibility of communications, some research does support trial commentators' use of pauses as a paralinguistic strategy. For example, research indicates that meaningful, controlled silence can be used for impact (Bruneau, 1973; Johannesen, 1974; R. S. Ross, 1986). Silence can also serve as a tool for conveying dominance. For example, people give others the "silent treatment" or use lengthy pauses to remind others of their status in relationships. In addition, subordinates wait for their superiors to speak first or indicate their permission for the subordinate to speak (Burgoon & Bacue, 2003; see Burgoon, Buller, & Woodall, 1996; Jaworski, 1993). Thus, strategically pausing may be useful for attorneys, but more research is necessary to understand pausing in the trial context. On the other hand, regular, extended pauses in attorneys' verbal communications are not recommended by the research findings.

Avoiding Speechification

Trial commentators advise attorneys against speechifying. *Speechifying* means overemphasizing tone and pace. Although no research has been done specifically on speechifying, there appear to be similarities between speechifying and the exaggerated characteristics of baby talk, discussed in Chapter 3. The research on baby talk suggested that an exaggerated speech intonation and an exaggerated speech rate are unlikely to negatively affect jurors' decision making. The research on baby talk did suggest that it may negatively influence the jurors' perceptions of the attorney and possibly negatively affect jurors' experience in the courtroom, but other factors are likely to minimize the damage. In addition, in their decision making, jurors probably rely more on the evidence presented than on their negative perceptions of an attorney who uses an exaggerated speech style. However, given the lack of information on speechifying, research is necessary before our hypothesis can be considered accurate.

Accents

Trial commentators believe that accents may be both beneficial and harmful. This notion has support in the scientific literature. Research indicates that regional group accents and dialects are usually perceived as trustworthy and likable and are preferred by ingroup members in informal contexts (Giles & Street, 1985). Likewise, speakers of nonstandard dialects rate those dialects more highly on "friendliness" scales (Clopper & Pisoni, 2005; see Linn & Piche, 1982; Luhman, 1990). When one researcher asked participants to judge the correctness, pleasantness, and intelligibility of English spoken in all 50 states, participants rated their own speech as most intelligible and most pleasant (Preston, 1989; see Clopper & Pisoni, 2005). One explanation for why accents are perceived positively is that accents serve to emphasize group cohesion (e.g., Tiersma, 1999) and speaker–listener similarity (Delia, 1972; Giles & Street, 1985). This implies, for example, that a lawyer representing a client in a small Southern town may wish to implement a southern twang to communicate to the jurors that he and his client are part of the local community (Tiersma, 1999).

On the other hand, standard dominant or prestigious group accents and dialects typically receive higher ratings on dimensions of perceived competence, status, intelligence, and success (Giles & Street, 1985). Speakers of Standard English are usually perceived to be more highly educated and to hold a higher status than speakers of nonstandard varieties. Unlike Standard English speakers, speakers who use a variation of English, such as Brooklynese, Black Vernacular or Ebonics, or cockney, are perceived to be less well educated and to hold a lower socioeconomic status (Tiersma, 1999).

This preference for Standard English is reflected in numerous studies. For example, studies using a matched-guise methodology, in which the same speaker uses multiple guises (e.g., dialects, varieties, languages) when talking, are informative. Because listeners are rating the same talker, variation in quality can be attributed to phonological properties of language instead of differences in voice qualities. These studies found that listeners rate standard varieties of language higher on scales of "intelligence" than nonstandard language varieties (Clopper & Pisoni, 2005). Similarly, negative evaluations of others based on nonstandard language varieties have been found in the research. For example, British subjects' ratings of the competence and social attractiveness of a speaker differed as a function of the speaker's use of a British Standard, South Welsh-, or Somerset-accented English (Giles, 1971; see Giles & Street, 1985).

Although these findings suggest that accents can lead to negative judgments of the speaker, the issue contains additional layers of complexity. The use of nonstandard language cues is likely to reflect the role of stereotypes in decision making (Giles & Street, 1985). However, when the message is on an issue relevant to the stereotype cued by accent or dialect, receivers may be more influenced than they would be otherwise (Giles & Street, 1985). For example, Southern speakers were more persuasive when speaking on desegregation than on grain reserves (Schenck-Hamun, 1978). When applied to a trial situation, this finding suggests that lawyers may want to use an accent when they are representing an issue that violates a stereotype. For example, if a Texas attorney were representing Texas cattlemen in their lawsuit against Oprah Winfrey for defaming the U.S. beef industry by airing a program on mad cow disease (e.g., Oprah free speech rocks, 1998), this research suggests that he or she would likely want to avoid speaking with a Texas twang. On the other hand, if a Texas attorney were representing Oprah in the lawsuit, speaking with a twang may improve persuasiveness. However, jurors presumably are going to scrutinize the message carefully because of their responsibility in the outcome of the case and will be less likely to rely on quick decision cues such as stereotypes. For example, one study found that stereotypes based on speech cues were likely to be given less weight when new information was added that put the speech stimulus into context (Delia, 1972; see Giles & Street, 1985). Research focused on attorney communications is needed to help identify the conditions under which the use of accent is desirable in the courtroom.

Because trial commentators perceive that accents can be either beneficial or detrimental under different circumstances, trial commentators encourage lawyers to develop the ability to selectively use their accents before the jury. This strategy is called *code switching,* and people who speak more than one language (i.e., code) often switch from one code to another depending on the topic, context, or participants. Code switching can also be applied to accents, dialects, or other specialized terminology (Tiersma, 1999).

Tiersma (1999) noted that lawyers are adept at code switching. For example, lawyers must distinguish themselves as a member of the legal field by using legal language, but they may need to avoid unnecessary jargon with witnesses in the courtroom. A study of North Carolina courts offers some empirical support for Tiersma's belief. The study revealed that lawyers and other participants use a range of language varieties in court, including formal legal language, Standard English, colloquial English, and the local dialect (O'Barr, 1982). The effect appears to have not been otherwise empirically substantiated, although one study analyzed how an African American attorney used the stylistic and rhetorical dimensions of her background in her rebuttal (Hobbs, 2003). In sum, developing the ability to code switch is likely to be an advantage for attorneys, but more empirical evidence is critical in understanding the effectiveness of code switching as a strategy.

Copying Opponents' Vocal Patterns

Trial commentators are concerned that trial attorneys will inadvertently pick up their opponents' vocal patterns. Repetition of words, expressions, whole utterances (Tannen, 1987, 1989), rhythm, tempo (Couper-Kuhlen, 1993), content, and intonation (Chafe, 1988) are common types of vocal matching (see Couper-Kuhlen, 1996). Although research does not specifically address whether picking up the vocal patterns of an opponent will have negative effects on persuasion, research does suggest people do "match" their speech behavior to one another as an adaptive strategy (Couper-Kuhlen, 1996; Namy, Nygaard, & Sauerteig, 2002).

Matching can be beneficial for communicators. For example, one can enhance communicative effectiveness and be perceived favorably by adjusting his or her speech rate level to the rate level that is characteristic of one's audience (Giles & Street, 1985). In addition, similarity in speech rate was found to mediate social attractiveness judgments (Giles & Smith, 1979; Putnam & Street, 1984; Street, 1982), and similar response latencies were significantly related to participants' favorable evaluations of communicators (Street, 1984). For example, when an interviewee adjusted his original response latency (3 seconds) to that of the interviewer (1 second) rather than maintaining the original latency or making it more dissimilar, he was perceived as more socially attractive and confident. But, it is not clear from the research if these findings are due to length of latencies or to latency similarity (Street, 1982; see Giles & Smith, 1985). In sum: "If their vocal characteristics match, listeners and speakers endorse positive attributes of one another. Mismatching characteristics appear to socially distance conversational partners from one another and may send a message of individual identity" (Nygaard, 2005, p. 393; Shepard, Giles, & Le Poire, 2001). However, in some circumstances matching may not lead to more favorable judgments (e.g., when a male speaker sounds too feminine; Goffman, 1974).

Despite the research suggesting that people may imitate others with whom they interact and persuasive benefits may result from the interactions, the application of this research to trial settings is limited. Although people may pick on the vocal patterns of others, most of the studies focused on interactive communications. Because trial attorneys will not typically interact with one another during trial, it is questionable whether attorneys are likely to pick up the other attorney's vocal patterns simply by observing the other attorney's trial presentations. And, even if an attorney does pick up the other's vocal patterns, the research does not indicate whether this will have negative consequences. Possibly jurors will not even be aware of the matching or know which attorney is matching the other. Therefore, more research is necessary to understand the impact of trial commentators' belief about this strategy.

CONCLUSION

Trial commentators argue that the distance that lawyers must stand from jurors necessitates a higher vocal volume, and for the most part the research supports these claims. Increased distance does require that speakers increase their volume to accommodate the audience's hearing. In addition, increased volume has been associated with other positive benefits, such as persuasiveness, confidence, and authority, which could benefit attorneys.

Little research has addressed the recommendation to alternate vocal volume to emphasize important points. However, vocal stress appears to have some influence on the comprehension and recall of spoken discourse, at least for elderly listeners, and loudness may serve to emphasize words or phrases for some jurors. Trial commentators discourage attorneys from being overly loud. According to research, loudness is associated with dominance, which has persuasive benefits, although it is also associated with expressions of hostility. Therefore, attorneys should exercise caution when they increase their vocal volume, so that it does not come across to jurors as anger or hostility.

Vocal tone is important for conveying meaning because listeners are proficient at assessing emotion from another's speech. Intonation also appears to influence views of the communicator's persuasiveness, but this effect may depend on individual differences among receivers. Tone and inflection are also recommended for holding jurors' attention, but research on this point is unclear. Linguistic processing is likely influenced by the processing of the emotional tone of voice, and lexical selection is influenced by the tone of voice. These findings suggest that attorneys can aid jurors' ability to follow and understand the message, if they use an emotional tone that is consistent with the information being conveyed. In addition, trial commentators correctly favor changes in tone over monotone. However, less obvious advantages emerge when comparing a normal with a more dynamic speaking style. Changing tone may be beneficial for emphasizing important ideas and can also convey cross-modal associations between pitch and visual–spatial properties, such as vertical location, size, and brightness. The implication of the findings is that attorneys may be able to convey ideas more effectively through adjustments in their tone of voice.

Trial commentators are concerned that attorneys with high voices will not be pleasant for jurors to listen to. However, research shows both positive and negative impressions with higher pitch, which indicates that high voices are not necessarily perceived to be unpleasant. In addition, research indicates that the size of the vocal tract influences the pitch of the voice, so attorneys may be limited in their ability to adjust this aspect of their speech.

People who speak at faster rates are perceived more favorably but are not necessarily more effective. In some studies, slower speech has been associated with improvements in the intelligibility of sentences, but other studies do not support this finding. Context may also influence whether slower speech is perceived negatively, and slower speech appears to be more acceptable in formal settings. Based on this research, attorneys may want to use a slower speaking rate to help some listeners' comprehension in the formal trial context. Trial commentators also recommend that attorneys make changes in pace to emphasize key ideas. Similar to tone, research indicates that visual comprehension can be improved by mapping visual information onto acoustic-auditory properties of speech. Therefore, pace and other elements of prosody may be tools that attorneys can manipulate for emphasizing key points.

Pauses are another technique that trial commentators recommend. According to research, favorable speaker evaluations and the length of internal pauses are inversely related. Context appears to influence how pauses are received, and when legitimate reasons for the pauses are apparent, then observers do not perceive them negatively. Although research is inconclusive, pausing does not appear to consistently increase the clearness and intelligibility of speech. Despite this research, some studies have shown that silence can be used for impact and to convey dominance. Thus, the research suggests that attorneys may be able to use pausing strategically, but regular extended pauses should be avoided.

Another recommendation of trial commentators is that attorneys say one word at a time. For the most part, however, listeners are not impaired by reduced word forms. Even so, listeners may still make errors if they fail to recover the intended utterance or if they incorrectly perceive a reduced pronunciation when one is not intended. However, it appears that jurors are likely to acclimate to many speech reductions that will occur.

According to trial commentators, lawyers should not speechify. Research on baby talk suggests that exaggerated speech intonation and speech rate are unlikely to affect jurors' decision making because jurors will probably be focused on the evidence, but they could lead jurors to perceive the attorney and the courtroom experience negatively, depending on whether mitigating factors are in place.

Trial commentators attribute both negative and positive results to accents, and the research is consistent with their intuition. Those who share the accent (either naturally or through code-switching) are likely to associate the accent with favorable qualities. Although this finding implies that the lawyer may be able to draw upon an accent shared with jurors to communicate group cohesion or similarity, speakers with standard or prestigious accents typically receive higher ratings on competence, status, intelligence, and success dimensions. Stereotype violation is one strategy, according to the research, that may be particularly persuasive for attorneys. Because the accent or dialect is likely to cue a stereotype, attorneys who draw upon their accent to invoke a stereotype (e.g., Southerner) and then violate it (e.g., with the issue that they are representing, such as equal protection for minorities) may increase their persuasiveness.

Finally, trial commentators warn attorneys against inadvertently copying their opponents' vocal patterns. Vocal matching does occur during communications and may have benefits for the communicators. However, applying the research on vocal matching to trial settings is currently impossible because no evidence is available on how vocal matching will affect third-party perceptions of the communicators.

5

ATTORNEY KINESIC COMMUNICATIONS

People seem to easily recognize that someone with a big smile is happy, whereas someone with a furrowed brow and hunched shoulders appears troubled or sad. We regularly use kinesic communications or body language (e.g., movements of the head, eyes, arms, and body) to convey meaning to others. Trial commentators accept that attorneys' nonverbal communications influence jurors and offer strategies for trial attorneys to employ in using these cues to their advantage in the courtroom. This chapter starts by reviewing the recommendations of trial commentators regarding kinesic communications. It then critically considers the science relevant to those recommendations and the likely effectiveness of those recommendations.

ATTORNEY KINESIC COMMUNICATIONS IN THE LEGAL LITERATURE

Trial commentators offer suggestions for kinesic communications to augment courtroom persuasiveness. For example, lawyers are advised to use body language to convey confidence (Haydock & Sonsteng, 1991; Murray, 1995). Good posture is considered key (Ball, 1993; Jeans, 1993; Murray, 1995; Packel

& Spina, 1984). One strategist asserted that "slouching makes you look tired, sloppy, un-alert, and uninvolved. Maybe arrogant or sneaky, too" (Ball, 1993, p. 4; 1997, p. 4). Similarly, other trial commentators have asserted that slouching may convey weakness or instability (Haydock & Sonsteng, 1991; Murray, 1995). Shifting weight from one leg to another is thought to make attorneys appear nervous and insecure. To avoid giving any bad impressions while standing, trial strategists advise lawyers to "stand solidly upright on both feet" (Murray, 1995, p. 78; see also Ball, 1993, 1997; Haydock & Sonsteng, 1991) and to keep their heads up (Ball, 1993, 1997). However, being overly stiff is thought to alienate jurors (Ball, 1993, 1997).

According to the legal literature, trial lawyers should also be mindful while sitting. Leaning back in the chair or crossing one's legs is believed to give the impression that the lawyer is not paying attention to or does not care about what is happening during the trial (Haydock & Sonsteng, 1991; Murray, 1995). Instead, trial lawyers are advised to sit upright with feet on the floor and legs directly underneath, so they can rise quickly to make an objection (Haydock & Sonsteng, 1991; Murray, 1995).

Although stillness is thought to be important for conveying confidence and strength (Ball, 1993, 1997), some trial commentators propose that deliberate body movements can concentrate the jury's attention and, therefore, purposeful movement is thought to be useful for communicating transition and emphasis in court (Lubet, 2000). For example, one trial commentator suggests that lawyers should take a step or two to one side or the other when transitioning from one point to another, make a movement toward the jury (without crowding the jurors) to emphasize a point and move away from the jury to deemphasize a point, and make sure that every step has a purpose (Lubet, 2000). Trial commentators discourage pacing because it will distract the jury (Lubet, 2000; Mauet, 1992, 2005), make it difficult for them to listen to the attorney, and reduce the attorney's authority (Lubet, 2000). Similarly, wiggling and fidgeting are thought to paint a negative picture of the attorney by making the attorney look bored, vacant, or ambivalent (Ball, 1993, 1997).

Another important kinesic factor addressed by trial commentators concerns the appropriate use of one's hands during the trial. The consensus appears to be that one's hands should be positioned out of the way, held naturally, or used purposefully (Haydock & Sonsteng, 1991; Murray, 1995). Trial commentators advise attorneys, when sitting, to simply rest the hands on the table, with one hand on each side of their notepad. Folding the hands, fiddling with the hands, and leaning the elbows on the table are considered improper (Ball, 1993, 1997). When the hands are being used for a purpose, trial commentators advise that they be firm and steady and that arm movements be controlled. When this is done effectively, it is believed to help convey confidence to jurors (Haydock & Sonsteng, 1992).

Some trial commentators argue that by simply changing the position of his or her hands, the lawyer can convey a multitude of messages to the jury. For example, crossing the hands in front of the chest is thought to convey aloofness or stubbornness (Murray, 1995). Similarly, attorneys are warned against letting their right arm cross to the left or their left cross to the right because this gives the appearance that the lawyer is defensively closing himself or herself off (Ball, 1993, 1997). In addition, clasping the hands or positioning them in a praying position is thought to convey tentativeness and insecurity; placing the hands in pockets is believed to convey nonchalance (Murray, 1995). Gestures related to hygiene also are to be avoided. In other words, fixing hair, rubbing one's eyes, poking one's ears, picking one's nose, or cleaning fingernails are all considered inappropriate during a trial (Ball, 1993, 1997). In addition, chewing on a pen and covering one's face are considered inappropriate. If an attorney covers his or her face, the attorney may look like he or she is "trying to hide something other than [the] face—such as the truth" (Ball, 1993, p. 6; 1997, p. 6).

Eye contact is another kinesic factor highlighted in the legal literature for communicating effectively in court. Trial attorneys are advised to make eye contact with each juror (Ball, 1993, 1997; Berg, 2003/2006) because "eye contact is the primary means by which a speaker transmits belief, sincerity, and commitment" (Fontham, 2002, p. 28). Other reasons cited in for maintaining comfortable eye contact with jurors include increasing the likelihood that one will sound natural by helping the trial attorney feel and appear as though he or she is talking to actual people, increasing the likelihood that listeners will more easily trust the attorney, and helping to relax nervous attorneys (Ball, 1993, 1997). To achieve comfortable eye contact, attorneys are instructed not to stare (Fontham, 2002) and to move their gaze easily and comfortably from juror to juror (Ball, 1993, 1997). In addition, trial attorneys are advised to avoid activities that may reduce eye contact with the jury, such as reading (Fontham, 2002) or taking notes during voir dire or the trial (Jossen, 1986).

Physical appearance is considered key for communicating information about the attorney to the jurors. According to trial commentators, inadequate attention to one's appearance will detract from successfully communicating in court. Appropriate care with regard to physical appearance is believed to make the attorney appear professional and credible to the jury (Haydock & Sonsteng, 1991). In addition, dressing inappropriately is thought to distract from the client's case (Haydock & Sonsteng, 1991) and increase the perceived distance between the attorney and the jurors (Fontham, 2002). To dress effectively, trial commentators advise lawyers to "look like a decent person any juror would want to have lunch with" (Ball, 1993, p. 7; 1997, p. 7), which requires attorneys to be well groomed (Haydock & Sonsteng, 1991), wear clothes that are clean and conservative (Berg, 2003/2006; Easton, 1998; Jeans, 1993), and select tasteful and unobtrusive accessories (Ball, 1993, 1997; Perrin, Caldwell, & Chase, 2003). The goal, according to trial commentators, is to blend in (Perrin et al., 2003). Wearing items that cause the attorney to stand out is discouraged. Overly stylish clothes and excessive jewelry (Berg, 2003/2006; Easton, 1998; Jeans, 1993), clunky jewelry (Ball, 1993; Perrin et al., 2003), pins or ribbons that have political or social significance (Perrin et al., 2003), and overly expensive clothing (Ball, 1993, 1997; Perrin et al., 2003) and pens (Ball, 1993, 1997) are all items cited in the legal literature as ineffective for communicating with the jury.

Additional suggestions for dressing to achieve effective communications are included in the legal literature. Attorneys are advised to dress comfortably (Ball, 1993, 1997; Haydock & Sonsteng, 1991) and consistently with their personality and approach (Haydock & Sonsteng, 1991). Once in court, trial attorneys are told to ignore their clothes (Ball, 1993, 1997) and be neat (Easton, 1998). Other advice includes choosing clothing colors to help emphasize the attorney's face because of the belief that the jurors' visual attention would be drawn to the attorney's face and, therefore, the jurors will be more apt to listen to the attorney. For example, attorneys are instructed to wear dark clothing to help frame their eyes and mouth if the courtroom walls are light (Ball, 1993, 1997).

Trial commentators also appear to be concerned about things that may block the jurors' view of the trial lawyer. For example, one trial strategist advises that the attorney's face be clearly visible from the front and sides. Therefore, attorneys are instructed to keep their hair out of and away from their faces because of the belief that the more the jurors can see the lawyer's face, the easier it is for them to trust and possibly hear the attorney (Ball, 1993, 1997). However, beards and moustaches are thought to be acceptable if they communicate trustworthiness (Ball, 1993, 1997). Another item that requires attention, according to the legal literature, is eyeglasses, which should be chosen to emphasize one's eyes. Women are also instructed to "use a little eye make-up to . . . subtly draw the viewer's gaze toward the eyes" (Ball, 1993, p. 9; 1997, p. 9). Other requirements for eyeglasses include choosing glasses that have antiglare coating and are untinted and with extra-thin lenses (Ball, 1993, 1997).

Finally, having stacks of papers and lecterns is also discouraged in the legal literature. Stacks of paper are thought to make jurors think the attorney will "talk forever" and thereby increase the likelihood that they will not listen carefully (Ball, 1993, p. 4; 1997, p. 4). Standing behind a lectern is believed to give the impression that the trial attorney is someone who is uncomfortable, has something to hide, or is planning to talk too long (Ball, 1993, 1997).

SCIENCE RELEVANT TO TRIAL COMMENTATORS' CLAIMS

Although almost no direct science addresses attorneys' kinesic communications, substantial research on nonverbal communications can be used to assess the recommendations of trial commentators. This section compares that science with the recommendations of trial commentators.

Good Posture

Trial commentators argue that good posture is critical for attorneys because slouching has negative connotations, such as weakness or instability. Trial commentators do not specifically define "good" posture, but presumably they mean that attorneys should hold themselves up straight. In addition, trial commentators recommend that attorneys stand solidly to avoid appearing nervous and insecure. They also warn that overly stiff postures will scare jurors. Similarly, trial commentators recommend that lawyers sit in an erect position for the purpose of facilitating quick objections and indicating attentiveness.

In general, trial commentators' beliefs about the benefits of posture in the courtroom are unsupported in the research literature. A straight back and an upright trunk are associated with an unrelaxed posture, and this type of postural rigidity appears to convey less power (Mehrabian, 1968b; Mehrabian, 1969; Mehrabian & Friar, 1969). Relaxed posture (e.g., arm position, asymmetry, sideways lean, leg position asymmetry, hand relaxation, neck relaxation, slight reclining angles; Suggs & Sales, 1978) signifies status (e.g., Mehrabian, 1969, 1970) and dominance (Burgoon & Bacue, 2003; Burgoon et al., 2002). For example, a relaxed posture when sitting, such as slumping in a chair and putting the feet up on the desk, is a habit of higher ranking individuals. One proposed explanation for these findings is that high-ranking individuals have less need to attend to others because they are relatively secure. On the other hand, people with lower status must exhibit more postural restraint, presumably to be watchful for potential threats from others (Andersen & Bowman, 1999; Burgoon et al., 1996; Burgoon et al., 2002; Burgoon et al., 2010).

Although wider and taller stances are associated with dominance (Burgoon & Bacue, 2003), dominance is not necessarily threatening and can be a communication style that is effective in influencing others when the nonverbal behaviors show social skill and competence (Burgoon et al., 2010; e.g., Burgoon & Dunbar, 2000). Despite what trial commentators appear to indicate, people appear to find the most attractive communication style to be one that combines dominance with relaxation (Burgoon & Bacue, 2002; Norton, 1983). This finding suggests that an unrelaxed, authoritarian style may also be associated with dominance, but people will want dominant individuals to be relaxed.

Therefore, postural relaxation may operate as a positive expectancy violation (Burgoon & Bacue, 2002; see Burgoon & Dunbar, 2000). Other research also supports the communicative advantage of dominance and relaxation. For example, people perceive others who are poised and relaxed to be more dominant, powerful, and persuasive (Burgoon et al., 2010). Similarly, people appear to find those communicating at reduced reclining angles to be more persuasive (Hargie, Saunders, & Dickson, 1994; see Mehrabian, 1972; Washburn & Hakel, 1973).

On the other hand, extremes in postural relaxation are perceived as negative expectancy violations and generate the formation of negative impressions. For example, a low-ranking person who appears too relaxed may be perceived poorly because this individual would contradict the expectation that subordinates should display proper deference to dominant individuals. Conversely, tense or underrelaxed high-status individuals may be perceived negatively because poise is expected of powerful individuals (Burgoon & Bacue, 2003).

An individual's attitude toward another person can be determined by the concepts of immediacy and postural relaxation. Immediacy is conveyed by "the distance between individuals, forward lean, eye contact, and whether or not an individual squarely faces" the receiver (Suggs & Sales, 1978, p. 636). Increased levels of immediacy demonstrate more positive regard towards another. A relaxed body posture when interacting with another person is associated with positive attitudes toward him or her. Extreme reclining angles can convey hostile or negative attitudes (Suggs & Sales, 1978; see Mehrabian, 1967b, 1968b, 1969; Mehrabian & Friar, 1969).

Men and women are likely to use different posture patterns. Men's posture is often more relaxed and powerful than women's. For example, although backward leaning is typical of men, backward leaning by women may indicate less involvement instead of dominance (Burgoon et al., 2010; see Kennedy & Camden, 1983; Shuter, 1977). Men also tilt their heads forward, thrust their chins out, and orient their heads more directly than women. In contrast, women are more likely to cock their heads to the side (Burgoon et al., 2010; see Dovidio, Brown, Keating, Heltman, & Ellyson, 1988; Kendon & Ferber, 1973).

Although this research suggests that a relaxed posture, in addition to other behaviors, will help achieve a favorable impression with jurors, currently there is a lack of research on jurors' expectations of appropriate behavior from attorneys. For example, jurors may expect a certain amount of postural correctness from the attorney given the formality of the courtroom. Therefore, it is unclear whether a lawyer's relaxed posture conforms to jurors' expectations and, if not, whether relaxed posture in this context would be perceived as a positive or a negative expectancy violation. Ultimately, more research is necessary to understand the courtroom applications of posture. However, based on the research outside of the courtroom setting, it appears that a moderate amount of relaxation in posture will be perceived positively by jurors.

Most research on posture is dated (Burgoon et al., 2010), so conclusions are tentative, but some can be drawn. Consistent with trial commentators' beliefs, standing solidly and appearing relaxed is likely to be the most advantageous standing posture. However, research does not support trial commentators' reasoning behind avoiding stiffness. Although trial commentators indicate that stiffness is aggressive, a stiff posture appears to be more characteristic of low status. In addition, contrary to what trial commentators favor, an upright seated position may not be perceived as well as a relaxed posture, at least for men. Finally, the research suggests that it is less appropriate for women than for men to display postural relaxation.

Stillness

Trial commentators recommend that to appear confident and strong, attorneys remain still. Research supports this contention. Body movements serve as a cue to emotional arousal (Suggs & Sales, 1978; see Ekman, 1965; Ekman & Friesen, 1967). When a person is experiencing low levels of arousal, the body remains relatively still. However, trial attorneys would be remiss to assume that stillness always conveys positive qualities. For example, a person may also be still when prevented from moving, which creates a tense position (Suggs & Sales, 1978; see Scheflen, 1964). In sum, an attorney who is nervous may fidget, or he or she may also be still but tense; thus, a relaxed stillness will probably be perceived more favorably.

People typically perceive less body movement as indicative of composure, poise, relaxation, and self-assurance, which are, in turn, associated with power, dominance, and persuasiveness (Burgoon et al., 1998). One study, which analyzed the 1976 presidential debates between Gerald Ford and Jimmy Carter, coded and rated the candidates' nervous behaviors such as lip licking, postural sway, and eye blinks. The segments that showed less tension were rated more favorably. For example, Ford showed fewer of these tension-related behaviors and received the more favorable ratings from observers (Exline, 1985; see e.g., Burgoon et al., 2010). The implication of this study is that nervous behaviors like fidgeting are not perceived positively, but research directly with attorneys is needed.

For example, trial commentators discourage pacing and fidgeting. Pacing is believed to distract jurors and weaken the attorney's authority in their eyes. Likewise, these commentators believe that fidgeting contributes to negative perceptions of the attorney by jurors. Research appears to support the proposition that pacing and fidgeting lead to negative perceptions. As noted above, power is associated with relaxation and poise. Shuffling feet are indicative of nervousness (Burgoon et al., 2010; see Bull, 1987; Guerrero & Floyd, 2006; Planalp, DeFrancisco, & Rutherford, 1996; Segrin, 1998), while a minimum of behaviors such as swiveling and random leg and foot movements are indicative of relaxation (Mehrabian, 1969; Mehrabian & Ksionzky, 1972).

Although fidgeting is typically perceived negatively, one study suggests that jurors may be more forgiving of nervous behaviors because of the formality of the courtroom context. In the study, when "anxiety cues, such as saying 'um,' fidgeting, and speaking too fast, coupled with low levels of eye contact and a lack of nonverbal expressiveness" were present, the participants were most likely to judge the context as formal (Burgoon et al., 2010, p. 339; Burgoon & Newton, 1991). These findings suggest that people expect others to be more nervous in formal settings when compared with informal settings. Applying this conclusion to trial settings, which are formal, suggests that jurors may be more accepting of nervous behaviors on the part of the attorney at trial.

Purposeful Movements

Because of overlaps in the scientific literature, purposeful movements and hand gestures are discussed in this section. For example, typically scholarship in the area of nonverbal communication has focused on hand gestures, but gestures may also refer to facial, postural, or ocular displays (Burgoon et al., 2010). Trial commentators advise attorneys to move their body positions purposefully as a technique for transitioning between ideas and emphasizing ideas. Purposeful hand movements are believed to convey confidence to jurors, and the scientific literature supports the conclusion that random and nervous gestures are not as powerful. Since the previous section on stillness focused on the positive perceptions associated with relaxed and controlled movements, this section focuses on the various meanings body movements can impart.

Research supports the concept that body movements can be used to assist the understanding of spoken language or to communicate information on their own. Trial commentators' belief that movement can be used for transitions and emphasis is similar to Birdwhistell's (1955, 1970) concept of parakinesics. This framework of understanding nonverbal behaviors is structured to reflect linguistic components. Therefore, parakinesics is similar to syntax in language. In other words, facial expressions or gestures perform parakinesic functions, such as emphasizing, punctuating, and pausing, when they assist in the understanding of spoken language. For example, one may gesture backwards with his or her head when talking in the past tense or may raise his or her eyebrows to emphasize a word (e.g., Burgoon et al., 2010). Changing positions during a transition or to emphasize an idea, as suggested by trial commentators, could work in a similar fashion.

Although Birdwhistell's (1955, 1970) framework is more closely related to trial commentators' beliefs about movement, other frameworks of nonverbal behavior exist. One framework that is also useful is that of Ekman and Friesen (1969), which focuses on the different functions of nonverbal behavior. According to this approach, kinesic behaviors can be categorized as emblems, illustrators, adaptors, regulators, and affect displays. These categories are not mutually exclusive.

In Ekman and Friesen's (1969) approach, *emblems* are movements with a clear symbolic meaning that do not need words for understanding. For example, waving hello is an example of an emblem. Next, *illustrators* are movements that coincide with speech. These types of movements assist the speaker in elaborating on the speech content, among other things. There are several types of illustrators. For example, *pictographs* are movements that draw the shape of the object being discussed in the air and deictic movements point to an object, place, or event. *Adaptors* are movements that satisfy needs. For example, self-adaptors involve personal maintenance and care (e.g., grooming and cleansing), object-adaptors involve the noninstrumental task of an object (e.g., tapping a pen), and alter-direct adaptors are movements directed toward another person during conversation (e.g., brushing lint off the other person's shirt). In contrast to emblems and illustrators, adaptors are performed with little intentionality or awareness. *Regulators* are behaviors that maintain or regulate how those engaged in conversation take turns. These behaviors are usually produced automatically, with very little awareness. Finally, *affect displays* indicate emotion (see Burgoon et al., 2010).

Other approaches to studying nonverbal behavior as communication elaborate on, add to, or deviate from the approaches discussed in this section (e.g., Bavelas & Chovil, 2000, 2006; Burgoon & Newton, 1991; McNeill, 1992). Although an in-depth review of all the possible approaches to nonverbal behavior is beyond the scope of this chapter, the approaches exemplify some of the possibilities for how nonverbal movements function as communication. In short, trial commentators' instructions about purposeful movements to assist jurors' understanding appear to contain some general support. However, research is necessary to understand exactly how attorneys can use their gestures, posture, and facial cues to increase their communicative and persuasive abilities.

Appropriate Hand Gestures

Trial commentators caution attorneys to use their hands appropriately. Although the commentators do not explicitly define what they mean by appropriate, they recommend that hands be held naturally and unobtrusively or used purposely. This section explores what hand gestures are likely to be the most appropriate and whether limiting hand movements is likely to be an effective approach during trial.

Gestures appear to contribute to increased persuasiveness, understanding, and recognition and memory about the speech content (Beattie & Shovelton, 2006; Graham & Argyle, 1975; Maricchiolo, Gnisci, Bonaiuto, & Ficca, 2009; Meharabian, 2009). Of the kinesic behavior categories just discussed, illustrators appear to serve as a resource that helps receivers clarify the speaker's intended meaning when it is ambiguous (Beattie & Shovelton, 2005; Holle & Gunter, 2007; Holler & Beattie, 2003). However, gestures in the research literature may refer to movements other than hand movements specifically.

Some studies have explored the role of hand gestures in the perceived effectiveness of the speaker. One study on hand movements indicated that illustrators are more likely to be used when the receiver is visibly present (Cohen & Harrison, 1973), which supports that the gestures are intended to assist in the communication and explanation of the verbalized message. Because of the limited research on the role of hand gestures in persuasion, some researchers are trying to explore this area of study in more detail. One recent study assessed undergraduate responses to video-message conditions that manipulated only the hand gestures of the speaker through the use of a professional actress (Maricchiolo et al., 2009). Participants were randomly assigned to one of the following five experimental conditions: ideational (i.e., illustrative) gestures, conversational gestures (i.e., an expansion of regulators), object-addressed adaptors, self-addressed adaptors, and the absence of gesture (i.e., hands kept on the table). Receivers evaluated the message persuasiveness, the effectiveness of the speaker's communication style, and the speaker's composure and competence.

The results of this study indicated that hand gestures cause differences in audience perceptions of the communicator and the persuasiveness of the message. The findings support that hand gestures that linked to speech (e.g., ideational and conversational) are more effective than hand gestures that were not related to speech (e.g., self- and object-addressed adaptors). Overall, ideational gestures had the strongest positive effects, increasing the perceptions of speaker competence and composure in addition to conveying a more effective style and more persuasive message. Adaptors had negative effects on composure, but the presence of ideational and object-addressed hand gestures on evaluations of speaker competence was comparable. Interestingly, self-addressed adaptors received higher positive evaluations than expected for message persuasiveness, which implies that any type of gestures are more persuasive than the absence of gestures. A second controlled study confirmed the effects of visible gestures (Maricchiolo et al., 2009).

It appears that gestures need to be synchronized with the verbal message, or receivers may become distracted and less attentive. For instance, one study tested how synchronized and unsynchronized body gestures influenced receiver perceptions of verbal messages. When verbal messages were highly synchronized with kinesic cues, they were perceived to be more persuasive than when verbal messages were accompanied by unsynchronized gestures. Receivers also found the source to be less credible for the unsynchronized message than for the synchronized message (Woodall & Burgoon, 1981). In support of this finding, studies indicate that hand gestures and the corresponding speech typically occur very close together (Treffner, Peter, & Kleidon, 2008; see Mayberry & Jacques, 2000). In addition, coordinating gestures and speech affects the perceived focus of a sentence and increases the certainty with which people perceive the communication. Coordinating or slightly preceding the gesture with the articulation adds emphasis. When the gesture precedes the start of the utterance, it is likely to cue the listener to should pay attention and anticipate where the speaker's intended emphasis will occur (Treffner, Peter, & Kleidon, 2008).

Although these studies tend to support the value of appropriate hand gestures in communication, drawing firm conclusions about the research on hand gestures is complicated by design limitations. For example, it is difficult for researchers to examine only the effects of hand gestures on perceptions of speaker effectiveness because other gestures (e.g., facial cues) may occur unintentionally in the communication. Research on hand gestures is limited by correlational studies, use of broad styles that included several different nonverbal signals, or inclusion of more than one type of hand gesture in the same experimental condition (Maricchiolo et al., 2009). In addition, some studies have not used appropriate control groups (e.g., audio only or no hand gestures; e.g., Woodall & Burgoon, 1981), and others have used only small subject samples (e.g., Treffner et al., 2008, N =14; Maricchiolo et al., 2009, N = 50). Therefore, more research is needed to improve upon the current research studies as well as contribute to the understanding of the role of hand movements in courtroom communications. However, a provisional conclusion is that by synchronizing their hand gestures and speech, attorneys are likely to assist jurors' understanding of attorneys and perhaps increase attorney persuasiveness.

When Seated

When sitting, attorneys are told in the legal literature to rest their hands on the table, with a hand on either side of their notepad, and advised not to fiddle, fold their hands, or lean on their elbows. Although there appears to be a lack of research about where hands should be placed on a table during communications, as noted above, research does indicate that fidgeting is associated with less positive perceptions. In addition, self-adaptors, such as wringing hands, may contribute to perceptions of anxiety, nervousness, and deception (Henningsen, Valde, & Davies, 2005; Maricchiolo et al., 2009; but see, e.g., Caso, Maricchiolo, Bonaiuto, Vrij, & Mann, 2006), but there is no evidence that simply placing the hands on top of one another would result in perceptions associated with self-adaptors. Finally, as noted earlier, a moderately relaxed position while seated, such as a backward or sideways lean, communicates a positive attitude or high status (Mehrabian & Friar, 1969). This research suggests that attorneys may present a more favorable impression to jurors if they sit comfortably, with the hands relaxed, instead of rigidly adhering to a set placement.

Purposeful Hand Movements

Because of the overlap in research on movements and gestures, purposeful hand movements were discussed above in conjunction with purposeful hand gestures.

Not Crossing the Hands in Front of the Chest (Not Appearing Defensive)

Crossing the hands in front of one's chest is believed to convey aloofness or stubbornness to the jury. In addition, crossing an arm from one side of the body to the other is believed to give the appearance of defensiveness. The research literature does not indicate that these specific qualities are conveyed by crossing the hands over one's chest, but findings do indicate that an open body position (i.e., one in which the body is accessible) is likely to be the most advantageous one in terms of conveying positive qualities (Burgoon et al., 2010). As noted in the previous section, relaxation is also indicated by the asymmetrical placement of the limbs. In contrast, people are likely to perceive a communicator with crossed arms less positively. When people cross their arms, hide their face, or stand behind objects, they are likely to be communicating that they are distrustful, vulnerable, and unsociable (Burgoon et al., 2010). Folded arms across one's chest can communicate displeasure and disagreement as well as contribute to perceptions that the source is "cold, rejecting, unyielding, shy, and passive" (Mehrabian, 1969, p. 120; Machotka, 1965). Although trial commentators appear to correctly understand that jurors are unlikely to perceive an attorney's crossed arms as reflecting positive feelings, this finding does not necessarily generalize to crossed legs, which appear to indicate positive affect and relaxation (Burgoon et al., 2010; see Bull, 1987; Guerrero & Floyd, 2006; Planalp et al., 1996; Segrin, 1998).

The implications of this research appear to conform to trial commentators' initial hunch. However, more specific information about exactly how jurors perceived crossed arms and whether altering the circumstances under which the attorney has his or her arms crossed is likely to influence jurors' perceptions of what the attorney is communicating, is needed prior to concluding whether this gesture can be used strategically. For example, if an attorney crosses his or her arms during key pieces of an opposing witness's testimony, will this convey disapproval to the jury?

Not Clasping Hands

Trial commentators instruct lawyers not to clasp their hands or place their hands in a praying position because these gestures make the attorney look tentative and insecure. According to the relevant research, though, these behaviors are more likely to convey dominance than insecurity. The following hand gestures are associated with dominance: "pointing at another person, using expressive and expansive gestures, steepling the hands, and using gesturing while directing others" (Burgoon et al., 2002, p. 455; see Andersen & Bowman, 1999; Burgoon, 1994). Therefore, the trial commentators' belief is not supported by the research. However, more research is necessary to understand how these expressions are perceived in the trial context, including whether dominance facilitates persuasiveness.

Avoiding Movements Related to Hygiene

According to the trial commentary, attorneys should not make gestures related to hygiene during trial. On this point, trial commentators' beliefs are supported by several studies. Self-adaptors, discussed earlier, are negatively correlated with perceived persuasiveness (Burgoon, Birk, & Pfau, 1990; Maricchiolo et al., 2009), and fewer self-manipulations appear more persuasive to others (Mehrabian, 1972; Washburn & Hakel, 1973). In addition, research indicates that self-adaptors in others are associated with perceptions of anxiety, nervousness, and possibly deception (Maricchiolo et al., 2009; see Henningsen, Valde, & Davies, 2005). In general, this information verifies trial commentators' beliefs that the absence of self-adaptors from attorney behaviors is likely to be perceived more favorably by jurors than including those behaviors. However, questions remain because not all studies have found the same connection between these qualities and self-adaptors (e.g., Caso et al., 2006; DePaulo, 2003) and because these relationships have not been tested in the trial context.

Not Covering the Face

Trial commentators also warn attorneys against covering their faces during trial because jurors will perceive that gesture as a sign of deceptiveness. Yet, a meta-analysis that considered cues of deception found no difference in the amount of facial shielding that occurred during lies and truths (DePaulo et al., 2003). People may cover all or parts of their faces for several reasons, but deception is not one that has been identified in the literature. Covering one's face is more characteristic of women than men and may be used to flirt; reduce environmental stimuli; or convey shyness, coyness, submissiveness, or self-consciousness (Burgoon et al., 2010; see Eibl-Eibesfeldt, 1972; Morris, 1977; Morsbach, 1973; Ramsey, 1981). Potentially related to facial shielding is facial fidgeting, which is defined as "speakers . . . touching or rubbing their faces or playing with their hair" (DePaulo et al., 2003, p. 115). This form of self-adaptor may also address trial commentators' concern about attorneys covering their faces because facial fidgeting may cause the attorney to block his or her face. DePaulo et al. (2003) found that there is no clear relationship between fidgeting (of any kind, including facial fidgeting) and lying.

Although trial commentators are likely incorrect about the relationship between facial shielding and lying, perhaps they are correct that jurors will focus on facial shielding or movements that block the face as a cue to deception. In other words, jurors may perceive an attorney who fidgets with or shields his or her face to be lying, regardless of whether this gesture is actually an indication of deception. However, more research is necessary to draw clear conclusions about this.

Eye Contact

Trial commentators believe that appropriate eye contact is critical for an attorney's communications with the jury because it will increase perceptions of sincerity, committedness, naturalness, and trustworthiness. In fact, research shows that increased eye gaze carries positive meanings, including "intimacy, attraction, inclusion, involvement, composure, informality, and similarity (Burgoon, Coker, & Coker, 1986, p. 506). In addition, increased eye contact indicates a positive feeling toward an individual (Suggs & Sales, 1978; see Argyle & Dean, 1965; Mehrabian, 1970, 1969). People tend to perceive the combination of eye contact and smiling as a sign of attraction (Burgoon & Bacue, 2003; see Burgoon et al., 1984; Kleinke, Bustos, Meeker, & Staneski, 1973; Rubin, 1970). The absence of eye contact can indicate that the relationship is in distress (Burgoon et al., 2002; see Noller, 1980). However, sex differences may influence the extent to which eye contact is perceived positively. For example, males tend to view continuous eye contact from another as threatening (Suggs & Sales, 1978; see Ellsworth & Ross, 1975). We discuss this more in the following section.

Eye contact with others is also associated with perceptions of credibility. For example, speakers using moderate to high gaze were perceived as significantly more credible on a qualification factor than speakers with low eye contact (Beebe, 1974; see Burgoon et al., 1986). In addition, increased eye gaze may affect persuasiveness. Several studies demonstrate an increase of compliance rates when people's requests are accompanied with eye gaze (e.g., Burgoon et al., 1986; Burgoon et al., 2002; Segrin, 1993). For instance, extended eye gaze has been associated with receiving recommendations for employment (Burgoon, Manusov, Mineo, & Hale, 1985), getting more rides while hitchhiking (Snyder, Grether, & Keller, 1974), getting more dimes for phone calls (Kleinke, 1980), and receiving help (Valentine & Ehrlichman, 1979). However, factors, such as gender (Valentine & Ehrlichman, 1979) and legitimacy of the request (Kleinke, 1980), may influence these results.

Overall, extended eye contact appears to be perceived positively and result in positive outcomes, supporting trial commentators' contention. However, eye gaze may have several meanings that vary with situational, cultural, and communicator variables, and these factors may lead to eye gaze being perceived negatively (e.g., dominant, threatening, aggressive). We discuss in more depth some of the negative implications of extended eye contact below.

Not Staring (Moving Gaze Easily and Comfortably)

Trial commentators instruct lawyers to avoid staring at jurors, although they do not indicate a specific reason why. As noted previously, research results indicate that increased eye contact typically carries positive meanings (Argyle & Dean, 1965; Burgoon et al., 1986; Mehrabian, 1969, 1970). However, continuous eye contact may be perceived negatively. For example, staring may be perceived to be a challenge or a threat (Ellsworth & Carlsmith, 1973), especially by males (Ellsworth & Ross, 1975). Staring can communicate dominance, power, and status (Burgoon et al., 2002). Higher status individuals spend more time looking while speaking and less time looking while listening, and this behavior is seen as more powerful by observers (Burgoon et al., 2002; see Dovidio & Ellyson, 1982, 1985; Ellyson, Dovidio, Corson, & Vinicur, 1980). Dominant people also break eye contact last (Burgoon et al., 2002). In contrast, gaze aversion is likely to communicate submission, deference, and attentive listening (Burgoon & Bacue, 2003).

Another instruction in the trial commentary is that attorneys should move their gaze comfortably from juror to juror. Based on the potential risks of over- and undergazing, this recommendation appears valid. However, lawyers should probably avoid "shifty eyes," which are not perceived favorably. For example, a decrease in the amount of visual interaction with others is characteristic of individuals who are being deceitful (Suggs & Sales, 1978; see Ekman & Friesen, 1974; Exline, Thibaut, Brannon, & Gumpert, 1961; Mehrabian, 1971). In addition, frequent lateral eye movements may indicate anxiousness (Day, 1967; see Suggs & Sales, 1978). Eye blink rate also increases when anxiety-arousing topics are discussed, although this increased rate declines with time (Kanfer, 1960; see Suggs & Sales, 1978).

Overall, a specific conclusion about the effects of staring and easy eye contact among jurors is difficult to draw. Attorneys who stare at jurors may risk being perceived as domineering or threatening. On the other hand, jurors may believe lawyers who make prolonged eye contact to hold a high status; thus, they may expect these attorneys' communications to be characterized by direct eye contact, frequent eye contact when speaking, and less eye contact when listening. If jurors hold these expectations, they would be less likely to negatively evaluate attorneys who exercise dominant forms of eye contact in their communications. Even if jurors do not hold these expectations for attorneys, consistent eye gaze may not be perceived negatively under certain conditions. The expectancy model of communication predicts that if the reward level of interacting with the communicator is high, the jurors will interpret the gaze violation positively (e.g., Burgoon et al., 1986). Some research supports this prediction, but no research has addressed what the jurors would consider a reward in regard to listening to attorneys. In addition, the gender of the communicator may influence these results. Male communicators may receive more favorable interpretations assigned to their behavior (see, e.g., Burgoon et al., 1986). Furthermore, it may be more advantageous for attorneys to focus eye contact on the perceived leader of the group on the assumption that she or he will have the greatest influence during jury deliberations. The dilemma is that the attorney can never be sure in advance who that person may be.

Not Reading or Taking Notes

Trial commentators believe that attorneys should avoid reading, taking notes, or engaging in any other activities during trial that will keep them from making eye contact with the jury. As noted above, less eye gaze is typically perceived negatively. For example, interviewees who used continuous gaze were judged to be "more composed, competent, attractive, and of higher character" than those who averted their gaze during the interview (Burgoon et al., 1986, p. 503; see Andersen & Coussoule, 1980). In addition, it appears that diverting gaze to objects like a book can have a similar effect. For example, oral interpreters with good eye contact were perceived as more effective than those who kept their eyes on a book (Cobin, 1962; see Burgoon et al., 1986). Overall, it appears that eye gaze aversion is perceived negatively, which suggests that trial attorneys should try to avoid diverting their gaze as much as possible. However, if jurors focus on the evidence presented instead of whether they perceive the communicator positively, as would be predicted by the dual processing models (see Chapter 2, this volume), attorneys should not be afraid to divert their eyes if necessary to make sure that they address the key points of their case. Research is needed to evaluate this hypothesis.

Physical Appearance

Trial commentators believe that physical appearance is an important component of persuasive nonverbal communication. Trial commentators focus on the controllable features of physical appearance, such as dressing appropriately, and believe that appropriate care to physical appearance will help the attorneys appear professional and credible to jurors. Research supports trial commentators' belief that appearance is an important factor in how people evaluate others.

People may be born with many qualities relating to attractiveness, which are uncontrollable. For example, tall height in men (Asthana, 2000) is an uncontrollable feature that is associated with attractiveness. However, other qualities can be manipulated to a certain degree through cosmetics, grooming, and clothing choices. For example, women may try to achieve youthful-looking skin, a characteristic related to physical attractiveness (Fink, Grammer, & Thornhill, 2001), through cosmetics (Burgoon et al., 2010). Therefore, trial commentators appear correct that attorneys have a certain amount of control over their appearance, but how important is appearance in nonverbal communication?

Typically, those who appear attractive to others also have other favorable qualities attributed to them. This is known as the *halo effect* (Burgoon and Bacue, 2002; Dion, Berscheid, & Walster, 1972), which was discussed in Chapter 2. For example, attractiveness is associated with friendliness, ambition, likability, and intelligence (Burgoon et al., 2010; see Dion, 1986; Dion et al., 1972; Hatfield & Sprecher, 1986). In addition, attractive people are often perceived as having high social and intellectual competency (Eagly, Ashmore, Makhijani, & Longo, 1991), although attractive people may not actually possess the positive characteristics others attribute to them (Feingold, 1992; see Burgoon et al., 2010). In addition, studies have found that physical attractiveness does not always generate positive evaluations on all dimensions. For instance, attractiveness is not related to judgments of expertise and is likely to only have weak effects on judgments of trustworthiness (O'Keefe, 2002; e.g., Chaiken, 1979; Horai, Naccari, & Fatoullah, 1974; Snyder & Rothbart, 1971; see also Norman, 1976; Widgery, 1974; cf. Patzer, 1983) and may be associated with the negative quality of self-centeredness (Burgoon et al., 2010; see Dermer & Thiel, 1975).

In sum, although it appears that physical attractiveness is typically associated with positive characteristics (see also Chapter 2), source attractiveness appears to have its greatest influence in relatively unimportant situations (Chaiken, 1986). Although mock jury research has shown that jurors may use simple cues, like physical attractiveness, in reaching their decisions (e.g., Zebrowitz & McDonald, 1991), people may still be motivated to process the message with care when in a trial situation (see Chapter 2). Therefore, the information communicated by the attorney's physical appearance may not have a large impact on jurors' decision making.

As noted in Chapter 2, most mock jury research is unlikely to provide adequate testing of central, careful processing of trial information because the simulations are typically unlikely to involve the subject in the way real jurors are likely to be involved in their responsibilities. Mock jury research typically involves brief vignettes, no jury deliberations, and a presentation of information that has little to do with what actually occurs in a real trial (Sales & Krauss, 2011). This is not to say that mock jury research could not be made more realistic and actually encourage the research participants to take their responsibilities as seriously as that of real jurors (see, e.g., Elwork, Sales, & Alfini, 1982). When mock jury research involves such realistic simulations, it can provide an appropriate vehicle for testing the central versus peripheral processing hypotheses in the trial contexts.

Dressing Decently

Trial commentators advise attorneys on how to dress. They recommend that attorneys be well-groomed, dress conservatively, and wear only unobtrusive accessories. In fact, one's dress may affect perceptions of the individual. For example, people tend to find grooming and fashionable attire as more attractive, while unconventional attire and poor grooming may have detrimental effects when expectancies for the person's attire are violated (Burgoon & Bacue, 2003; for summaries, see, e.g., Burgoon, 1978, 1991, 1993; Burgoon, Buller, & Woodall, 1996; Burgoon & Hale, 1988).

According to research on clothing in the workplace, conservative dress is related to impressions of effectiveness and dominance (Burgoon et al., 2010). For example, women who dressed professionally (e.g., skirted suit) are perceived positively (e.g., Rucker, Taber, & Harrison, 1981; Gjerdingen, Simpson, & Titus, 1987). Dressing too conservatively, however, may backfire, and the woman may be seen as uncreative (e.g., Johnson & Roach-Higgins, 1987). Women should select clothing that is both professional and feminine in order to create a positive impression (e.g., Johnson, Crutsinger, & Workman, 1994; Rucker et al., 1981). Men are usually limited to wearing a suit or a professional-looking shirt and pants in colors that are neutral, dark, or blue (e.g., Burgoon et al., 2010).

Many studies have shown that the speaker's attire influences both recipient compliance gaining and helping behaviors (Burgoon et al., 2002; see Bickman, 1971; Giles & Chavasse, 1975; Lambert, 1972; Lefkowitz, Blake, & Mouton, 1955). As noted in Chapter 2, one study found that pedestrians followed a man against the traffic light more frequently when he was wearing a suit as opposed to casual clothes (Lefkowitz et al., 1955). Similarly, "numerous studies have demonstrated that instructors who dressed informally command limited respect and are viewed by students as not especially knowledgeable and less intelligent but also more friendly and fun than their formally dressed counterparts" (Burgoon et al., 2002, p. 457; see Butler & Roesel, 1989; Workman, Johnson, &

Hadeler, 1993). Moreover, men and women who dressed formally were perceived to be of higher intelligence (Behling & Williams, 1991).

Other research also supports the conclusion that dress can influence people's perceptions of communicators. In a study of perceptions of women running as political candidates, candidates who dressed conservatively, appeared older, had almond-shaped eyes, and wore their hair short were rated as more competent than other women (Rosenberg, Kahn, & Tran, 1991). In another study, a young woman was dressed and made up attractively for one group of receivers. For a similar audience, the same woman was made to appear unattractive. The audience found the attractively presented communicator to be more charming, likable, and persuasive when compared to the unattractively presented communicator (Mills & Aronson, 1965).

For trial commentators, part of the recommended dress code is to avoid standing out, and research supports this assertion. For example, one study researched the success of well-dressed and casually dressed solicitors in gaining compliance of others at an airport and at a bus stop. In the airport, where targets are typically well-dressed, the well-dressed solicitor was more successful than the casually dressed solicitor. In contrast, the casually dressed solicitor was more successful at the bus stop, where targets are typically more casually dressed (Hensley, 1981; see Burgoon et al., 2002). In a courtroom, both attorneys and jurors are in a formal setting and are expected to be more formally dressed. In addition, clothing is one type of item that social groups use to symbolize their ingroup status (Bickman, 1971, 1974; Brownlow & Zebrowitz, 1990; Pallak, 1983; Pallak, Murroni, & Koch, 1983). For instance, team members wear uniforms to indicate affiliation. Presumably, similar dress facilitates persuasion because the clothing fosters identification with the source. As Hensley (1981) noted, similarity of attire appears to facilitate persuasion.

Most important, high-status clothing, uniforms, and conventional appearance have been shown to increase persuasiveness (Burgoon & Bacue, 2003; Burgoon et al., 2002; see Bickman, 1971, 1974; Brownlow & Zebrowitz, 1990; Pallak, 1983; Pallak et al., 1983). See Chapter 2 for our discussion of credibility. If the items such as stylish clothes, excessive jewelry, expensive clothing, and expensive pens (all items that trial commentators discourage) are scarce, valuable, or used by high-prestige groups, they may subtly remind jurors of the attorney's status. By indicating the source's status, these artifactual cues may imply the source has special knowledge or expertise (Burgoon & Bacue, 2003). In addition, these cues may give the attorney an "expectation advantage" (Burgoon & Bacue, 2003, p. 204), where the status reminders will enhance juror expectations that the attorney will contribute valuable information to the case.

In sum, the attorney's dress may communicate information nonverbally to the jury. Professional dress appears to have the greatest benefits in formal settings where such dress is expected. Perhaps individuals wearing formal clothing are viewed as more attractive, persuasive, credible, and intelligent because "high-status and privileged members of society tend to wear formal forms of dress more often than do low-status members" (Burgoon et al., 2002, p. 457). Despite findings that support the value of formal dress, as noted in Chapter 2, source characteristics may have less of an influence on decision making when the issue is important. Therefore, further research is required to determine the amount of influence that attorney dress has in actual trials.

Dressing Like Yourself

Trial commentators argue that trial attorneys should dress like themselves. Presumably, dressing in a way that is consistent with his or her personality may help the attorney feel more comfortable and relaxed, which will contribute to more effective nonverbal communication in court, although trial commentators do not specifically indicate a reason for this strategy. Unfortunately, no empirical research about whether this strategy contributes to an attorney's persuasiveness appears to be available. In addition, dressing like oneself may conflict with the conservative dress styles that are likely to be more favorably perceived in work environments.

Dressing Comfortably (Ignoring Clothes in the Courtroom)

Another trial strategy that lacks research is whether dressing comfortably or ignoring one's clothes helps the attorney's nonverbal communication. Again, trial commentators do not indicate a reason for this recommendation, but they probably believe that these recommendations will help the attorney avoid unnecessary fidgeting and be more relaxed. As noted previously, fidgeting may indicate nervousness and deception, which suggests that if comfortable dress and ignoring one's clothes help avoid fidgeting then the commentators' recommendation will likely help attorneys create a better impression on jurors. In addition, as noted above, relaxation is associated with positive perceptions of power. Research is needed to test our conclusions.

Using Clothes to Draw Attention to One's Face

Trial commentators advise attorneys to draw attention to the face, recommending that they wear dark colors when speaking in the lighted courtroom, in the belief that jurors will then be more likely to listen to the attorney. Although there appears to be no research specifically addressing whether dark colors facilitate this goal, there is anecdotal evidence on this issue from photographers. Photographers suggest that making it the point of greatest contrast draws attention to the face. Their strategy, however, is slightly different from that of trial commentators. Instead of wearing clothing that contrasts with background, photographers suggest that subjects wear clothing that is the same shade as the background, so that the face is what stands out the most (e.g., McDonald, 2002). Whether photographers' or trial commentators' strategy will prevail in the live, 3-D arena of the courtroom is an open question.

Despite the unanswered question of what clothing colors will emphasize faces, research indicates that trial commentators rightly acknowledge the value of facial cues in nonverbal communication. Emotions, such as happiness, sadness, anger, surprise, disgust, fear, warmth, sympathy, or confusion, are expressed through facial cues as people communicate verbally (e.g., Ekman, 1964; Grahe & Bernieri, 2002; Reynolds & Gifford, 2001). For example, smiling can communicate liking (Kraut & Johnston, 1979; Palmer & Simmons, 1995) and demonstrate interpersonal warmth (Andersen & Guerrero, 1998). However, sex differences in the facial expression of emotions exist. For instance, compared with men, women are more facially expressive (e.g., Eakins & Eakins, 1978), use warmer cues (Weitz, 1976), and smile more for all emotions (Dovidio et al., 1988).

Facial cues communicate a person's attitudes more effectively than verbal or paralinguistic information (Lieberman & Sales, 2007; Mehrabian, 1971; Zaidel & Mehrabian, 1969). People's intuition about what constitutes negative or positive emotions in the face appears accurate (Ekman, Friesen, & Ellsworth, 1972). In addition, people appear to rely more heavily on facial cues than vocal cues. One study investigated the interaction between speech, vocal cues, and facial cues. The researchers recorded three female speakers saying "maybe" in a positive, neutral, or negative tone, and took photographs of three female models while they tried to convey liking, neutrality, and disliking toward another person. Next, the researchers selected three vocal communications (i.e., positive, neutral, and negative) from each of two speakers and three facial communications (i.e., positive, neutral, negative) of two models on the basis of the participants' judgments of the vocal and facial communications. Researchers then paired the three vocal communications with the facial communications for 36 experimental conditions. Participants were individually presented all experimental conditions at random and rated the attitude of the speaker. According to the results, people relied more heavily on the facial cues in their judgments, and no significant interaction was observed between the facial and vocal components (Mehrabian & Ferris, 1967). Therefore, trial commentators' emphasis on the face is justified by the research.

Jurors' Clear View of Lawyer

Finally, trial commentators recommend that attorneys take steps to be visible to jurors at all times. They are especially concerned that things do not block the jurors' view of the lawyer.

Keeping Hair Off the Face

Trial commentators recommend that attorneys keep their hair off their face to increase trust and potentially the ability of the jurors to hear them. When hair falls in one's face, it is likely to increase facial fidgeting, which may be perceived negatively. In addition, as noted in the previous section, facial cues appear to communicate information that may contribute to the understanding of the spoken words. Therefore, trial commentators' suggestions may have merit.

Hair may also lead jurors to draw other conclusions about the attorney. For example, people perceive long-haired women as younger and sexier than women with shorter hair (e.g., Hinsz, Matz, & Patience, 2001), which may contribute to less positive perceptions from coworkers (Burgoon et al., 2010). In addition, according to a study of physician appearance, long hair on men is likely to be perceived as unprofessional (Gjerdingen et al., 1987). However, how attorneys are affected by hair length is still unclear. Some notable attorneys (e.g., William Kuntzler) had long hair, and women can tie their hair in a bun. In addition, professional attire may compensate for any effects of hair length. Further research directed at attorney kinesic communications is necessary to determine whether hair length affects attorney communications.

Beards, Moustaches, and Attorney Trustworthiness

Trial commentators find beards and moustaches acceptable if they help the attorney look trustworthy. However, research does not appear to support trial commentators' belief that facial hair can make men appear trustworthy. Although one study found that ratings on masculinity, maturity, self-confidence, dominance, courage, liberality, nonconformism, industriousness, and good looks increased as facial hair increased (Pellegrini, 1973; see Burgoon et al., 2010), trustworthiness was not a quality associated with facial hair. In addition, at least in the contemporary United States, a strong preference is expressed for short hair and the absence of facial hair on men. These characteristics are associated with professional success (Burgoon et al., 2010). For example, compared with men who had longer hair, beards, and moustaches, men with short hair and no facial hair were rated as more businesslike, serious (Gjerdingen et al., 1987), competent, and socially mature (Muscarella & Cunningham, 1996). Thus, it appears that facial hair for attorneys is not likely to be perceived positively.

Eye Emphasis

Trial commentators instruct trial attorneys to choose eyeglasses and, for women, makeup that emphasizes eyes. Presumably, trial commentators suggest this strategy based on their belief about the importance of eye contact.

Research does not appear to exist that specifically addresses whether eyeglasses and eye makeup help increase eye contact.

However, there is research on the perceptions of makeup. Certain features, like smooth, evenly textured, and youthful-looking skin, are considered attractive, and women use cosmetics to appear more feminine and cover up flaws (Burgoon et al., 2010; Fink et al., 2001). Makeup helps women feel more attractive and self-confident during social interactions (Burgoon et al., 2010; Miller & Cox, 1982). Therefore, makeup may help female trial attorneys appear more confident in front of the jury.

Makeup also appears to have positive effects on others' perceptions of a woman's attractiveness. People rated the average-looking women as more attractive when they used cosmetics (Osborn, 1996). Women wearing makeup are typically judged to be more "attractive, feminine, friendly, healthy, and sexy" compared to women not wearing makeup (Burgoon et al., 2010, p. 103; Cash, Dawson, Davis, Bowen, & Galumbeck, 1989; Cox & Glick, 1986; Dellinger & Williams, 1997). However, research indicates that too much makeup in the workplace is viewed unfavorably. For example, one study examined how the hair color and makeup use of female job applicants influenced people's perceptions of them. Participants looked at identical resumes with one of six photographs. All photos were of the same 40-year-old woman, but her hair and makeup were varied. The photographs were divided into three sets of different hair colors: blond, brown, and red. In each set of photographs, the women appear either without makeup or with a moderate amount of makeup. Although the participants found all three hair colors equally natural, and they rated the various versions of the woman as equally attractive, friendly, happy, healthy, or stressed, the woman received a lower starting salary when she was wearing makeup, regardless of her hair color. Perhaps the association between makeup and femininity leads to perceptions of less competence in the workplace (Kyle & Mahler, 1996; see Burgoon et al., 2010). Thus, women may convey a professional image best by using a minimal amount of cosmetics. In sum, more research is necessary to substantiate trial commentators' claims about the benefits of using makeup to emphasize eyes, but minimal makeup that creates a natural look and enhances the women's femininity is likely to be perceived the most positively for female lawyers.

No Stacks of Paper or Lecterns

Trial commentators want attorneys to make sure that other elements in their environment, such as stacks of paper or a lectern, do not block the jurors' view of them. The logic underlying this strategy is that jurors will perceive obstacles between themselves and the attorney as indications that the attorney is going to speak a long time or that he or she has something to hide.

Although there appears to be no research directly on this point, research does support that the contention that one's physical environment (i.e., characteristics and conditions of the physical surroundings) and artifacts (i.e., physical objects that are in the environment for either functional or aesthetic purposes) can serve as messages.

Mehrabian (1976) proposed that emotional responses to the environment vary across three dimensions: pleasure–displeasure, dominance–submissiveness, and arousal–nonarousal. The pleasure–displeasure dimension concerns whether environments make people feel happy, satisfied, and contented, or annoyed, melancholic, or distressed. The dominance–submissiveness dimension concerns whether the environment contributes to feelings of control and importance or weakness and impotence. Finally, the arousal–nonarousal dimension evaluates the degree to which the environment lends to active and alert feelings versus relaxed or sluggish feelings. The way that the environment is manipulated may influence people's perceptions (Burgoon et al., 2010).

Attorneys are likely to have limited ability to manipulate the courtroom environment. For the most part, the furniture in the courtroom is fixed, and in some courtrooms the lawyer may be required to stand behind the lectern. Although there appears to be no research specifically addressing the accuracy of the trial commentators' beliefs about how jurors perceive the lectern, the lectern may have the advantage of serving as a focal point for the jurors. As the judge's elevated position in the front of the room is intended to indicate his or her importance, standing behind the podium may draw the jurors' attention to the attorney and establish his or her importance (e.g., Burgoon et al., 2010). Thus, the attorney's use of a podium may not be perceived negatively by jurors.

The elements that attorneys are most likely to have control over are their personal belongings, such as their briefcases and papers. How a person arranges objects and artifacts can communicate information about the person and his or her values (Burgoon et al., 2010; e.g., Werner, Peterson-Lewis, & Brown, 1989). In particular, trial commentators' concern with avoiding stacks of papers appears to be supported, but not necessarily for the reasons they listed. One study examined the influence that an instructor's tidiness and organization had on perceptions of his or her credibility and communication style (Teven & Comadena, 1996). Some participants were shown an office that was attractive, clean, and neat, while others saw an office that was disorganized, untidy, and unattractive. After watching a videotaped lecture of the same instructor, the participants rated the instructor. The participants who visited the neat office rated the instructor on trustworthiness, authoritativeness, and friendliness more favorably than the participants who visited the unorganized office, perhaps because raters projected the qualities of the office onto the instructor. Therefore, it appears that attorneys may want to avoid stacks of papers because it may lead jurors to perceive the attorney less positively. However, research is needed on how attorney papers, books, and other personal belongings at the courtroom table affects jurors' perceptions and decision making, and how this factor is affected by the strength of the evidence and the complexity of the case.

CONCLUSION

A relaxed posture while standing and sitting is likely to convey status and dominance. A rigid posture is more typical of lower status, perhaps to be on guard from threats from others. Dominance, if relaxed, is attractive as a communication style. In addition, increased immediacy of body orientation to another demonstrates positive regard. On the other hand, extreme reclining angles demonstrate negative attitudes. Stillness is also perceived positively. Body movements are indicative of emotional arousal; however, a tense stillness may also be indicative of emotional arousal. Therefore, relaxed stillness is probably ideal.

Frameworks for understanding nonverbal behaviors support the proposition that hand movements be purposeful. Birdwhistell's (1955, 1970) concept of parakinesics, Ekman and Friesen's (1969) framework, and other approaches to studying nonverbal behavior support that movements can function as communication. Although purposeful movements appear likely to create a positive impression, pacing and fidgeting are usually perceived negatively. Shuffling and random leg and foot movement are indicators that one is nervous. However, people may expect others to display nervous behaviors, such as fidgeting, in formal settings. If jurors expect attorneys to be more nervous in the formal, courtroom environment, then attorneys who display nervous behaviors may not be viewed negatively.

Trial commentators favor placing the hands on either side of a notepad, but current research findings do not support these contentions. Appearing comfortable and relaxed instead of adhering to strict rules for hand placement is more likely to create a favorable impression with jurors. In addition, attorneys are likely to assist jurors' understanding, and perhaps increase attorney persuasiveness, if their hand gestures and speech are synchronized. Trial commentators also advise against crossing the hands in front of one's chest, believing that this posture will lead jurors to perceive the attorney as aloof or stubborn. Although the research does not indicate that these specific qualities are implied by crossed arms, an open body position is likely preferable. Research indicates that crossed arms communicate displeasure and disagreement as well as other unfavorable qualities. Yet, this gesture needs to be examined in the courtroom setting to determine whether attorneys can use it strategically.

Clasping the hands is also discouraged because it makes the attorney look tentative and insecure. However, research does not support this belief. Instead, pointing, expressive and expansive gesturing, steepling hands, and gesturing while directing others are associated with dominance. Trial commentators also indicate that attorneys should not make movements related to hygiene. These movements, called self-adaptors, are negatively correlated with perceived persuasiveness and are associated with perceptions of nervousness.

Eye contact is believed to be critical for trial communications. Eye gaze typically carries positive meanings and is associated with perceptions of credibility. It may also affect persuasiveness. However, how eye gaze is perceived may depend on situational, cultural, and communicator factors. For example, extended eye contact may be perceived negatively, especially by males. Unfortunately, it is still unclear how jurors perceive attorney eye contact. Likewise, trial commentators are concerned that diversion of eye contact from the jury will reflect negatively on the attorney. Although research indicates that diverting one's eyes to objects is not typically perceived as positively as continuous or good eye contact, the importance of evidence for jury decisions suggests that attorneys should divert their eyes if necessary to address key points in their case.

Physical appearance can play an important role in how people evaluate others. Attractiveness can have a halo effect, with additional favorable qualities being attributed to the attractive person. Source attractiveness is likely to have its biggest influence when the performance situation is relatively unimportant, which may undercut its value in a trial. However, attire may be important at trial because it can serve as an indication of affiliation and status, which may increase persuasiveness. For the most part, conservative and professional dress in the workplace conveys the appearance of effectiveness and dominance. For women, dress that is also feminine projects the most positive image.

Trial commentators insist that attorneys try to be visible to jurors at all times. Keeping hair out of the attorney's face may be important because facial cues are a key aspect of communication and jurors may negatively perceive fidgeting with hair. In addition, the attorney's hairstyle may convey an impression to the jury. Typically, long hair on both men and women appears to be perceived less positively. Research also indicates that facial hair is typically perceived less positively.

Emphasizing the eyes through eyeglasses and makeup (for women) is another recommendation of trial commentators. Although research does not address whether these factors will increase eye contact, makeup may help women feel more attractive and confident in social situations. As long as the look is natural, research indicates that others may perceive women wearing makeup to be more attractive, but too much makeup may be viewed unfavorably.

Finally, trial commentators want attorneys to avoid displaying stacks of paper or using lecterns. Research indicates that one's physical environment and artifacts can communicate information. Trial lawyers are unlikely to have much control over the courtroom environment, but one possible advantage of a lectern is that it could serve as a focal point for the jurors and may not be perceived negatively by them. In addition, attorneys will have some control over their personal belongings, and how a person arranges those objects and artifacts can communicate information about the person and his or her values. According to research, tidiness and organization of these objects appear to communicate trustworthiness, authoritativeness, and friendliness compared with unorganized objects.

6

ATTORNEY–CLIENT RELATIONSHIP

In the courthouse, jurors will observe many exchanges between the client and the attorney. Before the trial starts, the attorney may pat the worried client on the back or exchange a laugh about a non-trial-related issue. When the trial starts, jurors will see attorneys sitting next to their clients. Every now and then during the trial, the attorney and client may simply look pertinently at one another. Maybe the attorney jots down a note for the client to read, leans over to whisper something in the client's ear, or questions the client on the witness stand. At the end of the day, the attorney and client may shake hands, with the attorney reassuring the client that everything is going smoothly.

How do jurors view these exchanges? Trial commentators assume that the jurors observe the interactions between the client and the attorney and that the observations factor into the jurors' evaluations of the case. This chapter investigates the type of displays between trial attorneys and clients that is encouraged by trial commentators, discusses the believed benefits a positive relationship with a client can have in successfully presenting a case, and considers the science relevant to these beliefs.

ATTORNEY–CLIENT RELATIONSHIP
IN THE LEGAL LITERATURE

Trial commentators suggest that the attorney–client relationship can affect the trial in two ways. It can benefit the attorney's work and alter the jurors' perceptions and decisions.

According to the legal literature, one benefit of a close relationship with the client is that the information gathered by the attorney from the client can help the trial attorney present a better case. Trial commentators assert that by paying attention to the client and developing a relationship with the client, the lawyer will be more successful in communicating the client's emotions to the jurors (Singer, 2000) and better at "humanizing" the client at trial. Humanizing the client and the case requires the trial attorney to find and stress the human element in the case, regardless of the particular facts involved (Perrin, Caldwell, & Chase, 2003). For example, defense attorneys are advised to start establishing in the minds of the jury, from the very beginning of the trial, a warm relationship with the client and to make sure that the jurors see the client as a human being and not as a stereotype. This advice is founded on the belief that jurors judge someone they know much differently than they would strangers, so it is the attorney's responsibility to help the jury see the client as a real person (Goodpaster, 1983).

Because jurors' perceptions are paramount according to the legal literature, the client must be seen in a favorable light to garner favor with the jurors. Trial commentators believe that one way jurors develop a favorable view of the client is by observing the trial attorney's relationship with the client. Generally, most trial commentators encourage attorneys to display a "close relationship" with the client as a way to increase the jurors' perception of the client as a "credible or good" person (Haydock & Sonsteng, 1991, p. 52). The underlying reasoning behind this belief is that jurors will pick up any negative feelings between the attorney and client, which will influence their judgments of the client. The legal literature, therefore, admonishes that trial advocates convey through words and actions that they like their clients, believe in them, and trust them (Association of Trial Lawyers of America, 2003). More specifically, the trial attorney is advised to be seen at each recess or adjournment talking with the client (Jeans, 1993), appearing to like him or her (Haydock & Sonsteng, 1991). Some commentators note that it is acceptable for the trial lawyer to recognize the client's imperfections, as long as the attorney conveys his or her pride in representing the client despite the imperfections. Therefore, it is up to the trial attorney to show the jurors what they should like about the client (Easton, 1998).

In cases where the attorney believes that the jurors will not identify with or like a client, trial commentators express two opposing views. One view is that attorneys should distance themselves from the client as much as possible because the appearance of a close relationship with the client will hurt the attorney's standing with the jury. The other view is that the attorney should still be visibly supportive of the client, because otherwise jurors may think that if a client's own attorney wants nothing to do with the client, then they also should not support him or her (Haydock & Sonsteng, 1991).

SCIENCE RELEVANT TO TRIAL COMMENTATORS' CLAIMS

When the attorney–client relationship is characterized by trust and cooperation, an attorney's work should become easier and more satisfying because the client is more willing to disclose useful information (Atkins & Boyle, 1976, as cited in Boccaccini & Brodsky, 2001). However, the exact benefits of a positive attorney–client relationship, and the likely success of trial commentators' strategies for using this relationship to the attorney's advantage, are complex and must be teased out in more detail to fully understand the likely validity of the trial commentators' assertions.

Attorney–Client Rapport

Trial commentators argue that lawyers who develop a close relationship with the client will benefit by having greater access to client information, which will be useful for presenting a better case to the jury. Unfortunately, creating that close relationship does not appear easy for most lawyers or clients. Many criminal defendants report dissatisfaction with the relationship they had with previous attorneys. In one study, only 22% reported being satisfied. Not only do these respondents report dissatisfaction, but they also report that they did not feel trust for their previous attorney (Boccaccini & Brodsky, 2001). Another study found that prisoners believed it was important that their attorney like them and that they like their attorney, but attorneys who were surveyed were not concerned about liking their clients or their clients liking them (Boccaccini, Boothby, & Brodsky, 2002). If nothing else, criminal attorneys and their criminal clients do not appear to be on the same page with regard to their expectations about and satisfaction with the relationship.

Lawyers' interpersonal skills appear to be an important component in client satisfaction with the attorney and the attorney–client relationship. A survey of criminal defendants revealed that although clients in litigation are concerned about their attorneys' legal knowledge, experience, and skills, these criminal defendants are especially concerned with the attorney's client-relations skills (Boccaccini & Brodsky, 2001). The majority of these defendants expected their attorney to not only represent them but to also relate to them as human beings. In a study on the interpersonal skills of lawyers, college students rated attorneys' legal competence and relational skills after viewing a simulated, videotaped attorney–client interview. The attorney having high legal competence and high relational skills was rated as more expert, attractive and trustworthy, having more potential to satisfy the client, and more likely to be used in the future. The attorney having low legal competence but high relational skills received the second highest ratings on almost all measures, while the attorney with high legal competence and low relational skills ranked in third place (Feldman & Wilson, 1981). Although this study relied on ratings from undergraduate students instead of actual clients, the results are similar to the research findings using criminal defendants noted above and affirm the importance of the attorney's personal ability to establish rapport with the client. In addition, they suggest that if the client had to choose either legal competence or high relational skills, the latter matter more to the client than the former.

It appears that the lack of rapport between attorneys and clients can contribute to clients' reluctance to disclose information, impairing attorneys' ability to effectively represent the client. For example, lawyers who represented public clients claim that these clients are "more skeptical and less willing to accept their professional authority than are private clients," with the lack of trust making public clients the most difficult to represent (Flemming, 1986, p. 253). In interviews of defense attorneys (29 full-time public defenders, 34 part-time defenders, 44 court-appointed or court-assigned attorneys, and 48 private attorneys) and their criminal defendant clients, criminal defendants saw public defenders "as part of the system, overly eager to plead them guilty, disinclined to spend much time with them, and not concerned about their welfare" (Flemming, 1986, p. 254).

If public clients distrust their attorneys, it is logical to expect that they would be hesitant to share information with them. For example, one study asked inmates to indicate how they would respond to an attorney who displayed ideal client relational skills (e.g., caring about the client, spending time with the client). Most participants (66%) reported that they would act differently with an ideal attorney. For example, many participants (18%) reported that they would share more information about the alleged crime, be more active in aiding their ideal attorney (17%), and be more trustful and respectful of their ideal attorney (13%; Boccaccini & Brodsky, 2001). These reports support trial commentators' belief that a good attorney–client relationship will help attorneys gather information useful to the case.

The difficulty that many attorneys seem to have in establishing rapport with clients may stem from the attorney's personality. According to the research on the personality characteristics of attorneys and law students, attorneys and law students tend to be less interested in people, emotions, and interpersonal issues compared with the general population (Boccaccini & Brodsky, 2001; e.g. Daicoff, 1997). Research using the Myers-Briggs Type Indicator (MBTI) reveals that attorneys naturally are more inclined to think logically and less emotionally than other people. When the MBTI was administered to 3,000 practicing attorneys, results showed that 81% of men and 66% of women lawyers preferred thinking over feeling, compared with 60% of men and 35% of women in the general population (Richard, 1993). Lawyers' personal preference for purely cognitive thinking over cognitive and affective thinking may help explain why criminal defendants in the survey complained about a low level of rapport-building effort by the attorney.

What techniques would help build attorney–client rapport? The scientific literature suggests the following three possibilities.

Values Supporting the Attorney–Client Relationship

Research with criminal defendants reveals that they value, in their order of importance, the attorney (a) talking up in court, (b) knowing the law, (c) being aware of what is occurring the courtroom, (d) "rap[ping] with" the client, (e) explaining the case to the client, and (f) contacting the client outside the courtroom (O'Brien, Pheterson, Wright, & Hostica, 1977; see also Boccaccini & Brodsky, 2001). Unfortunately, these findings contradict those reported by Feldman and Wilson (1981), discussed above, and we have no direct research addressing the actual influence of particular client values on their rapport or disclosure with their attorney.

Client Involvement in Case Decision Making

Some public defenders attempt to develop a personal relationship with the criminal defendant client by involving her or him in the case's tactical decision-making process. Obviously, this approach protects the attorney from a defendant appealing on the grounds that "I told the lawyer I wasn't guilty, but all he ever wanted to talk about was how I should plead guilty to this charge" (Flemming, 1986, p. 265). In addition, some public defenders actively involve the client in all phases of the proceedings, allowing them to make all of the key decisions in their case (Flemming, 1986). Lawyers who allowed the client to participate in the case by asking clients for suggestions are more trusted than attorneys who do not do this (e.g., Dinerstein, 1990). Allowing client participation also increases the amount of time the lawyer has to spend with the client in person or over the phone, requires the use of listening skills, and requires that the lawyer respect his or her client's opinions—all of which are client relational (Boccaccini & Brodsky, 2001). However, we do not know if these approaches improved client disclosure to their attorney.

Affirmative Behaviors in Interpersonal Relationships

Although research has not determined a particular method or manner that consistently works to create rapport with all clients (Minichiello, Aroni, Timewill, & Alexander, 1990), research on behaviors in interpersonal relationships is instructive. This research shows that interviewees spoke significantly longer in response to the personal questions of the interviewer when the interviewer displayed certain mannerisms (Collins, Lincoln, & Frank, 2002), such as using short verbal utterances (e.g., "yeah" and "okay" or vocal "mm's"), a direct body orientation, head nods, and eye contact (Feldman & Wilson, 1981). According to research, the relationally skilled attorney employs similar strategies, introducing himself or herself using first names; shaking hands; making small talk; letting the client talk; leaning forward; looking at the client; reflecting upon the client's verbal content and affect; and appearing warm, reactive, and animated. In contrast, the relationally unskilled attorney often fails to introduce him or herself, shake hands, participate in small talk, be a good listener, use good posture, make eye contact, or reflect the client's content or affect; he or she may appear distant, aloof, or nonreactive (Feldman & Wilson, 1981). Future research needs to assess the relationship between affirmative behaviors in interpersonal relationships and disclosure.

Juror Perceptions and Decision Making and Attorney–Client Rapport

A number of additional strategies, some of which may help build attorney–client rapport, trust, and disclosure, may also influence juror perceptions of the attorney, the client, the case, and jury decision making. For this reason we include them in this section.

Showing That the Attorney Likes the Client

One strategy the legal literature recommends is that trial advocates use words to show liking for the client. Research shows that the jury can infer the communicator's feelings through the degree of nonimmediacy in verbal communications (Suggs & Sales, 1978). *Nonimmediacy* is a measure of when the communicator's word choice decreases "the degree of directness and intensity between the communicator and the referent" (Mehrabian, 1966, p. 28; Mehrabian & Weiner, 1966). For example, referring to the client as "this person" or "the defendant" rather than using his name demonstrates a measure of nonimmediacy (Mehrabian & Weiner, 1966; Suggs & Sales, 1978). Even untrained observers, such as jurors, can correctly identify the nonimmediate form of two statements and associate it with a degree of more negative feelings relative to the object of the communication (Mehrabian, 1966). In addition, relatively nonimmediate communications about an immediate relationship are assumed by the listener to imply more negative communicator attitudes in regard to the objects being communicated about (Mehrabian, 1967a). This research suggests that the attorney seeking to use words to convey to the jury his or her liking for the client can convey the message through an intentional choice of more immediate language in reference to the client.

Research also suggests that words and actions can convey liking. When the attorney is trying to make the client more sympathetic or influence the jury on behalf of the client, he or she can use voice, gesture, and personality to persuade and to communicate his attitude toward the client (Mehrabian, 1966). For example, to communicate warmth, trial attorneys can try expressing positive attitudes, smiling, increasing eye contact, and demonstrating interest in the other person (Guerrero, Anderson, & Afifi, 2011; see Anderson & Guerrero, 1998; Folkes & Sears, 1977; Friedman, Riggio, & Casella, 1988). Compared to very low or very high amounts of talk, moderate amounts are most associated with liking (Daly, McCroskey, & Richmond, 1977; see Palmer & Simmons, 1995). In addition, object-focused gestures convey involvement in the interaction (Coker & Burgoon, 1987; see Palmer & Simmons, 1995).

Another approach attorneys can use to convey liking for their client is though opinionated statements. Persuasive speech can contain nonopinionated or opinionated language. Nonopinionated language conveys information relating solely to the source's attitude. In contrast, opinionated language conveys the source's attitude, as well as his or her attitude toward those who agree or disagree with him or her (Miller & Lobe, 1967). Opinionated language consists of two forms: opinionated rejection or opinionated acceptance. Opinionated rejection statements "imply rejection of a given belief and also rejection of those who accept that belief," while opinionated acceptance "refers to statements that imply acceptance of a particular belief and of those who also accept the belief" (Miller & Lobe, 1967, p. 333). There is research comparing the amount of attitude change resulting from exposure to opinionated language with the amount of attitude change resulting from nonopinionated communication. This research finds that opinionated language has a greater persuasive effect than nonopinionated language when the source is highly credible (Miller & Lobe, 1967). In addition, the results indicate that the persuasive efficacy of opinionated language is not diminished by either the open- or closed-mindedness of the message receivers (Miller & Lobe, 1967). For the attorney, this research suggests that opinionated statements may convey more liking of the client to the client and the jury. Unfortunately, this line of research has not included measurement of its effect on client trust and disclosure or on juror and jury decision making. Attorneys should also exercise caution when making opinions before the jury according to American Bar Association's (2009) Model Rules of Professional Conduct, Rule 3.4(e): "A lawyer shall not . . . assert personal knowledge of facts in issue . . . or state a personal opinion as to the justness of a cause, the credibility of a witness, the culpability of a civil litigant or the guilt or innocence of an accused."

Talking to the Client at Recess

Trial commentators recommend that the attorney talk to the client at recess to build client trust and to convey to the client and the jury the appearance that the attorney likes the client. Although there is no direct research on this specific recommendation, there is research on kinesic behaviors that are supportive of it. Specifically, research on the inference of attitudes from the posture, orientation, and distance of a communicator suggests that when in the seated position, showing greater relaxation, a forward lean of trunk toward one's addressee and a smaller distance to the addressee will communicate a more positive attitude than an increased backward lean of posture and a larger distance (Mehrabian & Friar, 1969). In a standing position for male communicators, more eye contact, smaller distance, and less "arms-akimbo" position (fist on hips with elbows turned outward) communicate a more positive attitude (Mehrabian, 1968a, p. 305). For females, less arms-kimbo position, smaller distance, and arm openness are cues for a more positive attitude. For standing positions, a tense posture communicates a more negative attitude compared to a moderately relaxed posture that communicates a more positive attitude (Mehrabian, 1968a). The research supports that there is a greater tendency to use an "arms-akimbo" position (fists on hips with elbows turned outward) with disliked addressees (Mehrabian, 1968a, p. 305). However, the research did not find much support for the use of more open posture and more direct shoulder orientation to indicate a more positive attitude (Mehrabian, 1968a). This research supports the trial commentators' view that talking to the client can help the jury infer that the attorney–client relationship is based on liking; however, the attorney must be aware of posture and the position of head and arms, as well as degree of eye contact, for the jury to infer a positive attitude from observing the conversation. Once again unfortunately, this line of investigation has not included measurement of the effects on client trust and disclosure or on juror and jury decision making.

Developing a Positive Affective Attorney–Client Relationship

Research on the affective relationship between attorney and client shows that the jury is more willing to consider mitigation for a capital case if the attorney and the client display a warm and friendly relationship throughout the trial. The manner in which they interact in front of the jury can delay early guilt determinations in capital cases, which will benefit defense attorneys (Brewer, 2005). In addition, the research indicates that the more a juror perceives the the attorney–client relationship as affectively warm, the more willing the juror is to consider mitigation evidence at the sentencing phase of the trial. If respondents perceived the attorney–client relationship to be warm, "the odds of being receptive to mitigation evidence increased by 66.3%" (Brewer, 2005, p. 356).

This research revealed another benefit of a warm relationship between the attorney and client. When the two worked closely together as a team, jurors perceived the attorney to be less credible and were less receptive to mitigation, with receptivity to mitigation decreasing by 25.3% (Brewer, 2005). When the attorney did not appear too close to the client, maintaining a more detached manner toward the client, jurors perceived him or her as being more honest and objective (Brewer, 2005). The only time jurors did not view a close working relationship between the attorney and client negatively was when they determined that the attorney and client had genuine warmth in their relationship. According to research, "modeling a warm relationship between attorney and client has the effect of suppressing the negative effects of a close relationship" (Brewer, 2005, p. 358).

According to research on relationships (Kelley et al., 1983), closeness is indicated by three factors: emotional involvement, intimacy (i.e., sharing of feelings and experiences), and interdependence (i.e., mutual and causal interconnectedness between two people; see Clark & Reiss, 1988). Because warmth appears to alleviate the negative effects of jurors' perceptions of attorney–client closeness, perhaps when emotional involvement is low but the other factors are present jurors perceive the attorney–client relationship to be insincere. In fact, one study found that people's perceptions about whether an individual was a friend of a prominent person significantly affected the target individual's reputation, regardless of whether an actual friendship existed (Kilduff & Krackhardt, 1994; see Krackhardt & Kilduff, 1999). Jurors may also be relying on a schema about appropriate interactions among friends and appropriate interactions among attorneys and clients (Krackhardt & Kilduff, 1999; see e.g., DiMaggio, 1991; Swidler, 1986).

Research on how people resolve inconsistencies is potentially relevant to understanding why attorney–client closeness is not always viewed positively. People have to spend time thinking about information to integrate it into an overall impression. Because of the complex process people use to try to understand the information, the inconsistent information stands out more (Hastie & Kumar, 1979; Trafimow & Finlay, 2001). When attorneys dislike their client but try to appear close to him or her in front of the jury, jurors may notice the inconsistency and focus on that information as they develop their impressions of the case.

In sum, the research strongly suggests that, at least for capital cases, the attorney has "more to gain in terms of receptivity to mitigation evidence by modeling a warm but not particularly close relationship with the defendant" (Brewer, 2005, p. 357). The client is likely to benefit only if the jury perceives that there is an actual friendship between the attorney and the client. Whether a warm, affective relationship between the attorney and the client has an effect on client trust and disclosure still needs to be studied.

Creating Positive Associations Between Jurors and the Client

The value of attorney–client closeness may also show itself in another way. If jurors feel positively about the attorney, it is possible that attorney–client closeness will cause jurors to also feel positively about the client (see Cialdini, 1993). Advertisers try to capitalize on positive associations by putting an attractive woman in an advertisement with a car (e.g., Smith & Engel, 1968), while people assume that friends share the same personality traits they themselves have (Miller, Campbell, Twedt, & O'Connell, 1966). Research suggests that negative associations can also influence one's perceptions in the same way that positive association can (Forgas, 1995; Lott & Lott, 1965). For example, people tend to dislike someone who brings unpleasant news, even when the person is otherwise unrelated to the information (Manis, Cornell, & Moore, 1974), with negative information about a person tending to weigh more heavily in the impression formation process (Coovert & Reeder, 1989; Taylor, 1991; Yzerbyt & Leyens, 1991). In other words, if jurors perceive that the attorney dislikes the client, it is possible they will focus on this negative piece of information when reaching their judgments about the client.

Conveying Pride in the Client

Trial commentators encourage trial lawyers to convey the impression of pride in the client and the feeling of being honored to represent the client despite his or her imperfections. Researchers speculate that pride may be useful for conveying information about an individual's current social status. For example, pride may promote high self-esteem after a personal accomplishment, which can inform a person of his or her social value. Pride may also "function to reinforce and motivate . . . socially valued behaviors" (Tracy & Robins, 2007a, p. 149). For example, pride may serve as a psychological motivator to make people act in altruistic ways, which can improve one's social status (Tracy & Robins, 2007a).

Pride is described as a "self-conscious' emotion involving complex self-evaluative processes" (Tracy & Robins, 2007a, p. 147). Typically, research has focused on personal pride (e.g., Tracy & Robins, 2007a), but researchers note that individuals also feel pride when someone close to them achieves success (Ortony, Clore, & Collins, 1988). In addition, individuals may "bask in reflected glory" when their ingroup outshines an outgroup (Cialdini, et al., 1976, p. 1; see Harth, Kessler, & Leach, 2008). Therefore, the pride response appears to be felt at personal, relational, and collective levels (e.g., Brewer & Gardner, 1996). However, research has yet to tease out differences among these various levels of pride (e.g., Tracy & Robins, 2007a). *Group-based pride* is an ingroup's achievement of a legitimate advantage over an outgroup, and depending on individuals' ingroup associations, relational and collective levels of pride could fall under this category (Harth et al., 2008; Leech, Snider, & Iyer, 2002). Research on group-based pride is limited (for a review, see Leach et al., 2002), but initial research results support the conceptualization of group-based pride and found that group-based pride led to greater ingroup favoritism in a resource distribution task (Harth et al., 2008).

An additional consideration in analyzing pride in the context of the courtroom is the two facets of pride: authentic, which is associated with "genuine feelings of self-worth" and actual accomplishments, and hubristic, which is more "loosely tied to actual accomplishments" and is less reflective of one's actual self (Tracy & Robins, 2007a, p. 149). Research on this issue found that participants consistently distinguished between authentic and hubristic pride dimensions when thinking about semantic meanings of words relating to pride and describing their pride feelings in situations that elicited pride. Authentic pride appears associated with success attributed to internal, unstable, and controllable causes; on the other hand, hubristic pride occurs when success is attributed to internal, stable, and uncontrollable causes, and it is related to distorted and self-aggrandized self-views (Tracy & Robins, 2007c). These initial findings suggest that the attorney's pride in the client may be perceived either positively or negatively by jurors depending on whether it is viewed as authentic or hubristic. For example, jurors may perceive an attorney as appearing genuinely proud of his or her client for working hard on the case or being brave as displaying authentic pride; in contrast, an attorney who unjustifiably conveys pride at her client for being "great" may be perceived by the jurors as displaying hubristic pride. At this point in the research, however, it is impossible to know whether jurors will perceive an attorney's pride in his or her client as authentic or hubristic and what circumstances or behaviors factor into their judgments.

Nonverbal expressions for demonstrating pride appear superior to verbal expressions (Hawk, van Kleef, Fischer, & van der Schalk, 2009). Research on pride expressions indicates that the prototypical pride expression includes a "small smile, slightly head tilted . . . back, expanded posture, and arms akimbo with hands on hips" (Tracy & Robins, 2007b, p. 793). Although pride can be recognized in the absence of all prototypical components, research demonstrates that the small smile must be paired with at least one other nonverbal component of pride or arms that are down at the sides must include two additional components of pride (Tracy & Robins, 2007b). Interestingly, researchers only found one nonverbal expression for the two facets of pride. Eye gaze directed upward appears to be a subtle cue for authentic pride, but eye gaze direction may simply reflect that individuals who gaze upward with pride are perceived as "less dominate and assertive," which may correspond better to the less dominate, nonaggressive features of authentic pride (Tracy & Robins, 2007b,

p. 798). Thus, upward eye gaze is not a clear distinguishing feature of authentic pride.

Perhaps when jurors perceive attorneys to have pride in their client, they will use pride as an indicator that the client is deserving of social status and acceptance. However, without more research about the effects of pride for others, it is impossible to know if this hypothesis is valid. Clearly, many questions about pride in the trial context remain unanswered. For example, would trial commentators' strategy for attorneys to display pride in the client be perceived as a type of personal pride? In other words, are attorneys trying to convey to jurors that they are proud of their choice to represent the client or their work in representing the client? Or would attorney's pride in the client be a form of group-based pride? In other words, do the attorney and client form a type of ingroup that serves as a basis for pride? Depending on whether jurors perceive the attorney's pride for the client to be personal, relational, or individual, should the attorney adjust his or her pride displays? Is pride for one's client considered authentic or hubristic pride? Should attorneys adjust their pride displays in the attorney–client relationship depending on which facet of pride is perceived by jurors?

Communicating Client Emotions to the Jurors

One benefit of attorneys developing a strong understanding of their clients is that they should be more successful at identifying the client's legally relevant emotions and communicating those emotions to the jurors. However, no direct research addresses these claims by trial commentators or explores whether the effectiveness of conveying emotions accurately affects juror decision making.

Even research on sympathy and social distances, which is indirectly related, is not helpful in assessing the veracity of the above claims. Specifically, the sympathy and social distance literature indicates that reducing social distance (i.e., by increasing feelings of closeness between individuals can promote sympathy (i.e., emotional concern for others) and helpful behavior (Small & Simonsohn, 2007; see Loewenstein & Small, 2007). For example, people are more willing to help identified victims in contrast to nonidentifiable or statistical victims (Small & Simonsohn, 2007; see e.g., Kogut & Ritov, 2005a, 2005b; Small, Loewenstein, & Slovic, 2007). In addition, victims who are similar to them (e.g., Krebs, 1975) or are part of their ingroup garner more sympathy from people than victims who are not (Small & Simonsohn, 2007; see Dovidio et al., 1997; Krebs, 1975). Other research has found that even indirect feelings of closeness can influence feelings of sympathy. For example, closeness with a victim of a misfortune enhances sympathy and prosocial behaviors toward other similar victims. Also, when compared to more distant relationships, closer relationships with unfortunate others appear to contribute to increased sympathies toward similar victims. Although this research suggests that trial advocates will have greater feelings of sympathy for their clients with whom they develop a close relationship, closeness does not guarantee that the attorney will be able to accurately identify or understand the client's legally relevant emotions.

Normative expectations may interfere with the comprehension of others' emotions (Wyer & Adaval, 2003). For example, married couples frequently misinterpreted expressions of hostility in their partners—a finding that researchers attribute to men's and women's different expectations for how the opposite sex should respond emotionally (Gaelick, Bodenhausen, & Wyer, 1985; see Wyer & Adaval, 2003). Moreover, people appear to have difficulty accurately inferring emotions in naturally occurring facial expressions (Motley, 1993; Motley & Camden, 1988; see Wyer & Adaval, 2003).

Even if the attorney accurately identifies and interprets the client's emotions, conveying those emotions effectively to the jury may be difficult; no research has addressed this issue. In short, the current research literature does not indicate that becoming close or sympathizing with one's client will increase an attorney's ability to communicate emotions effectively to the jury or that it will affect jury decision making.

This is problematic because emotion can play an important role in the outcome of a trial. Some laws require jurors to distinguish degrees of the defendant's emotions in deciding his or her level of culpability. In these situations, the ability of the attorney to communicate the emotion of the client effectively to the jury may have direct ramifications on the verdict. For example, "in the heat of passion" or "under the influence of extreme mental or emotional disturbance" are factors used to distinguish murder from manslaughter (Kahan & Nussbaum, 1996, p. 305). Manslaughter decisions rely on what constitutes appropriate emotions and how they can be expressed in an acceptable manner in society (i.e., Dressler, 1992; Nourse, 1997). In addition, understanding client emotions both at the time of the crime and during the trial may be critical during jury decision making for extralegal reasons. For example, jury nullification (i.e., the power of the jury to ignore the law when reaching its decision) may occur in situations where the defendant is emotionally sympathetic (e.g., euthanasia or "mercy killings"; Finkel, 1995).

Jurors appear to have expectations about appropriate emotions in court. When researchers investigated jurors' expectations regarding emotional testimony from crime victims, they discovered that victims who are less emotional are not viewed as favorably by jurors (Hills & Thomson, 1999). In particular, juries expect female victims' emotional reactions to match the seriousness of the crime. For example, research using videotaped variations of victim testimony in rape cases found that victim's emotional display testimony strongly influenced observer's perceptions of their credibility.

Research also indicates that jurors are persuaded by defendants' emotions and feelings in their decision making. One study examined the effects of a juvenile offender's facial expressions while giving testimony by varying his expression as angry, happy, sad, or neutral. The offender's facial expression did influence jurors' perceptions of guilt. Participants responded more favorably to the defendant when he exhibited a sad or neutral expression compared with when he displayed a happy or angry face, and the angry facial expression resulted in the most unfavorable reaction. In addition, when the offender's expression was sad instead of happy or angry, participants viewed the crime as less serious and saw the defendant as less likely to reoffend (Savitsky & Sim, 1974). Other research on facial expression analyzed the effect of smiling versus not smiling. According to this research, people demonstrated more lenient treatment towards others who were smiling than toward those who were not smiling (i.e., neutral), but this finding may depend on the appropriateness of the context (Forgas, O'Connor, & Morris, 1983). Another study examined the effect of a defendant's level of anxiety during testimony on juror ratings of credibility and the verdict. In this research situation, the defendant was seen as most credible and least guilty in the low-anxiety condition (Pryor & Buchanan, 1984).

One caveat to these findings is that they relied on juror simulations, which could influence the generalizability to actual jurors. For example, the type of case used in the study may influence the effect of the emotions on the jurors' decision. In addition, as discussed in Chapter 2, Attorney Demeanor, decision makers are less likely to rely on emotion and will use systematic processing when the issue is important (e.g., Chaiken & Trope, 1999; Petty & Cacioppo, 1986). In fact, research findings support that when perceivers are highly accountable for their inferences, they use more systematic processing of the information from the target, regardless of the emotional inferences in the situation (Lerner, Goldberg, & Tetlock, 1998; Ottati, Terkildsen, & Hubbard, 1997). Therefore, although research indicates that mock jurors may focus on the emotion of the defendant in their decision making, this effect may be less apparent in an actual trial if jurors are motivated to systematically process the information.

Research on the role of mood in persuasion also has implications for trial lawyers. The mood of message receivers has been shown to influence how they process a persuasive message. The message recipient may use affective reactions as criteria for evaluating the message. For example, when evaluating a message that either favored or opposed comprehensive exams, people developed attitudes in line with the message when they were in a positive mood instead of a negative mood (Albarracín & Kumkale, 2003). However, in line with the dual processing models, the extent to which jurors' affective reactions will influence the evaluation of the trial message, including the client's and witnesses' emotions, may depend on whether jurors are unable or unwilling to process more complex information (Albarracín & Kumkale, 2003; see e.g., Petty, Schumann, Richman, & Strathman, 1993). Another factor that could influence the use of affect in information processing is whether a person is able to identify his or her affective reaction in the first place. In other words, the mood of the message receivers appears to have the strongest effects on the message evaluations under conditions where the emotion is perceived by the receivers and not discounted as irrelevant (Albarracín & Kumkale, 2003).

In sum, emotion is clearly important in a trial, and it can potentially influence jurors' legal decisions. Unfortunately, the current research does not offer any clear understanding of whether developing a close relationship with one's client will assist the attorney in conveying the client's emotions to the jury. However, research suggests one strategy that could be useful for getting jurors to understand the client's emotions: asking or priming jurors to take the client's perspective. This strategy may reduce perceptions of social distance and enhance sympathetic feelings and altruistic behaviors with the jury (Small & Simonsohn, 2007; see Batson, Early, & Salvarani, 1997; Batson, Van Lange, Ahmad, & Lishner, 2003).

Humanizing the Client

Finally, another strategy to influence juror and jury perception and decision making is for the attorney to humanize the client. As with many terms used by trial commentators, *humanizing* is not defined. In lay terminology, to humanize means to attribute human qualities or attribute humaneness (e.g., compassion, sympathy, and a consideration of other persons) to a person (*Merriam-Webster's Collegiate Dictionary*, 2009). Two scientific literatures appear relevant to understanding the potential effects of humanizing the client to a jury: ingroup/outgroup effects and framing.

One frequent kind of categorizing that people do is dividing others into ingroups and outgroups; research indicates that ingroup members are given more positive evaluations, rewarded more, and found to be more persuasive (Brewer & Brown, 1998). These group affiliations can occur under minimal conditions (Tajfel, Billig, Bundy, & Flament, 1971). For example, when students were told that they were assigned to a group that shared their art preferences, their attitudes and behaviors were more favorable toward members of their ingroup than members of the outgroup despite never having actually interacted with people in either group (Tajfel et al., 1971). Another study manufactured group membership by arbitrarily telling British schoolboys they were overestimators or underestimators, after asking them to guess how many dots were on a slide. The boys were then asked to work alone in a cubicle on another task, but they could give points to other boys identified as overestimators or underestimators. The boys assigned more points to others that were categorized the same way (i.e., an overestimator or an underestimator) as themselves (Tajfel et al., 1971). When the boys emerged from their cubicles, the others would ask "Which were you?" and receive cheers from their group members and boos from the other group (Tavris & Aronson, 2007). One implication of this research is that to the extent that the attorney can successfully humanize the client by drawing parallels between the client and the jurors, the more likely it is that the jurors will view the client and his or her story more favorably.

Trial commentators' recommended strategy of humanizing the client is also closely related to the scientific literature on framing. *Framing* involves the selection of "aspects of a perceived reality" and increasing their salience (Entman, 1993, p. 52). By highlighting information about a person, thing, or event, the frame raises the salience or the apparent importance of certain ideas. The increased salience "enhances the probability that the receivers will perceive the information, discern meaning and thus process it, and store it into memory" (Entman, 1993, p. 53; see also Fiske & Taylor, 1991). Framing then activates schemas, or beliefs about the world, that encourage the receivers to think, feel, and decide in a particular way about the message's content (Entman, 2007). Not surprisingly, framing is a common strategy used by advertisers (e.g., Levin & Gaeth, 1988), media (e.g., Entman & Rojecki, 2000), and politicians (e.g., Entman, 2004) to convey their messages, with frames being used to define problems, diagnose causes, make moral judgments, and suggest remedies (Entman, 1993).

Kahneman and Tversky (1984) offered one example of the power of framing, presenting participants with the following scenario:

> Imagine that the U.S. is preparing for the outbreak of an unusual Asian disease, which is expected to kill 600 people. Two alternative programs to combat the disease have been proposed. Assume that the exact scientific estimates of the consequences of the programs are as follows: If Program A is adopted, 200 people will be saved. If Program B is adopted there is a one-third probability that 600 people will be saved and a two-thirds probability that no people will be saved. Which of the two programs would you favor? (p. 343)

Seventy-two percent of subjects chose Program A and 28% chose Program B. In the next experiment, the identical options were offered, but framed in terms of likely deaths rather than likely lives saved. Framing the question in terms of likely deaths led to an inverse of percentages for the two options.

Framing's effect has been duplicated in advertising research. Consumers' judgments of products can vary depending on the verbal labels used for highly specific product attributes (Johnson & Levin, 1985; Levin, Johnson, Russo, & Deldin, 1985). For example, in Levin (1987), consumers indicated that they made more favorable associations to ground beef and were more likely to purchase ground beef when the beef was framed in terms of percent leanness (75% lean) rather than percent fatness (25% fat). However, the framing effects are influenced by actual consumer experiences with the product. For example, in one study, consumers rated several qualitative attributes (e.g., good tasting/bad tasting, greasy/greaseless, high quality/low quality, fat/lean) of ground beef framed as either "75% lean" or "25% fat." Although consumer evaluations were more favorable toward the beef labeled 75% lean, tasting the meat lessened the magnitude of the framing effect. Researchers offer an averaging model to explain these findings, in which unambiguous product experiences will dilute the impact of framing, with stronger framing effects occurring when the product experience is more ambiguous. In other words, if the ground beef tastes terrible, then a positive frame is unlikely to lead to a favorable evaluation (Levin & Gaeth, 1988).

A clear implication of this research is that an attorney could use framing to humanize his or her client in the eyes of the jurors. For example, defense attorneys may try to connect their clients' crimes to past abuses as a strategy for humanizing their clients. This strategy appeared to be successful in the 2007 trial of Mary Winkler for murdering her husband Matthew, a preacher. The defense introduced testimony from Winkler and others about how her husband repeatedly abused her physically, emotionally, and sexually during their 10-year marriage. Presumably the reports of abuse resonated with the jury, which chose to convict Winkler of the lesser charge of voluntary manslaughter instead of first-degree murder (Candiotti & Dornin, 2007). Despite the potential power of using framing to humanize the client, framing's effectiveness as a persuasive strategy may have some limitations. Frames are unlikely to have a universal effect on all jurors (Entman, 1993). In addition, research suggests that jurors' initial expectations derived from the frame may change as they become more familiar with the client through the presentation of evidence in the trial. In other words, the attorney can create an expectation, but jurors will confirm or disconfirm the expectation based on their exposure to objective information (Deighton, 1984). However, even with the limitations, framing is likely to serve as a useful tool for creating ingroup favoritism among jurors.

Opposing attorneys should also be able to use framing and group status (i.e., ingroup versus outgroup) to influence juror decision making. For example, the flip side of ingroup favoritism is outgroup derogation. When authoritarian jurors viewed defendants as differing from them in values and lifestyle, they were likely to be categorized as criminal and receive more severe verdicts and sentences (Mitchell & Byrne, 1973).

Dehumanizing, taking away the human qualities of another, is one form of outgroup derogation. Two types of dehumanization can occur. *Mechanistic* dehumanization compares others to automata and denies them human characteristics (Haslam, 2006). *Animalistic* dehumanization suggests that others do not possess the dimensions— intelligence, reasoning, language, and uniquely human emotions—that make humans unique from other animal species (e.g., love, hope, contempt, resentment; Haslam, 2006; Leyens et al., 2003; Vaes, Paladino, Castelli, Leyens, & Giovanazzi, 2003). Uniquely human emotions are also referred to as *secondary* emotions because the primary emotions (e.g, anger, aggressive feelings, pain, pleasure) are found in many animal species. Research has shown that people ascribed the secondary emotions to their ingroup while attributing primary emotions to the outgroup, a phenomenon called *infrahumanization* (Leyens et al., 2003; Vaes, Paladino, & Leyens, 2006). Even when members of an outgroup are ascribed secondary emotions, ingroup members processed the secondary emotions associated with the outgroup in a different manner (Gaunt, Leyens, & Demoulin, 2002; see Leyens et al., 2003). In addition, people were less cooperative "in terms of altruism, imitation, and approach" with outgroup members, even when they used secondary emotions to express themselves (Leyens et al., 2003, p. 703). Finally, people were more inclined to help members of their ingroup who expressed secondary emotions (Vaes et al., 2002; see Vaes, Paladino, Castelli, Leyens, & Giovanazzi, 2003; Vaes, Paladino, & Leyens, 2002).

Infrahumanization has been studied in the context of intergroup violence and conflict, with the denial of the humanness of the outgroup theorized to motivate aggression and to result from aggressive behaviors (Paladino & Vaes, 2009; see e.g., Bar-Tal, 1989; Fiske, Harris, & Cuddy, 2004; Opotow, 1990). For example, in one study, researchers successfully manipulated aggression—a primary emotion. The experimental group received derogatory comments while engaging in a frustrating challenge, but the control group was complimented while engaging in an easier task. Afterwards, both groups were exposed to an article on juvenile delinquency. The experimental group (i.e., those who were made to feel aggressive) were more punitive than those in the control group (Weiss & Fine, 1956).

This research, and the use of framing, has implications for attorney use of infrahumanization. According to research in capital cases, many jurors begin to consider the defendant's punishment before the defendant's guilt had been determined. In one study, nearly half of jurors made up their mind prior to the end of the guilt phase, even before aggravating or mitigating evidence was presented (Bowers, 1996; see English & Sales, 2005). Because the plaintiff's attorney (or prosecutor) presents evidence first, his or her efforts to categorize the client (or victim) as part of jurors' ingroup and infrahumanize the defendant will be heard first. Assuming the plaintiff's attorney (or prosecutor) is successful at this goal, then the research implies that there could be negative consequences for the defense. Generating anger and aggressive feelings in jurors for the defendant's motives and actions could result in greater punishments for the defendant. In addition, defense attorneys who emphasize secondary emotions of their client may actually receive less cooperation from jurors once the defendant is framed as a member of the outgroup and perceived that way by the jurors.

Defense attorneys are not completely helpless in counteracting the effects of infrahumanization. First, research indicates that a warm attorney–client relationship can increase the likelihood that jurors will be receptive to the defense's evidence (see above for more detailed discussion). Second, infrahumanization appears less likely to occur when members of the outgroup can be individualized and separated from their group (Leyens et al., 2003). For example, one study reported that dehumanization did not occur if a stranger was introduced by his or her first and last name (Cortes, Rodriguez, Rodriguez, Demoulin, & Leyens, unpublished work, 2002, as cited in Leyens et al., 2003). Perhaps attorneys can achieve similar results by introducing their clients by their first and last names to the jury and referring to their client by name during trial. Third, convincing jurors to take the perspective of the outgroup member may assist in individualizing him or her and diminish the effects of infrahumanization (Leyens et al., 2003). Although it is impermissible for attorneys to appeal to jury members to imagine themselves in their client's position because it encourages the jury to depart from its neutral role (e.g., *Spray-Rite Services Corp. v. Monsanto Co.*, 1982), attorneys may be able to induce jurors to take the perspective of their clients in other ways. For example, an attorney may be able to accomplish this goal by playing on common human behaviors: "We have all been stressed out and done something irrational under pressure. That is what happened to Mrs. Smith the night her husband died." Another possibility is that rhetorical questions may encourage jurors to think of things from the client's perspective: "Mrs. Smith testified that she was stressed out after her husband died, which is why she did not call the police immediately. Who hasn't done something irrational under stress?" However, the effectiveness of these strategies and other strategies for counteracting infrahumanization in the trial setting needs to be explored empirically. Despite the potential benefits of individualization, it may not be sufficient to keep one from being identified with a general negative category, which may make it impossible for jurors to ignore and change the defendant's categorization as a member of the outgroup or see the facts from the defendant's perspective. For example, a child rapist may be identified with a general category of pedophiles (Leyens et al., 2003). Fourth, the attorney could influence jurors to recategorize ingroup and outgroup status. For example, in one study, men and women in different university departments infrahumanized the other group and attributed more secondary emotions to their ingroup than to the outgroup. In contrast, men and women who were classmates (i.e., members of a superordinate inclusive group) did not infrahumanize the opposite sex (Leyens et al., 2002). Therefore, it appears that finding a way to restructure jurors' perceptions to include the defendant in the ingroup could assuage jurors.

Moreover, although direct research does not exist to draw implications about the validity of trial commentators' belief about humanizing the client, some reasonable conclusions about the effectiveness of humanizing the client can be made. Framing the client (or victim) in a way that highlights his or her positive characteristics and dehumanizing the opposing side is likely to be especially beneficial for the plaintiff (or prosecutor). It seems key that plaintiffs (or prosecutors) get jurors to perceive the defendant as a member of the outgroup. However, a warm relationship between defense counsel and the defendant appears to delay jurors' guilt determinations. In addition, the defense lawyer may have some success countering the opposing side's efforts if he or she individualizes the defendant or recategorizes the defendant's status as an ingroup member.

CONCLUSION

Trial commentators believe that one benefit of a close attorney–client relationship is greater access to information that will be useful for the trial. However, research indicates that many lawyers and clients have difficulty creating a close relationship. Deficits in lawyers, interpersonal skills appear to contribute to clients' dissatisfaction, with clients highly valuing attorneys' relational skills possibly even more than their legal skills. Studies reporting both lawyers' and clients' perspectives indicate that clients are reluctant to disclose information to their lawyers, which suggests that the lack of rapport between them is affecting the quality of the representation. One cause for the discordance is that attorneys and law students are more prone to be purely cognitive thinkers than people in the general population, which suggests that attorneys' personalities may be influencing their ability to effectively establish rapport with their clients. Attorneys are likely to have more success in developing rapport with clients if they understand what the client values in the professional relationship, involve the client in the decision making about the case, and use affirmative behaviors during communications with the client.

The attorney–client relationship may influence juror perceptions and decision making. Trial commentators recommend that lawyers demonstrate liking for the client. Research indicates that people are able to infer others' feelings through the degree of nonimmediacy in verbal communications. Attorneys may be able to convey liking of their clients through their voice, gestures, and interactions with them. Opinionated statements to the jury about the client may also convey greater liking than nonopinionated statements, but attorneys will have to use this strategy carefully because of constraints imposed by legal rules.

Another recommendation of trial commentators is that lawyers talk to their clients during recesses to build trust with the client and convey liking of the client to the jury. Research indicates that attitudes can be inferred from kinesic behaviors. Attorneys' posture, position of head and arms, and degree of eye contact appear to be most likely to contribute to an inference that the attorney holds a positive attitude toward the client.

Developing a positive, affective attorney–client relationship appears to have beneficial effects for attorneys and clients with regard to jurors' willingness to consider their information. It is important to note that these positive results appear to be limited to attorney–client relationships that are perceived as warm. Jurors react negatively when they perceive an attorney and client to be working closely together without genuine warmth in their relationship, but not if the attorney maintains a professional distance in the absence of warmth. At least in capital cases, attorneys' safest practice is to display a warm but not particularly close relationship with defendants.

Trial commentators also believe that if jurors feel positively about the attorney, these feelings will cause them to also feel positively about the client if they perceive that the attorney and client are close. Research supports that positive affect attributed to one object may be transferred to other objects that are associated with it, which tentatively substantiates trial commentators' beliefs. In addition, negative associations also appear to work the same way as positive ones but may weigh more heavily in the impression-formation process.

Conveying pride in the client is another recommendation of trial commentators. It is possible that jurors will perceive an attorney's pride in the client as an indication that the client is deserving of social status and acceptance. However, the available research leaves many questions unanswered, so it is currently impossible to gauge how jurors will respond to perceptions of attorneys' pride in their client.

Trial commentators list the ability to identify and effectively communicate the clients' emotions as another benefit of a close attorney–client relationship. Although emotion is clearly important in trials and may influence jurors' legal decisions (e.g., consider the research on emotional displays from defendants), the associated research issues are complex, and the available research cannot offer concrete conclusions. Currently, no research substantiates the belief that becoming close with one's client or sympathizing with the client will either (a) increase attorneys' ability to identify and communicate emotions effectively to the jury or (b) influence jury decision making. One strategy that is likely to be successful is implied by research, however. Asking or priming jurors to take the client's perspective may help jurors to understand the client's emotions, reduce their perceptions of social distance, and enhance their sympathetic feelings and altruistic behaviors.

Humanizing the client is the last recommendation of the trial commentators. People's tendency to categorize others into ingroups and outgroups suggests that one way attorneys can humanize the client is by drawing parallels between him or her and jurors. Similarly, framing can highlight information that helps activate schemas, which can influence the way that jurors cognitively process the message. Likewise, dehumanizing is a strategy that can be used to emphasize negative aspects of the opponent. Opposing attorneys may be able to deflect some of these effects if (a) they have a warm attorney–client relationship and (b) they are able to individualize their client or recategorize him or her as an ingroup member.

7

ATTORNEY STORYTELLING

Famed defense counsel Johnnie Cochran in his legal representation of O. J. Simpson, who was accused of murdering his ex-wife Nicole Brown Simpson and her friend Ronald Goldman, exemplifies a master storyteller in the courtroom. "If it doesn't fit, you must acquit," was Cochran's catchy quip in his closing argument. It quickly became a mantra for poking holes in the prosecution's version of what happened the night Simpson and Goldman were murdered. This pithy statement focused the jury's attention on a serious shortcoming in the police department's investigation of the killings (i.e., O. J. Simpson's difficulty in getting on the gloves, which were a key piece of the State's evidence for linking Simpson to the murders; e.g, Angeles, 1995).

In addition to his quip, Cochran strategically evoked the memory of the Rodney King beating trial, only 4 years earlier, as part of his storytelling in the Simpson trial. By alluding to the commonality between King and Simpson, Cochran was able to create a shared story of police misconduct, thereby enabling jurors to see Simpson as a victim. The prosecution, apparently underestimating the symbolic and emotional impact that the memory of King would have on jurors in the Simpson trial, failed to offer a viable counterstory to disassociate King and Simpson (Jacobs, 2002). Cochran, who probably crafted his catchy slogan and version of events to remind the jurors as they went into the deliberations that the flaw in the prosecution's case amounted to reasonable doubt, likely hit his mark with the jury. Not only was O. J. Simpson acquitted but Americans still remember Cochran's defense of Simpson long after the trial, as evidenced by Cochran's being parodied and his mantra endlessly repeated in popular culture (e.g., "Defense superstar," 2005).

Since there are generally at least two sides to every case, it is no surprise that trial commentators insist that trial lawyers must be good storytellers (Berg, 2003/2006) to recreate the events that happened to parties and facts in a way that is comprehensible and persuasive to the jury (Lubet, 2000; Mauet, 1992, 2005; Murray, 1995). This chapter (a) develops the storytelling elements, which include the theory and theme of a case and their attendant strategies, (b) discusses the supposed persuasive benefits of storytelling, and (c) considers whether scientific research and theory support the legal strategists' recommendations.

ATTORNEY STORYTELLING IN THE LEGAL LITERATURE

Storytelling is considered a performance to draw the jury into the story: "an artfully enacted event, a skilled display of communication that holds an audience, stimulates their senses, provokes their emotions . . . evokes and comments on aspects of reality yet remains at a distance from it" (Schrager, 1999, p. 4). Ultimately, the story should lead "[jurors] to forget they are jurors . . . at trial . . . but instead believe they are observers at an event unfolding before them" (Haydock & Sonsteng, 1991, p. 48).

Relationship of the Theory to the Story

To be an effective storyteller at trial, trial attorneys must make sure that they have the elements of a story in place, with the theory and theme of the case guiding the choice of the stories (Lubet, 2000; Mauet, 1992, 2005; Murray, 1995). The theory of the case is a "word picture" that provides the trial lawyer's version of "what really happened" (Fontham, 2002, p. 95; see also Bocchino, 2001; Haydock & Sonsteng, 1991; Lubet, 2000; Mauet, 1992, 2005; Murray, 1995) and presents the reason why the jurors will want to find in favor of the lawyer's client (Haydock & Sonsteng, 1991). In some of the legal literature, attorneys, even those who discuss theory, refer to the attorney's "story" as interchangeable with their theory of the case. Both *theory* and *story* words are used to refer to the attorney's explanation of events. For example, one commentator explains that the theory of the case is "each party's version of what really happened" (Mauet, 2005, p. 8); this same commentator explains that "good stories show, not tell, what happened" (Mauet, 2005, p.10).

However, some trial commentators explain that there is a difference between a theory and a story: "Stories tend to be particularized, theories to be more general" (Gewirtz, 1996, p. 6). Other commentators explain that the story presents the theory in a coherent manner (Lubet, 2000; Mauet, 1992, 2005; Murray, 1995). The theory is an organizing framework for developing the story that will be conveyed at trial. Detail is then added to the theory to create a story, which serves as a persuasive device (Gewirtz, 1996). For example, the theory is believed to guide the lawyer's factual investigation (Burns, 1999); help the lawyer develop an outline of key points that need to be presented at trial; and guide the development of the opening statements, closing arguments, and decisions about which witnesses will testify (Haydock & Sonsteng, 1991). When the underlying theory is well developed, the jury will be more likely to accept the lawyer's version of events; if the jurors buy into the attorney's version of events, they will use it to fill in the evidentiary gaps in a way that is favorable to the lawyer (Fontham, 2002; see also Gilden 2001).

Why a Story Is Important

Trial commentators offer several reasons why a story form is beneficial for presenting information at trial: The story form is a good way to draw the jury's interest and attention because stories make people want to listen (Ball, 1993, 1997; see also Burns, 1999), help make complicated trial information understandable (Schrager, 1999), establish a context for understanding the information presented at trial (Jeans, 1993; Haydock & Sonsteng, 1991), aid learning and understanding the case (Burns, 1999; Perrin, Caldwell, & Chase, 2003; Schrager, 1999), and improves jurors' retention of the information (Burns, 1999) because people "think with stories" rather than "massive compilations" of disparate evidence (Schrager, 1999, p. 7). Memory for the information presented at trial may also be enhanced by the meaning given to the things that happen to people through the story (Schrager, 1999). "Jurors quickly shut down mentally if the data presented are excessively difficult to follow" (Singer, 2000, p. 80); using a story reminds jurors that their duty to evaluate the evidence in the trial is doable (Burns, 1999).

The story form also has the advantage of connecting actions or evidence together into a "convincing whole" (Schrager, 1999, p. 29). Because jurors are believed to be influenced by whether the message is perceived as credible, using the story to connect the trial information in a convincing manner is thought to increase its persuasiveness (Mauet, 1992). Stories are believed to be particularly advantageous for explaining an attorney's evidence (Fontham, 2002) because they allow the attorney to highlight the elements that are considered important in the jury's decision making while downplaying information that is irrelevant by excluding those pieces from the story (Burns, 1999).

Therefore, using a story format may help attorneys shape jurors' attitudes and impressions of the case (Wells, 1988).

Strategies for Developing the Theory and Story

Given that both theory and story are the lawyer's explanation of what happened in the case, there are similarities between the two concepts and significant overlap in trial commentators' recommendations for them. Therefore, we discuss trial commentators' recommended strategies for the theory and story together to avoid repetition.

Developing a theory for the story first requires identifying facts (Perrin et al., 2003). The story elements that need to be presented at trial are the circumstances of time and place, the protagonists, the problem, and the solutions to the problem (Haydock & Sonsteng, 1991). Some commentators suggest asking three questions as part of the process of gathering this information: What happened, why did it happen, and why does that mean my client should win (Lubet, 2000; see also Bocchino, 2001; Haydock & Sonsteng, 1991; Perrin et al., 2003)? Another commentator suggests asking the client questions, beginning with open-ended ones to determine the client's problem and desired resolution, then moving to more directive questions to construct a chronology of central events, and concluding with theory-driven questions to help test the viability of possible narratives (Burns, 1999). A timeline is considered useful in this process (Bocchino, 2001). In addition, it is recommended that the attorney test the proposed theory on others who are not related to the case, but trial lawyers should still ultimately rely on their own judgment (Haydock & Sonsteng, 1991). The facts that the attorney chooses must explain the motives of key witnesses (Bocchino, 2001), account for the differences among the witnesses and other evidence, favor the attorney's client (Bocchino, 2001), and address why the jury should believe this version of the events (Mauet, 1992, 2005). In addition, having moral or political appeal gives the jury a reason to rule favorably on the lawyer's case (Burns, 1999; see also Schrager, 1999).

Trial commentators also identify other considerations, such as making sure that the story is comprehensive (Perrin et al., 2003) and includes any facts and law (Perrin et al., 2003) that are necessary to convince the trier of fact that the theory and story accurately describe what happened (Haydock & Sonsteng, 1991). In other words, commentators believe that the underlying theory and story should not only fit the available facts (Burns, 1999; Haydock & Sonsteng, 1991; Lubet, 2000; Murray, 1995) that can be supported by "admissible, credible, and ethically presentable evidence" (Burns, 1999, p. 45; see also, Haydock & Sonsteng, 1991; Perrin et al., 2003) but also be supported by a legal rule favorable to the lawyer's position (Burns, 1999; Haydock & Sonsteng, 1991;

Lubet, 2000; Murray, 1995). For example, it is important that the selected theory and story avoid problems of proof and survive a motion for summary judgment (i.e., which allows the judge in civil litigation to decide the case on the basis of the law because there is no dispute as to the material facts) or motion for directed verdict (i.e., which allows the judge in a civil or criminal trial to direct the verdict because the party with the burden of proof has failed in providing sufficient evidence to prove his or her case; Easton, 1998; Haydock & Sonsteng, 1991). In addition, an attorney should anticipate the opponent's theory and theme (Burns, 1999). The attorney must be able to overcome the opposing side's explanation for the events and withstand defenses that may be raised, including denials and affirmative defenses (Haydock & Sonsteng, 1991).

Although a comprehensive version of events is important, trial commentators also assert that the story should be simple (Burns, 1999; Lubet, 2000; Mauet, 1992, 2005; Murray, 1995; Perrin et al., 2003). Simple, straightforward explanations are thought to be more believable to jurors than convoluted explanations (Haydock & Sonsteng, 1991). Another reason simplifying cases is important is that jurors' reportedly have difficulty comprehending information at trial. For example, trial commentators explain that jury comprehension levels are negatively affected by brief attention spans (Haydock & Sonsteng, 1991; Mauet, 1992). In addition, comprehension levels are believed to be affected by long trials, which disrupt the lives of the jurors and exhaust them (Kidd, 1991). Because of these challenges, lawyers should strive for a version of events that is easy for the juries to follow (Fontham, 2002; Lubet, 2000; Mauet, 1992, 2005; Perrin et al., 2003). Lawyers can make the case easier for the jury to comprehend by simplifying the facts and explanations (Haydock & Sonsteng, 1991).

Another consideration is whether the underlying theory and story are plausible (Burns, 1999) and compelling/persuasive (Mauet, 1992, 2005); in other words, one that the jury will be likely to find true and that maximizes the chances of prevailing at trial (Perrin et al., 2003). There are two primary types of factual plausibility: internal and external. According to the legal literature, internal plausibility means the necessary elements are included; the relationships between items of information are defined; and the setting, characters, and means or motive are adequately developed (Burns, 1999). When telling the story, the focus should be on the people (Ball, 1993, 1997; Lubet, 2000; Mauet, 1992, 2005; Perrin et al., 2003) because trial attorneys want the jurors to understand that the case involves people instead of abstract legal problems and to increase the acceptability and believability of the theory and story for the jurors (Haydock & Sonsteng, 1991). In sum, an internally plausible story is one that appears to illustrate reality given the attorneys' explanation of the facts and events of the case. For an explanation of events to be externally plausible, it must make sense to the jury given what they know about how people typically act in a given situation (Burns, 1999) and capture "the drama, emotion, and spontaneity of life" (Fontham, 2002, p. 94). The objective of external plausibility is that attorneys should develop a version of events that aligns with the jurors' attitudes and commonsense beliefs about the way persons typically act under similar circumstances (Bocchino, 2001; Burns, 1999; Haydock & Sonsteng, 1991; Lubet, 2000; Mauet, 1992, 2005; Murray, 1995). Considering jurors' common sense is believed to be important because jurors "are both schooled and skilled in what are fair and common sense notions of who should be responsible in given situations" (Bocchino, 2001, p. 7). Trial commentators recommend paying attention to the existing evidence and law and tying those pieces to plotlines jurors already hold (Schrager, 1999, p. 7). Stated another way, lawyers who consider jurors' innate schema for the organization and interpretation of experience and maintain consistency with jurors' common sense (i.e., "a store of empirical generalizations concerning human behavior") can convey a story that is likely to be more believable to jurors (Burns, 1999, p. 169). For example, civil attorneys portraying the client as acting in a way that exhibits good character, and prosecutors portraying the defendant as exhibiting bad character, may appeal to jurors (e.g., Burns, 1999). One perceived pitfall in implementing this strategy is correspondence bias (i.e., assuming that jurors will automatically perceive the case the same way that the attorney does; Singer, 2000). Trial commentators warn attorneys that jurors are unlikely to accept a lawyer's complete version of events, but instead will fill in the story with additional pieces of information and judgments that are purely historical, moral, and human/political (Burns, 1999).

According to the legal literature, the lawyer's version of events also needs to be logical (Burns, 1999; Lubet, 2000; Mauet, 1992; Murray, 1995; Perrin et al., 2003). Avoiding contradictions (Burns, 1999; Easton, 1998; Haydock & Sonsteng, 1991) and achieving a coherent and consistent structure for the attorneys' facts and arguments (Fontham, 2002) are key to developing a logical explanation. Lawyers can achieve consistency by (a) avoiding inconsistent alternative factual accounts (Bocchino, 2001; Easton, 1998; Haydock & Sonsteng, 1991), (b) avoiding weak arguments (Perrin et al., 2003) or positions that would require jurors to make a difficult choice (Haydock & Sonsteng, 1991), (c) not contradicting any disputed fact that the jurors will likely find to be true (Perrin et al., 2003), and (d) rejecting any claims or defenses that are inconsistent with other claims or defenses (Perrin et al., 2003). Attorneys can also avoid contradictions by refraining from the use of words such as "but," "however," and "even if" because statements containing these types of words "may unintentionally concede the validitiy of the other side's explanation" (Haydock & Sonsteng, 1991, p. 47). Similarly, lawyers are warned against arguing in the alternative because "real people interpret this as an admission that the attorney is indeed wrong about point one. Even worse, the attorney's lengthy but now conceded argument about point one diminishes his credibility on point two" (Easton, 1998, p. 19). For situations that require lawyers to present alternative explanations at trial, trial commentators suggest presenting those arguments in a way that does not contradict. For example, attorneys can affirmatively state a position and then add another explanation, using words such as *moreover* or *furthermore*, to maintain consistency (Haydock & Sonsteng, 1991).

Logic can also be achieved through organizational mechanisms (Lubet, 2000; Mauet, 1992; Perrin et al., 2003). Trial commentators remind lawyers that a cogent story has a good beginning involving people, a middle that gets the people step-by-step from the beginning to the end (i.e., linear organization; Gilden, 2001), and a strong ending centered on the people (Ball, 1993, 1997; Gilden, 2001). Attorneys should begin with their main contention (Ball, 1993). Next, the trial attorney should use a narrative of the case's main issues as the middle of the story and conclude with an emotional ending that makes the jurors feel the importance of deciding the main issue in the attorney's favor and responding to the attorney's requested relief (Ball, 1993). Another recommendation is that the attorney use the following order to explain his or her version of what happened in the case: characters, events, chronology, causality, and purpose (Gilden, 2001). Causality (i.e., the belief that one event brings about another; all events should be causally connected to one another) and teleology (i.e., the idea that things happen for a reason or at least as part of a system that is moving in a particular direction) are presumably useful when creating a convincing version of events (Gilden, 2001).

Selecting a Theme for the Case

If one considered the theory to be akin to a movie script, then the theme would be the equivalent of the movie's tagline (e.g., "Just when you thought it was safe to go back in the water" from *Jaws 2* [Zanuck, Brown, Alves, Szwarc, & Alves, 1978]; "In space, no one can hear you scream" from *Alien* [Carroll, Giler, Hill, & Scott, 1979]). A tagline, which is often seen or heard in movie advertisements, gives a glimpse into the show and reinforces the audiences' memory of a movie. Similarly, the theme of a case is supposed to express an attorney's gist or nub of a case (i.e., one central theme for the case that incorporates the facts used in the theory; Perrin et al., 2003) and contain an accompanying moral (Burns, 1999). For example, a lawyer may choose a theme such as "This is a case about cheating" (Mauet, 1992, p. 42). Like the example, many possible themes discussed in the legal literature only imply the desired outcome in the case (i.e., if the case is about cheating, and most people agree cheating is wrong, then whoever cheated should be punished). Most trial commentators do not insist that the theme explicitly state what the attorney is hoping to achieve. However, attorneys could in fact articulate a theme that does direct a clear course of action for the jury (e.g., "Cheaters should not prosper").

Trial commentators recommend presenting a theme or themes at trial because they believe that jury deliberations center around one or more of them (e.g., Association of Trial Lawyers of America, 2003; see end of section for an account of the acceptability of multiple themes in the legal literature). A theme provides the "essence of the case" (Association of Trial Lawyers of America, 2003) and a way for the jurors to organize and understand the evidence (Association of Trial Lawyers of America, 2003; Murray, 1995), thereby making the lawyer's case more credible, or at least acceptable, in the minds of the jurors (Murray, 1995). Themes are also thought to summarize the lawyer's position on the evidence (Mauet, 1992, 2005).

Trial commentators suggest emphasizing the theme throughout the presentation of the case (Fontham, 2002) and recommend that attorneys "use [the theme] as early and often in the trial as [they] can" (Easton, 1998, p. 219). Thus, trial commentators instruct lawyers to introduce their theme in voir dire (Perrin et al., 2003; Wells, 1988) and build their opening statement (Fontham, 2002) and closing argument on it (Fontham, 2002; Perrin et al., 2003; Wells, 1988). Repeating the theme often throughout the course of the trial is emphasized as a way for the theme to "take hold" in the jurors' minds (Perrin et al., 2003, p. 43).

To maximize the benefits of using a theme, the lawyer should begin to think about a theme as soon as he or she decides to take the case and continually fine-tune it throughout the trial process (Murray, 1995). A primary consideration is whether the theme is consistent with the attorney's "credibility as the truth-giver in the courtroom" (Fine, 1998, p. 8). In determining which theme the jury will find most persuasive, trial commentators look to many sources for ideas: symbols (Murray, 1995), song titles, bible phrases, slogans, lyrics, proverbs, parables, children's rhymes (Association of Trial Lawyers of America, 2003), and literary sources (Perrin et al., 2003) such as stories, religious writings, and parental lessons (Bocchino, 2001). However, obscure literary references should be avoided because they may be lost on less sophisticated jurors (Perrin et al., 2003). Likewise, one commentator suggests that a theme should not be allegorical (i.e., a comparative device to illustrate a point about the facts) or purely conceptual (Fontham, 2002). An allegorical theme at trial can confuse the jury by diverting attention from the facts in the case, distract the attorney from the case at hand, and provide a potential opportunity for opposing counsel to manipulate the theme to help his or her argument (Fontham, 2002). Brainstorming with colleagues is recommended when developing ideas for a theme (Association of Trial Lawyers of America, 2003).

Successful themes "psychologically sum up [the lawyer's] case in the light most favorable to [his or her client]," (O'Quinn, 2001, p. 3). A theme may be persuasive to jurors because it focuses them on a particular fact, element, or pattern (Murray, 1995) that the lawyer wishes to emphasize and on different aspects of the lawyer's arguments (Fontham, 2002). Some trial commentators recommend devising a theme that is consistent with all the important facts, even the facts that do not favor the client's case. The factual points that are believed to be most important to stress are those that highlight and contrast the differences between sides (Association of Trial Lawyers of America, 2003). For example, in creating the theme, if the trial attorney is representing the plaintiff in the case, he or she should focus the jury on the wrongful conduct of the defendant while taking into account any personal responsibility of the plaintiff in the situation. This strategy is founded on the belief that jurors are predisposed to scrutinize both litigants and their conduct (Association of Trial Lawyers of America, 2003). Overall, however, attorneys are advised to resist reliance on any facts that are inconsistent with the central theme (Fine, 1998; Perrin et al., 2003).

Despite the emphasis given to the factual considerations, trial attorneys are warned against becoming overly engrossed with the facts and details of the case because they can produce an unsatisfactory theme. One trial commentator advises attorneys to analyze the case for the purpose of developing a theme after taking a "step back" from the facts. Along this line of reasoning, a theme should address the facts in a compelling way (Association of Trial Lawyers of America, 2003), combining logic with emotion to accomplish two things: (a) telling the jury why the lawyer's client should win and (b) connecting the jury to some reason why it should care about the party winning (Perrin et al., 2003). Achieving these goals will likely tap into the jurors' reasoning and decision making, using both cognitive and affective (i.e., emotion based) thought processes.

The affective processes may be triggered by having the theme "provide . . . a reason, deeply rooted in common experience, why a client should prevail"(Bocchino, 2001, p. 12) and state "universal truths about people and events that [they] learn during [their] lives" (Mauet, 1992, p. 42; see also Fine, 1998; Perrin et al., 2003). For example, one commentator suggests choosing a theme that "play[s] on common psychological traits" (Murray, 1995, p. 53). Other commentators suggest directing the theme to the jurors' set of values (Perrin et al., 2003) or sense of morality, such as achieving justice in the case (Lubet, 2000; see also Association of Trial Lawyers of America, 2003; Fine, 1998). One way to appeal to morality or justice is by using a theme that makes the case appear bigger than the immediate parties involved, or by helping the jury realize the importance of the case to society (Perlman, 1986; Perrin et al., 2003; Wells, 1988).

The legal literature indicates that themes should be simple, concise, understandable (Association of Trial Lawyers of America, 2003), and easily remembered (Perrin et al., 2003). However, there is disagreement over what the exact length should be. Some consider the theme to be only a few words (Easton, 1998; O'Quinn, 2001) or, even better, one word (Easton, 1998); others consider one (Lubet, 2000) to two sentences an acceptable length for a theme (Perrin et al., 2003).

Along with length, another point of disagreement among trial commentators is whether more than one theme is considered appropriate. The majority of trial commentators appear to believe that cases should contain only one overall theme (Association of Trial Lawyers of America, 2003; Lubet, 2000), but several commentators suggest that most cases have more than one theme (called *subthemes*; Fontham, 2002; Mauet, 2005; Murray, 1995). The difference in opinion about the acceptability of multiple themes may be accounted for in how specifically the term *theme* or *subtheme* is used by individual commentators. For example, some legal strategists suggest using "labels" (Mauet, 1992, p. 47), "impact" or "buzz" words (Perrin et al., 2003, p. 43), or "viscerals" (Ball, 1993, p. 60; 1997, p. 94) to refer to parties, events, and other important things during trial. It is possible that the commentators in favor of employing multiple themes or additional subthemes are using the theme category broadly to encompass labels or buzz words. Whatever the terminology used, the purposes for using these words or statements at trial appears to be similar: to give impact to a statement (Ball, 1993, 1997). For example, instead of referring to a vehicle collision as an "accident," labeling it as a "wreck" or a "crash" will have more impact on the jury's decision making. Another purpose for these words is to emphasize key issues (Perrin et al., 2003) and project the lawyer's theory and theme of the case to the trier of fact (Mauet, 1992). It appears that for the commentators who use them, specific words or phrases take on some responsibilities of the theme.

In conclusion, the following questions highlight many of the key points of interest expressed in the legal literature for selecting a theme: (a) Does the theme summarize the story? (b) Does the theme have factual as well as emotional appeal? (c) Does the theme paint a visual image for the jury? (d) Does the theme blend with the life experiences, values, and perception of the jurors? (e) Does the theme apply the classical and rhetorical principles of ethos [i.e., source of the message], pathos [i.e., emotion], and logos [i.e., reason]? (f) Does the theme guide the jurors' decision-making process? (g) Does the theme treat the jurors like thinking adults? (h) Is the theme consistent with the applicable legal instructions? (i) Does the theme point out the injustices in the case and allow jurors to view a victory for the client as advancing community interests? (j) Does the theme have universal application and appeal? (Association of Trial Lawyers of America, 2003).

Other Strategies for Successful Trial Performance

After a satisfactory theory, theme, and story are in place, trial commentators offer additional strategies to achieve a successful trial performance. Like a good actor, the trial attorney's performance in court must create an atmosphere that affects jurors' emotions at the right time by leading the audience to the "threshold of emotion" and making sure "the culmination of the emotion is felt by the audience" (Haydock & Sonsteng, 1991, p. 48). Techniques that are believed to influence jurors' emotional responses include positive and negative emotional messages, rhetorical questions, one-sided and two-sided arguments, forewarning techniques, labels and themes, repetition, reinforcement, and order effects. Trial commentators also stress that a performance that mentally and emotionally involves the jurors in the case will be more interesting to jurors and will help them remember evidence (Haydock & Sonsteng, 1991).

When telling the story, trial commentators recommend that attorneys start strongly. Attorneys should immediately draw the audience into the story and maintain the audience's attention throughout (Haydock & Sonsteng, 1991). Jurors view lawyers who begin dramatically as worth listening to (Jeans, 1993). In addition, the jury's attention is thought to be highest at the beginning of the trial, and lawyers can initiate the persuasive process when jurors are most likely to pay attention (Jeans, 1993). Beginning dramatically is also beneficial because trial commentators believe that jurors reach decisions quickly and resist changing their minds (Haydock & Sonsteng, 1991; Mauet, 1992). In fact, one trial commentator notes that most people make up their minds quickly—in a minute or less (Fontham, 2002).

Trial commentators also suggest other strategies to make the story interesting to jurors. These commentators warn that the quickest way to lose a jury's attention is by being boring (O'Quinn, 2001). To protect against this, attorneys are advised to monitor how well the jury is engaged by scanning for nonverbal cues of boredom from the jury (e.g., glassy-eyed stares, lack of eye contact, or excessive fidgeting; Singer, 2000). Humor, anger, pathos, gestures, eye contact, voice (O'Quinn, 2001), and use of literary devices such as foreshadowing, irony, and comparing and contrasting (Perrin et al., 2003) can add elements of interest to the trial. In addition, attorneys can maintain the jurors' attention with visual exhibits and simplicity and by using the principles of primacy and recency (Haydock & Sonsteng, 1991; Mauet, 1992, 2005). Attorneys can also cue the jury that something is important as a technique for emphasizing topics (Mauet, 1992, 2005). Underlying this strategy is the presumption that jurors will only pay attention when they think something is important (Mauet, 1992).

Trial commentators favor creating clear, vivid images of the event as another technique for adding interest to the story (Mauet, 1992, 2005; Murray, 1995). Trial attorneys claim that such initial images created at trial attract jurors' attention and help their understanding (Haydock & Sonsteng, 1991). To aid the jury in vividly and accurately imagining the event, critical images should be enhanced to make them as realistic and complete as possible (Haydock & Sonsteng, 1991). According to trial commentators, a realistic story is detail oriented (Perrin et al., 2003), including all details of the event as well as tapping into the jurors' senses (Haydock & Sonsteng, 1991). One commentator claims that this kind of "visceral" communication "elicit[s] a mental/emotional/physical reflex which occurs like a knee-jerk reaction" and influences jurors because "evolution or God (or both) created this unsuppressible defense mechanism to make us seek or avoid such survival-determinate things" (Ball, 1997, p. 94).

SCIENCE RELEVANT TO TRIAL COMMENTATORS' CLAIMS

The research literature acknowledges two primary approaches to storytelling. The first approach is a literary one, which views the story as "dramaturgical" (Mandelbaum, 2003, p. 597). Under this approach, the storyteller takes an active role, serving as a performer or speaker, while the audience comprises passive listeners (Mandelbaum, 2003). In addition, a literary perspective to storytelling approaches the story according to "scripts" based on chosen activities (Mandelbaum, 2003, p. 597). On the other hand, communication scholars approach storytelling as an interaction between storyteller and audience. According to this approach,

> storytelling is a basic method by which we share experiences, and in sharing experiences we undertake such important social processes as joking, performing delicate activities, complaining, accounting, telling troubles, gossiping, and constructing relationships, social roles, and social and institutional realities. (Mandelbaum, 2003, p. 596)

The storyteller and story recipient work together to construct the meanings of past events according to their relevance in the present (Mandelbaum, 2003).

In addition to the different approaches to storytelling, the research on storytelling is ambiguous when it comes to operationalizing terms. Researchers frequently fail to distinguish literary storytelling from interactive storytelling: "the stories produced orally as performance, those produced in casual interactional settings, and those that are written are treated as the same thing—

kinds of discourse organized around the passage of time in some world" (Mandelbaum, 2003, p. 597–598). In addition, narrative, narration, discourse, story, anecdote, and storytelling are reportedly used interchangeably in the research literature (Mandelbaum, 2003) and are not necessarily used to distinguish one approach to storytelling from another.

Furthermore, empirical studies on storytelling by attorneys in actual trials are nonexistent. The closest available research is limited to (a) stories made by litigants in small claims courts, where litigants typically appear without legal representation (O'Barr & Conley, 1985); (b) stories made during plea bargains, where attorneys tell a story in order to negotiate a resolution for their clients outside of trial (Maynard, 1988); and (c) nonempirical, scholarly discussions of the use of stories by lawyers in trials (e.g., Bennett, 1978; Bennett & Feldman, 1981). Thus, knowledge about how attorneys use stories and how those stories are structured is lacking. For example, although the literary approach is most closely akin to trial commentators' description of the attorney's role as a performer, some also acknowledge that interactions occur with storytelling. As Burns (1999) acknowledged, jurors will complete the lawyer's version of events with other beliefs they hold.

Despite the explicit indication by trial commentators that storytelling is a performance, we will not focus on this aspect here. Several reasons justify this approach. First, trial commentators largely focus on broad claims instead of specific strategies for storytelling as a performance. For example, one recommendation was to begin dramatically, but commentators do not acknowledge exactly what actions will accomplish this goal. In addition, many performance-associated aspects of trial advocacy (but not specifically directed as such by commentators, e.g., tone of voice and gestures) were addressed in Chapters 4 and 5 on nonverbal communication strategies. Therefore, we refer readers to those chapters in lieu of repeating the information here. Last, and most important, much of the trial commentary related to storytelling really addresses how lawyers should develop a convincing account of the events. Thus, instead of focusing on the performance, this chapter is focused on the stories themselves—more specifically, the content of the story and its effect on jury decision making.

Attorney's Case Theory in Relation to the Story

Trial commentators indicate that a theory explains the attorney's version of "what really happened." However, the word *theory* has other definitions in the scientific literature. To the scientist, a theory is "an explanation of a set of related observations or events based upon proven hypotheses and verified multiple times by detached groups of researchers" (Wilson, 2007). On the other hand, according to the commonsense meaning, a theory embodies a supposition or strategy based on intuition, instinct, or experience (*Merriam-Webster's Collegiate Dictionary*, 2009; e.g., "I have a theory about that."). The definition of theory asserted by trial commentators may fall into the common usage of the word *theory* because it attempts to tap into jurors' intuition about the likely sequence of events, but it does not conform to how scientists typically use the term.

In addition to theory, trial commentators also discuss a related concept: *story*. The scientific literature supports trial commentators' claims that stories are detailed and coherent accounts of "what really happened." In the scientific literature, a story is considered "a structured, coherent retelling of an experience or a fictional account of an experience" (Schank & Berman, 2002, p. 288). Researchers indicate that a story consists of a series of events that contain a physical setting and participants. Additional details would also be included as part of the story (e.g., the participants' psychological states, actions, and relationships to other participants; Rumelhart, 1977; Schank & Abelson, 1977).

The story model for juror decision making (discussed in greater detail below), which proposes that jurors create a story in order to understand the evidence and reach a verdict, is instructive on the issue of how theory and story relate (Pennington & Hastie, 1991). Story episodes are composed of purposeful events that are connected by causal relationships (Pennington & Hastie, 1991, 1993). For example, "initiating events cause characters to have psychological responses and to form goals that motivate subsequent actions which cause certain consequences and accompanying states" (Pennington & Hastie, 1991, p. 525; 1993, p. 127). The story model views the story as a hierarchy of embedded episodes, with the highest level episodes highlighting "the most important features of 'what happened'" (Pennington & Hastie, 1991, p. 527). The lower level episodes contain more detailed event sequences that explain causal and intentional relationships for purposes of elaborating on the highest level episodes (Pennington & Hastie, 1986; see Thorndyke & Yekovich, 1980). This model appears consistent with trial commentators' explanation of theory and story. Trial commentators' theory would be analogous to the highest level episodes in the story, whereas story would be the entire hierarchy of embedded episodes, including the additional details provided by the lower level episodes.

The story model, like the trial commentators' theory and story, relates to the psychological concept of schemas that people hold. *Schemas*, which refer to how people mentally organize information, represent mental categories about a particular subject and include knowledge about the subject, relationships among cognitions, and specific examples (Fiske & Taylor, 1991; Thorndyke & Yekovich, 1980). For instance, people may hold a schema about getting a speeding ticket. This schema is likely to include hearing sirens, looking in the review mirror to see the police car with flashing lights, pulling off to the side of the road, and waiting nervously with license in hand for the uniformed officer to approach the car. Scripts (i.e., a schema for situation and event sequences; Abelson, 1976; Thorndyke & Yekovich, 1980) and prototypes (i.e., a schema that is based on specific features of the subject; Smith, 1991) are kinds of schemas that will be discussed in more detail below as they relate to theory and story.

Schemas simplify and organize complex information following a hierarchical structure. One way in which a hierarchy may emerge is through the varying degrees of specificity in which related concepts are connected (Thorndyke & Yekovich, 1980). In other words, the upper level will comprise abstract concepts, while the lowest levels will contain specific, dependent information (Schank & Abelson, 1977; Thorndyke & Yekovich, 1980). For example, a general schema for "party" is likely to include a property of "food," but a more specific schema of "party" is "birthday party," which is likely to contain a more specific food property of "cake and ice cream" (Thorndyke & Yekovich, 1980). Hierarchical organization occurs when schemas contain lower order structures embedded within higher order structures. The lower order structures serve as elements of the higher order structure (e.g., Thorndyke & Yekovich, 1980). This structure is sometimes referred to as a *goal–subgoal hierarchy* (Read, 1985; see Abbott, Black, & Smith, 1985; Bower, Black, & Turner, 1979). For example, an episode schema for a "birthday party" may have embedded within it another episode schema for "opening presents." Within these episode schemas and their constituent elements, there are also schemas for the story structure ("story schemata"; Thorndyke & Yekovich, 1980, p. 28) that provide rules and constraints for organizing the sequence of events within stories. For example, each rule will have a schema for the higher level element (e.g., an episode for achieving a goal) that directs which constituent elements are necessary and their order (e.g., subgoal + attempt + outcome; Thorndyke & Yekovich, 1980). Therefore, it appears that the inherent organizational structures found within a theory and story are useful for organizing the trial attorney's case.

Another benefit of schemas is that they will fill in missing information when gaps exist in one's knowledge. For example, because scripts are schemas that identify the typical sequence of actions to attain a particular goal, the script will provide relevant information about (a) goals, (b) actors and roles, (c) instruments and objects that are important for performing actions, (d) the location, and (e) the sequence of actions (Read, 1987). Exemplars (i.e., mental representations of a category that include its significant attributes) also help people fill in missing information (Sia, Lord, Blessum, Thomas, & Lepper, 1999). For example, even without information about a police officer's clothing, an exemplar of a "police officer" may supply that the officer is likely to be wearing a navy uniform, hat, and badge. Therefore, knowledge about schemas, alternative schemas, scripts, and exemplars can help attorneys identify facts that need further development. Scripts and the other knowledge structures will be discussed in more detail later in this chapter.

The story model is consistent with trial commentators' claims. The model proposes that the degree to which the certainty principles (discussed further below) are fulfilled will influence the jurors' perceptions of the story's acceptability. Pennington and Hastie's (1988, 1991) research on the story model also supports trial commentators' belief that jurors will rely on the accepted version of events to complete missing information and appear to favor the story that is easiest for them to construct Their study manipulated the order of evidence presented in a trial according to either a story order, which followed temporal and causal ordering between evidence, or a "witness by witness" order (Pennington & Hastie, 1991, p. 528). Participants' verdicts favored the evidence that was presented in story form. In addition, this study found that participants' perceptions of evidence strength and their confidence in the decision were influenced by the presentation order and the strength of alternative explanations (Pennington & Hastie, 1988).

Another reason lawyers believe theories are important is their usefulness in highlighting key points that should be presented at trial. As noted above, the hierarchical structure of schemas is useful for identifying key ideas and summarizing the information (Schank & Abelson, 1977; Thorndyke & Yekovich, 1980). Research supports the conclusion that the perceived importance of information increases with higher levels of the hierarchy. For example, Thorndyke and Yekovich (1980) found that higher order information was more likely to be recalled. Another study asked participants to write short summaries from memory about stories they read. The information in the abstracts was usually consistent with important, higher level information in the story (Thorndyke &Yekovich, 1980; see Rumelhart, 1975, 1977; Thorndyke, 1977). Thus, it appears that theories will assist attorneys in identifying key points.

Trial commentators also instruct lawyers to use the theory to develop their opening statements, closing arguments, and decisions about which witnesses will testify, but they do not specify how the theory should guide lawyers' organizational decisions. However, research suggests that the lawyers should not necessarily adhere too strictly to the theory's temporal framework at all of these trial phases. For example, Spiecker and Worthington (2003) investigated the influence of two organizational structures, a narrative (i.e., a story using temporal structuring to place significant events in chronological order) and a legal-expository format (i.e., "delineation of the judicial instructions and legal elements governing the dispute" that explains "why the evidence in the case either supports or refutes the applicable law;" p. 440), on structuring opening statements and closing arguments for both the plaintiff and the defendant). This study found that a mixed organizational strategy that used a narrative structure in the opening statement and legal-expository structure in the closing argument was more effective than a strict narrative strategy for the plaintiff. For the defense, a mixed organizational strategy or strictly legal-expository organizational strategy was more effective than a strict narrative strategy. Several limitations existed in this study, including but not limited to the following: It only investigated civil verdict and damage awards; the study used videotaped presentations instead of an actual trial or simulation; the effect of group dynamics was not assessed; and the subject population did not represent a typical jury. While more research is necessary to assess the impact of these limitations, it appears that trial attorneys should only consider using the theory as the framework for the opening statement. For the closing arguments, it appears that it is more critical that lawyers identify the relevant legal criteria and judicial instructions and explain how the evidence meets (for the plaintiff) or fails to meet (for the defense) these elements.

Benefits of Theory and Story to Jurors

Trial commentators believe that the theory and its story tap into jurors' learning mechanisms and connect actions and trial information together in a convincing manner. The legal literature asserts that jurors use stories to organize the information, provide a context for understanding the information, help them remember the information, and enhance the meaning of the information.

The research literature is consistent with trial commentators' beliefs about the value of a theory and its story in organizing information for jurors. "There is a large body of empirical literature supporting the superiority of the narrative structure in a variety of areas including comprehension and memory" (Spiecker & Worthington, 2003, p. 438; see Mandler, 1984). As noted above, scripts and other generalizations help people use their minds efficiently (Schank & Abelson, 1977). People not only prefer to recall information in a story form but also have great difficulty in recalling information in any other way (Mandler & DeForest, 1979). In addition, people hold expectations and make plans and predictions based on scripts (Schank & Berman, 2002; see Hammond, 1989; Schank & Abelson, 1977). People also rely on scripts to make judgments, understand new situations, and solve problems (Schank & Berman, 2002; see Gick & Holyoak, 1980; Lalljee, Lamb, & Abelson, 1992; B. Ross, 1987; L. Ross, 1977).

In addition, the benefits of the story form have been extended to theories on juror decision making. As explained by Bennett and Feldman (1981), who first pointed out that jurors use stories to synthesize evidence, jurors rely on stories for several reasons (Finkel, 1995). Stories enable jurors to break down large amounts of information to be more easily managed; serve as a framework for organizing, placing, and connecting evidence to understand it; provide a framework for lay citizens and trained legal professionals to communicate;

and provide a social context to give meaning to events that would otherwise be ambiguous if viewed in isolation (Finkel, 1995).

Although several models of jury decision making exist and other psychological theories have implications for jury decision making (e.g., dual process models discussed in Chapter 2, this volume), two models—the story model and commonsense justice—are especially relevant for understanding the potential benefits of stories to jurors. These models are discussed in more detail next, and when applicable, connections are drawn to address the points made in the trial commentary.

Story Model

Explanation-based decision making begins by reviewing relevant evidence to construct a causal model that contains key information and relationships (Pennington & Hastie, 1987). For example, a physician may construct a medical diagnosis of a patient's illness from his or her symptoms (Pennington & Hastie, 1988, 1992, 1993; see Pople, 1982). The story model of jury decision making is characteristic of explanation-based decision making because it constructs a causal explanation of evidence through the combination of information with real-world knowledge and expectations (Pennington & Hastie, 1986, 1988, 1992). In other words, the story model explains that jurors process and organize trial information into stories that follow preexisting knowledge and expectation structures. The constructed story is then used to reach a decision about the verdict (Groscup & Tallon, 2009).

The story model includes three processes: (a) story construction for evidence evaluation, (b) representation of the decision alternatives by learning the attributes and elements of the verdict categories, and (c) reaching an ultimate decision on the verdict by classifying the story into the category that fits best (Pennington & Hastie, 1986, 1991, 1992, 1993). The model's primary claim is that the story the juror constructs ultimately determines his or her decision. The model also contains certainty principles, which account for the extent to which the story will be accepted by jurors and the level of confidence that they have in their ultimate decision (Pennington & Hastie, 1991, 1992, 1993; see Groscup & Tallon, 2009).

Under the story model, jurors use a story form to actively organize, elaborate on, and interpret the evidence during the course of the trial (Pennington & Hastie, 1988, 1991, 1992, 1993). Constructing a story is believed to be critical in legal trials for several reasons. First, there is a large amount of evidence presented, usually over the course of several days (Pennington & Hastie, 1988, 1991, 1992, 1993). In addition, the evidence is often presented in a disconnected format. For example, (a) the information is obtained through a question-and-answer format, (b) different witnesses are usually necessary to present connected information, and (c) the information obtained from various witnesses is unlikely to follow a temporal or causal order. Last, the available evidence is likely to be incomplete because the information is based on reconstructed events and witnesses are usually not allowed to speculate on connecting events, motives, or emotional reactions (Pennington & Hastie, 1988, 1991, 1992, 1993).

Accordingly, jurors formulate a complete picture of the case by constructing stories from three types of knowledge: (a) case-specific trial information (e.g., witness testimony), (b) knowledge about events that are similar to those at issue in the trial (e.g., a similar crime in the community), and (c) generic expectations about what makes a complete story (e.g., knowledge that goals often motivate human actions) (Pennington & Hastie, 1988, 1991, 1992, 1993). This aspect of the story model conforms to trial commentators' concern that the evidence be combined to make a "convincing whole." The structure of stories plays an important role in the comprehension and decision making of the jurors (Pennington & Hastie, 1992, 1993). The organizational structure of the story assists jurors in deriving a subset of events and causal relationships from the evidence presented at trial, which they combine with additional events and causal relationships that they infer to fill in the story gaps (Pennington & Hastie, 1988, 1991, 1993). Although the attorney may suggest some of the inferences that jurors should draw, the juror may draw his or her own inferences (Pennington & Hastie, 1991, 1993).

According to the story model, the story structure has several advantages for jurors. The knowledge about story structures helps the juror make judgments about whether the evidence is complete. In addition, the story construction is consistent with how people understand human action, which allows jurors to compare the evidence with their prior knowledge. Furthermore, the story's hierarchical episodic and causal structure highlights its important pieces of evidence (Pennington & Hastie, 1986, 1988, 1991, 1992, 1993). Thus, the story model affirms trial commentators' belief that jurors use stories to organize, contextualize, remember, and enhance the meaning of trial information (Pennington & Hastie, 1988, 1991, 1993).

Trial commentators also believe that the story will have persuasive advantages. According to the story model, jurors may develop multiple stories to explain the evidence, but one of the stories is considered to be the best. The decision about what story is "best" is accounted for by the "certainty principles" (Pennington & Hastie, 1991, p. 527; 1993, p. 129). Three principles contribute to the acceptability of the story and the confidence placed in the story: coverage, coherence, and uniqueness.

A story's *coverage* concerns how well the story accounts for the trial evidence. For example, a story that leaves a lot of the evidence unaccounted for would have poor coverage, but a story that addresses most of the evidence will have good coverage (Pennington & Hastie, 1993). According to the story model, "the greater the coverage, the more acceptable the story [is] as an explanation of the evidence, and the more confidence the juror will have in the story as an acceptable explanation, if accepted" (Pennington & Hastie, 1992, p. 190; see Groscup & Tallon, 2009). The concept of coverage is consistent with trial commentators' view that the story must be comprehensive, which means that the lawyer should account for all of the evidence (Pennington & Hastie, 1991, 1992, 1993; see Finkel, 1995; Groscup & Tallon, 2009). Trial commentators also assert that a comprehensive version of events will account for the relevant law, an element that is not included under coverage but that is included in the story model in the verdict representation phase.

Coherence has three components according to the story model: consistency, plausibility, and completeness (Pennington & Hastie, 1991, 1993; see Graesser, Olde, & Klettke, 2002; Grosscup & Tallon, 2009). The degree of fulfillment of these three components determines the level of coherence of the story. The consistency component refers to the extent that the story lacks internal contradictions about the evidence presented as truthful or other parts of the explanation. Trial commentators also focus on avoiding contradictions and maintaining consistency as well as coherency, but they appear to frame this as a logic issue. Under the story model, the story is plausible when it is consistent with the juror's knowledge about typical occurrences in the real world (Pennington & Hastie, 1991, 1992; see Finkel, 1995). Plausibility is also addressed in the trial commentary. Trial commentators' use of external plausibility, which is explained as making sense given the jurors' knowledge about people's typical actions in a particular situation, is most consistent with the explanation provided by the story model. Completeness occurs when the story is considered to have the necessary parts of episodic structure (see the discussion above under Attorney's Case Theory in Relation to the Story). If the story structure is incomplete or lacks plausible inferences about any important components, then jurors' confidence in the explanation will be decreased (Pennington & Hastie, 1988, 1991). The story model's completeness component is similar to two concepts discussed in the legal literature. The first is internal plausibility, which trial commentators explain as the inclusion of the necessary story elements and the relationships between them. The second is the organizational mechanisms that are part of logic. Although trial attorneys do not specifically explain story structure in terms of episodes, their discussion is analogous to the story structure presented in the story model. For example, trial commentators assert that a good story should have a beginning, a middle, and an end; similarly, initiating events, the goal-motivated actions, and the resulting consequences make up an episodic structure. Likewise, both the story structure that trial commentators favor and the episodic structure of the story model focus on causal relationships that connect episodes.

Uniqueness of the story increases the juror's confidence in his or her decision (Pennington & Hastie, 1991, 1993). For example, if only one story is coherent, then the juror will not have difficulty accepting that story as the explanation of the case; on the other hand, if more than one story is coherent, then the juror may not have a strong belief in any of them (Pennington & Hastie, 1991, 1993). Note that an element corresponding to uniqueness is not found in the legal literature.

After the story construction phase, jurors begin the verdict representation phase, in which they must comprehend the decision alternatives. For example, in criminal trials, they are typically responsible for understanding the mental state (mens rea), the actions (actus reas), and the circumstances of the crime (Finkel, 1995). The judge provides the verdict definitions in the substantive instructions on the law. However, jurors may rely on prior knowledge of crime categories, which could interfere with jurors' ability to understand the verdict options as presented to them in the jury instructions (Pennington & Hastie, 1991, 1993; see Groscup & Tallon, 2009).

Once jurors understand the verdict options, they must make a decision about the verdict. During the third phase of the story model, jurors match the accepted story with each of the verdict options. Jurors apply a goodness-of-fit evaluation to determine which verdict category is selected and the level of confidence that they will place in their decision. A good fit between the story and the verdict will result in that verdict being selected. On the other hand, if the goodness of fit is insufficient, then jurors will not be confident in their decision and will vote for the other party's position (Pennington & Hastie, 1986, 1991, 1993).

There is support for the story model in the research literature. Early research on the story model, which asked jurors to describe their decision making, found that jurors' discussion and interpretations of the evidence followed the story structure. Jurors were less likely to discuss evidence that was not relevant to the stories or draw inferences to supplement any missing elements. In addition, differences in the story construction correlated with the verdicts (Pennington & Hastie, 1986; see Groscup & Tallon, 2009).

In a later study, participants completed a trial evidence recognition task after reading a mock trial summary and rendering a verdict (Pennington & Hastie, 1988). This task required participants to distinguish statements that had been presented as evidence from those that had not been included in the case but were plausible inferences. Participants were more likely to recognize sentences from the story that supported their verdict compared with sentences that were inconsistent with their story, regardless of whether these sentences were actually present in the case. In addition, they rated trial evidence items that were consistent with their story as being more important than facts that were inconsistent with their story (Pennington & Hastie, 1988; see Groscup & Tallon, 2009).

The next study on the story model expanded on prior research by manipulating the ease of story construction and the credibility of evidence (Pennington & Hastie, 1992). As in the previous research (Pennington & Hastie, 1988), which was discussed earlier, researchers manipulated the ease of story construction by varying the order in which the evidence was presented using either a story format that followed temporal sequencing or an issue-by-issue format. The credibility of one of the witnesses was also varied. Consistent with the previous study, participants more easily constructed stories when the evidence was presented in story order than when the evidence followed the alternative format. In addition, jurors' perceptions of credibility were influenced by the format used to present the information, with credibility having a greater effect on decision making when it could be easily integrated into a story (Pennington & Hastie, 1992; see Groscup & Tallon, 2009).

In the second experiment of this study, researchers wanted to explore how juror decision making would be affected by the point at which they were asked to make a decision about the evidence. Some participants read the case materials completely and then made a decision based on all of the evidence (i.e., global assessment), while others were asked to read the materials in sections and make cumulative evaluations of the evidence (i.e., item by item). The results indicated that participants' processing of the materials was consistent with the story model under the global assessment condition, but when evaluating evidence item by item, participants were more likely to use an anchoring and adjustment strategy in which they would change their beliefs as they received the new information. Changes in the evidence had increased effects on global judgments, which supports the proposition that the participants were constructing stories (Pennington & Hastie, 1992; see Groscup & Tallon, 2009).

Most of the studies on the story model have focused on scenarios involving criminal trials. When the story model has been explored in civil matters, researchers have found that mock jurors in civil cases also construct a narrative summary of the evidence that includes major events and causal linkages that are ordered temporally (Hastie, Schkade, & Payne, 1998).

In short, the story model supports trial commentators' claims that jurors use stories to understand the information presented at trial and accounts for many of the qualities trial commentators' believe are important for stories to possess. The story model needs further research development on the certainty principles and the internal processes of constructing stories and comparing them with verdict categories (Groscup & Tallon, 2009). Although this model suggests that attorneys who present information using a story format, including temporal organization and emphasis on causal connections, may enjoy a significant advantage (Pennington & Hastie, 1992), more research is necessary to connect aspects of the story model to lawyers' actual trial presentations and the approaches recommended by trial commentators.

Commonsense Justice

Trial commentators advise lawyers to consider jurors' common sense when devising their theory. In fact, one theory of jury decision making centers around jurors' common sense. *Commonsense justice* is "the ordinary citizen's notions of what is fair and just, and what is culpable and what is not" (Finkel & Groscup, 1997, p. 211). Commonsense justice is premised on the conceptualization that lay citizens may have a different understanding of the law than what is intended. In the context of jury decision making, the theory accounts for situations when jurors' notions of the fairness diverge from "black letter law" (i.e., the written law). According to experimental research, when discrepancies between the law and jurors' common sense occur, jurors may diverge from the black letter law, reconstrue the law and legal instructions, or possibly nullify the law (i.e., jury nullification; Finkel, 1996).

According to commonsense justice, the ingredients of the jurors' story are evidence, extralegal factors (i.e., legally irrelevant information), and prejudicial statements and legally inadmissible material, which may still affect jurors' decision making even if the judge instructs jurors to ignore that information. The final ingredient is jurors' prior knowledge. Prior knowledge consists of many types of cognitions that jurors hold (Finkel, 1995).

One type of prior knowledge is stereotypes or prototypes of "typical" crimes, criminals, and resulting harms. Although the mass media is likely to provide much of the information and crime-related images that jurors use to form their stereotypes and prototypes, the media portrayals are likely to be more extreme and violent than most of the crimes, criminals, and resulting harms (Finkel, 1995; see Hans, 1990). In addition to stereotypes and prototypes, the availability heuristic, a mental shortcut in which the most recently stored information in the memory is the most easily accessible, is likely to bias jury decision making (Finkel, 1995; see Tversky & Kahneman, 1974). Jurors more readily recall the recent, specific criminal cases from the media using the availability heuristic, but the most recent information is not necessarily representative of the typical case. Pretrial publicity is another way that the mass media may bias jurors' judgments (Finkel, 1995; see Kramer, Kerr, & Carroll, 1990). Finally, less sensational information that is typically more representative of actual crime scenarios is likely to come from jurors' interpersonal and personal experiences (Finkel, 1995; see Stalans, 1993).

Commonsense justice may be relevant to story construction in several ways. It may be present in terms of the information that jurors bring with them about (a) similar events and (b) expectations about whether the story is complete (Finkel, 1995). Case-specific information acquired during the trial is considered to be objective information that is also integrated with the subjective elements as part of story construction. Another way that commonsense justice may come into play is when jurors are determining which story is more acceptable. Finkel (1995) posited that coverage, consistency, completeness, and possibly uniqueness contribute to jurors' subjective evaluations because they address whether the story is a "good" one (p. 76). On the other hand, plausibility is considered the objective measure of the information because it serves as a reality check on the story (Finkel, 1995). Finally, commonsense justice may be key in determining the causal inferences and intentionality involved in the story, which may play a role in jurors' judgments of culpability or blameworthiness. For example, what happened and the mental state and motivation of the actor may influence the degree to which jurors will hold him or her responsible (Finkel, 1995).

In addition to the story construction phase, commonsense justice may also apply to the verdict possibility phase. Jurors may rely on information other than what is provided in the judge's substantive instructions. Smith (1991) asked subjects to write down all the attributes they associated with the crimes of assault, burglary, kidnapping, murder, and robbery. The features of the crimes that participants listed were significantly different from the legally correct features. For example, robbery involves using force to take property, but it does not require that the property be valuable. The researcher also asked participants to indicate the guilt of the defendant who was charged with either a typical or an atypical scenario for assault, burglary, kidnapping, murder, and robbery. Participants were more likely to assign guilt to the defendant in typical scenarios rather than atypical ones in cases involving assault, burglary, and kidnapping (Finkel, 1995).

One limitation of this research is that the prototypes held by jurors may not be as simple as the ones in this study. Follow-up research found that when participants wrote different crimes and verdicts into stories, they incorporated prototypical content. The motive and type of crime influence the prototypes that emerged in the stories, and each type of crime included multiple prototypes (Finkel & Groscup, 1997). All together, research on prototypes suggests that prototypes can be complex and may influence jurors' understanding of the verdict possibilities and, ultimately, their verdict decision (Finkel & Groscup, 1997).

Moreover, the commonsense justice approach may be informative for understanding jurors' inferences in the process of constructing stories (e.g., Huntley & Costanzo, 2003). In addition, this perspective may offer insight into improving the accuracy of jurors' understanding of crime categories and the way they reach decisions about criminal behavior and its punishment (e.g., Darley & Pittman, 2003; Gromet & Darley, 2009). For example, although it appears that the commonsense justice approach may be useful for understanding many elements of the story model, how the two models may be integrated needs further research.

Attorney Construction of the Theory and Story

Although the story model is an explanation-based model for jury decision making, which indicates that jurors infer events that are not represented in the testimony or evidence from frames of knowledge about the world (Pennington & Hastie, 1986), research has not developed or investigated an explanation-based model for attorney decision making. An attorney may rely on different sets of causal rules and structures to devise a case theory or select legal strategies based on the available testimony and evidence. If so, schemas are also likely to serve as the basis for the lawyer's theory because they afford reasoning from incomplete information (e.g., Thorndyke & Yekovich, 1980). For example, if one were told about a birthday party, he or she may infer that there were presents, even though that information was not explicitly stated. Accordingly, the attorney would probably follow a similar process to devise a case theory. In other words, he or she would use default information supplied by the applicable schema to fill in the missing pieces that were not explicitly supplied by available evidence and testimony. Researchers interested in studying attorney decision making will likely benefit from developing and investigating an explanation-based model for lawyers.

Until attorney decision making and construction of case theories and stories are studied empirically, research on the elements of stories and the construction of causal scenarios is informative for understanding how attorneys may develop their case theory and story. Trial commentators advise lawyers to include several elements in their story: circumstances of the time and place, the protagonists, the problem, and the solutions. Scholars studying narratives and stories appear to typically include similar components in their assessments of a well-formed story, yet a clear consensus in the literature is lacking. Consider two examples. Rumelhart (1975) explained story structure simply as including the setting and episode. According to this story structure, an episode would contain an event, which is further explained in terms of an event and resulting change of state, and a reaction, which is further explained in terms of the internal response and overt response. Hastie (2008; see also Pennington & Hastie, 1991, 1993), on the other hand, explained that the story should begin with a setting, which includes the protagonist, other actors, and their mental states; physical conditions; and the event that initiated the problem. Next, the story should explain the protagonist's reaction to the event, which should include his or her emotional states, intentions, and goals, before discussing his or her plans to achieve the goals. The story must then describe the actions taken to execute the plans, the consequences of the actions, and finally, a reaction to the consequences. In short, it appears that different researchers diverge in how they structure the story elements (Read, 1987; Thorndyke & Yekovich, 1980), although many of the elements proposed by the trial commentary are included in these accounts (e.g., setting, protagonists, the problem, and the responses). Therefore, a primary difference between the social science scholars and trial commentators is the emphasis that is placed on mental states.

In addition to information about story elements, the scenario construction in the research literature is useful for understanding how attorneys are likely to construct their theories and stories. Attorneys construct a story with information gathered from the client about what happened and why it happened, among other things. Read's (1987) causal reasoning model integrates knowledge structures into the comprehension of behavior sequences. There are four types of knowledge structures that are relevant for constructing scenarios in this model: scripts, plans, goals, and themes.

Scripts are a typical sequence of actions performed for the purposes of achieving a goal. The characteristics of scripts were explained earlier in this chapter, so we will not include a detailed description here. Script knowledge may explain the performance of the whole or part of the script in one of the following ways: (a) subsequent action it enables, (b) subgoal that it is part of, or (c) overall goal of the script (Read, 1987). The goal–subgoal hierarchy is instructive for this purpose. Higher level actions are usually explained in terms of the goal of the script, while explanations of lower level actions are likely to be more variable because there are a greater number of actions between the action and the goal (Read, 1987; see Galambos & Black, 1985; Graessser & Murachver, 1985).

In developing the lawyer's theory of the case, trial commentators recommend using theory-driven questions to help test the viability of possible narratives. Research appears to support the potential usefulness of this strategy. People may arrive at explanations by coming up with plausible hypotheses and then testing them, using the scientific definition of theory by analogy (Read, 1987; see e.g., Einhorn & Hogarth, 1978b; Hastie, 1983; Lalljee, 1981). For example, people may rely on their knowledge of the script to generate hypotheses, which can then be tested as explanations for the behavior (Read, 1987). Information about scripts may be particularly useful for explaining why behavior diverges from what is expected (Lalljee & Abelson, 1983).

When people encounter situations for which they lack an appropriate script, they rely on their knowledge of general types of actions that can be used to attain different goals, known as plans, to help them understand other people's actions or to plan their own future actions. For example, in a new situation, a person may rely on an *ask plan,* which would require approaching someone else and asking for help. Explanations may be developed through knowledge of plans, but to do so one must understand how an action fits in with other actions that form a plan to attain a desired goal. For example, approaching someone with the goal to talk to him or her is a precondition of the ask plan and explains that behavior. The goal–subgoal hierarchy in scripts also underlies the mental representation in plans by directing which actions are likely necessary to achieve subsequent actions (Read, 1987).

Goals are another kind of knowledge structure. Five kinds of goals have been proposed: (a) satisfaction goals to achieve biological needs such as hunger, (b) achievement goals to attain success, (c) enjoyment goals for relaxing or having fun, (d) preservation, and (e) crisis goals to maintain previously obtained goals (Read, 1987; see Schank & Abelson, 1977). Goals provide information that is useful for explanation. For example, knowledge of goals can help one to draw assumptions about typical plans, infer goals on the basis of behavior, and help one to infer the kinds of events that are likely to initiate that goal (Read, 1987).

Goals can also be related to other goals in some way, which may explain behavior. When people try to achieve a state that will facilitate recurring goals or achieving multiple goals, a goal subsumption relation occurs. For example, marriage is likely to subsume the goals of companionship, love, and sex (Read, 1987). Goals may also conflict. For example, resources may be limited. In these situations, a person may have to pick one goal over another (Read, 1987). Competing goals may arise between individuals in circumstances where achieving one person's goal will interfere with the fulfillment of another's goal. For example, limited resources may lead to conflicts between individuals. Finally, goal concordance occurs when people share the same goals and cooperate to attain them.

According to this perspective, themes are a grouping of related goals (see below for additional discussion of themes). Three types of themes may come into play. *Role* themes provide "information about expected characteristics of people in particular roles" (Read, 1987, p. 292; see also role schema; Fiske & Taylor, 1984). For example, a nurse should desire to help care for sick people. Another kind of theme is *interpersonal* themes, which refer to interpersonal relationships between people (Read, 1987). For example, friendship or marriage are types of interpersonal themes. *Life* themes, or a desirable objective for life, is the last type of theme (Read, 1987; Schank & Abelson, 1977). "Get rich" may be a life theme for some. All themes can provide information about typical goals, the instigation of these goals, typical plans used to attain the goals, and information about the typical behaviors of people in those roles (Read, 1987).

Causal syntax is also critical for constructing scenarios that connect the knowledge structures. Six rules of causal syntax are proposed: (a) actions and events can result in state changes (e.g., throwing a rock through a window will change the window); (b) states can enable actions and events (e.g., a broken window allows a criminal to unlock the door); (c) states can disable actions (e.g., the state of a sounding alarm prevents the criminal from breaking into the home); (d) states can initiate mental states (e.g., the homeowner was angered by the broken window); (e) acts can initiate mental states (e.g., the criminal's wife was saddened by his life of crime); (f) mental states can be reasons for actions (e.g., the homeowner decided to move to avoid to feel safer). Sometimes the intervening mental and physical states are implied (Read, 1987; see Schank & Abelson, 1977). For example, someone may explain that the parents punished the child because she did not do her homework; the parents' mental state is inferred.

Drawing on earlier research, Read's (1987) model explains "how these knowledge structures are integrated in the comprehension of sequences of behavior" (p. 293). The model is premised on a spreading activation process, which means that observations of interactions trigger relevant knowledge structures. Related structures will also be activated, and structures that are most closely associated with the input will receive the highest activation. Highly activated structures are more likely to be used in subsequent interpretations of information and will receive additional activation, while less useful structures will deteriorate (Read, 1987).

According to Read's (1987) model, constructing a scenario involves the following steps. First, people are sorted into basic categories according to race, gender, role, or other classification, and the situation is observed. Additional knowledge structures are activated by the new input. Second, subsequent actions are connected to the current scenario. Active knowledge structures and newly activated knowledge structures are used. Interpretations of previous actions shed light on understanding new actions. Third, new actions are examined to determine whether they could be part of a plan under the constructed scenario, and if so, then the connection is made. If the connection is not made, then the action is examined in light of general world knowledge to see if it could fit into another plan. If another plan exists, then a determination must be made as to whether the new plan can be connected to the existing scenario. Fourth, after the plan is identified, an effort is made to identify the goal of the plan. Fifth, a determination must be made as to whether the goal is sufficient or is part of a larger plan. Finally, the source for that goal must be identified, which is usually the theme or the event that instigates the goal.

This process is proposed for explaining why something went as expected (i.e., constructive explanation), but sometimes situations do not go as expected. In these situations, people will rely on a different process for explaining the discrepancy (i.e., contrastive explanation; Lalljee & Abelson, 1983; Read, 1987). First, people will figure out what the expected actions were. They will then use constructive explanation to insert these actions into a typical plan or script sequence that would culminate in the action. After this step, they will attempt to identify the most likely reason that the typical scenario failed. The goal relations discussed above offer categorizations of the possible failures. For example, goal conflict may explain why someone chooses not to lock the door to his or her house when running late for an important appointment (Lalljee & Abelson, 1983; Read, 1987).

The process described in Read's (1987) model is similar to the intuitive process described by trial commentators for constructing a story. As in the model, lawyers are supposed to develop from client information the situation and the people involved, their actions and goals, and the causal connections. Also incorporated in the third step of the model is how new scenarios can be developed if there are inconsistencies between the action and the scenario, which also corresponds to trial commentator's recommendation to test stories on others. The model's inclusion of a theme also is consistent with trial commentators' claim that the story should have moral or political appeal. Based on this model, trial commentators' beliefs about how to create a viable story for trial appear on target. However, research is necessary to better determine whether the model can help lawyers more effectively develop their case.

Trial commentators recommend asking *what?* and *why?* questions during the theory/story development phase. It appears that these types of questions may be useful in investigating causal scenarios. For example, some researchers asked subjects to read a story and then answer how and why questions about each story event (Read, 1987; see Graesser, 1981; Graesser & Clark, 1985; Graesser & Murachver, 1985). Participants' responses to why questions addressed their inferences about causes, goals, and initiating conditions. The answers and story information can be categorized into areas such as goals, events, and states and developed into a network representation that contains these categories along with the goal and causal relations connecting them. Predictions about answers to questions and recall and summarization of passages can be made by using these representations (Read, 1987; see Graesser & Clark, 1985; Graesser & Murachever, 1985).

In his discussion of constructing causal scenarios, Read (1987) presented summaries of five principles of story comprehension (Wilensky, 1983), which are believed to constrain how scenarios are constructed. The principle of *coherence* states that people should incorporate all necessary knowledge for producing a coherent interpretation. Next, the principle of *concretion* states that people will interpret the information using the most concrete knowledge available. In other words, more concrete structures will be favored over abstract ones. Another principle is that of *least commitment*, which "suggests that people make no more than the minimum assumptions necessary to produce a coherent interpretation" (Read, 1987, p. 294). The fourth principle, that of *exhaustion*, posits that people should try to account for the most data possible in their interpretations. Finally, the principle of *parsimony* says that people try to maximize the connections among data when interpreting information. Individual differences, short-term memory, and conflicts among these principles limit the degree to which they will be implemented (Read, 1987).

These principles, the trial commentary, and the story model's certainty principles overlap. For example, the principle of coherence appears to be analogous to the story model's coherence principle and its subparts and the related trial commentary (discussed under Story Model). The principle of least commitment also reflects the trial commentators' concern that the story be simple. In addition, the principle of exhaustion is similar to the story model's coverage principle and the related trial commentary (also discussed under the Story Model). However, Read addresses how these principles will constrain one's construction of a scenario, while the story model addresses how the constraints will influence the acceptability of the story for the receivers (i.e., the jury). Despite the apparent consensus for many of the constraints imposed on stories, more research is key for understanding the effect of these constraints in the context of legal advocacy. For example, research currently has not investigated whether attorneys consider the principles Read (1987) summarized in his model to construct their stories.

According to trial commentators, a timeline is a useful tool for attorneys in constructing the case theory and story. The linear development of action simplifies the organization of information and aids the identification of a central action and critical junctures in its development (Schank, 1975, pp. 241–254). In addition, as noted in the discussion of the story model research, jurors appear to favor information presented temporally instead of witness by witness. Also, plots in which the main causal chains develop chronologically are remembered longer than details (Graesser et al., 2002; see Graesser & Clark, 1985; Kintsch, 1998; Trabasso & van den Broek, 1985). These facts suggest that a timeline may be useful for trial attorneys in the process of developing their story in a manner that will appeal to jurors.

Trial commentators favor a collaborative approach to checking the acceptability of their theory. "Although the group brainstorming technique has been found to facilitate idea generation . . . , evidence has consistently illustrated that sets of individuals working in isolation . . . outperform interactive groups in both laboratory and organizational settings" (Dugosh, Paulus, Roland, & Yang, 2000, p. 722; see Parnes & Meadow, 1959; Taylor, Berry, & Block, 1958). More recently, three factors have been identified that influence productivity during brainstorming: enhancing attention to others' ideas, increasing one's exposure to ideas, and increasing discussion about relevant ideas (Dugosh et al., 2000). Although brainstorming with colleagues may generate some theories that the attorney thinks will be successful, it still may not actually result in a theory that the jurors accept.

While testing the theory on other lawyers may not be as helpful as trial commentators appear to indicate, testing the theory on mock jurors may be more useful. Hastie (2008) suggested that attorneys use mock jurors composed of citizens who are likely to serve on an actual jury to test their first-developed presentation of the case, including arguments relating to the trial information and conclusions. Three methodologies were recommended. First, the attorney should ask mock jurors to "think aloud as they heard the evidence" (p. 30). Mock jurors should next provide "global ratings for the legal elements" and summarize their reasons for their rating (p. 30). Finally, if no clear story or stories have emerged after the first tasks, then attorneys should ask mock jurors to recall and summarize the evidence. After gathering this information, the attorney should attempt to construct the most prevalent stories. In addition, attorneys are advised to ensure that the components of a well-formed narrative are included: setting, problem event, reaction, plans to achieve goals, actions to achieve plans, consequences, and reaction to the consequences. The defense attorney's task is potentially more challenging because he or she may need to offer multiple stories to the jury. For example, they have to not only account for the defendant's activities but also explain the events that led to the lawsuit.

Although this advice is geared toward lawyers in civil trials, it may have implications for criminal cases. This approach may be beneficial for discovering stories that were not anticipated. In addition, this method may allow attorneys to identify the weaknesses in the opposing party's stories. Identifying the weak points in the opposing arguments creates an opportunity for the lawyer to highlight the other side's unproven story elements in the closing argument (Hastie, 2008). Despite the apparent advantages of this strategy for developing the case story, it must be subject to empirical tests before its efficacy can be verified.

Theme

According to trial commentators, a theme is the gist of the case. Similarly, in the research on story construction, a theme refer to the "moral, adage, or main message that emerges from the plot configuration" (Graesser et al., 2002, p. 235). Themes are also considered to be mental organizing structures of an event that imply "fundamental elements of a story" and "the overall lesson to be learned" (Schank & Berman, 2002, p. 301; Schank, 1990).

Trial commentators believe that themes are useful for focusing jurors on elements of the story or arguments that the lawyers wish to emphasize. Researchers also posit that lawyers may facilitate jurors' information processing by introducing themes in the opening statement (Linz & Penrod, 1984). If jurors attempt to give context to the events they hear about a trial (Finkel, 1995, 1997), they likely seek out frameworks to provide context for behaviors and actions (Finkel, 1997). Case themes may act as a framework that helps jurors remember the facts (Tversky & Kahneman, 1974; see Chapter 6, this volume, for additional discussion of frames).

Thematic frameworks refer to "any subset of existing knowledge, based on prior experience and relevant to a limited domain, which people use as a framework to guide their observation, organization, and retrieval from memory of perceived events" (Lingle & Ostrom, 1981, p. 401; Pyszczynski & Wrightsman, 1981). According to this perspective, themes are labels attached to informational arrays. The arrays could trigger schemas that could assist the jurors with processing the large amount of disjointed testimony and evidence that is presented throughout the trial and may color how jurors interpret this information (Pyszczynski & Wrightsman, 1981; see also Lieberman & Sales, 2007).

Only one study attempted to account for the influence of themes on jury decision making. In this study, mock jurors read a transcript recreating an actual criminal trial that contained opening statements, direct and cross examinations, judicial instructions, and closing arguments. The opening statements were manipulated to be either a brief preview introducing the attorney and clients or an extensive preview that fully summarized the expected evidence and inferences. After reading the transcript, mock jurors gave their verdict and level of certainty in their decision. Results indicated that the effect of the amount of information presented in either side's opening statement depended on the amount of information presented by the other side. In other words, it appeared that "jurors were heavily influenced by the first strong presentation they read" (Pyszczynski & Wrightsman, 1981, p. 309). The researchers speculated that the first strong persuasive communication created a thematic framework that jurors used to interpret trial information and reach their final verdict. However, other possible explanations (e.g., a primacy effect) and limitations with the study (e.g., generalizability to actual courtrooms) require further research to understand whether the results could be accounted for by the use of themes (Pyszczynski & Wrightsman, 1981).

Other studies lend support to the proposition that the use of themes will influence the way that information is constructed and interpreted by jurors. For example, themes do appear to "have a major influence on the comprehension and memory of story events" when one is identified (Graesser et al., 2002, p. 236; Narvaez, 1998; Williams, 1993). This research suggests that trial commentators are correct that jurors need the theme to be highlighted. In addition, placing a thematic title before sentences and prose was found to improve recall (Bransford & Johnson, 1972; Dooling & Mullet, 1973; Pyszczynski & Wrightsman, 1981). Similarly, another study showed that people were more likely to remember information consistent with the schema or theme they were given as a frame of reference before watching an event. This research found that observers recalled more intention-relevant than intention-irrelevant information when they received prior information about the actors' intentions. Prior to being shown a videotape of two people interacting in an apartment, participants were told that the people were waiting for a friend, planning to rob the apartment, or were expecting a drug bust. Depending on what information they received in advance, they remembered different aspects of the scene (Zadny & Gerard, 1974; see Pyszczynski & Wrightsman, 1981).

Although trial commentators believe that it is important to emphasize the theme as part of effective storytelling, listeners are capable of judging whether a theme is appropriate for a story. However, generating a theme during and after comprehension presents difficulties for many adults and children (Graesser et al., 2002; see Goldman, 1985; Williams, 1993).

Trial commentators recommend using repetition for emphasizing the theme to jurors. Advertising researchers found a *truth effect* (i.e., "repeated statements are believed more than new statements"), and increased exposure to the statements increases the person's perceptions of their truthfulness (Roggeveen & Johar, 2002, p. 72; Cacioppo & Petty, 1989). According to the persuasion literature, three repetitions of a message impacted attitude change more than stating the message only once, but many repetitions of the message decreased attitude change (Cacioppo & Petty, 1979). The literature on persuasion indicates that repeating the same argument three times resulted in more attitude change than did a single presentation. However, five repetitions resulted in decreased attitude change (Cacioppo & Petty, 1979). Researchers hypothesized that some repetition allows the listener time to think about the information. Boredom is likely to have a negative impact on the audience's agreement after the message has been repeated four or five times (Cacioppo & Petty, 1979). Research in advertising confirms that persuasive messages should be presented no more than four times. For example, likability for a television commercial increases over the first four exposures but tends to fall back and flatten out after additional exposures (Joyce, 1991). In addition, attorneys may be more successful at emphasizing the theme if they connect it to various episodes in the story, rather than simply repeating the same theme multiple times (Chang, 2009). Repetition is likely to be most effective for strong arguments because repeating weak ones will only serve to highlight any issues (Cacioppo & Petty, 1979). In sum, research supports that at least some repetitions will help the juror accept and understand the intended theme, but more research is necessary to understand the extent to which this conclusion translates to trial advocacy.

Another recommendation by trial commentators is that lawyers draw on many sources, such as biblical phrases, slogans, proverbs, and parables, for selecting their theme. Researchers appear to support their conclusion: Themes concern "general life topics" (Schank, 1990, p. 86), integrate important components of the story, and convey the point of the message (Graesser et al., 2002). Proverbs or fables are noted as containing culturally common themes (Schank & Berman, 2002). However, empirical studies are still lacking about whether these sources for themes will appeal in trial situations.

Whichever topic is chosen for the theme, trial commentators also emphasize that the theme should contain an affective component. If an affective theme were achieved, it could theoretically affect jurors' decision making through four processes. First, emotions may act as heuristics (see Cacioppo & Petty, 1989; Chaiken, 1980, 1987; Petty, Cacioppo, & Kasmer, 1988; Petty, Cacioppo, Sedikides, & Strathman, 1988; Petty, Gleicher, & Baker, 1991). Positive or extremely arousing emotions appear most likely to promote heuristic decision making (Nabi, 2002). Second, emotions may stimulate careful information processing. Under the dual process models (the elaboration likelihood model and the heuristic-systematic model), first discussed in Chapter 2 of this volume, people process information carefully and systematically when they are motivated and have the time and ability to do so (Chaiken, 1980). Emotion may influence the direction or depth of information processing in situations where the person is moderately to highly motivated (see Cacioppo & Petty, 1989; Petty, Cacioppo, & Kasmer, 1988; Petty, Cacioppo, Sedikides, & Stranthman, 1988; Petty et al., 1991). Next, emotions may invite selective information processing. In other words, emotions may serve as frames that highlight selective pieces of information (Nabi, 1999; 2002). Last, the transportation-imagery model (discussed in more depth below) proposes that, along with mental imagery and attention, emotions may help promote transportation (or immersion) into stories, which may induce narrative-based belief change (Green & Brock, 2000). Themes that have emotional appeal may influence jury decision making through one of these processes. However, it is necessary to investigate the influence of emotion on decision making in trials, and whether emotional themes will encourage decision making through one of these processes in trials.

Trial commentators recommend appealing to jurors' sense of morality or justice, among other things, to achieve an emotionally appealing theme. Although this type of theme appears to be common (see the discussion above), issues surrounding the emotional appeals still emerge in the persuasion literature. For example, it is unclear whether emotional appeals work because of message characteristics or the receiver's responses to the message. Ideally, the message characteristics will achieve the desired emotional response, but research has yet to explore which message characteristics for various topics will promote particular emotional reactions from specific receivers (Nabi, 2002). Therefore, before one can trust trial commentators' recommendations about which themes are emotionally charged, more research is needed on theme development, emotional responses to themes, and the influence of individual receiver's characteristics.

Finally, trial commentators dispute whether it is valuable to use one or more themes. In addressing this dispute, the story structure is instructive. As previously discussed, the hierarchical structure of a story is organized so that the lower level concepts are more specific and the higher level concepts are more abstract and thematic. Themes are high coverage if a high proportion of the explicit episodes in the text is covered by the theme's subordinate structures (Graesser et al., 2002; see Lehnert, 1981; Schank, 1982), with good thematic points being able to cover a large proportion of the episodes (Graesser et al., 2002; see Graesser & Clark, 1985; Lehnert, 1981). For example, adults are easily able to classify short stories (approximately 80 words) according to similar themes, and the stories are grouped on the basis of shared abstract structures (e.g. goals), rather than surface features (Seifert, McKoon, Abelson, & Ratcliff, 1986; see Graesser et al., 2002). This research suggests that one overarching theme may be better than many. However, researchers raise the point that because listeners bring to the story their unique backgrounds, each listener may come to his or her own conclusion about the theme, even when it was not intended by the storyteller (Schank & Berman, 2002). This factor invites the question of whether several themes may be useful to tap into the story banks of different jurors or explicitly stating the desired theme facilitates jurors' adoption of that theme for their stories. Last, trial commentators' debate about one versus multiple themes appears to stem from whether trial commentators use the term "theme" to also include labels for different components of the case. Research discussed in Chapter 6 indicates that labels are likely to help attorneys establish frameworks for jurors to understand the information. For example, an attorney representing a wife charged with murdering her husband, who had Alzheimer's disease, may choose to label the killing a "mercy killing" or an "act of kindness" in an effort to encourage jurors to see the defendant in a positive light.

Additional Strategies

Trial commentators recommend several additional strategies that they believe are a part of effective storytelling, which center around strategies to develop an emotional, interesting, and vivid story. The transportation-imagery model is relevant for merging trial commentators' strategies in this section.

Transportation-Imagery Model

The transportation-imagery model posits that people exposed to narrative stories will experience a state of transportation (Green & Brock, 2002). *Transportation* means that while reading, watching, or listening to a narrative, receivers focus mental systems and capacities on the narrative events (Appel & Richter, 2010; Green & Brock, 2000). In simpler terms, transportation means that receivers become immersed in the story. This attention to the story may facilitate narrative-based belief change. Transportation effects appear to be a combination of three main components: emotional reactions, mental imagery, and a loss of access to real-world information (Green & Brock, 2000).

The transportation-imagery model contrasts with the dual processing models (e.g., elaboration likelihood model [Petty & Cacioppo, 1986] and heuristic-systematic model [Chaiken, 1987]) discussed in Chapter 2. The dual processing models propose that message recipients will rely on careful and systematic processing when they are motivated and are not constrained by time and ability; they will rely on simple decision rules if they are unmotivated or lack time or ability to process the information. Although the mechanisms for persuasion described in dual process models will apply to narratives as well, they may not fully explain narrative persuasion because of differences between narratives and argumentative texts. *Narratives* consist of "a story that raises unanswered questions, presents unresolved conflicts, or depicts not yet completed activity; characters may encounter and then resolve a crisis or crises. A story line, with a beginning, middle, and end, is identifiable" (Green & Brock, 2000, p. 701). On the other hand, *argument texts* are advocacy messages consisting of nonnarrative or nonfiction accounts of beliefs (Appel & Richter, 2010). Instead of achieving attitude change through careful consideration of arguments, researchers hypothesize that transportation relies on different mechanisms for achieving persuasion (Appel & Richter, 2010). Specifically, transportation is hypothesized to reduce negative cognitive responding (e.g., disbelief, counterarguments) and elaboration (e.g., careful attention to major argument points) that contribute to resistance to persuasion and invite less counterarguments. It is also believed that transportation can achieve a realistic experience for forming attitudes and create strong feelings toward story characters that can influence receivers' beliefs (Green, 2004). Last, unlike high-elaboration situations that may establish connections to previously held schemas and experiences, high transportation may encourage receivers to distance themselves from those schemas and experiences (Green & Brock, 2000).

Researchers investigating the transportation-imagery model presented participants with a story called "Murder at the Mall," which provided a graphic account of a college student, Joan, whose little sister, Katie, was stabbed to death by a psychiatric patient while they were at the mall. Participants read this story and then answered questions to address dependent measures. The initial research lends support to the transportation-imagery model. Participants who were more highly transported into the story showed greater belief change and more positive evaluations of sympathetic major characters. For example, transported readers were more likely to indicate that malls were dangerous places and that the world was unjust than were less transported readers. In addition, transportation appears to affect the willingness of the reader to accept the authenticity of the story (Green et al., 2008). Acceptance of the story was tested using a measure researchers called *Pinocchio circling* (Green & Brock, 2000, p. 708). After reading the story and completing dependent measures, researchers asked receivers to go back over the story and circle any parts of the story that did not appear to be true to them. Results indicated that highly transported individuals were less likely to find falsehoods in the story. These findings were replicated with both measured and manipulated differences in transportation (Green & Brock, 2000).

This model parallels trial commentators' belief that a good story, composed of attention-grabbing devices, vivid imagery, and emotional elements, will have persuasive benefits. Research on the transportation-imagery model has explored the effectiveness of different story factors for engaging receivers in the transportation process. Using a similar methodology to the one listed above, participants received instructions about how to approach the reading task and then read a story about a homosexual man who returned to his college fraternity reunion, where none of his former friends were aware that he is gay (Green, 2004).

Following the story presentation, participants answered questions. This study revealed no difference between groups of participants who were given no instructions, instructions encouraging participants toward transportation, or instructions encouraging participants toward careful consideration (Green, 2004). This finding suggests that asking jurors to think carefully about the information may not limit the effects of transportation. The study also found that prior information or personal experience with the topic was associated with transportation. Individuals who knew someone who was homosexual or were familiar with fraternity life were more transported into the story. Based on this finding, lawyers may increase transportation into their story if they devise a story with elements that many jurors are familiar with, perhaps through the selection of themes. In addition, some types of prior knowledge or familiarity will be more effective for achieving transportation. For example, manipulating the gender of the main character to be the same as the participant did not influence transportation (Green, Butler, & Britt, 2003). The perceived realism of the story also influences how easily individuals were transported, but the finding was based on measured transportation, so the direction of causality was not determined. In addition, the relationship between realism and transportation is unclear. A regression analysis did not find that realism mediated the effects of transportation on beliefs. Thus, it appears that transportation and realism are related, but the effect of transportation on beliefs is more complex than making the events, settings, and characters in the story more realistic.

According to trial commentators, exhibits may help lawyers capture the interest of the jurors, and research appears to support this recommendation. Researchers investigated the effect on transportation of repeat exposure to print and film stories. In the first session, participants were randomly assigned to read or watch an excerpt of a story. In the second session, they were randomly assigned to read or watch the same story again. Participants who watched the movie after reading the book were more transported into the movie version. Perhaps this effect emerges because readers must produce their own mental imagery, which is not true for film. This finding suggests that lawyers may increase jurors' transportation into their story if they first develop the story verbally and then follow up the story with visual aids. However, the study used print and film, so the results may not extend to a trial presentation, which presents the story verbally; further study is required. These findings also suggest that lawyers may want to explore computer-generated reenactments of their story as a strategy for increasing transportation. Again, more research is needed to understand how advances in technology may influence transportation for trial lawyers' stories.

In addition, this study found that repeated exposures do not necessarily diminish transportation. At first glance, this information appears to conflict with previous research indicating that excessive repetition may decrease persuasion. Increased repetitions in advertising appear to bore or irritate message receivers, which curbs the advantages of repeating information. It is possible that the same result may occur with repeated exposure to stories, especially if the person has no control over the repeated exposure (Green et al., 2008), but research has yet to explore this question. In sum, trial commentators should probably avoid belaboring the information, even if presenting it with different media.

The research on the transportation-imagery model suggests that using a story may effectively merge cognitive and affective processes for persuasive purposes (Green & Brock, 2000). The transportation-imagery model indicates that trial commentators correctly identify the importance of emotion, imagery, and cognitive involvement for positively influencing jurors toward their case. However, future research should explore the transportation in the disconnected story format of trials, more specific strategies for inducing transportation particularly in legal settings, and whether different modes of presentation will influence the inducement of transportation.

Trial commentators offered several additional strategies under the broad objectives combined in the transportation-imagery model: emotion, attention (i.e., interest), and imagery. Many of the specific strategies offered by trial commentators for achieving these objectives were discussed or developed previously in this chapter or prior chapters. For example, humor and rhetorical questions were discussed in Chapter 2 of this volume; imagery was discussed in Chapter 3; voice was discussed in Chapter 4; gestures and eye contact were discussed in Chapter 5; and labels, themes, and repetition was discussed earlier in this chapter. Therefore, only selected strategies will be developed further: potential emotional responses from jurors, positive/negative emotional messages, one- and two-sided arguments, forewarning, and starting strongly.

Potential Emotional Responses From Jurors. The research indicates that emotions are complex processes, and many aspects of emotion remain unstudied. For example, the role of emotions in jury decision making has not been thoroughly explored (Loewenstein & Lerner, 2003). Some mental processes through which emotions may influence decision making were discussed above under Theme. More specifically, emotion may influence jury decision making in several ways. For one, jurors may be influenced by their incidental emotions (e.g., being in a general state of sadness; Hastie, 2001), and people may consult their emotions as part of their decision making (Forgas, 1995). One study found that, compared with people who were in a sad or neutral mood, people who were induced to be angry were likely to perceive a Hispanic person as more guilty than a non-Hispanic person after reading case evidence

(Bodenhausen, Sheppard, & Kramer, 1994), but this effect may be limited to situations in which the stereotype is perceived as relevant to the decision (Moons & Mackie, 2007). The implication of this finding in trial settings is that jurors may reference their feelings, even those that are unrelated to the case, when interpreting the meaning of trial information. Research on terror management theory in jury decision making supports this conclusion. According to this research, when mortality is salient, personality attributes and individual biases that affect juror decision making may be activated and interact with aspects of the case and trial. For example, when jurors were reminded of their morality, those who believed procedural fairness was highly important were more likely to follow judicial instructions to ignore inadmissable evidence (Cook, Arndt, & Lieberman, 2004; see Lieberman & Sales, 2007).

Decision-relevant emotions may also influence jurors' decision making (Hastie, 2001). Emotionally affected jurors may have more difficulty focusing and elaborating on information (e.g., Wilder & Simon, 1996). Evidence that has strong emotional content may lead jurors to focus their attention on negative information that is consistent with the defendant's guilt instead of positive information (Feigenson & Park, 2006). Another possibility is that stress may influence the amount of effort the juror will use to process the trial information, perhaps prompting jurors to rely on simple decision cues. However, this topic has not been studied systematically, especially in trial contexts (Hastie, 2001). Jurors may also be influenced if they make predictions about the emotions that will result from their decision. For example, punishing a sympathetic defendant may result in feelings of guilt, and jurors may evaluate their anticipated emotional responses as part of their decision making (Hastie, 2001).

Using the story model, Hastie (2001) also explained that emotion may come into play at several points in the trial. Jurors' emotions may sway them at the story construction stage by inducing them to retrieve biased information from long-term memory. For example, if a juror is feeling angry, he or she may focus on negative information from the case and construct a story of the case based on a previous story that produced an angry reaction. Emotions may also bias jurors' inferences when they attempt to complete the story details or influence their later decisions about the acceptability of the story or the fit to the verdict categories. Potentially, emotion may play an even larger role in jury decision making under the story model in situations when the evidence is undeveloped or so vague that jurors are unable to construct a story and must make a decision on other factors (Hastie, 2001). More research is needed to understand possible emotional responses from jurors, how those emotional responses will influence their decision making, the applications of this information to the story model and the other models discussed in this chapter, and ultimately whether and under what case conditions lawyers can use this information to enhance persuasiveness.

Positive/Negative Emotional Messages. Trial commentators assert that positive and negative emotional messages will influence jurors' emotional responses. The literature indicates that persuasion may be achieved by arousing an emotional state in combination with advocating an action that provides "a means for the receiver to deal with those aroused feelings" (O'Keefe, 2002, p. 228). However, the research on emotional appeals is mainly limited to fear appeals (Nabi, 2002; O'Keefe, 2002), and research has only superficially explored other emotions such as pride and guilt (for a summary, see Nabi, 2002). In addition, negative stories appear to have a more powerful effect on beliefs than positive stories, but transportation may still occur with positive ones (Green & Brock, 2000). In the trial context, jurors in one study (Hans & Swiegart, 1993) "reported disliking extreme levels of emotion (i.e. too much or too little) that were inconsistent with the severity of the plaintiff's injuries and disliked the badgering of witnesses" (Devine, Clayton, Dunford, Seying, & Pryce, 2001, p. 684). Another study investigated the effectiveness of attorneys' communication and impression making in the courtroom by rating their presentations in opening statements. This study revealed that none of the opening statement variables, including emphasis on emotional issues, was effective for predicting the trial outcome (Linz, Penrod, & McDonald, 1986; see Devine et al., 2001). Future research should strive to understand the effects of positive and negative appeals in trial contexts and the techniques that are most likely to achieve the desired responses.

Despite lacking a definitive response about how positive and negative appeals influence jurors' emotions, research does suggest that once a message achieves an emotional reaction, it may be difficult to change, even when the cognitions that underlie that reaction are invalidated (Sherman & Kim, 2002; see Zajonc, 1980). Instead, it appears that invalidating information is better at replacing previously held affective beliefs if it is also affective in nature, rather than rational (Sherman & Kim, 2002). This finding suggests that attorneys will not be able to counteract an emotional jury with logic and will have more success if they can connect their rational appeal with a related emotion.

One-Sided and Two-Sided Arguments. One-sided arguments present only supporting arguments. In contrast, two-sided arguments discuss both supporting and opposing arguments (O'Keefe, 2002). Trial commentators argue that both types of argument can be used to create an emotional response in jurors. According to the research literature, both types of argument are roughly equivalent in terms of persuasiveness, until two-sided arguments are further distinguished as refutational (i.e., attempts to refute opposing arguments) or nonrefutational (i.e., raises opposing considerations but does not directly attempt to refute the opposing side's arguments). When compared with one-sided messages, refutational two-sided messages are significantly more persuasive, but nonrefuational two-sided messages are significantly less persuasive

(O'Keefe, 1999, 2002). Therefore, it appears that attorneys should refute opposing arguments instead of ignoring them or just mentioning the counter-arguments, which is an even worse strategy. The research on one- or two-sided arguments has focused on the persuasive aspects as opposed to the emotional aspects. Thus, further research is needed here.

Forewarning. Another proposed strategy for influencing jurors' emotional responses is forewarning. Research indicates that when listeners have prior knowledge of another's persuasive intent, the message is less effective (Linz & Penrod, 1984; see Brock, 1967; Petty & Cacioppo, 1977, 1979). Individuals who are warned that they are about to be subjected to a persuasive attempt are believed to immediately begin generating counterarguments to the anticipated message (Linz & Penrod, 1984; McGuire & Papageorgis, 1962). The credibility of the source and the level of listener involvement are factors that can influence the effectiveness of the forewarning strategy. In sum, forewarning appears to be a successful strategy for refuting an argument or appeal before the opponent presents his or her argument, but it remains unclear whether forewarning as a strategy has emotional consequences for jurors.

Another line of research is relevant here, although it has not yet considered the emotional effect on jurors. *Stealing thunder* refers to an attorney revealing negative information about his client, the evidence, or himself to defuse the effect of opposing counsel revealing it to the jury (Howard, Brewer, & Williams, 2006). The original research on stealing thunder (Howard et al., 2006; Williams, Bourgeois, & Croylet, 1993) showed that it significantly lowered the negative impact of the information because it raised the attorney's credibility in the eyes of mock jurors (Howard, Brewer, & Williams, 2006; Williams et al., 1993). The stealing thunder effect occurred even without framing because it led mock jurors to interpret the information more favorably (Dolnik, Case, & Williams, 2003), probably because the increased credibility of the attorney presenting the information enhanced the persuasiveness of her or his argument (Howard et al. 2006). However, there are two important limitations to the value of attorneys using this strategy. When opposing counsel revealed that the tactic was being used on the jurors, it was no longer effective (Dolnik et al., 2003). In addition, it only works under conditions where mock jurors are peripherally rather than centrally processing the trial information (Howard et al., 2006).

Start Strongly. Although attorneys' strategies for starting strongly are unspecified, trial attorneys believe that attorneys should begin their case in this way. *Primacy effects,* or the idea that there is an intrinsic advantage to information heard first, are relevant to understanding whether attorneys should start strongly.

Some research suggests that primacy effects can influence judgments. One experiment investigated the impact of primacy effects on later judgments of overall impressions. Two paragraphs were created about "Jim," a fictitious character. One paragraph described Jim as outgoing and extraverted, and the other described him as introverted and withdrawn. One group of participants received only the paragraph describing Jim as introverted, while one group received only the paragraph describing Jim as extraverted. Another group of participants received the paragraph describing Jim as extraverted followed by the paragraph describing him as introverted, and the fourth group received the paragraph describing Jim as introverted followed by the paragraph describing him as extraverted. The extroversion only group rated Jim as friendly; the introversion only group rate Jim as unfriendly. For participants who received both paragraphs, Jim's rating as friendly or unfriendly was consistent with whether the first paragraph described Jim as introverted or extraverted (Luchins, 1957; see Linz & Penrod, 1984; Luchins, 1958).

Social psychologists argue that information heard first may be important in providing a schema for interpreting and integrating subsequent information in a meaningful way (Linz & Penrod, 1984; see Bartlett, 1932; Fiske & Taylor, 1991). Schemas applied at the outset appear to have more powerful influencing effects than when the schema is applied afterward (Linz & Penrod, 1984; see Fiske & Taylor, 1991). For example, people may attend to facts about the person that are consistent with the schema but disregard behaviors that are inconsistent with the schema. Alternatively, people may remember aspects of the person that were inconsistent with the schema because they stand out, or they may assign a new interpretation to incongruent information to achieve consistency with the schema (Linz & Penrod, 1984; see Hastie, 1980). In the trial context, transcripts of interviews with 99 jurors from 14 civil cases revealed that the opening statements provided a framework for understanding and interpreting the evidence (Hans & Swiegart, 1993; see Devine et al., 2001).

On the other hand, research indicates that there is no general persuasive advantage for arguments heard first or second (O'Keefe, 2002; see Rosnow, 1966). Primacy effects appear more likely to occur when topics are interesting, controversial, and familiar, whereas recency effects are more likely to be found with uninteresting, noncontroversial, or unfamiliar topics (Rosnow, 1966). Some researchers have suggested that primacy effects are more likely to occur under conditions of high elaboration because "the first message can produce attitudes that are relatively more resistant to persuasion" (O'Keefe, 2002, p. 253). In contrast, conditions of low elaboration are more likely to result in recency effects because the information "heard last is more prominent in memory" (O'Keefe, 2002, pp. 253–254; see Haugtvedt & Wegener, 1994). However, the argument strength may influence the outcome, and the side with the stronger arguments may have an advantage in whatever order the position is presented (O'Keefe, 2002; see Rosnow & Robinson, 1967).

In short, research on primacy effects appears to tentatively support trial commentators' recommendation of starting strongly as a way to create a good first impression with the jury that will establish the lawyer as someone worth listening to. In addition, an interesting presentation is likely to contribute to primacy effects in situations in which there is a need for elaboration, such as in trials. However, the primacy effect appears to have the most advantage in cases with strong arguments, which suggests that attorneys should not try to replace quality arguments with dramatic flourishes.

One reason trial commentators favor beginning strongly is the belief that jurors make up their minds quickly and resist changing their minds. One study asked mock jurors to make liability judgments at various points during a trial and concluded that the judgments made after the opening statements tended to reflect the final verdict (Weld & Danzig, 1940). This is similar to the Pyszczynski and Wrightsman (1981) study, discussed previously, that found that mock jurors tended to vote consistently with the first party that presented an extensive opening statement. However, another study "failed to find a relationship between the content or style of the opening statements and first-ballot votes during deliberations or final verdicts" (Devine et al., 2001, p. 684; Linz et al., 1986).

Other studies have found that verdicts are determined sometime prior to deliberations. In an early study, mock jurors reported reaching their decisions before the deliberations. About one third of the jurors began the process of making their decision quite early in the trial process, and 82% of the jurors had reached a definite conclusion before deliberations began (Weld & Roff, 1938). In post-trial interviews of 65 actual jurors who had participated in 10 felony trials, jurors identified at what point they had determined the defendant's guilt or innocence. Of the jurors, 23 (35%) answered "near the beginning" or "near the middle" of the trial; 31 (47%) answered "by the end of the trial" but before deliberations, and only 11 (17%) jurors reported they were still undecided when the trial proper ended (Bridgeman & Marlowe, 1979). Another study that conducted interviews of randomly selected jurors in death penalty trials found that many begin to consider punishment even before the defendant's guilt had been decided (Bowers, 1996). Other studies strongly indicate that jurors' verdicts are determined by their votes in the first ballot (Devine et al., 2001; see Kalven & Zeisel, 1966; Sandys & Dillehay, 1995). For example, the first-ballot verdicts predicted final verdicts 93% of the time (Sandys & Dillehay, 1995).

These studies indicate that jurors decide the verdict sometime before the end of the trial and are unlikely to change their mind in deliberations. However, it is still largely unclear at what point these decisions are determined, and the studies certainly do not indicate that jurors decide the case in a minute or less, as one commentator (Fontham, 2002) claimed. In addition, many of these studies are limited by small sample sizes, the use of mock jurors, and the reliance on unrealistic trial materials. Many studies that used actual jurors are limited by small sample sizes and the use of jurors' recollections of past events, which may lead to inaccuracies. Finally, the research indicates a strong positive association between strength of evidence and juror verdicts of guilt or liability (see Devine, Clayton, Dunford, Seying, & Pryce, 2001), which appears to indicate that a strong start and good first impression are not enough to counter a weak case. In sum, it appears that starting strongly may help provide a framework for jurors to rely on in their decision making (Linz et al., 1986), but it cannot overcome weakness in the evidence.

CONCLUSION

This chapter reviewed research addressing trial commentators' claims about storytelling in the courtroom. Four storytelling models were most relevant: the story model (Pennington & Hastie, 1991), the commonsense justice model (Finkel & Groscup, 1997), the construction model (Read, 1987), and the transportation-imagery model (Green & Brock, 2000).

The story model accounts for jurors' processing and organizing of trial information into stories that involve preexisting knowledge and expectation structures. The story is then used to reach a decision about the verdict. The story model incorporates three primary processes: (a) constructing the story for evidence evaluation, (b) representing the decision alternatives by learning the attributes and elements of the verdict categories, and (c) reaching an ultimate decision on the verdict by classifying the story into the category that fits best (Pennington & Hastie, 1991, 1993). The model's certainty principles account for the extent to which the story will be accepted by jurors and the level of confidence that they have in their ultimate decision (Pennington & Hastie, 1991, 1993). Because jurors often receive incomplete and disjointed information during trial, jurors construct stories to help them fill in missing information. The current state of research on the story model supports trial commentators' claims that jurors use stories to understand the information presented at trial and accounts for many of the qualities trial commentators believe are important for stories to possess.

The commonsense justice model is critical for understanding how jurors are likely to diverge from what is intended by the law. Under commonsense justice, factors that are likely to influence jurors are the evidence, extralegal factors, prejudicial statements and legally inadmissible material, and jurors' prior knowledge (Finkel, 1995). For example, stereotypes or prototypes of typical crimes, criminals, and resulting harms are a type of prior knowledge that may influence jurors' decision making. Commonsense justice concepts may have implications for the story model in terms of, for example, the types of information that jurors rely on to construct their story or which verdict they choose.

The construction model (Read, 1987) is relevant to understanding trial commentators' strategies for developing their theory and story of the case because it addresses how knowledge structures are used to construct behavioral sequences. Four types of knowledge structures are relevant for constructing scenarios: scripts, plans, goals, and themes. In addition, causal syntax rules explain how knowledge structures are connected together into scenarios. According to the model, observations of interactions trigger relevant knowledge structures, which will trigger other related structures. Research that explores the relationship of the construction model to the story model and commonsense justice is still necessary for gaining insight into how lawyers and jurors are likely to construct their stories of the case. Trial commentators and the construction model both posit the importance of the theme to storytelling. Themes are believed to guide one's observation and organization of events in memory, and research supports that themes influence the way that information is constructed and interpreted. However, only one study has attempted to address the influence of themes on jury decision making, and the results were unclear given the study's methodology.

The last model, the transportation-imagery model (Green & Brock, 2000), proposes that people exposed to narrative stories will experience a state of transportation or immersion in the story. Transportation is believed to facilitate persuasion by reducing negative cognitive responding and elaboration and invite less counterarguments. The research on the transportation-imagery model suggests that stories may effectively merge cognitive and affective processes for persuasive purposes; emotion, imagery, and cognitive involvement are key aspects of using transportation to positively influence receivers.

All of these models, as well as the additional recommendations discussed in the chapter, have implications for attorneys when constructing the case theory, theme, and story. Ultimately, stories appear to be an important aspect of how jurors understand the information presented at trial, and attorneys who understand what factors jurors are likely to attend to should have an advantage at trial.

8

CONCLUSION

Trial strategy and advocacy have been implemented by attorneys in court and portrayed in TV dramas (e.g., *Perry Mason* [Jackson & Jackson, 1957] and *Matlock* [Hargrove, Silverman, Hargrove, Steiger, & Griffith, 1986]) and movies (e.g., *Primal Fear* [Lucchesi & Hoblit, 1996] and *My Cousin Vinny* [Launer, Schiff, & Lynn, 1992]). However, what strategies are actually effective in real trials, in which real people's lives and money are at stake? Trial commentators think they know what is likely to be persuasive to the jury and offer many intuition-based strategies on attorney demeanor, verbal and nonverbal communication, the attorney–client relationship, and storytelling. This volume offered insight into the question of effective strategies by using social scientific research and theory to critically evaluate the trial commentators' recommendations, suggest research-based advocacy techniques that are likely to persuade the jury, and encourage a new generation of research in this important area of professional behavior and practice.

A few overarching conclusions can be drawn from the current evaluation of trial commentators' recommended strategies. Attorneys' best strategy is to develop the evidence and their arguments. In situations where jurors do not understand the evidence and arguments, or are not motivated or are unable to process the trial information, they are likely to focus on other nonlegal information such as source cues in their decision making. For example, interpersonal skills appear key for getting greater disclosure from clients, which may potentially benefit lawyers in developing their evidence and arguments (e.g., Boccaccini & Brodsky, 2001). In addition, stories appear to be a vehicle through which attorneys can convey information to jurors, so storytelling skills are important for attorneys to possess. For more specific lessons, the reader must carefully review each of the prior chapters.

METHODOLOGICAL PROBLEMS WITH TRIAL ADVOCACY RESEARCH

Although our conclusions are based on the available research, there are methodological limitations in applying this work to trial advocacy. Several broad points about limitations with the current state of research are worth highlighting. The problems in the research can largely be classified as accessibility problems, internal validity problems, external and ecological validity problems, and operational definition problems. Readers should also keep in mind that many of the specific limitations with individual studies were discussed within each chapter, and readers should reference each chapter for greater detail.

Accessibility Problems

Very little research has been conducted on trial advocacy: Judges are often reluctant to permit variations in courtroom procedures because of constitutional concerns (Fifth, Sixth, Seventh, and Fourteenth Amendments) or permit recording of court proceedings for research purposes (Drew, 1985). In addition, the litigating attorneys may decline to cooperate with researchers out of concern for maintaining attorney–client confidentiality or strategic advantages for the current or future trials (e.g., Danet, Hoffman, & Kermish, 1980). The fact that jurors are observers only complicates research because the effect of courtroom communications cannot easily be observed in "naturally occurring data" (Drew, 1985, p. 134), and jury deliberations are usually secluded from observation. Therefore, finding legal and creative ways for overcoming these obstacles is crucial for research in trial advocacy.

Internal Validity Problems

Even if researchers are able to gain access to the courtroom to study trial advocacy, the inability of researchers to conduct true experiments in this environment may negatively affect the informativeness of the research. Internal validity problems "inhibit researchers from interpreting direct causal relationships between changes in the independent variable or variables and changes in the dependent or outcome variable" (Krauss & Sales, 2000, p. 850). To overcome internal validity problems, researchers need to be able to control all other variables except the ones that they are trying to study to determine whether there is a direct relationship between the variables of interest. Otherwise, the results will be confounded by the outside factors (e.g., Krauss & Sales, 2000).

To study attorney advocacy in trial settings, researchers may have to account for many types of variables that could have confounding effects. For example, dimensions of credibility should be manipulated individually. Consider research on source cues. It has typically assessed the trustworthiness and expertise aspects of credibility in combination even though they are conceptually distinct, which means that their effects on persuasive outcomes should be examined separately as well (O'Keefe, 2002). However, manipulating how a lawyer presents in the courtroom can undermine the party's right to a fair trial (e.g., English & Sales, 2005). In addition, researchers trying to investigate trial advocacy in courtrooms cannot randomly assign defendants to different situations or use control groups to establish whether a particular strategy made a significant difference in outcomes. As a result, it is virtually impossible for researchers to control or manipulate the possible factors that may come into play in an actual trial (e.g., Krauss & Sales, 2000). Moreover, focusing solely on a particular part of the trial is no solution because it may not reflect influences from the entire trial (Drew, 1985).

External and Ecological Validity Problems

Given the obstacles imposed by the court system and the difficulty in controlling variables, research has typically relied on mock jury studies that involve simulated materials to study trial issues (Devine, Clayton, Dunford, Seying, & Pryce, 2001). Simulations have the advantage of allowing the experimenter to control variables that could not be controlled in an actual trial and allowing access to the deliberation process (Devine et al., 2001). However, some fear that mock jurors may differ from actual jurors in their decision making and that these studies are not generalizable to actual jurors (e.g., *Lockhart v. McCree*, 1986). The concerns with mock jury research methodologies include recruiting students instead of community members in the sample (Bornstein, 1999; Devine et al., 2001; Diamond, 1997), using written trial summaries instead of more realistic simulations, using laboratory settings instead of the courtroom, failing to include typical trial elements (e.g., deliberations), failing to account for the consequentiality of the task (i.e., a hypothetical versus real decision), using dependent variables that are inconsistent with the law (e.g., probability-of-guilt judgments vs. dichotomous verdicts; Bornstein, 1999; Diamond, 1997), and using dependent measures and measurement techniques that fail to address the legal constructs and outcomes that are of concern to trial commentators and practicing lawyers. For example, in regard to attorney demeanor, factor analysis scales have been used to identify the dimensions of source characteristics, but these studies are too focused on semantic differential scales instead of alternative measurement techniques. Cronkhite and Liska (1976) criticized the procedures for selecting and naming credibility scales; the conclusions drawn by researchers and generalizability of raters, concepts, and factoring procedures; and the lack of properly addressing the effect of context and the role of the source in the communication. In addition, research typically focuses on both expertise and trustworthiness in assessing credibility because the interaction is what leads to reliable communications. Although some research has tried to separate the dimensions, the results are not clearly generalizable (e.g., O'Hara, Netemeyer, & Burton, 1991). Focusing research on separately manipulating individual dimensions of credibility would be informative. For example, trustworthiness and expertise are conceptually distinct aspects of credibility, which means that their effects on persuasive outcomes should be examined separately and not just in combination. Credibility assessments could also be developed for addressing specific circumstances because the judgments and emphasis on particular dimensions underlying credibility may vary under different circumstances (O'Keefe, 2002). Studies comparing high- and low-credibility communicators have also failed to tease out what makes one lawyer more or less credible than another when arguing diverse topics in the different areas of litigation (e.g., divorce claims versus products liability claims), while controlling for the counter- versus proattitudinal character of the message when compared to juror's preexisting beliefs. Addressing these components would allow for relevant contrasting conditions, whereas studying these factors concurrently could provide additional information about how factors influence the magnitude and direction of credibility effects. For instance, studies that do not find high-credibility communicators to be more successful than low-credibility sources have altered one of three conditions: (a) source identification made prior to the message, (b) relevance of the topic, and (c) messages contrasted with receivers' positions. Varying these factors interactively may lead to different effects in credibility assessments (O'Keefe, 2002).

Although ideally researchers should want to obtain corroborative field data (Diamond, 1997), they can maximize the external validity of their studies by using realistic reenactments, a realistic trial setting (e.g., videotape of an actual trial), large samples, and participants from a real jury pool. Deliberations to reach a verdict are also key in ensuring that the results are generalizable to real trials (Devine et al., 2001; Diamond, 1997; English & Sales,

2005). Although these techniques are considered the best methodologies, the necessity of more realistic simulation methods is questionable because some research findings have suggested that more realistic simulation methods do not produce reliable differences in jury behavior (e.g., Bornstein, 1999; Hastie, Penrod, & Pennington, 1983). Because studies need to generalize to the behavior of real jurors, more research is needed on the external validity of mock jury methodologies. Specifically, researchers need to investigate whether methodological variations affect the results of studies, explore whether possible interactions between variables will affect the results (e.g., deliberations and consequentiality of the task), and develop a theoretical basis for understanding the effects of different methodologies on mock jurors' decisions (Bornstein, 1999; Devine et al., 2001; Diamond, 1997).

The lack of ecological validity also compromises researchers' ability to generalize the findings to the real world of attorneys' interactions with their clients. Existing studies of attorney–client relationships, trust, and disclosure typically use prison inmates as participants (e.g., Boccaccini & Brodsky, 2001). Although these participants are convenient, defendants who were not sentenced to prison (i.e., those who received probation or were found not guilty) are not represented, which could bias client attitudes toward defense attorneys and therefore skew research results. Also, some studies of attorney–client relationships focused on the attorneys' and clients' opinions concerning legal skills, which could differ from the attorneys' actual behavior. Behavioral measures that rely on self-reports are also potentially limiting because people may not accurately recount their behaviors (Boccaccini, Boothby, & Brodsky, 2002). In addition, some studies did not inquire about many key aspects of attorney–client interactions (e.g., whether attorneys would have preferred to establish deeper client relationships; e.g., Hosticka, 1979; Uphoff & Wood, 1998). Studies that inquire about attorneys' perceptions of client interactions could help develop theories on the dynamics that help establish cooperative attorney–client teams.

A related limitation concerns the comprehensiveness of lists for the rating of lawyering skills by attorneys and clients. For instance, one study investigating the attitudes of attorneys and convicted clients toward the attorney–client relationship did not include several skills that are considered important for effective lawyers (e.g., only six legal skills were listed, and these were not clearly defined; Boccaccini et al., 2002). To be able to generalize research findings on this topic, more information is needed about (a) the nature of the attorney–client relationship and whether there are differences in attorney–client relationships for type of case (e.g., criminal or civil) and type of client (e.g., public or private), (b) attorneys' knowledge and use of effective communication techniques, (c) whether communication strategies need to be modified based on the type of case or type of client, and (d) how juror perceptions of the attorney–client relationship in actual cases affect the attorney's ability to persuade.

Operational Definition Problems

A final methodological limitation in current research studies is a lack of clear operationalization of terms. When concepts are operationalized, they require an unambiguous and uniform definition, which enables researchers to break down the idea into components that are easily identifiable and assessable. This level of definitional specificity allows researchers to effectively study and measure the concept with social scientific techniques. Without specifying exactly what a concept means, researchers' ability to develop valid measurement techniques, standardize assessment instruments, compare different studies, and summarize the existing research on point is jeopardized (Krauss & Sales, 2000).

Issues with operationalization may emerge in several areas in trial advocacy. For example, nonverbal behaviors carrying the same labels are not consistently defined or the operational definitions are vague (e.g., the difference between "loud" and "soft" voices; Burgoon et al., 1990). Another example of an operationalization issue occurs in a study investigating clients' perceptions of attorneys' legal skills. One skill was "standing up for client's rights"; without an explanation, this statement could be construed as asking whether the lawyer objected when appropriate, presented every possible defense, negotiated a fair plea bargain for the client, all of these possibilities, or something else entirely. Because no definition was offered, participants had to rely on their own judgment of the meaning (Boccaccini et al., 2002). Finally, the lack of operational definitions of the attorney strategies and behaviors that are intended to increase persuasiveness, along with accepted means for measuring them, will impede the ability of researchers to understand and improve attorney advocacy.

FUTURE RESEARCH AND SOLUTIONS TO PROBLEMS

As discussed in Chapter 7, "there is ample evidence supporting the conclusion that [strength of evidence] is the primary determinant of jury verdicts in criminal trials in most circumstances" (Devine et al., 2001, p. 686). Although one implication from this research finding is that lawyers should focus on developing strong evidence and arguments for trial, this conclusion does not imply that trial advocacy skills are not important. Indeed, trial advocacy skills most likely affect jury decision making in situations where neither side has a clear advantage or when jurors are unmotivated to process the trial information or unable to do so. Therefore, future research on trial advocacy is critical for improving attorney goals and strategies for developing better trial advocacy.

Targeting Research to Improve Attorney Strategies and Behaviors

This volume has explored trial commentators' recommendations from the perspective of current research studies, many of which are only indirectly on point because they did not attempt to directly study or simulate attorney behavior. Although the validity of many of trial commentators' recommendations is not yet known given the available research, the current research summarized in each chapter is useful for targeting areas for further study to improve attorney strategies and behaviors.

In addition, some types of studies are worth pursuing. Developing specific tests of when particular strategies will be most useful to attorneys under varying conditions (e.g., trial length, evidentiary type, evidentiary complexity). When conducting the above research, future studies should also look at the main and interaction effects of the individual modes of communication (verbal, vocal, and kinesic) on jurors' accurate understanding of the attorney's message and their susceptibility to persuasion, with attention paid to individual differences among jurors. For example, among the individual factors that have been shown to influence the decoding of nonverbal behaviors are intelligence, culture, age, gender, and personality (Burgoon & Bacue, 2003). By understanding how individual differences influence persuasion and comprehension, researchers may be able to develop strategies and trial advocacy skills that will have the greatest impact on different types of jurors. Future studies should also explore new technologies that may have effects on trial advocacy. For example, computer reenactments of the attorneys' cases may impact their ability to be convincing storytellers.

Researchers also can adapt and improve upon available scientific research methods and models to test hypotheses about attorney advocacy. For example, one model that could be adapted to studying trial advocacy is Krauss and Sales's (2001) study on the effects of scientific expert testimony on jury decision making. Participants served as jury members in a simulated capital case, with participants hearing actuarial or clinical expert testimony. At the various stages of trial, participants completed questionnaires that offered insight into the influence of the expert testimony on jurors' beliefs of the mock defendant's guilt. Researchers could use a similar methodology for studying trial advocacy. In addition, given the limitations of individual experimental designs, replicating experimental findings using multiple methods will be imperative for justifying the validity of results.

Using Theory to Improve Research on Attorney Strategies and Behaviors

To increase the usefulness of research on trial advocacy, attention must be focused on developing theory-driven studies of real trials or closely related simulations. Theory is important for understanding what is happening and why. Otherwise, any results that are discovered may be due to the unique conditions of the experiment. By using theory, researchers can be more confident in their conclusions and know whether the results are generalizable to all trials or some trials, and why.

Theories applicable to the study of trial advocacy are the dual process models. Under both the elaboration likelihood model (Petty & Cacioppo, 1986) and the heuristic-systematic model of persuasion (Eagly & Chaiken, 1984), source factors have less weight in decision making when the decision is highly important to receivers. Given the importance of their likely role in the trial and outcome of some cases, these models suggest that jurors are unlikely to resort to simple decision rules, like source cues, as the basis for their trial decisions. Rather, they are more likely to rely on evidence and substantive arguments. However, as noted earlier, whether this analysis accurately describes juror behavior in all types of trials, and for all types of jurors, is an open question. Future research needs to assess the following: under what conditions jurors resort to simple decision cues, juror perceptions of trial importance, their motivation to actively participate, their ability to do so across all types of cases, the importance they place on their decision-making responsibilities, how their role perception influences their decision making, the factors that influence all of the above outcomes, the influence of attorney source characteristics on jury decision making when jurors are relying on peripheral processing, and how all of the above issues vary depending on the trial circumstances. For example, studies should develop specific tests of when specific strategies may be most useful to attorneys under varying conditions (e.g., trial length, evidentiary type, evidentiary complexity). Most important, however, we need to start developing rich theory or theories to explain the likely effects of attorney behavior on jurors that can guide rigorous programmatic research on the topic.

Other theories mentioned throughout the book that could serve as a basis for future studies include the story model (Pennington & Hastie, 1991), commonsense justice (Finkel & Groscup, 1997), the construction model (Read, 1987), and the transportation-imagery model (Green & Brock, 2000). Other theories, such as the HEXACO model (Ashton & Lee, 2007; Lee & Ashton, 2008), should also be considered. The HEXACO model proposes a six-dimensional structure of personality: honesty-humility (H), emotionality (E), extraversion (X), agreeableness (A), conscientiousness (C), and openness to experience (O). This model could serve as a framework for understanding the effect of the attorney's personality on clients' willingness to disclose information, jurors' perceptions of attorneys and their case, and jurors' decision making. In addition, researchers need to consider developing new theoretical models or integrating parts of existing models to better explain the relationships between the influence of trial advocacy techniques (see, e.g., Lieberman & Sales, 2007). As noted previously in this chapter, many factors (e.g., individual differences among jurors, strength of evidence, type of case) may affect the ultimate jury decision. Therefore, it is critical that researchers broaden their theoretical focus to encompass all potential factors that could explain attorney effectiveness.

Developing Attorney–Researcher Partnerships

Finally, greater collaboration between attorneys and academic researchers is necessary to understand the efficacy of trial commentators' beliefs. As noted previously, a lack of cooperation from attorneys and judges greatly impedes the ability of researchers to study the behavior of legal actors in legal settings. Collaboration between fields would allow researchers to go beyond what the trial commentators say and learn what the practicing bar believes and does. This opportunity is critical for establishing whether the strategies discussed in the trial commentary are in fact the same ones that are actually implemented during trials and for identifying what variations in strategy and behaviors are occurring. In addition, access to attorneys' records and perceptions of their trial work may facilitate the investigation of new issues that could have an impact on trial advocacy.

Greater collaboration would also allow for better measurement of the effectiveness of the proposed strategies or actually implemented strategies. For example, research on mock juries would be improved if participants include practicing attorneys, actual judges, and a full-sized panel of prospective jurors who accurately represented the characteristics of the juror pool. For example, the attorneys could inform researchers in developing the simulated case, evidence, and arguments, as well as provide input for how particular trial techniques would most likely be implemented during an actual trial. In addition, lawyers could help researchers make sure that their case is legally accurate and help them expand their research focus to areas of trial advocacy that are less well studied. These techniques would allow researchers to make mock jury simulations more realistic and increase the generalizability of results.

Several possible solutions could encourage attorney–researcher collaborations. Interdisciplinary education and training would educate future attorneys about the value of social science research in improving advocacy strategies and behaviors and would help both lawyers and social science researchers understand the other discipline's concerns. This type of education and training could occur within legal education and during postgraduate meetings (e.g., at bar association meetings and judicial conferences). In addition, it would be helpful to develop conferences devoted to overcoming any attorney–social scientist communication and goal problems. Finally, it would substantially help if law firms developed a national program of funding to support social science research on attorney advocacy, although this suggestion is not without its own problems during a time of fiscal austerity.

Another way to increase our knowledge of attorney advocacy is to get attorneys and judges to allow the use of shadow juries. Shadow juries are composed of individuals who match the characteristics of the actual jury members. The shadow jurors stay in the courtroom during the actual trial, listen to the testimony, and report their reactions each day to the trial investigators (Lieberman & Sales, 2007). Although shadow juries may be seen as controversial or problematic by the public (Loh, 1984), the advantages of this technique are that the shadow jury is already used by jury consultants in some cases and is exposed to the same trial elements and advocacy that the real jury is exposed to. Thus, they can provide researchers with a mechanism for understanding attorney behaviors that were found to be influential and the point at which the jurors were influenced toward a particular verdict. In addition, the validity of the shadow jury may be determined by comparing its verdict with the actual jury verdict and by conducting posttrial interviews of actual jurors and comparing their responses with those of the shadow jurors (Lieberman & Sales, 2007). Potentially, posttrial interviews can provide confirmation of the successfulness of the trial advocacy techniques that researchers hypothesize will have an influence on jurors' decision making.

Another possibility for conducting research in an actual courtroom environment is using the electronically activated recorder (EAR). Participants wear the EAR as they conduct their daily activities, and it unobtrusively records ambient sound bites (e.g., Mehl, Pennebaker, Crow, Dabbs, & Price, 2001; Mehl, Vazire, Holleran, & Clark, 2010). Potentially, the EAR could overcome limitations with studies that investigate attorney behavior on the basis of opinions or self-reports by attorneys, clients, and jurors. In addition, the EAR may overcome concerns with maintaining attorney–client confidentiality and jurors' privacy during deliberations because the EAR only provides snippets of information. For example, attorneys or clients could wear the EAR during their meetings, and perhaps for a time before and after the meetings. Researchers could code the recorded sound bites to substantiate results of previous studies including clients' and attorneys' self-reports, as well as potentially study paralinguistic aspects of the communication. Jurors could also wear the EAR during deliberations, which could allow researchers to monitor the deliberations for references to attorney advocacy techniques used during trial or quality of the evidence. However, this latter approach raises due process and equal protection concerns that would have to be addressed by the attorneys and judges.

Use of shadow juries, posttrial interviews and possibly the EAR, would allow researchers the opportunity to replicate findings from mock jury simulations in the courtroom environment. Even with the limitations of these research techniques when analyzed individually, if the results are supported through several different mechanisms (i.e., convergent methodologies), then researchers can be confident in the accuracy of their findings and conclusions.

To develop more effective trial advocates, it is important that attorneys look to the social sciences for input on the effectiveness of currently recommended strategies and behaviors and for developing new trial advocacy techniques. Although methodological limitations exist with current research approaches, future studies can overcome these limitations by using theory as the basis for developing studies, creating more realistic simulations, replicating laboratory findings in the courtroom, and applying new techniques and technologies to studying the influence of trial advocacy on jury decision making. Moreover, it is critical that the study of trial advocacy be approached as a collaboration between attorneys and researchers. Such collaborations are the best way that researchers and attorneys will obtain accurate and useful information on attorney advocacy.

REFERENCES

Abbott, V., Black, J. B., & Smith, E. E. (1985). The representation of scripts in memory. *Journal of Memory and Language, 24*, 179–199. doi:10.1016/0749-596X (85)90023-3

Abelson, R. P. (1976). Script processing in attitude formation and decision making. In J. S. Carroll & J. W. Payne (Eds.), *Cognition and social behavior* (pp. 33–45). Hillsdale, NJ: Erlbaum.

Adams, G. R. (1977). Physical attractiveness research: Toward a developmental social psychology of beauty. *Human Development, 20*, 217–239. doi:10.1159/000271558

Addington, D. W. (1971). The effect of vocal variation on ratings of source credibility. *Speech Monographs, 38*, 242–247. doi:10.1080/03637757109375716

Aiello, J. R. (1987). Human spatial behavior. In D. Stokols and I. Altman (Eds.), *Handbook of environmental psychology* (pp. 359–504). New York, NY: John Wiley & Sons.

Akinnaso, F. N. (1982). On the differences between spoken and written language. *Language and Speech, 25*, 97–125.

Albarracín, D., & Kumkale, G. T. (2003). Affect as information in persuasion: A model of affect identification and discounting. *Journal of Personality and Social Psychology, 84*, 453–469. doi:10.1037/0022-3514.84.3.453

Alden, D. L., & Crowley, A. E. (1995). Improving the effectiveness of condom advertising: A research note. *Health Marketing Quarterly, 12*, 25–38. doi:10.1300/J026v12n04_04

Amano, S. (1996). Some observations on neighborhood statistics of spoken English words. In D. B. Pisoni (Ed.), *Research on spoken language processing: Progress report no. 21* (1996–1997; pp. 440–453). Speech Research Laboratory, Department of Psychology, Indiana University, Bloomington, IN.

American Bar Association (1980). *Model code of professional responsibility*. Retrieved from http://www.abanet.org/cpr/mrpc/mcpr.pdf

American Bar Association (2009). *Model rules of professional conduct*. Retrieved from http://www.americanbar.org/groups/professional_responsibility/publications/model_rules_of_professional_conduct.html

American heritage dictionary of the English language (4th ed.). (2000). New York, NY: Houghton Mifflin. Retrieved from http://www.thefreedictionary.com

Andersen, P. A., & Bowman, L. L. (1999). Positions of power: Nonverbal influence in organizational communication. In L. K. Guerrero, J. A. DeVito, & M. L. Hecht (Eds.), *The nonverbal communication reader: Classic and contemporary readings* (pp. 317–334). Prospect Heights, IL: Waveland.

Andersen, P. A., & Coussoule, A. (1980). The perceptual world of the communication apprehensive: The effect of communication apprehension and interpersonal gaze on interpersonal perception. *Communication Quarterly, 28,* 44–54. doi:10.1080/01463378009369357

Andersen, P. A., & Guerrero, L. K. (1998). The bright side of relational communication: Interpersonal warmth as a social emotion. In P. A. Andersen & L. K. Guerrero (Eds.), *Handbook of communication and emotion: Research, theory, applications, and contexts* (pp. 303–329). San Diego, CA: Academic Press.

Anderson, J. R. (1974). Verbatim and propositional representation of sentences in immediate and long-term memory. *Journal of Verbal Learning & Verbal Behavior, 13,* 149–162. doi:10.1016/S0022-5371(74)80039-3

Angeles, D. M. (1995). Simpson's lawyer tells jury that evidence doesn't fit. *The New York Times.* Retrieved from http://www.nytimes.com

Anisfeld, M., & Knapp, M. (1968). Association, synonymity, and directionality in false recognition. *Journal of Experimental Psychology, 77,* 171–179. doi:10.1037/h0025782

Appel, M., & Richter, T. (2010). Transportation and need for affect in narrative persuasion: A mediated moderation model. *Media Psychology, 13,* 102–135. doi:10.1080/15213261003799847

Applbaum, R. L., & Anatol, K. W. E. (1972). The factor structure of source credibility as a function of the speaking situation. *Speech Monographs, 39,* 216–222. doi:10.1080/03637757209375760

Apple, W., Streeter, L. A., & Krauss, R. M. (1979). Effects of pitch and speech rate on personal attributions. *Journal of Personality and Social Psychology, 37,* 715–727. doi:10.1037/0022-3514.37.5.715

Argyle, M., & Dean, J. (1965). Eye-contact, distance and affiliation. *Sociometry, 28,* 289–304. doi:10.2307/2786027

Arkes, H. R. (2001). Overconfidence in judgmental forecasting. In J. S. Armstrong (Ed.), *Principles of forecasting: A handbook for researchers and practitioners* (pp. 495–515). Boston, MA: Kluwer Academic.

Aronovitch, C. D. (1976). The voice of personality: Stereotyped judgments and their relation to voice quality and sex of speaker. *The Journal of Abnormal and Social Psychology, 99,* 207–220. doi:10.1080/00224545.1976.9924774

Aronson, E., Turner, J. A., & Carlsmith, J. M. (1963). Communicator credibility and communication discrepancy as a determinant of opinion change. *Journal of Abnormal and Social Psychology, 67,* 31–36. doi:10.1037/h0045513

Ashton, M. C., & Lee, K. (2007). Empirical, theoretical, and practical advantages of the HEXACO model of personality structure. *Personality and Social Psychology Review, 11,* 150–166. doi:10.1177/1088868306294907

Association of Trial Lawyers of America. (2003). *Communicating to the jury that your client deserves to win before the client says a word.* Advocacy track: Communicating with the jury—repackaging your message. Winter Convention Reference Materials. Retrieved from Westlaw. http://www.westlaw.com

Asthana, S. (2000). Female judgement of male attractiveness and desirability for relationships: Role of waist-to-hip ratio. *Psycho-Lingua, 30,* 61–64.

Atkins, B. M., & Boyle, E. W. (1976). Prisoner satisfaction with defense counsel. *Criminal Law Bulletin, 12*, 427–31. As reported in Boccaccini, M. T., & Brodsky, S. L. (2001). Characteristics of the ideal criminal defense attorney from the client's perspective: Empirical findings and implications for legal practice. *Law & Psychology Review, 25*, 81–117.

Atkinson, D. R., Winzelberg, A., & Holland, A. (1985). Ethnicity, locus of control for family planning, and pregnancy counselor credibility. *Journal of Counseling Psychology, 32*, 417–421. doi:10.1037/0022-0167.32.3.417

Austin, A. D. (1984). *Complex litigation confronts the jury system: A case study.* Frederick, MA: University Publications of America.

Axthelm, P. (1978, Nov. 20). A 'racehorse' for Cullen Davis. *Newsweek, 92*, 83–84.

Bachoud-Lévi, A. C., Dupoux, E., Cohen, L., & Mehler, J. (1998). Where is the length effect? A cross linguistic study of speech production. *Journal of Memory and Language, 39*, 331–346. doi:10.1006/jmla.1998.2572

Baddeley, A. D., & Scott, D. (1971). Word frequency and the unit sequence interference hypothesis in short-term memory. *Journal of Verbal Learning & Verbal Behavior, 10*, 35–40. doi:10.1016/S0022-5371(71)80090-7

Baddeley, A. D., Thomson, N., & Buchanan, M. (1975). Word length and the structure of short-term memory. *Journal of Verbal Learning & Verbal Behavior, 14*, 575–589. doi:10.1016/S0022-5371(75)80045-4

Baldwin, M. W., Carrell, S. E., & Lopez, D. F. (1990). Priming relationship schemas: My advisor and the pope are watching me from the back of my mind. *Journal of Experimental Social Psychology, 26*, 435–454. doi:10.1016/0022-1031(90)90068-W

Ball, D. (1993). *Theater tips and strategies for jury trials.* Notre Dame, IN: National Institute for Trial Advocacy.

Ball, D. (1997). *Theater tips and strategies for jury trials.* South Bend, IN: National Institute for Trial Advocacy.

Barber, C. (1962/1988). Some measurable characteristics of modern scientific prose. In J. Swales (Ed.), *Episodes in ESP* (pp. 1–16). New York, NY: Prentice Hall.

Baron, R. A. (1978). Invasions of personal space and helping: Mediating effects of invader's apparent need. *Journal of Experimental Social Psychology, 14*, 304–312. doi:10.1016/0022-1031(78)90018-5

Baron, R. A., & Bell, P. A. (1976). Physical distance and helping: Some unexpected benefits of "crowding in" on others. *Journal of Applied Social Psychology, 6*, 95–104. doi:10.1111/j.1559-1816.1976.tb01316.x

Bar-Tal, D. (1989). Deligitimization: The extreme case of stereotyping. In D. Bar-Tal, C. F.Grauman, A. Kruglanski, & W. Stroebe (Eds.), *Stereotyping and prejudice: Changing conceptions* (pp. 151–167). New York, NY: Springer-Verlag.

Bartlett, F. C. (1932). *Remembering: A study in experimental and social psychology.* Cambridge, England: Cambridge University Press.

Baskett, G. D., & Freedle, R. O. (1974). Aspects of language and the social perception of lying. *Journal of Psycholinguistic Research, 3*, 117–131. doi:10.1007/BF01067571

Batson, C. D., Early, S., & Salvarani, G. (1997). Perspective-taking: Imagining how another feels versus imagining how you would feel. *Personality and Social Psychology Bulletin, 23*, 751–758. doi:10.1177/0146167297237008

Batson, C. D., Van Lange, P. A. M., Ahmad, N., & Lishner, D. A. (2003). Altruism and helping behavior. In M. A. Hogg & J. Cooper (Eds.), *Sage handbook of social psychology* (pp. 279–295). Thousand Oaks, CA: Sage.

Baudhuin, E. S., & Davis, M. K. (1972). Scales for the measurement of ethos: Another attempt. *Speech Monographs, 39*, 296–301. doi:10.1080/03637757209375769

Baumeister, R. F., Smart, L., & Boden, J. M. (1996). Relation of threatened egotism to violence and aggression: The dark side of high self-esteem. *Psychological Review, 103*, 5–33. doi:10.1037/0033-295X.103.1.5

Bavelas, J. B., & Chovil, N. (2000). Visible acts of meaning. An integrated message model of language use in face-to-face dialogue. *Journal of Language and Social Psychology, 19*, 163–194. doi:10.1177/0261927X00019002001

Bavelas, J. B., & Chovil, N. (2006). Hand gestures and facial displays as part of language use in face-to-face dialogue. In V. Manusov & M. Patterson (Eds.), *Handbook of nonverbal communication* (pp. 97–115). Thousand Oaks, CA: Sage.

Beattie, G., & Shovelton, H. (2005). Why the spontaneous images created by the hands during talk can help make TV advertisements more effective. *British Journal of Psychology, 96*, 21–37. doi:10.1348/000712605X103500

Beattie, G., & Shovelton, H. (2006). A critical appraisal of the relationship between speech and gesture and its implications for the treatment of aphasia. *Advances in Speech Language Pathology, 8*, 134–139. doi:10.1080/14417040600667392

Beatty, M. J., & Behnke, R. R. (1980). Teacher credibility as a function of verbal content and paralinguistic cues. *Communication Quarterly, 28*, 55–59. doi:10.1080/01463378009369358

Beebe, S. A. (1974). Eye contact: A nonverbal determinant of speaker credibility. *The Speech Teacher, 23*, 21–25.

Begg, I., & Paivio, A. (1969). Concreteness and imagery in sentence meaning. *Journal of Verbal Learning & Verbal Behavior, 8*, 821. doi:10.1016/S0022-5371 (69)80049-6

Begg, I., & Rowe, E. J. (1972). Continuous judgments of word frequency and familiarity. *Journal of Experimental Psychology, 95*, 48–54. doi:10.1037/h0033272

Behling, D. U., & Williams, E. A. (1991). Influence of dress on perception of intelligence and expectations of scholastic achievement. *Clothing & Textiles Research Journal, 9*, 1–7. doi:10.1177/0887302X9100900401

Beighley, K. C. (1952). An experimental study of the effect of four speech variables on listener comprehension. *Speech Monographs, 19*, 249–258. doi:10.1080/03637755209375068

Belch, G. E. (1981). An examination of comparative and noncomparative television commercials: The effects of claim variation and repetition on cognitive response and message acceptance. *Journal of Marketing Research, 18*, 333–349. doi:10.2307/3150974

Bell, B. E., & Loftus, E. F. (1988). Degree of detail of eyewitness testimony and mock juror judgments. *Journal of Applied Social Psychology, 18*, 1171–1192. doi:10.1111/j.1559-1816.1988.tb01200.x

Bell, B. E., & Loftus, E. F. (1989). Trivial persuasion in the courtroom: The power of (a few) minor details. *Journal of Personality and Social Psychology, 56*(5), 669–679. doi:10.1037/0022-3514.56.5.669

Bell, R. A., Zahn, C. J., & Hopper, R. (1984). Disclaiming: A test of two competing views. *Communication Quarterly, 32*, 28–36. doi:10.1080/01463378409369528

Bennett, W. L. (1978). Storytelling in criminal trials: A model of social judgment. *The Quarterly Journal of Speech, 64*, 1–22. doi:10.1080/00335637809383408

Bennett, W. L., & Feldman, M. S. (1981). *Reconstructing reality in the courtroom: Justice and judgment in American culture*. New Brunswick, NJ: Rutgers University Press.

Benoit, W. L. (1991). A cognitive response analysis of source credibility. In B. Dervin & M. J. Voight (Eds.), *Progress in communication sciences* (Vol. 10, pp. 1–19). Norwood, NJ: Ablex.

Benoit, W. L., & Benoit, P. J. (2008). *Persuasive messages: The process of influence*. Malden, MA: Blackwell.

Benoit, W. L., & Kennedy, K. A. (1999). On reluctant testimony. *Communication Quarterly, 47*, 367–387.

Benson, P. L., Karabenic, S. A., & Lerner, R. A. (1976). Pretty pleases: The effects of physical attractiveness on race, sex, and receiving help. *Journal of Experimental Social Psychology, 12*, 409–415. doi:10.1016/0022-1031(76)90073-1

Benson, R. W. (1985). The end of legalese: The game is over. *Review of Law and Social Change*. New York University, 13, 519–573.

Berg, D. (2003/2006). *The trial lawyer: What it takes to win*. Chicago, IL: American Bar Association.

Bergin, A. E. (1962). The effect of dissonant persuasive communications upon changes in self-referring attitude. *Journal of Personality, 30*, 423–438. doi:10.1111/j.1467-6494.1962.tb02314.x

Berlo, D. K., Lemert, J. B., & Mertz, R. J. (1969). Dimensions for evaluating the acceptability of message sources. *Public Opinion Quarterly, 33*, 563–576. doi:10.1086/267745

Berman, R. A., & Verhoeven, L. (2002). Cross-linguistic perspectives on the development of text-production abilities: Speech and writing. *Written Language and Literacy, 5*, 1–43. doi:10.1075/wll.5.1.02ber

Bernstein, I. H., & Edelstein, B. A. (1971). Effects of some variations in auditory input upon visual choice reaction time. *Journal of Experimental Psychology, 87*, 241–247. doi:10.1037/h0030524

Berscheid, E. (1985). Interpersonal attraction. In G. Lindsey & E. Aronson (Eds.), *Handbook of social psychology* (3rd ed., Vol. 2, pp. 413–484). New York, NY: Random House.

Berscheid, E., & Walster, E. (1974). Physical attractiveness. In L. Berkowitz (Ed.), *Advances in experimental social psychology* (Vol. 7, pp. 157–215). New York, NY: Academic Press.

Bickman, L. (1971). The effect of social status on the honesty of others. *The Journal of Social Psychology, 85*, 87–92. doi:10.1080/00224545.1971.9918547

Bickman, L. (1974). The social power of a uniform. *Journal of Applied Social Psychology: Essays on body motion communication, 4*, 47–61.

Birdwhistell, R. L. (1955). Background to kinesics. *ETC: A Review of General Semantics, 13*, 10–18.

Birdwhistell, R. L. (1970). *Kinesics and context: Essays on body motion communication*. Philadelphia, PA: University of Pennsylvania Press.

Blankenship, J. (1962). A linguistic analysis of oral and written style. *The Quarterly Journal of Speech, 48*, 419–422. doi:10.1080/00335636209382571

Bliss, L. S. (2002). *Discourse impairments: Assessment and intervention applications*. Boston, MA: Allyn & Bacon.

Bloomer, R. H. (1961). Concepts of meaning and reading and spelling difficulty of words. *The Journal of Educational Research, 54*, 249–258.

Blount, H. P., & Johnson, R. E. (1971). Syntactic influences in the recall of sentences in prose. *Proceedings of the 79th Annual Convention of the American Psychological Association, 6*(Pt. 2), 529–530.

Blumenthal, A. L. (1966). Observation with self-embedded sentences. *Psychonomic Science, 6*, 453–454.

Boccaccini, M. T., Boothby, J. L., & Brodsky, S. L. (2002). Client-relations skills in effective lawyering: Attitudes of criminal defense attorneys and experienced clients. *Law & Psychology Review, 26*, 97–121.

Boccaccini, M. T., Boothby, J. L., & Brodsky, S. L. (2004). Development and effects of client trust in criminal defense attorneys: Preliminary examination of the congruence model of trust development. *Behavioral Sciences & the Law, 22*, 197–214. doi:10.1002/bsl.584

Boccaccini, M. T., & Brodsky, S. L. (2001). Characteristics of the ideal criminal defense attorney from the client's perspective: Empirical findings and implications for legal practice. *Law & Psychology Review, 25*, 81–117.

Bocchino, A. J. (2001). Ten touchstones for trial advocacy. *Temple Law Review, 74*, 1–26.

Bochner, S., & Insko, C. A. (1966). Communicator discrepancy, source credibility, and opinion change. *Journal of Personality and Social Psychology, 4*, 614–621. doi:10.1037/h0021192

Bock, D. G., & Saine, T. J. (1975). The impact of source of credibility, attitude valence, and task sensitivity on trait errors in speech evaluation. *Speech Monographs, 42*, 229–236. doi:10.1080/03637757509375898

Bodenhausen, G. V., Sheppard, L. A., & Kramer, G. P. (1994). Negative affect and social Judgment: The differential impact of anger and sadness. *European Journal of Social Psychology*, *24*, 45–62. doi:10.1002/ejsp.2420240104

Bolinger, D. L. (1989). *Intonation and its use: Melody in grammar and discourse*. Stanford, CA: Stanford University Press.

Bond, C. F. (2008). A few can catch a liar, sometimes: Comments on Ekman and O'Sullivan (1991), as well as Ekman, O'Sullivan, and Frank (1999). *Applied Cognitive Psychology*, *22*, 1298–1300. doi:10.1002/acp.1475

Bond, Jr., C. F. & DePaulo, B. M. (2006). Accuracy of deception judgments. *Personality and Social Psychology Review*, *10*, 214–234. doi:10.1207/s15327957pspr1003_2

Bond, Jr., C. F. & DePaulo, B. M. (2008a). Individual differences in judging deception: Accuracy and bias. *Psychological Bulletin*, *134*, 477–492. doi:10.1037/0033-2909. 134.4.477

Bond, Jr., C. F. & DePaulo, B. M. (2008b). Individual Differences in Judging Deception: Reply to O'Sullivan (2008) and Pigott and Wu (2008). *Psychological Bulletin*, *134*, 501–503. doi:10.1037/0033-2909.134.4.501

Bond, Jr., C. F. & Uysal, A. (2007). On lie detection "wizards". *Law and Human Behavior*, *31*, 109–115. doi:10.1007/s10979-006-9016-1

Bond, G. D. (2008). Deception detection expertise. *Law Human Behavior*, *32*, 339–351. doi:10.1007/s10979-007-9110-z

Bond, Z. S. (2005). Perception of intonation. In D. B. Pisoni & R. E. Remex (Eds.), *The handbook of speech perception* (pp. 236–263). Malden, MA: Blackwell.

Bond, Z. S., & Moore, T. J. (1994). A note on the acoustic-phonetic characteristics of inadvertently clear speech. *Speech Communication*, *14*, 325–337. doi:10.1016/0167-6393(94)90026-4

Borchers, G. (1936). An approach to the problem of oral style. *The Quarterly Journal of Speech*, *22*, 114–117. doi:10.1080/00335633609380170

Bornstein, B. H. (1999). The ecological validity of jury simulations: Is the jury still out? *Law and Human Behavior*, *23*, 75–91. doi:10.1023/A:1022326807441

Bornstein, B. H., Rung, L. M., & Miller, M. K. (2002). The effects of defendant remorse on mock juror decisions in a malpractice case. *Behavioral Sciences and the Law*, *20*, 393–409. doi:10.1002/bsl.496

Bourassa, D. C., & Besner, D. (1994). Beyond the articulatory loop: A semantic contribution to serial order recall of subspan lists. *Psychonomic Bulletin & Review*, *1*, 122–125. doi:10.3758/BF03200768

Bousfield, W. A., & Cohen, B. H. (1955). The occurrence of clustering the recall of randomly arranged words of different frequencies of usage. *Journal of General Psychology*, *52*, 83–95. doi:10.1080/00221309.1955.9918346

Bower, G. H., Black, J. H., & Turner, T. J. (1979). Scripts in memory for text. *Cognitive Psychology*, *11*, 177–220. doi:10.1016/0010-0285(79)90009-4

Bowers, J. W., & Phillips, W. A. (1967). A note on the generality of source-credibility scales. *Speech Monographs*, *34*, 185–186. doi:10.1080/03637756709375542

Bowers, W. J. (1996). The capital jury: Is it tilted toward death? *Judicature, 79,* 220–223.

Bradac, J. J., Courtright, J. A., Schmidt, G., & Davies, R. A. (1976). The effects of perceived status and linguistic diversity upon judgment of speaker attributes and message effectiveness. *Journal of Psychology: Interdisciplinary and Applied, 93,* 213–220. doi:10.1080/00223980.1976.9915815

Bradac, J. J., Davies, R. A., Courtright, J. A., Desmond, R. J., & Murdock, J. I. (1977). Richness of vocabulary: An attributional analysis. *Psychological Reports, 41,* 1131–1134.

Bradac, J. J., Desmond, R. J., & Murdock, J. I. (1977). Diversity and density: Lexically determined evaluative and informational consequences of linguistic complexity. *Communication Monographs, 44,* 273–283. doi:10.1080/03637757709390139

Bradac, J. J., Hemphill, M. R., & Tardy, C. H. (1981). Language style on trial: Effects of "powerful" and "powerless" speech upon judgments of victims and villains. *Western Journal of Speech Communication, 45,* 327–341.

Bradac, J. J., & Wisegarver, R. (1984). Ascribed status, lexical diversity, and accent: Determinants of perceived status, solidarity and control of speech style. *Journal of Language and Social Psychology, 3,* 239–255. doi:10.1177/0261927X8400300401

Bradlow, A. R., Kraus, N., & Hayes, E. (2003). Speaking clearly for learning impaired children: Sentence perception in noise. *Journal of Speech, Language, and Hearing Research, 46,* 80–97. doi:10.1044/1092-4388(2003/007)

Bradlow, A. R., Torretta, G. M., & Pisoni, D. B. (1996). Intelligibility of normal speech I: Global and fine-grained acoustic-phonetic talker characteristics. *Speech Communication, 20,* 255–272. doi:10.1016/S0167-6393(96)00063-5

Braithwaite, D. O., & Thompson, T. L. (2000). Disability and communication research: A productive past and a bright future. In D. O. Braithwaite & T. L. Thompson (Eds.), *Handbook of communication and people with disabilities: Research and application* (pp. 507–513). Mahwah, NJ: Erlbaum.

Bransford, J. D., & Johnson, M. D. (1972). Contextual prerequisites for understanding: Some investigations of comprehension and recall. *Journal of Verbal Learning & Verbal Behavior, 11,* 717–726. doi:10.1016/S0022-5371(72)80006-9

Brewer, M. (1979). In-group bias in the minimal intergroup situation: A cognitive-motivational analysis. *Psychological Bulletin, 86,* 307–324. doi:10.1037/0033-2909.86.2.307

Brewer, M. B., & Brown, R. J. (1998). Intergroup relations. In D. T. Gilbert & S. T. Fiske (Eds.), *The handbook of social psychology* (4th ed., Vol. 2, pp. 554–594). New York, NY: McGraw-Hill.

Brewer, M. B., & Gardner, W. L. (1996). Who is this "we"? Levels of collective identity and self-representations. *Journal of Personality and Social Psychology, 71,* 83–93. doi:10.1037/0022-3514.71.1.83

Brewer, T. W. (2005). The attorney–client relationship in capital cases and its impact on juror receptivity to mitigation evidence. *Justice Quarterly, 22,* 340–363. doi:10.1080/07418820500219169

Bridgeman, D. L., & Marlowe, D. (1979). Jury decision making: An empirical study based on actual felony trials. *Journal of Applied Psychology, 64,* 91–98. doi:10.1037/h0078046

Broadbent, D. E. (1967). Word frequency effect and response bias. *Psychological Review, 74,* 1–15. doi:10.1037/h0024206

Brock, T. C. (1965). Communicator-recipient similarity and decision change. *Journal of Personality and Social Psychology, 36,* 650–654. doi:10.1037/h0022081

Brock, T. C. (1967). Communication discrepancy and intent to persuade as determinants of counterargument production. *Journal of Experimental Social Psychology, 3,* 296–309. doi:10.1016/0022-1031(67)90031-5

Brockner, J., & Lloyd, K. (1986). Self-esteem and likability: Separating fact from fantasy. *Journal of Research in Personality, 20,* 496–508. doi:10.1016/0092-6566(86)90128-5

Brodsky, S. L., & Cannon, D. E. (2006). Ingratiation in the courtroom and in the voir dire process: When more is not better. *Law & Psychology Review, 30,* 103–117.

Brodsky, S. L., Griffin, M. P., & Cramer, R. J. (2010). The Witness Credibility Scale: An outcome measure for expert witness research. *Behavioral Sciences & the Law, 28,* 892–907. doi:10.1002/bsl.917

Brown, B. L. (1980). Effects of speech rate on personality attributions and competency evaluations. In H. Giles, W. P. Robinson, & P. M. Smith (Eds.), *Language: Social psychological perspectives* (pp. 293–300). Oxford, England: Pergamon Press.

Brown, G. D. A., & Hulme, C. (1995). Modeling item length effects in memory span: No rehearsal needed? *Journal of Memory and Language, 34,* 594–621. doi:10.1006/jmla.1995.1027

Brownlow, S., & Zebrowitz, L. A. (1990). Facial appearance, gender, and credibility in television commercials. *Journal of Nonverbal Behavior, 14,* 51–60. doi:10.1007/BF01006579

Bruneau, T. J. (1973). Communication silences: forms and functions. *Journal of Communication, 23,* 17–46. doi:10.1111/j.1460-2466.1973.tb00929.x

Bryant, J., Brown, D., Silberberg, A., & Elliott, S. (1981). Effects of humorous illustrations in college textbooks. *Human Communication Research, 8,* 43–57. doi:10.1111/j.1468-2958.1981.tb00655.x

Buchanan, R. W., Pryor, B., Taylor, K. P., & Strawn, D. U. (1978). Legal communication: An investigation of juror comprehension of pattern instructions. *Communication Quarterly, 26,* 31–35. doi:10.1080/01463377809369311

Bull, P. E. (1987). *Posture and gesture* (Vol. 16). Oxford, England: Pergamon Press.

Buller, D. B. (1987). Communication apprehension and reactions to proxemic violations. *Journal of Nonverbal Behavior, 11,* 13–25. doi:10.1007/BF00999603

Buller, D. B., & Aune, R. K. (1986). The effects of vocalics and nonverbal sensitivity on compliance. *Human Communication Research, 13,* 301–332. doi:10.1111/j.1468-2958.1988.tb00159.x

Buller, D. B., & Burgoon, J. K. (1986). The effects of vocalics and nonverbal sensitivity on compliance. *Human Communication Research, 13,* 126–144. doi:10.1111/j.1468-2958.1986.tb00098.x

Buller, D. B., LePoire, B. A., Aune, R. K., & Eloy, S. V. (1992). Social perceptions as mediators of the effect of speech rate similarity on compliance. *Human Communication Research, 19,* 286–311. doi:10.1111/j.1468-2958.1992.tb00303.x

Bunn, C. (1964). How lawyers use speech. *Communication Education, 13,* 6–9. doi:10.1080/03634526409377331

Burgoon, J. K. (1978). A communication model of personal space violations: Explication and an initial test. *Human Communication Research, 4,* 129–142. doi:10.1111/j.1468-2958.1978.tb00603.x

Burgoon, J. K. (1985). Nonverbal signals. In M. L. Knapp & G. R. Miller (Eds.), *Handbook of interpersonal communication* (pp. 344–390). Beverly Hills, CA: Sage.

Burgoon, J. K. (1991). Relational message interpretations of touch, conversational distance, and posture. *Journal of Nonverbal Behavior, 15,* 233–259. doi:10.1007/BF00986924

Burgoon, J. K. (1993). Interpersonal expectations, expectancy violations, and emotional communication. *Journal of Language and Social Psychology, 12,* 30–48. doi:10.1177/0261927X93121003

Burgoon, J. K. (1994). Nonverbal signals. In M. L. Knapp & G. R. Miller (Eds.), *Handbook of interpersonal communication* (2nd ed., pp. 344–390). Beverly Hills, CA: Sage.

Burgoon, J. K., & Bacue, A. (2003). Nonverbal communication skills. In B. R. Burleson & J. O. Greene (Eds.), *Handbook of communication and social interaction skills* (pp. 179–219). Mahwah, NJ: Erlbaum.

Burgoon, J. K., Birk, T., & Pfau, M. (1990). Nonverbal behaviors, persuasion, and credibility. *Human Communication Research, 17,* 140–169. doi:10.1111/j.1468-2958.1990.tb00229.x

Burgoon, J. K., Buller, D. B., Hale, J. L., & deTurck, M. A. (1984). Relational messages associated with nonverbal behaviors. *Human Communication Research, 10,* 351–378. doi:10.1111/j.1468-2958.1984.tb00023.x

Burgoon, J. K., Buller, D. B., & Woodall, W. G. (1996). *Nonverbal communication: The unspoken dialogue.* New York, NY: McGraw-Hill.

Burgoon, J. K., Coker, D. A., & Coker, R. A. (1986). Communicative effects of gaze behavior: A test of two contrasting explanations. *Human Communication Research, 12,* 495–524. doi:10.1111/j.1468-2958.1986.tb00089.x

Burgoon, J. K., & Dunbar, N. E. (2000). An interactionist perspective on dominance-submission: Interpersonal dominance as a dynamic, situationally contingent social skill. *Communication Monographs, 67,* 96–121. doi:10.1080/03637750009376497

Burgoon, J. K., Dunbar, N. E., & Segrin, C. (2002). Nonverbal Influence. In J. P. Dillard & M. Pfau (Eds.), *The persuasion handbook: Developments in theory and practice* (pp. 445–473). Thousand Oaks, CA: Sage.

Burgoon, J. K., Guerrero, L. K., & Floyd, K. (2010). *Nonverbal communication*. Boston, MA: Allyn & Bacon/Pearson.

Burgoon, J. K., & Hale, J. L. (1988). Nonverbal expectancy violations: Model elaboration and application to immediacy behaviors. *Communication Monographs, 55*, 58–79. doi:10.1080/03637758809376158

Burgoon, J. K., Johnson, M. L., & Koch, P. T. (1998). The nature and measurement of interpersonal dominance. *Communication Monographs, 65*, 308–335. doi:10.1080/03637759809376456

Burgoon, J. K., Manusov, V., Mineo, P., & Hale, J. L. (1985). Effects of eye gaze on hiring, credibility, attraction and relational message interpretation. *Journal of Nonverbal Behavior, 9*, 133–146. doi:10.1007/BF01000735

Burgoon, J. K., & Newton, D. A. (1991). Applying a social meaning model to relational messages of conversational involvement: Comparing participant and observer perspectives. *The Southern Communication Journal, 56*, 96–113.

Burke, K. (1961). Attitudes toward history. Boston, MA: Beacon. (Original work published 1937).

Burns, A. C., Biswas, A., & Babin, L. A. (1993). Operation of visual imagery as a mediator of advertising effects. *Journal of Advertising, 22*, 71–85.

Burns, R. P. (1999). *A theory of the trial*. Princeton, NJ: Princeton University Press.

Burrell, N. A., & Koper, R. J. (1998). Explicit and implicit conclusions in persuasive messages. In M. Allen & R. W. Preis (Eds.), *Persuasion: Advances through meta-analysis* (pp. 203–215). Cresskill, NJ: Hampton Press.

Bushman, B. J. (1984). Perceived symbols of authority and their influence on compliance. *Journal of Applied Social Psychology, 14*, 501–508. doi:10.1111/j.1559-1816.1984.tb02255.x

Bushman, B. J., & Baumeister, R. F. (1998). Threatened egotism, narcissism, self-esteem, and direct and displaced aggression: Does self-love or self-hate lead to violence? *Journal of Personality and Social Psychology, 75*, 219–229. doi:10.1037/0022-3514.75.1.219

Butler, S., & Roesel, K. (1989). The influence of dress on students' perceptions of teacher characteristics. *Clothing & Textiles Research Journal, 7*, 57–59. doi:10.1177/0887302X8900700309

Byrne, D. (1969). Attitudes and attraction. In L. Berkowitz (Ed.), *Advances in experimental social psychology* (Vol. 4, pp. 35–89). New York, NY: Academic Press.

Byrne, D. (1971). *The attraction paradigm*. New York, NY: Academic Press.

Byrne, D., Ervin, C. R., & Lamberth, J. (1970). Continuity between the experimental study of attraction and real-life computer dating. *Journal of Personality and Social Psychology, 16*, 157–165. doi:10.1037/h0029836

Byrne, D., Rasche, L., & Kelley, K. (1974). When "I like you" indicates disagreement: An experimental differentiation information and affect. *Journal of Research in Personality, 8*, 207–217. doi:10.1016/0092-6566(74)90032-4

Byrne, D., & Rhamey, R. (1965). Magnitude of positive and negative reinforcements as a determinant of attraction. *Journal of Personality and Social Psychology, 2,* 884–889. doi:10.1037/h0022656

Cacioppo, J. T., Marshall-Goodell, B., Tassinary, L., & Petty, R. E. (1992). Rudimentary determinants of attitudes: Classical conditioning is more effective when prior knowledge about the attitude stimulus is low than high. *Journal of Experimental Social Psychology, 28,* 207–233. doi:10.1016/0022-1031(92) 90053-M

Cacioppo, J. T., & Petty, R. E. (1979). Effects of message repetition and position on cognitive response, recall, and persuasion. *Journal of Personality and Social Psychology, 37,* 97–109. doi:10.1037/0022-3514.37.1.97

Cacioppo, J. T., & Petty, R. E. (1987). Stalking rudimentary processes of social influence: A psychophysiological approach. In M. P. Zanna, J. M. Olson, & C. P. Herman (Eds.), *Social influence: The Ontario symposium* (Vol. 5, pp. 41–74). Hillsdale, NJ: Erlbaum.

Cacioppo, J. T., & Petty, R. E. (1989). Effects of message repetition on argument processing recall, and persuasion. *Basic and Applied Social Psychology, 10,* 3–12. doi:10.1207/s15324834basp1001_2

Candiotti, S., & Dornin, R. (2007, August 14). Wife who killed preacher set free. *CNN.* Retrieved from http://www.cnn.com

Caplan, D., & Waters, G. S. (1994). Articulatory length and phonological similarity in span tasks: A reply to Baddeley and Andrade. *The Quarterly Journal of Experimental Psychology A, 47,* 1055–1062.

Caporael, L. R. (1981). The paralanguage of caregiving: Baby talk to the institutionalized aged. *Journal of Personality and Social Psychology, 40,* 876–884. doi:10.1037/ 0022-3514.40.5.876

Caporael, L. R., Lukaszewski, M. P., & Culbertson, G. H. (1983). Secondary baby talk: judgments by institutionalized elderly and their caregivers. *Journal of Personality and Social Psychology, 44,* 746–754. doi:10.1037/0022-3514.44.4.746

Carli, L. L. (1990). Gender, language, and influence. *Journal of Personality and Social Psychology, 59,* 941–951. doi:10.1037/0022-3514.59.5.941

Carnaghi, A., & Maass, A. (2007). In-group and out-group perspectives in the use of derogatory group labels. *Journal of Language and Social Psychology, 26,* 142–156. doi:10.1177/0261927X07300077

Carnaghi, A., Maass, A., Bianchi, M. B., Castelli, L., & Brentel, M. (2005). Gay or fag? On the cognitive and affective consequences of derogatory group labels. Manuscript submitted for publication. As reported in Carnaghi, A., & Maass, A. (2007). In-group and out-group perspectives in the use of derogatory group labels. *Journal of Language and Social Psychology, 26,* 142–156. doi:10.1177/ 0261927X07300077

Carroll, G., Giler, D., & Hill, W. (Producers) & Scott, R.(Director). (1979). *Alien* [Motion picture]. USA: Brandywine.

Carroll, J. C. (1958). Process and content in psycholinguistics. In R. A. Patton (Ed.), *Current trends in the description and analysis of behavior* (pp. 175–200). Pittsburgh, PA: University of Pittsburgh Press. doi:10.1037/11445-007

Cash, T. F., Dawson, K., Davis, P., Bowen, M., & Galumbeck, C. (1989). Effects of cosmetics use on the physical attractiveness and body image of American college women. *The Journal of Social Psychology, 129,* 349–355. doi:10.1080/00224545.1989.9712051

Caso, L., Maricchiolo, F., Bonaiuto, M., Vrij, A., & Mann, S. (2006). The impact of deception and suspicion on different hand movements. *Journal of Nonverbal Behavior, 30,* 1–19. doi:10.1007/s10919-005-0001-z

Casper, J. D. (1978). Having their day in court: Defendant evaluations of the fairness of their treatment. *Law & Society Review, 12,* 237–251. doi:10.2307/3053234

Caza, N., & Belleville, S. (1999). Semantic contribution to immediate serial recall using an unlimited set of items: Evidence for a multi-level capacity view of short-term memory. *International Journal of Psychology, 34,* 334–338. doi:10.1080/002075999399657

Cecil, J. S., Lind, E. A., & Bermant, G. (1987). *Jury services in lengthy civil trials.* Washington, DC: Federal Judicial Center.

Cermak, G., Schnorr, J., Buschke, H., & Atkinson, R. C. (1970). Recognition memory as influenced by differential attention to semantic and acoustic properties of words. *Psychonomic Science, 19,* 79–81.

Chafe, W., & Danielewicz, J. (1987). Properties of spoken and written language. Comprehending oral and written language. In R. Horowitz & S. J. Samuels (Eds.), *Comprehending oral and written language* (pp. 83–113). San Diego, CA: Academic Press.

Chafe, W. L. (1988). Linking intonation units in spoken English. In J. Haiman & S. A. Thompson (Eds.), *Clause combining in grammar and discourse* (pp. 1–27). Philadelphia, PA: Benjamins.

Chaiken, S. (1979). Communicator physical attractiveness and persuasion. *Journal of Personality and Social Psychology, 37,* 1387–1397. doi:10.1037/0022-3514.37.8.1387

Chaiken, S. (1980). Heuristic versus systematic information processing and the use of source versus message cues in persuasion. *Journal of Personality and Social Psychology, 39,* 752–766. doi:10.1037/0022-3514.39.5.752

Chaiken, S. (1986). Physical appearance and social influence. In C. P. Herman, M. P. Zanna, & E. T. Higgins (Eds.), *Physical appearance, stigma, and social behavior: The Ontario symposium* (Vol. 5, pp. 143–177). Hillsdale, NJ: Erlbaum.

Chaiken, S. (1987). The heuristic model of persuasion. In M. P. Zanna, J. M. Olsen, & C. P. Herman (Eds.), *Social influence: The Ontario symposium* (Vol. 5, pp. 3–39). Hillsdale, NJ: Erlbaum.

Chaiken, S., & Eagly, A. H. (1983). Communication modality as a determinant of persuasion: The role of communicator salience. *Journal of Personality and Social Psychology, 45,* 241–256. doi:10.1037/0022-3514.45.2.241

Chaiken, S., & Trope, Y. (1999). *Dual-process theories in social psychology*. New York, NY: Guilford Press.

Champagnol, R. (1971). Genetic evolution of the reading speed of words in relation to their frequency. *L'Année Psychologique, 71*, 407–416. doi:10.3406/psy.1971.27750

Chan, K. Y., & Vitevitch, M. S. (2009). The influence of the phonological neighborhood clustering-coefficient on spoken word recognition. *Journal of Experimental Psychology: Human Perception and Performance, 35*, 1934–1949. doi:10.1037/a0016902

Chang, C. (2009). Repetition variation strategies for narrative advertising. *Journal of Advertising, 38*, 51–66. doi:10.2753/JOA0091-3367380304

Chang, M.-J., & Gruner, C. R. (1981). Audience reaction to self-disparaging humor. *Southern Speech Communication Journal, 46*, 419–426.

Charrow, R., & Charrow, V. (1979). Making legal language understandable: A psycholinguistic study of jury instructions. *Columbia Law Review, 79*, 1306–1374. doi:10.2307/1121842

Chebat, J.-C., Filiatrault, P., Laroche, M., & Watson, C. (1988). Compensatory effects of cognitive characteristics of the source, the message, and the receiver upon attitude change. *The Journal of Psychology: Interdisciplinary and Applied, 122*, 609–621. doi:10.1080/00223980.1988.9915535

Cialdini, R. B. (1987). Compliance principles of compliance professionals: Psychologists of necessity. In M. P. Zanna, J. M. Olson, & C. P. Herman (Eds.), *Social influence: The Ontario symposium* (Vol. 5, pp. 165–184). Hillsdale, NJ: Erlbaum.

Cialdini, R. B. (1993). *Influence: Science and practice* (3rd ed.). New York, NY: Harper-Collins.

Cialdini, R. B., Borden, R. J., Thorne, A., Walker, M., Freeman, S., & Sloan, L. (1976). Basking in reflected glory: Three (football) field studies. *Journal of Personality and Social Psychology, 34*, 366–375. doi:10.1037/0022-3514.34.3.366

Clark, M. S., & Reis, H. T. (1988). Interpersonal processes in close relationships. *Annual Review of Psychology, 39*, 609–672. doi:10.1146/annurev.ps.39.020188.003141

Clemons, W. (1979, August 13). Murder most Texan; Blood will tell: The murder trials of T. Cullen Davis. *Newsweek*, 70.

Clopper, C. G., & Pisoni, D. B. (2005). Perception of dialect variation. In D. B. Pisoni & R. E. Remez (Eds.), *The handbook of speech perception* (pp. 312–337). Oxford, England: Blackwell. doi:10.1002/9780470757024.ch13

Cobin, M. (1962). Response to eye-contact. *The Quarterly Journal of Speech, 48*, 415–418. doi:10.1080/00335636209382570

Cochran, M. (1977a, August 23). [Associated Press report]. Retrieved from http://www.lexisnexis.com/

Cochran, M. (1977b, August 31). [Associated Press report]. Retrieved from http://www.lexisnexis.com/

Cohen, A. A., & Harrison, R. P. (1973). Intentionality in the use of hand illustrators in face-to-face communication situations. *Journal of Personality and Social Psychology, 28,* 276–279. doi:10.1037/h0035792

Cohen, G., & Faulkner, D. (1986). Does "elderspeak" work? The effect of intonation and stress on comprehension and recall of spoken discourse in old age. *Language & Communication, 6,* 91–98. doi:10.1016/0271-5309(86)90008-X

Cohen, H., Douaire, J., & Elsabbagh, M. (2001). The role of prosody in discourse processing. *Brain and Cognition, 46,* 73–82. doi:10.1016/S0278-2626(01)80038-5

Coker, D. A., & Burgoon, J. K. (1987). The nature of conversational involvement and nonverbal encoding patterns. *Human Communication Research, 13,* 463–494. doi:10.1111/j.1468-2958.1987.tb00115.x

Collins, R., Lincoln, R., & Frank, M. (2002). The effect of rapport in forensic interviewing. *Psychiatry, Psychology and Law, 9,* 69–78. doi:10.1375/pplt.2002.9.1.69

Collins, R. L., Taylor, S. E., Wood, J. V., & Thompson, S. C. (1988). The vividness effect: Elusive or illusory? *Journal of Experimental Social Psychology, 24,* 1–18. doi:10.1016/0022-1031(88)90041-8

Comadena, M. E. (1982). Accuracy in detecting deception: Intimate and friendship relationships. In M. Burgoon & N. E. Doran (Eds.), *Communication yearbook 6* (pp. 446–472). Beverly Hills, CA: Sage.

Compact Oxford English dictionary of current English (3rd Ed.). (2005). Oxford, England: Oxford University Press. Retrieved from http://www.askoxford.com

Conley, J. M., O'Barr, W. M., & Lind, E. A. (1979). The power of language: Presentational style in the courtroom. *Duke Law Journal, 1978,* 1375–1399.

Conrad, C. (1974). Context effects in sentence comprehension—a study of the subjective lexicon. *Memory & Cognition, 2,* 130–138. doi:10.3758/BF03197504

Cook, A., Arndt, J., & Lieberman, J. D. (2004). Firing back at the backfire effect: The influence of mortality salience and nullification beliefs on reactions to inadmissible evidence. *Law and Human Behavior, 28,* 389–410. doi:10.1023/B:LAHU.0000039332.21386.f4

Coovert, M. D., Reeder, G. D. (1989). Negativity effects in impression formation: The role of unit formation and schematic expectations. *Journal of Experimental Social Psychology, 26,* 49–62. doi:10.1016/0022-1031(90)90061-P

Costanzo, F. S., Markel, N. N., & Costanzo, P. R. (1969). Voice quality profile and perceived emotion. *Journal of Counseling Psychology, 16,* 267–270. doi:10.1037/h0027355

Couper-Kuhlen, E. (1993). *English speech rhythm. Form and function in everyday verbal interaction.* Philadelphia, PA: Benjamins.

Couper-Kuhlen, E. (1996). The prosody of repetition: On quoting and mimicry. In E. Couper-Kuhlen & M. Selting (Eds.), *Prosody in conversation: Interactional studies* (pp. 366–405). New York, NY: Cambridge University Press. doi:10.1017/CBO9780511597862.011

Couper-Kuhlen, E., & Selting, M. (1996). Towards an interactional perspective on prosody and a prosodic perspective on interaction. In E. Couper-Kuhlen (Ed.),

Prosody in conversation (pp. 11–56). New York, NY: Cambridge University Press. doi:10.1017/CBO9780511597862.003

Cowan, N. (1994). Mechanisms of verbal short-term memory. *Current Directions in Psychological Science, 3*, 185–189. doi:10.1111/1467-8721.ep10770705

Cox, C. L., & Glick, W. H. (1986). Resume evaluations and cosmetics sue: When more is not better. *Sex Roles, 14*, 51–58. doi:10.1007/BF00287847

Cox, R. M., Alexander, G. C., & Gilmore, C. (1987). Intelligibility of average talkers in typical listening environments. *The Journal of the Acoustical Society of America, 81*, 1598–1608. doi:10.1121/1.394512

Cronkhite, G., & Liska, J. (1976). A critique of factor analytic approaches to the study of credibility. *Communication Monographs, 43*, 91–107. doi:10.1080/03637757609375920

Cronkhite, G., & Liska, J. (1980). The judgment of communicator acceptability. In M. E. Roloff & G. R. Miller (Eds.), *Persuasion: New directions in theory and research* (pp. 101–139). Beverly Hills, CA: Sage.

Cruse, D. A. (1990). Language, meaning and sense: Semantics. In N. E. Collinge (Ed.), *An encyclopaedia of language* (pp. 139–172). London, England: Routledge.

Crystal, D. (2002). *The English language: A guided tour of the language* (2nd ed.). London, England: Penguin Books.

Curriden, M. (2009, March). Richard "Racehorse" Haynes. *ABA Journal*. Retrieved from http://www.abajournal.com/magazine/article/richard_racehorse_haynes

Cutler, A. (1994). Segmentation problems, rhythmic solutions. *Lingua, 92*, 81–104. doi:10.1016/0024-3841(94)90338-7

Cutler, A., & Butterfield, S. (1990). Durational cues to word boundaries in clear speech. *Speech Communication, 9*, 485–495. doi:10.1016/0167-6393(90) 90024-4

Daicoff, S. (1997). Lawyer, know thyself: A review of empirical research on attorney attributes bearing on professionalism. *American University Law Review, 46*, 1337–1427.

Daly, J. A., McCroskey, J. C., & Richmond, V. (1977). Relationship between vocal activity and perception of communicators in small group interaction. *Western Journal of Speech Communication, 41*, 175–187.

Danet, B. (1980). Language in the legal process. *Law & Society Review, 14*, 445–564. doi:10.2307/3053192

Danet, B., Hoffman, K. B., & Kermish, N. C. (1980). Obstacles to the study of lawyer–client interaction: The biography of a failure. *Law & Society Review, 14*, 905–922. doi:10.2307/3053213

Darley, J. M. & Pittman, T. S. (2003). The psychology of compensatory and retributive justice. *Personality and Social Psychology Review, 7*, 324–336. doi:10.1207/S15327957PSPR0704_05

Day, M. E. (1967). An eye-movement indicator of individual differences in the psychological organization of attentional processes and anxiety. *Journal of Psychology: Interdisciplinary and Applied, 66*, 51–62.

Defense superstar Johnnie Cochran dead at 67: Client list include O. J. Simpson, Michael Jackson. (2005). *MSNBC*. Retrieved from http://www.msnbc.msn.com/id/7330234/

Deffenbacher, K. A. (1980). Eyewitness accuracy and confidence: Can we infer anything about their relationship? *Law and Human Behavior, 4*, 243–260. doi:10.1007/BF01040617

Deighton, J. (1984). The interaction of advertising and evidence. *Journal of Consumer Research, 11*, 763–770. doi:10.1086/209012

de Klerk, V. (2003). The language of truth and reconciliation: Was it fair to all concerned? *Southern African Linguistics and Applied Language Studies, 21*, 1–14. doi:10.2989/16073610309486324

Delia, J. G. (1972). Dialects and the effects of stereotypes on interpersonal attraction and cognitive processes in impression formation. *The Quarterly Journal of Speech, 58*, 285–297. doi:10.1080/00335637209383125

Dellinger, K., & Williams, C. L. (1997). Make-up at work: Negotiating appearance rules in the workplace. *Gender & Society, 11*, 151–177. doi:10.1177/089124397011002002

DePaulo, B. M., & Bonvillian, J. D. (1978). The effect on language development of the special characteristics of speech addressed to children. *Journal of Psycholinguistic Research, 7*, 189–211. doi:10.1007/BF01067042

DePaulo, B. M., & Coleman, L. M. (1981). Evidence for the specialness of the "Baby Talk" register. *Language and Speech, 24*, 223–231.

DePaulo, B. M., & Coleman, L. M. (1986). Talking to children, foreigners, and retarded adults. *Journal of Personality and Social Psychology, 51*, 945–959. doi:10.1037/0022-3514.51.5.945

DePaulo, B. M., & Coleman, L. M. (1987). Verbal and nonverbal communication of warmth to children, foreigners, and retarded adults. *Journal of Nonverbal Behavior, 11*, 75–88. doi:10.1007/BF00990959

DePaulo, B. M., Lindsay, J. J., Malone, B. E., Muhlenbruck, L., Charlton, K., & Cooper, H. (2003). Cues to deception. *Psychological Bulletin, 129*, 74–118. doi:10.1037/0033-2909.129.1.74

Dermer, M., & Thiel, D. I. (1975). When beauty may fail. *Journal of Personality and Social Psychology, 31*, 1168–1176. doi:10.1037/h0077085

Devine, D. J., Clayton, L. D., Dunford, B. B., Seying, R., & Pryce, J. (2001). Jury decision making 45 years of empirical research on deliberating groups. *Psychology, Public Policy, and Law, 7*, 622–727. doi:10.1037/1076-8971.7.3.622

Dholakia, R. R. (1987). Source credibility effects: A test of behavioral persistence. *Advances in Consumer Research, 14*, 426–430.

Diamond, S. S. (1997). Illuminations and shadows from jury simulations. *Law and Human Behavior, 21*, 561–571. doi:10.1023/A:1024831908377

Dillard, J. P., & Pfau, M. (2002). *The persuasion handbook: developments in theory and practice*. Thousand Oaks, CA: Sage.

DiMaggio, P. (1991). The macro-micro dilemma in organizational research: Implications of the role system theory. In J. Huber (Ed.), *Macro-micro linkages in sociology* (pp. 76–98). Newbury Park, CA: Sage.

Dinerstein, R. D. (1990). Client-centered counseling: Reappraisal and refinement. *Arizona Law Review, 32,* 501–604.

Dion, K. K. (1986). Stereotyping based on physical attractiveness: Issues and conceptual perspectives. In C. P. Herman, M. P. Zanna, & E. T. Higgins (Eds.), *Physical appearance, stigma and social behaviour: The Ontario symposium* (Vol. 3, pp. 7–21). Hillsdale, NJ: Erlbaum.

Dion, K. K., Berscheid, E., & Walster, E. (1972). What is beautiful is good. *Journal of Personality and Social Psychology, 24,* 285–290. doi:10.1037/h0033731

Dixon, T. R., & Dixon, J. F. (1964). The impression value of verbs. *Journal of Verbal Learning & Verbal Behavior, 3,* 161–165. doi:10.1016/S0022-5371(64)80035-9

Dolnik, L., Case, T., & Williams, K. D. (2003). Stealing thunder as a courtroom tactic revisited: Processes and boundaries. *Law and Human Behavior, 27,* 267–287. doi:10.1023/A:1023431823661

Dooling, D. J., & Mullet, R. L. (1973). Locus of thematic effects in retention of prose. *Journal of Experimental Psychology, 97,* 404–406. doi:10.1037/h0034100

Dovidio, J. F., Brown, C. E., Keating, C. F., Heltman, K., & Ellyson, S. L. (1988). Power displays between women and men in discussions of gender-linked tasks: A multichannel study. *Journal of Personality and Social Psychology, 55,* 580–587. doi:10.1037/0022-3514.55.4.580

Dovidio, J. F., & Ellyson, S. L. (1982). Decoding visual dominance: Attributions of power based on the relative percentages of looking while speaking and looking while listening. *Social Psychology Quarterly, 45,* 106–113. doi:10.2307/3033933

Dovidio, J. F., & Ellyson, S. L. (1985). Patterns of visual dominance in humans. In S. L. Ellyson & J. F. Dovidio (Eds.), *Power, dominance, and nonverbal behavior* (pp. 129–149). New York, NY: Springer-Verlag.

Dovidio, J. F., Gaertner, S. L., Validzic, A., Matoka, A., Johnson, B., & Frazier, S. (1997). Extending the benefits of recategorization: Evaluations, self-disclosure, and helping. *Journal of Experimental Social Psychology, 33,* 401–420. doi:10.1006/jesp.1997.1327

Dovidio, J. F., Kawakami, K., Johnson, C., Johnson, B., & Howard, A. (1997). On the nature of prejudice: Automatic and controlled processes. *Journal of Experimental Social Psychology, 33,* 510–540. doi:10.1006/jesp.1997.1331

Downs, V. C., Kaid, L. L., & Ragan, S. (1990). The impact of argumentativeness and verbal aggression on communicator image: The exchange between George Bush and Dan Rather. *Western Journal of Speech Communication, 54,* 99–112.

Drachman, D., deCarufel, A., & Insko, C. A. (1978). The extra credit effect in interpersonal attraction. *Journal of Experimental Social Psychology, 14,* 458–465. doi:10.1016/0022-1031(78)90042-2

Dressler, J. (1992). Rethinking heat of passion: A defense in search of a rationale. *Journal of Criminal Law and Criminology, 73,* 421–470. doi:10.2307/1143104

Drew, P. (1985). Analyzing the use of language in courtroom interaction. In T. Van Dijk, *Handbook of discourse analysis, Vol. 3: Discourse and dialogue* (pp. 133–147). London, England: Academic Press.

Druckman, J. N. (2001). The implications of framing effects for citizen competence. *Political Behavior, 23,* 225–256. doi:10.1023/A:1015006907312

Dugosh, K. L., Paulus, P. B., Roland, E. J., & Yang, H.-C. (2000). Cognitive stimulation in brainstorming. *Journal of Personality and Social Psychology, 79,* 722–735. doi:10.1037/0022-3514.79.5.722

Dumas, J. E., Johnson, M., & Lynch, A. M. (2002). Likableness, familiarity, and frequency of 844 person-descriptive words. *Personality and Individual Differences, 32,* 523–531. doi:10.1016/S0191-8869(01)00054-X

Duncan, C. P. (1973). Storage and retrieval of low frequency words. *Memory & Cognition, 1,* 129–132. doi:10.3758/BF03198081

Eagly, A. H., Ashmore, R. D., Makhijani, M. G., & Longo, L. C. (1991). What is beautiful is good, but . . . : A meta-analytic review of research on the physical attractiveness stereotype. *Psychological Bulletin, 110,* 109–128. doi:10.1037/0033-2909.110.1.109

Eagly, A. H., & Chaiken, S. (1975). An attribution analysis of the effect of communicator characteristics on opinion change: The case of communicator attractiveness. *Journal of Personality and Social Psychology, 32,* 136–144. doi:10.1037/h0076850

Eagly, A. H., & Chaiken, S. (1984). Cognitive theories of persuasion. In L. Berkowitz (Ed.), *Advances in experimental social psychology* (Vol. 17, pp. 267–359). New York, NY: Academic Press.

Eagly, A. H., Wood, W., & Chaiken, S. (1978). Causal inferences about communicators and their effect on opinion change. *Journal of Personality and Social Psychology, 36,* 424–435. doi:10.1037/0022-3514.36.4.424

Eagly, A. H., Wood, W., & Chaiken, S. (1981). An attribution analysis of persuasion. In J. H. Harvey, W. Ickes, & R. F. Kidd (Eds.), *New directions in attribution research* (Vol. 3, pp. 37–62). Hillsdale, NJ: Erlbaum.

Eakins, B. W., & Eakins, R. G. (1978). *Sex differences in communication.* Boston, MA: Houghton Mifflin.

Easton, S. D. (1998). *How to win jury trials: Building credibility with judges and jurors.* Philadelphia, PA: ALI-ABA.

Eibl-Eibesfeldt, I. (1972). Similarities and differences between cultures in expressive movement. In R. A. Hinde (Ed.), *Non-verbal communication* (pp. 297–312). Cambridge, England: Cambridge University Press.

Einhorn, H. J., & Hogarth, R. M. (1978a). Confidence in judgment: Persistence of the illusion of validity. *Psychological Review, 85,* 395–416. doi:10.1037/0033-295X.85.5.395

Einhorn, H. J., & Hogarth, R. M. (1978b). Prediction, diagnosis, and causal thinking in forecasting. *Journal of Forecasting, 1,* 23–36.

Ekman, P. (1964). Body position, facial expression, and verbal behavior during interviews. *The Journal of Abnormal and Social Psychology, 68,* 295–301. doi:10.1037/h0040225

Ekman, P. (1965). Differential communication of affect by head and body cues. *Journal of Personality and Social Psychology, 2,* 726–735. doi:10.1037/h0022736

Ekman, P., & Friesen, W. V. (1967). Head and body cues in the judgment of emotion: A reformulation. *Perceptual and Motor Skills, 24,* 711–724.

Ekman, P., & Friesen, W. V. (1969). The repertoire of nonverbal behavior: Categories, origins, usage, and coding. *Semiotica, 1,* 49–98.

Ekman, P. & Friesen W. V. (1974). Detecting deception from the body or face. *Journal of Personality and Social Psychology, 29,* 288–298.

Ekman, P., Friesen, W. V., & Ellsworth, P. (1972). *Emotion in the human face: Guidelines for research and as an integration of findings.* New York, NY: Pergamon Press.

Ekman, P., O'Sullivan, M., & Frank, M. G. (1999). A few can catch a liar. *Psychological Science, 10,* 263–266. doi:10.1111/1467-9280.00147

Eldridge, F. M. (1986). An advocate's use of language. In D. L. Rumsey (Ed.), *Master advocates' handbook* (pp. 15–16). St. Paul, MN: National Institute for Trial Advocacy.

Ellsworth, P., & Carlsmith, J. M. (1973). Eye contact and gaze aversion in an aggressive encounter. *Journal of Personality and Social Psychology, 28,* 280–292. doi:10.1037/h0035779

Ellsworth, P., & Ross, L. (1975). Intimacy in response to direct gaze. *Journal of Experimental Social Psychology, 11,* 592–613. doi:10.1016/0022-1031(75)90010-4

Ellyson, S. L., Dovidio, J. F., Corson, R. L., & Vinicur, D. L. (1980). Visual dominance behavior in female dyads: Situational and personality factors. *Social Psychology Quarterly, 43,* 328–336. doi:10.2307/3033735

Elwork, A., Alfini, J. J., & Sales, B. D. (1982). Toward understandable jury instructions. *Judicature, 65,* 432–443.

Elwork, A., Sales, B., & Alfini, J. (1977). Juridic decisions: In Ignorance of the law or in light of it? *Law and Human Behavior, 1,* 163–189. doi:10.1007/BF01053437

Elwork, A., Sales, B. D., & Alfini, J. (1982). *Making jury instructions understandable.* Charlottesville, VA: Michie.

Emswiller, T., Deaux, K., & Willits, J. E. (1971). Similarity, sex, and requests for small favors. *Journal of Applied Social Psychology, 1,* 284–291. doi:10.1111/j.1559-1816.1971.tb00367.x

English, P. W., & Sales, B. D. (2005). *More than the law: Behavioral and social facts in legal decision making.* Washington, DC: American Psychological Association. doi: 10.1037/11163-000

Enkvist, N. E. (1964). On defining style. In J. W. Spencer (Ed.), *Linguistics and style* (pp. 3–56). London, England: Oxford University Press.

Entman, R. M. (1993). Framing: Toward clarification of a fractured paradigm. *The Journal of Communication, 43,* 51–58. doi:10.1111/j.1460-2466.1993.tb01304.x

Entman, R. M. (2004). *Projections of power: Framing news, public opinion, and U.S. foreign policy*. Chicago, IL: University of Chicago Press.

Entman, R. M. (2007). Framing bias: Media in the distribution of power. *Journal of Communication, 57*, 163–173. doi:10.1111/j.1460-2466.2006.00336.x

Entman, R. M., & Rojecki, A. (2000). *The black image in the white mind: Media and race in America*. Chicago, IL: University of Chicago Press.

Erickson, B., Lind, E. A., Johnson, B., & O'Barr, W. (1978). Speech style and impression formation in a court setting: The effects of "powerful" and "powerless" speech. *Journal of Experimental Psychology, 14*, 266–279. doi:10.1016/0022-1031(78)90015-X

Eriksen, C. W., Pollack, M. D., & Montague, W. E. (1970). Implicit speech: Mechanism in perceptual encoding? *Journal of Experimental Psychology, 84*, 502–507. doi:10.1037/h0029274

Ernest, R. C., & Cooper, R. E. (1974). "Hey mister, do you have any change?": Two real world studies of proxemic effects on compliance with a mundane request. *Personality and Social Psychology Bulletin, 1*, 158–159. doi:10.1177/014616727400100154

Evans, F. B. (1963). Selling a dyadic relationship: A new approach. *American Behavioral Scientist, 6*, 76–79.

Exline, R. V. (1985). Multichannel transmission of nonverbal behavior and the perception of powerful men: The presidential debates of 1976. In S. L. Ellyson & J. F. Dovidio (Eds.), *Power, dominance, and nonverbal behavior* (pp. 183–206). New York, NY: Springer-Verlag.

Exline, R. V., Thibaut, J., Brannon, C., & Gumpert, P. (1961). Visual interaction in relation to Machiavellianism and an unethical act. *American Psychologist, 16*, 396.

Falcione, R. L. (1974). The factor structure of source credibility scales for immediate superiors in the organizational context. *Central States Speech Journal, 25*, 63–66.

Feigenson, N. R. (1997). Sympathy and legal judgment: A psychological analysis. *Tennessee Law Review, 65*, 1–78.

Feigenson, N. R., & Park, J. (2006). Emotions and attributions of legal responsibility and blame: A research review. *Law and Human Behavior, 30*, 143–161. doi:10.1007/s10979-006-9026-z

Feingold, A. (1992). Good-looking people are not what we think. *Psychological Bulletin, 111*, 304–341. doi:10.1037/0033-2909.111.2.304

Feldman, S., & Wilson, K. (1981). The value of interpersonal skills in lawyering. *Law and Human Behavior, 5*, 311–324. doi:10.1007/BF01044946

Ferguson, C. A. (1964). Baby talk in six languages. *American Anthropologist, 66*, 103–114. doi:10.1525/aa.1964.66.suppl_3.02a00060

Ferguson, C. A. (1977). Baby talk as a simplified register. In C. E. Snow & C. A. Ferguson (Eds.), *Talking to children* (pp. 209–235). Cambridge, England: Cambridge University Press.

Ferguson, C. A. (1981). "Foreigner talk" as the name of a simplified register. *International Journal of the Sociology of Language*, 1981, 9–18. doi:10.1515/ijsl.1981.28.9

Ferrand, L., & New, B. (2003). Syllabic length effects in visual word recognition and naming. *Acta Psychologica*, *113*, 167–183. doi:10.1016/S0001-6918(03)00031-3

Fiedler, K., Semin, G. R., & Koppetsch, C. (1991). Language use and attributional biases in close personal relationships. *Personality and Social Psychology Bulletin*, *17*, 147–155. doi:10.1177/014616729101700205

Fine, R. A. (1998). *The "how-to-win" trial manual: Winning trial advocacy in a nutshell*. Yonkers, NY: Juris.

Fink, B., Grammer, K., & Thornhill, R. (2001). Human (Homo sapiens) facial attractiveness in relation to skin texture and color. *Journal of Comparative Psychology*, *115*, 92–99. doi:10.1037/0735-7036.115.1.92

Finkel, N. J. (1995). *Commonsense justice: Jurors' notions of the law*. Cambridge, MA: Harvard University Press.

Finkel, N. J. (1996). Culpability and commonsense justice: Lessons learned betwixt murder and madness. *Notre Dame Journal of Law, Ethics & Public Policy*, *10*, 11–64.

Finkel, N. J. (1997). Commonsense justice, psychology, and the law: Prototypes that are common, senseful, and not. *Psychology, Public Policy, and Law*, *3*, 461–489. doi:10.1037/1076-8971.3.2-3.461

Finkel, N. J., & Groscup, J. L. (1997). Crime prototypes, objective versus subjective culpability, and a commonsense balance. *Law and Human Behavior*, *21*, 209–230. doi:10.1023/A:1024830413404

Fiske, S. T., Harris, L. T., & Cuddy, A. J. C. (2004, November 26). Why ordinary people torture enemy prisoners. *Science*, *306*, 1482–1483. doi:10.1126/science.1103788

Fiske, S. T., & Taylor, S. E. (1984). *Social cognition*. Reading, MA: Addison-Wesley.

Fiske, S. T., & Taylor, S. E. (1991). *Social cognition* (2nd ed.). New York, NY: McGraw-Hill.

Fleming, M. A., & Petty, R. E. (2000). Identity and persuasion: An elaboration likelihood approach. In D. J. Terry & M. A. Hogg (Eds.), *Attitudes, behavior, and social context: The role of norms and group membership* (pp. 171–199). Mahwah, NJ: Erlbaum.

Flemming, R. B. (1986). Client games: Defense attorney perspectives on their relations with criminal clients. *Law & Social Inquiry*, *11*, 253–277. doi:10.1111/j.1747-4469.1986.tb00241.x

Flesch, R. (1950). Measuring the level of abstraction. *Journal of Applied Psychology*, *34*, 384–390. doi:10.1037/h0058980

Flesch, R., & Lass, A. H. (1963). *A new guide to better writing*. New York, NY: Popular Library.

Fleshler, H., Ilardo, J., & Demoretcky, J. (1974). The influence of field dependence, speaker credibility set, and message documentation on evaluations of speaker and message credibility. *The Southern Communication Journal*, *39*, 389–402.

Fodor, J., & Garrett, M. (1967). Some syntactic determinants of sentential complexity. *Perception & Psychophysics, 2*, 289–296. doi:10.3758/BF03211044

Folkes, V. S., & Sears, D. O. (1977). Does everybody like a liker? *Journal of Experimental and Social Psychology, I*, 505–519. doi:10.1016/0022-1031(77)90050-6

Fonagy, I. (1978). A new method of investigating the perception of prosodic features. *Language and Speech, 21*, 34–49.

Fontham, M. (2002). *Trial technique and evidence*. Danvers, MA: LexisNexis.

Forgas, J. P. (1995). Mood and judgment: The affect infusion model (AIM). *Psychological Bulletin, 117*, 39–66. doi:10.1037/0033-2909.117.1.39

Forgas, J. P., O'Connor, K., & Morris, S. L. (1983). Smile and punishment: The effects of facial expression on responsibility attribution by groups and individuals. *Personality and Social Psychology Bulletin, 9*, 587–596. doi:10.1177/0146167283094008

Forster, K. I. (1966). Left-to-right processes in the construction of sentences. *Journal of Verbal Learning & Verbal Behavior, 5*, 285–291. doi:10.1016/S0022-5371(66)80032-4

Forster, K. I., & Chambers, S. M. (1973). Lexical access and naming time. *Journal of Verbal Learning & Verbal Behavior, 12*, 627–635. doi:10.1016/S0022-5371(73)80042-8

Forster, K. I., & Ryder, L. A. (1971). Perceiving the structure and meaning of sentences. *Journal of Verbal Learning & Verbal Behavior, 10*, 285–296. doi:10.1016/S0022-5371(71)80056-7

Forston, R. F. (1970). Judge's instructions: A quantitative analysis of jurors' listening comprehension. *Today's Speech, 18*, 34–38.

Fowler, C. A., & Galantucci, B. (2005). The relation of speech perception and speech production. In D. B. Pisoni & R. E. Remez (Eds.), *The handbook of speech perception* (pp. 632–652). Malden, MA: Blackwell. doi:10.1002/9780470757024.ch26

Frank, J., & Applegate, B. K. (1998). Assessing juror understanding of capital-sentencing instructions. *Crime & Delinquency, 44*, 412–433. doi:10.1177/0011128798044003005

Frauenfelder, U. H., Baayen, R. H., & Hellwig, F. M. (1993). Neighborhood density and frequency across languages and modalities. *Journal of Memory and Language, 32*, 781–804. doi:10.1006/jmla.1993.1039

Freedle, R., & Craun, M. (1970). Observations with self-embedded sentences using written aids. *Perception & Psychophysics, 7*, 247–249. doi:10.3758/BF03209371

Freedman, R. (1972). The analysis of movement behaviour during the clinical interview. In A. W. Siegman & B. Pope (Eds.), *Studies in dyadic communication* (pp. 153–175). New York, NY: Pergamon Press.

Freeman, J. B., & Ambady, N. (2011). A dynamic interactive theory of person construal. *Psychological Review, 118*, 247–279. doi:10.1037/a0022327

Frick, R. W. (1985). Communicating emotion: the role of prosodic features. *Psychological Bulletin, 97*, 412–429. doi:10.1037/0033-2909.97.3.412

Friedman, H. S. (1976). Effects of self-esteem and expected duration of interaction on liking for a highly rewarding partner. *Journal of Personality and Social Psychology, 33*, 686–690. doi:10.1037/0022-3514.33.6.686

Friedman, H. S., Riggio, R. E., & Casella, D. F. (1988). Non-verbal skill, personal charisma, and initial attraction. *Personality and Social Psychology Bulletin, 14*, 203–211. doi:10.1177/0146167288141020

Fry, D. B. (1958). Experiments in the perception of stress. *Language and Speech, 1*, 126–152.

Gaelick, L. Bodenhausen, G. V., & Wyer, R. S. (1985). Emotional communication in close relationships. *Journal of Personality and Social Psychology, 49*, 1246–1265. doi:10.1037/0022-3514.49.5.1246

Galambos, J. A., & Black, J. B. (1985). Using knowledge of activities to understand and answer questions. In A. C. Graesser & J. B. Black (Eds.), *The psychology of questions* (pp. 157–189). Hillsdale, NJ: Erlbaum.

Gaunt, R., Leyens, J.-P., Demoulin, S. (2002). Intergroup relations and the attribution of emotions: control over memory for secondary emotions associated with the ingroup and outgroup. *Journal of Experimental Social Psychology, 38*, 508–514. doi:10.1016/S0022-1031(02)00014-8

Gernsbacher, M. A. (1984). Resolving 20 years of inconsistent interactions between lexical familiarity and orthography, concreteness, and polysemy. *Journal of Experimental Psychology: General, 113*, 256–281. doi:10.1037/0096-3445.113.2.256

Gerver, D. (1969). Effects of grammaticalness, presentation rate, and message length on auditory short-term memory. *The Quarterly Journal of Experimental Psychology, 21*, 203–208. doi:10.1080/14640746908400214

Gewirtz, P. (1996). Victims and voyeurs: two narrative problems at the criminal trial. In P. Brooks & P. Gewirtz (Eds.), *Law's stories: Narrative and rhetoric in the law* (pp. 135–160). New Haven, CT: Yale University Press.

Gibson, J. W., Gruner, C. R., Kibler, R. J., & Kelly, F. J. (1966). A quantitative examination of differences and similarities in written and spoken messages. *Speech Monographs, 33*, 444–451. doi:10.1080/03637756609375510

Gick, M. L., & Holyoak, K. J. (1980). Analogical problem solving. *Cognitive Psychology, 12*, 306–355. doi:10.1016/0010-0285(80)90013-4

Giffin, K., & Ehrlich, L. (1963). Attitudinal effects of a group discussion on proposed change in company policy. *Speech Monographs, 30*, 377–379. doi:10.1080/03637756309375385

Gifford, R. (1982). Projected interpersonal distance and orientation choices: Personality, sex, and social situation. *Social Psychology Quarterly, 45*, 145–152. doi:10.2307/3033647

Gilden, D. L. (2001). Cognitive emissions of 1/f noise. *Psychological Review, 108*, 33–56. doi:10.1037/0033-295X.108.1.33

Giles, H. (1971). Patterns of evaluations to RP, South Welsh, and Somerset accented speech. *The British Journal of Social & Clinical Psychology, 10*, 280–281. doi:10.1111/j.2044-8260.1971.tb00748.x

Giles, H., & Chavasse, W. (1975). Communication length as a function of dress style and social status. *Perceptual and Motor Skills, 40,* 961–962.

Giles, H., & Smith, P. M. (1979). Accommodation theory: Optimal levels of convergence. In H. Giles & R. N. St. Clair (Eds.), *Language and social psychology* (pp. 45–65). Baltimore, MD: University Park Press.

Giles, H., & Street, R. L., Jr. (1985). Communication characteristics and behavior. In M. L. Knapp & G. R. Miller (Eds.), *Handbook of interpersonal communication* (pp. 205–261). Beverly Hills, CA: Sage.

Gjerdingen, D. K., Simpson, D. E., & Titus, S. L. (1987). Patients' and physicians' attitudes regarding the physician's professional appearance. *Archives of Internal Medicine, 147,* 1209–1212. doi:10.1001/archinte.147.7.1209

Glanzer, M., & Bowles, N. (1976). Analysis of the word-frequency effect in recognition memory. *Journal of Experimental Psychology: Human Learning and Memory, 2,* 21–31. doi:10.1037/0278-7393.2.1.21

Glanzer, M., & Ehrenreich, S. L. (1979). Structure and search of the internal lexicon. *Journal of Verbal Learning & Verbal Behavior, 18,* 381–398. doi:10.1016/S0022-5371(79)90210-X

Glasman, L. R., & Albarracin, D. (2006). Forming attitudes that predict future behavior: A meta-analysis of the attitude–behavior relation. *Psychological Bulletin, 132,* 778–822. doi:10.1037/0033-2909.132.5.778

Gleason, J. B., & Weintraub, S. (1978). Input language and the acquisition of communicative competence. In K. Nelson (Ed.), *Children's language* (Vol. 1, pp. 163–210). New York, NY: Gardner Press.

Glick, P., DeMorest, J. A., & Hotze, C. (1988). Keeping your distance: Group membership, personal space, and requests for small favors. *Journal of Applied Social Psychology, 18,* 315–330. doi:10.1111/j.1559-1816.1988.tb00019.x

Goethals, G. R., & Nelson, R. E. (1973). Similarity in the influence process: The belief–value distinction. *Journal of Personality and Social Psychology, 25,* 117–122. doi:10.1037/h0034266

Goffman, E. (1974). *Frame analysis: An essay on the organization of experience.* Cambridge, MA: Harvard University Press.

Goldman, S. R. (1985). Inferential reasoning in and about narrative texts. In A. C. Graesser & J. B. Black (Eds.), *The psychology of questions* (pp. 247–276). Hillsdale, NJ: Erlbaum.

Goldman-Eisler, F., & Cohen, M. (1971). Symmetry of clauses and the psychological significance of left branching. *Language and Speech, 14,* 109–114.

Goldswig, S. R., & Cody, M. J. (1990). Legal communication: An introduction to rhetorical and communication theory perspectives. In D. O'Hair & G. L. Kreps (Eds.), *Applied communication theory and research* (pp. 245–267). Hillsdale, NJ: Erlbaum.

Goodpaster, G. (1983). The trial for life: Effective assistance of counsel in death penalty cases. *New York University Law Review, 58,* 299–362.

Gordon, B. (1983). Lexical access and lexical decision: Mechanisms of frequency sensitivity. *Journal of Verbal Learning & Verbal Behavior, 22*, 24–44. doi:10.1016/S0022-5371(83)80004-8

Gorman, A. M. (1961). Recognition memory of nouns as function of abstractness and frequency. *Journal of Experimental Psychology, 61*, 23–29. doi:10.1037/h0040561

Gorney, C. (1978, September 24). More blood and money; The Texas tales—more blood, more money; The Texas tale of murder and millions, of the platinum blond, and the lawyer called "Racehorse." *The Washington Post*. Retrieved from http://www.lexisnexis.com/

Gough, P. B. (1966). The verification of sentences: The effect of delay on evidence and sentence length. *Journal of Verbal Learning & Verbal Behavior, 5*, 492–496. doi:10.1016/S0022-5371(66)80067-1

Graesser, A. C. (1981). *Prose comprehension beyond the word*. New York, NY: Springer-Verlag.

Graesser, A. C., & Clark, L. F. (1985). *The structures and procedures of implicit knowledge*. Norwood, NJ: Ablex.

Graesser, A. C., & Murachver, T. (1985). Symbolic procedures of question answering. In A. C. Graesser & J. B. Black (Eds.), *The psychology of questions* (pp. 15–88). Hillsdale, NJ: Erlbaum.

Graesser, A. C., Olde, B., & Klettke, B. (2002). How does the mind construct and represent stories? In M. C. Green, J. J. Strange, & T. C. Brock (Eds.), *Narrative impact: Social and cognitive foundations* (pp. 229–262). Mahwah, NJ: Erlbaum.

Graham, J. A., & Argyle, M. (1975). A crosscultural study of the communication of extraverbal meaning by gestures. *International Journal of Psychology, 10*, 57–67. doi:10.1080/00207597508247319

Grahe, J. E., & Bernieri, F. J. (2002). Self-awareness of judgment policies of rapport. *Personality and Social Psychology Bulletin, 28*, 1407–1418. doi:10.1177/014616702236872

Grant, C. A., & Gomez, M. L. (2001). *Campus and classroom: Making schooling multicultural*. Upper Saddle River, NJ: Merrill/Prentice.

Green, M.C. (2004). Transportation into narrative worlds: The role of prior knowledge and perceived realism. *Discourse Processes, 38*, 247–266. doi:10.1207/s15326950dp3802_5

Green, M. C., & Brock, T. C. (2000). The role of transportation in the persuasiveness of public narratives. *Journal of Personality and Social Psychology, 79*, 701–721. doi:10.1037/0022-3514.79.5.701

Green, M. C., & Brock, T. C. (2002). In the mind's eye: Imagery and transportation into narrative worlds. In M. C. Green, J. J. Strange, & T. C. Brock (Eds.), *Narrative impact: Social and cognitive foundations* (pp. 315–341). Mahwah, NJ: Erlbaum.

Green, M. C., Butler, D., & Britt, L. (2003). [Effect of character and reader similarity on transportation into narrative worlds]. Unpublished raw data. As reported in

Green, M. C. (2005). Transportation into narrative worlds: The role of prior knowledge and perceived realism. *Discourse Processes, 28*, 247–266.

Green, M. C., Kass, S., Carrey, J., Herzig, B., Feeney, R., & Sabini, J. (2008). Transportation across media: Repeated exposure to print and film. *Media Psychology, 11*, 512–539. doi:10.1080/15213260802492000

Greenberg, J. H., & Jenkins, J. J. (1967). Studies in the psychological correlates of the sound system of American English. In L. A. Jacobovits & M. S. Miron (Eds.), *Readings in the psychology of language* (pp. 186–200). Englewood Cliffs, NJ: Prentice Hall.

Greene, J. M. (1970). The semantic function of negatives and passives. *British Journal of Psychology, 61*, 17–22. doi:10.1111/j.2044-8295.1970.tb02797.x

Greenwald, A. G., Poehlman, T. A., Uhlmann, E. L., & Banaji, M. R. (2009). Understanding and using the Implicit Association Test: III. Meta-analysis of predictive validity. *Journal of Personality and Social Psychology, 97*, 17–41. doi:10.1037/a0015575

Gribben, M. (n.d.). T. Cullen Davis: The best justice money can buy. *TruTV Crime Library*. Retrieved from http://www.trutv.com/library/crime/notorious_murders/not_guilty/t_cullen_davis/index.html

Griffin, D., & Tversky, A. (1992). The weighing of evidence and the determinants of confidence. *Cognitive Psychology, 24*, 411–435. doi:10.1016/0010-0285(92)90013-R

Grimshaw, J. (1977). Complement selection and the lexicon. *Linguistic Inquiry, 10*, 279–326.

Gromet, D. M., & Darley, J. M. (2009). Retributive and restorative justice: The importance of crimes severity and shared identity on people's justice responses. *Australian Journal of Psychology, 61*, 50–57. doi:10.1080/00049530802607662

Groscup, J., & Tallon, J. (2009). Theoretical models of jury decision-making. In J. Lieberman & D. Krauss (Eds.), *Jury psychology: Social aspects of trial processes: Psychology in the courtroom* (Vol. 1, pp. 41–65). Burlington, VT: Ashgate.

Gruner, C. R. (1967). Effect of humor on speaker ethos and audience information gain. *Journal of Communication, 17*, 228–233. doi:10.1111/j.1460-2466.1967.tb01181.x

Gruner, C. R. (1970). The effect of humor in dull and interesting informative speeches. *Central States Speech Journal, 21*, 160–166.

Gruner, C. R., & Lampton, W. E. (1972). Effects of including humorous material in a persuasive sermon. *Southern Speech Communication Journal, 38*, 188–196.

Guerrero, L. K., Andersen, P. A., & Afifi, W. A. (2011). *Close encounters: Communication in relationships*. Thousand Oaks, CA: Sage.

Guerrero, L. K., & Floyd, K. (2006). *Nonverbal communication in close relationships*. Mahwah, NJ: Erlbaum.

Gustafsson, M. (1975). *Some syntactic properties of English law language*. Turku, Finland: University of Turku, Dept. of English.

Hall, E. T. (1959). *The silent language*. Garden City, NY: Doubleday.

Hall, J. A. (1980). Voice tone and persuasion. *Journal of Personality and Social Psychology, 38*, 924–934. doi:10.1037/0022-3514.38.6.924

Hamilton, H. W., & Deese, J. (1971). Comprehensibility and subject-verb relation in complex sentences. *Journal of Verbal Learning & Verbal Behavior, 10*, 163–170. doi:10.1016/S0022-5371(71)80008-7

Hamilton, M. A., & Hunter, J. E. (1998). The effect of language intensity on receiver evaluations of message, source, and topic. In M. Allen & R. W. Preiss (Eds.), *Persuasion: Advances through meta-analysis* (pp. 99–138). Cresskill, NJ: Hampton.

Hamilton, M. A., Hunter, J. E., & Burgoon, M. (1990). An empirical test of an axiomatic model of the relationship between language intensity and persuasion. *Journal of Language and Social Psychology, 9*, 235–255. doi:10.1177/0261927X9094002

Hammond, K. J. (1989). *Case-based planning: Viewing planning as a memory task*. Boston, MA: Academic Press.

Haney, C., & Lynch, M. (1994). Comprehending life and death matters: A preliminary study of California's capital penalty instructions. *Law and Human Behavior, 18*, 411–436. doi:10.1007/BF01499048

Hanley, R. F. (1986). The importance of being yourself. In D. L. Rumsey (Ed.), *Master advocates' handbook* (pp. 9–12). St. Paul, MN: National Institute for Trial Advocacy.

Hans, V. P. (1990). Law and the media: An overview and introduction. *Law and Human Behavior, 14*, 399–407. doi:10.1007/BF01044219

Hans, V. P., & Swiegart, K. (1993). Jurors' views of civil lawyers: Implications for courtroom communication. *Indiana Law Journal* (Indianapolis, Ind.), *68*, 1297–1332.

Hargrove, D. (Creator) & Silverman, F., Hargrove, D., Steiger, J., Griffith, A. (Producers). (1986). *Matlock* [Television series]. New York, NY: CBS Television Network.

Harmon, R. R., & Coney, K. A. (1982). The persuasive effects of source credibility in buy and lease situations. *Journal of Marketing Research, 19*, 255–260. doi:10.2307/3151625

Harth, N. S., Kessler, T., & Leach, C. W. (2008). Advantaged group's emotional reactions to intergroup inequality: The dynamics of pride, guilt, and sympathy. *Personality and Social Psychology Bulletin, 34*, 115–129. doi:10.1177/0146167207309193

Harwood, J., & Giles, H. (1996). Reactions to older people being patronized. *Journal of Language and Social Psychology, 15*, 395–421. doi:10.1177/0261927X960154001

Harwood, J., Giles, H., Fox, S., Ryan, E. B., & Williams, A. (1993). Patronizing young and elderly adults: Response strategies in a community setting. *Journal of Applied Communication Research, 21*, 211–226. doi:10.1080/00909889309365368

Harwood, J., Ryan, E. B., Giles, H., & Tysoski, S. (1997). Evaluations of patronizing speech and three response styles in a non-service-providing context. *Journal of Applied Communication Research, 25*, 170–195. doi:10.1080/00909889709365475

Haslam, N. (2006). Dehumanization: An integrative review. *Personality and Social Psychology Review, 10*, 252–264. doi:10.1207/s15327957pspr1003_4

Hass, R. G. (1981). Effects of source characteristics on cognitive responses and persuasion. In R. E. Petty, T. M. Ostrom, & T. C. Brock (Eds.), *Cognitive responses in persuasion* (pp. 44–72). Hillsdale, NJ: Erlbaum.

Hastie, R. (1980). Memory for behavioral information that confirms or contradicts a personality impression. In R. Hastie, T. M. Ostrom, E. B. Ebbesen, R. S. Wyer, Jr., D. L. Hamilton, & D. E. Carlston. (Eds.), *Person memory: The cognitive basis of social perception* (pp. 155–177). Hillsdale, NJ: Erlbaum.

Hastie, R. (1983). Social inference. *Annual Review of Psychology, 34*, 511–542. doi:10.1146/annurev.ps.34.020183.002455

Hastie, R. (2001). Emotions in jurors' decisions. *Brooklyn Law Review, 66*, 991–1009.

Hastie, R. (2008). What's the story? Explanations and narratives in civil jury decisions. In B. H. Bornstein, R. L. Wiener, R. Schopp, & S. L. Willborn (Eds.), *Civil juries and civil justice: Psychological and legal perspectives* (pp. 23–34). New York, NY: Springer. doi:10.1007/978-0-387-74490-2_2

Hastie, R., & Kumar, P. A. (1979). Person memory: Personality traits as organizing principles in memory for behavior. *Journal of Personality and Social Psychology, 37*, 25–38. doi:10.1037/0022-3514.37.1.25

Hastie, R., Penrod, S. D., & Pennington, N. (1983). *Inside the jury*. Clark, NJ: The Lawbook Exchange.

Hastie, R., Schkade, D., & Payne, J. W. (1998). A study of juror and jury judgments in civil cases: Deciding liability for punitive damages. *Law and Human Behavior, 22*, 287–314. doi:10.1023/A:1025754422703

Hatfield, E., & Sprecher, S. (1986). *Mirror, mirror: The importance of looks in everyday life*. New York, NY: SUNY Press.

Haugtvedt, C. P., & Wegener, D. T. (1994). Message order effects in persuasion: An attitude strength perspective. *Journal of Consumer Research, 21*, 205–218. doi:10.1086/209393

Hawk, S. T., van Kleef, G., Fischer, A. H., & van der Schalk, J. (2009). "Worth a thousand words": Absolute and relative decoding of nonlinguistic affect vocalizations. *Emotion, 9*, 293–305. doi:10.1037/a0015178

Haydock, R., & Sonsteng, J. (1991). *Trial: Theories, tactics, techniques*. St. Paul, MN: West.

Hayduk, L. A. (1983). Personal space: Where we now stand. *Psychological Bulletin, 94*, 293–335. doi:10.1037/0033-2909.94.2.293

Hazan, V., & Markham, D. (2004). Acoustic-phonetic correlates of talker intelligibility in adults and children. *The Journal of the Acoustical Society of America, 116*, 3108–3118. doi:10.1121/1.1806826

Heatherton, T. F., & Vohs, K. D. (2000). Interpersonal evaluations following threats to self: Role of self-esteem. *Journal of Personality and Social Psychology, 78*, 725–736. doi:10.1037/0022-3514.78.4.725

Hendry, L., & Tehan, G. (2005). An item/order trade-off explanation of word length and generation effects. *Memory, 13,* 364–371. doi:10.1080/09658210344000341

Henley, N. (1977). *Body politics: Power, sex, and nonverbal communication.* Englewood Cliffs, NJ: Prentice-Hall.

Henningsen, D. D., Valde, K. S., & Davies, E. (2005). Exploring the effect of verbal and nonverbal cues on perceptions of deception. *Communication Quarterly, 53,* 359–375. doi:10.1080/01463370500101329

Hensley, W. E. (1981). The effects of attire, location, and sex on aiding behavior: A similarity explanation. *Journal of Nonverbal Behavior, 6,* 3–11. doi:10.1007/BF00987932

Heslin, R., & Alper, T. (1983). Touch: A bonding issue. In J. M. Weimann & R. P. Harrison (Eds.), *Nonverbal communication* (pp. 47–75). Beverly Hills, CA: Sage.

Hill, J. C. (1986). The importance of sincerity. In D. L. Rumsey (Ed.), *Master advocates' handbook* (pp. 13–14). St. Paul, MN: National Institute for Trial Advocacy.

Hills, A. M., & Thomson, D. (1999). Should victim impact influence sentences? Understanding the community's justice reasoning. *Behavioral Sciences & the Law, 17,* 661–671. doi:10.1002/(SICI)1099-0798(199923)17:5<661::AID-BSL369>3.0.CO;2-N

Hiltunen, R. (1984). The type and structure of clausal embedding in legal English. *Text, 4,* 107–122. doi:10.1515/text.1.1984.4.1-3.107

Hinsz, V. B., Matz, D. C., & Patience, R. A. (2001). Does women's hair signal reproductive potential. *Journal of Experimental Social Psychology, 37,* 166–172. doi:10.1006/jesp.2000.1450

Hirsh-Pasek, K., & Treiman, R. (1982). Doggerel: Motherese in a new context. *Journal of Child Language, 9,* 229–237. doi:10.1017/S0305000900003731

Hobbs, P. (2003). "Is that what we're here about?": A lawyer's use of impression management in a closing argument at trial. *Discourse & Society, 14,* 273–290.

Hoff, E., & Tian, C. (2005). Socioeconomic status and cultural influences on language. *Journal of Communication Disorders, 38,* 271–278. doi:10.1016/j.jcomdis.2005.02.003

Hofling, C. K., Brotzman, E., Dalrymple, S., Graves, N., & Pierce, C. M. (1966). An experimental study of nurse–physician relationships. *Journal of Nervous and Mental Disease, 143,* 171–180. doi:10.1097/00005053-196608000-00008

Hollandsworth, S. D. (2001, December 30). The lives they lived: Priscilla Davis, B. 1941—Survivor's Gilt. *New York Times Magazine,* late edition, *31.* Retrieved from http://www.nytimes.com

Holle, H., & Gunter, T. C. (2007). The role of iconic gestures in speech disambiguation: ERP evidence. *Journal of Cognitive Neuroscience, 19,* 1175–1192. doi:10.1162/jocn.2007.19.7.1175

Holler, J., & Beattie, G. W. (2003). Pragmatic aspects of representational gestures: Do speakers use them to clarify verbal ambiguity for the listener? *Gesture, 3,* 127–154. doi:10.1075/gest.3.2.02hol

Holmes, V. M. (1973). Order of main and subordinate clauses in sentence perception. *Journal of Verbal Learning & Verbal Behavior, 12*, 285. doi:10.1016/S0022-5371(73)80072-6

Holtgraves, T. (1997). Yes, but . . . positive politeness in conversation arguments. *Journal of Language and Social Psychology, 16*, 222–239. doi:10.1177/0261927X970162006

Horai, J. M., Naccari, N., & Fatoullah, E. (1974). Effects of expertise and physical attractiveness upon opinion agreement and liking. *Sociometry, 37*, 601–606. doi:10.2307/2786431

Hornby, P. A. (1972). The psychological subject and predicate. *Cognitive Psychology, 3*, 632–642. doi:10.1016/0010-0285(72)90023-0

Hosman, L. A. (2002). Language and persuasion. In J. P. Dillard & M. Pfau (Eds.), *The persuasion handbook* (pp. 371–390). Thousand Oaks, CA: Sage.

Hosticka, C. J. (1979). We don't care about what happened, we only care about what is going to happen: Lawyer–client negotiations of reality. *Social Problems, 26*, 599–610. doi:10.1525/sp.1979.26.5.03a00100

Houseman, A. W., & Perle, L. E. (the Center for Law and Social Policy, November, 2003). *Securing equal justice for all: A brief history of civil legal aid in the United States* (revised Jan. 2007). Retrieved from http://www.clasp.org/admin/site/publications/files/0158.pdf

Hovland, C. I., Janis, I. L., & Kelley, H. H. (1953). *Communication and persuasion*. New Haven, CT: Yale University Press.

Hovland, C. I., & Weiss, W. (1951). The influence of source credibility on communication effectiveness. *Public Opinion Quarterly, 15*, 635–650. doi:10.1086/266350

Howard, M. V. A., Brewer, N., & Williams, K. D. (2006). How processing resources shape the influence of stealing thunder on mock-juror verdicts. *Psychiatry, Psychology and Law, 13*, 60–66. doi:10.1375/pplt.13.1.60

Howes, D. (1954). On the interpretation of word frequency as a variable affecting speed of recognition. *Journal of Experimental Psychology, 48*, 106–112. doi:10.1037/h0059478

Howes, D. (1957). On the relation between the intelligibility and frequency of occurrence of English words. *Journal of the Acoustical Society of America, 29*, 296–305. doi:10.1121/1.1908862

Howes, D. H., & Solomon, R. L. (1951). Visual duration threshold as a function of word-probability. *Journal of Experimental Psychology, 41*, 401–410. doi:10.1037/h0056020

Hulme, C., Roodenrys, S., Schweickert, R., Brown, G. D. A., Martin, S., & Stuart, G. (1997). Word frequency effects on short-term memory tasks: Evidence for a reintegration process in immediate serial recall. *Journal of Experimental Psychology: Learning, Memory, and Cognition, 23*, 1217–1232. doi:10.1037/0278-7393.23.5.1217

Hulme, C., Surprenant, A. M., Bireta, T. J., Stuart, G., & Neath, I. (2004). Abolishing the word-length effect. *Journal of Experimental Psychology: Learning, Memory, and Cognition, 30,* 98–106. doi:10.1037/0278-7393.30.1.98

Hummert, M. L., Garstka, T. A., Ryan, E. B., & Bonnesen, J. L. (2004). The role of age stereotypes in interpersonal communication. In J. F. Nussbaum & J. Coupland (Eds.), *Handbook of communication and aging research* (2nd ed., pp. 91–114). Mahwah, NJ: Erlbaum.

Hummert, M. L., & Ryan, E. B. (1996). Toward understanding variations in patronizing talk addressed to older adults: Psycholinguistic features of care and control. *International Journal of Psycholinguistics, 12,* 149–169.

Hummert, M. L., Shaner, J. L., Garstka, T. A., & Henry, C. (1998). Communication with older adults: The influence of age stereotypes, context, and communicator age. *Human Communication Research, 25,* 124–151. doi:10.1111/j.1468-2958.1998. tb00439.x

Hunt, K. W. (1970). Syntactic maturity in school children and adults. *Monographs of the Society for Research in Child Development, 35,* iii–iv, 1–67.

Huntley, J. E., & Costanzo, M. (2003). Sexual harassment stories: Testing a story-mediated model of juror decision-making in civil litigation. *Law and Human Behavior, 27,* 29–51. doi:10.1023/A:1021674811225

Hurwitz, S. D., Miron, M. S., & Johnson, B. T. (1992). Source credibility and the language of expert testimony. *Journal of Applied Social Psychology, 22,* 1909–1939. doi:10.1111/j.1559-1816.1992.tb01530.x

Huston, T. L., & Levinger, G. (1978). Interpersonal attraction and relationships. *Annual Review of Psychology, 29,* 115–156. doi:10.1146/annurev.ps.29.020178. 000555

Huttenlocher, J., Eisenberg, K., & Strauss, S. (1968). Comprehension: Relation between perceived actor and logical subject. *Journal of Verbal Learning & Verbal Behavior, 7,* 527–530. doi:10.1016/S0022-5371(68)80044-1

Huttenlocher, J., & Strauss, S. (1968). Comprehension and a statement's relation to the situation it describes. *Journal of Verbal Learning & Verbal Behavior, 7,* 300–304. doi:10.1016/S0022-5371(68)80005-2

Infante, D. A. (1978). Similarity between advocate and receiver: The role of instrumentality. *Central States Speech Journal, 29,* 187–193.

Isenberg, D., & Gay, T. (1978). Acoustic correlates of perceived stress in an isolated synthetic disyllable. *The Journal of the Acoustical Society of America, 64,* S21. doi:10.1121/1.2004098

Jackson, G. P., & Jackson, T. C. (Producers). (1957–1966). *Perry Mason* [Television broadcast or Television series]. New York, NY: CBS Television Network.

Jacobs, R. N. (2002). *Race, media, and the crisis of civil society: From Watts to Rodney King.* Cambridge, England: Cambridge University Press.

James, C. T. (1975). The role of semantic information in lexical decisions. *Journal of Experimental Psychology: Human Perception and Performance, 1*, 130–136. doi:10.1037/0096-1523.1.2.130

Jared, D., & Seidenberg, M. S. (1990). Naming multisyllabic words. *Journal of Experimental Psychology: Human Perception and Performance, 16*, 92–105. doi:10.1037/0096-1523.16.1.92

Jaworski, A. (1993). *The power of silence: Social and pragmatic perspectives*. Newbury Park, CA: Sage.

Jeans, J. W. (1993). *Trial advocacy* (2nd ed.). St. Paul, MN: West.

Jehle, A., Miller, M., & Kemmelmeier, M. (2009). The influence of accounts and remorse on mock jurors' judgments of offenders. *Law and Human Behavior, 33*, 393–404. doi:10.1007/s10979-008-9164-6

Johannesen, R. L. (1974). The functions of silence: A plea for communication research. *Western Speech, 38*, 25–35.

Johnson, H. H., & Torcivia, J. M. (1967). Group and individual performance on a single-stage task as a function of distribution of individual performance. *Journal of Experimental Social Psychology, 3*, 266–273. doi:10.1016/0022-1031(67)90028-5

Johnson, K. K. P., Crutsinger, C., & Workman, J. E. (1994). Can professional women appear too masculine? The case of the necktie. *Clothing and Textiles Research Journal, 12*, 27–31. doi:10.1177/0887302X9401200204

Johnson, K. K. P., & Roach-Higgins, M. E. (1987). Dress and physical attractiveness of women in job interviews. *Clothing and Textiles Research Journal, 5*, 1–8. doi:10.1177/0887302X8700500301

Johnson, R. C., Thompson, C. W., & Frincke, G. (1960). Word values, word frequency and visual duration thresholds. *Psychological Review, 67*, 332–342. doi:10.1037/h0038869

Johnson, R. D., & Levin, I. P. (1985). More than meets the eye: The effect of missing information on purchase evaluations. *Journal of Consumer Research, 12*, 169–177. doi:10.1086/208505

Jones, E. E., & Wortman, C. (1973). *Ingratiation: An attributional approach*. Morristown, NJ: General Learning Corp.

Jossen, R. J. (1986). Opening statements. In D. L. Rumsey (Ed.), *Master advocates' handbook* (pp. 61–71). St. Paul, MN: National Institute for Trial Advocacy.

Joyce, T. (1991). Models of the advertising process? *Marketing and Research Today, 19*, 205–213.

Just, M. A., & Carpenter, P. A. (1971). Comprehension of negation with quantification. *Journal of Verbal Learning & Verbal Behavior, 10*, 244–253. doi:10.1016/S0022-5371(71)80051-8

Just, M. A., & Clark, H. H. (1973). Drawing inferences from the presupposition and implications of affirmative and negative sentences. *Journal of Verbal Learning & Verbal Behavior, 12*, 21–31. doi:10.1016/S0022-5371(73)80057-X

Kahan, D., & Nussbaum, M. C. (1996). Two conceptions of emotion in criminal law. *Columbia Law Review, 96*, 269–374. doi:10.2307/1123166

Kahneman, D., & Klein, G. (2009). Conditions for intuitive expertise: A failure to disagree. *American Psychologist, 64,* 515–526. doi:10.1037/a0016755

Kahneman, D., & Tversky, A. (1973). On the psychology of prediction. *Psychological Review, 80,* 237–251. doi:10.1037/h0034747

Kahneman, D., & Tversky, A. (1984). Choice, values, and frames. *American Psychologist, 39,* 341–350. doi:10.1037/0003-066X.39.4.341

Kalbfleisch, J. G. (1985). *Probability and statistical inference.* New York, NY: Springer-Verlag.

Kalven, H., Jr., & Zeisel, H. (1966). *The American jury.* Boston, MA: Little, Brown.

Kamins, M. A., & Marks, L. J. (1988). An examination into the effectiveness of two-sided comparative price appeals. *Journal of the Academy of Marketing Science, 16,* 64–71. doi:10.1007/BF02723318

Kanfer, F. H. (1960). Verbal rate, eyeblink, and content in structured psychiatric interviews. *The Journal of Abnormal and Social Psychology, 61,* 341–347. doi:10.1037/h0038933

Kaufmann, G., Drevland, G. C. B., Wessel, E., Overskeid, G., & Magnussen, S. (2003). The importance of being earnest: Displayed emotions and witness credibility. *Applied Cognitive Psychology, 17,* 21–34. doi:10.1002/acp.842

Kelley, H. H., Berscheid, E., Christensen, A., Harvey, J. H., Huston, T. L., Levinger, G., . . . Peterson, D. R. (1983). *Close relationships.* New York, NY: Freeman.

Kemper, S., & Harden, T. (1999). Experimentally disentangling what's beneficial about elderspeak from what's not. *Psychology and Aging, 14,* 656–670. doi:10.1037/0882-7974.14.4.656

Kendon, A., & Ferber, A. (1973). A description of some human greetings. In R. P. Michael & J. H. Crook (Eds.), *Comparative Behaviour and Ecology of Primates* (pp. 591–668). London, England: Academic Press.

Kennedy, C. W., & Camden, C. T. (1983). A new look at interruptions. *Western Journal of Speech Communication, 47,* 45–58.

Kidd, J. E. (1991). *Jury trials and mock jury trials.* New York, NY: Practising Law Institute.

Kiesler, C. A., & Mathog, R. (1968). The distraction hypothesis in attitude change. *Psychological Reports, 23,* 1123–1133.

Kilduff, M., & Krackhardt, D. (1994). Bring the individual back in: A structural analysis of the internal market for reputation in organizations. *Academy of Management Journal, 37,* 87–108. doi:10.2307/256771

Kimble, C. E., & Musgrove, J. I. (1988). Dominance in arguing mixed-sex dyads: Visual dominance patterns, talking time, and speech loudness. *Journal of Research in Personality, 22,* 1–16. doi:10.1016/0092-6566(88)90021-9

King, S. W., & Sereno, K. K. (1973). Attitude change as a function of degree and type of interpersonal similarity and message type. *Western Speech, 37,* 218–232.

Kintsch, W. (1998). *Comprehension: A new paradigm for cognition*. New York, NY: Cambridge University Press.

Kitayama, S., & Howard, S. (1994). Affective regulation of perception and cognition. In P. M. Niedenthal & S. Kitayama (Eds.), *The heart's eye: Emotional influences in perception and attention* (pp. 41–65). New York, NY: Academic Press.

Klapp, S. T. (1971). Implicit speech inferred from response latencies in same-different decisions. *Journal of Experimental Psychology, 91*, 262–267. doi:10.1037/h0031852

Klapp, S. T., Anderson, W. G., & Berrian, R. W. (1973). Implicit speech in reading: Reconsidered. *Journal of Experimental Psychology, 100*, 368–374. doi:10.1037/h0035471

Klare, G. R. (1968). The role of word frequency in readability. In J. R. Bormuth (Ed.), *Readability, national conference on research in English* (pp. 7–17). New York, NY: National Council of Teachers of English.

Klein, G. (2007). Performing a project premortem. *Harvard Business Review* (September): 18–19.

Kleinke, C. (1980). Interaction between gaze and legitimacy or request on compliance in a field setting. *Journal of Nonverbal Behavior, 5*, 3–12. doi:10.1007/BF00987050

Kleinke, C. L., Bustos, A. A., Meeker, F. B., & Staneski, R. A. (1973). Effects of self-attributed and other-attributed gaze in interpersonal evaluations between males and females. *Journal of Experimental Social Psychology, 9*, 154–163. doi:10.1016/0022-1031(73)90007-3

Klenbort, I., & Anisfeld, M. (1974). Markedness and perspective in the interpretation of the active and passive voice. *The Quarterly Journal of Experimental Psychology, 26*, 189–195. doi:10.1080/14640747408400404

Klock, S. J., & Traylore, M. B. (1983). Older and younger models in advertising to older consumers: An advertising effectiveness experiment. *Akron Business and Economic Review, 14*, 48–52.

Koegel, O. E. (1951). Speech and the legal profession. *The Quarterly Journal of Speech, 37*, 471–472. doi:10.1080/00335635109381701

Kogut, T., & Ritov, I. (2005a). The "identified victim" effect: An identified group, or just a single individual? *Journal of Behavioral Decision Making, 18*, 157–167. doi:10.1002/bdm.492

Kogut, T., & Ritov, I. (2005b). The singularity effect of identified victims in separate and joint evaluations. *Organizational Behavior and Human Decision Processes, 97*, 106–116. doi:10.1016/j.obhdp.2005.02.003

Kosieradzki, M. R. (2001). Voir dire in the age of juror bias. *Trial* (Boston, Mass.), *37*, 65–69.

Krackhardt, D., & Kilduff, M. (1999). Whether close or far: Social distance effects on perceived balance in friendship networks. *Journal of Personality and Social Psychology, 76*, 770–782. doi:10.1037/0022-3514.76.5.770

Kramer, G. P., Kerr, N. L., & Carroll, J. S. (1990). Pretrial publicity, judicial remedies, and jury bias. *Law and Human Behavior, 14*, 409–438. doi:10.1007/BF01044220

Kramer, G. P., & Koening, D. M. (1990). Do jurors understand criminal jury instruction? Analyzing the results of the Michigan juror comprehension project. *Journal of Law Reform, 23*, 401–437.

Krause, J. C., & Braida, L. D. (2002). Investigating alternative forms of clear speech: The effects of speaking rate and speaking mode on intelligibility. *Journal of the Acoustical Society of America, 112*, 2165–2172. doi:10.1121/1.1509432

Krause, J. C., & Braida, L. D. (2004). Acoustic properties of naturally produced clear speech at normal speaking rates. *Journal of the Acoustical Society of America, 115*, 362–378. doi:10.1121/1.1635842

Krauss, D. A., & Sales, B. D. (2000). Legal standards, expertise, and experts in the resolution of contested child custody cases. *Psychology, Public Policy, and Law, 6*, 843–879. doi:10.1037/1076-8971.6.4.843

Krauss, D. A., & Sales, B. D. (2001). The effects of clinical and scientific expert testimony on juror decision-making in capital sentencing. *Psychology, Public Policy, and Law, 7*, 267–310. doi:10.1037/1076-8971.7.2.267

Kraut, R. E., & Johnston, R. (1979). Social and emotional messages of smiling: An ethological approach. *Journal of Personality and Social Psychology, 37*, 1539–1553. doi:10.1037/0022-3514.37.9.1539

Kraut, R. E., & Poe, D. (1980). On the line: The detection judgments of customs inspectors and laymen. *Journal of Personality and Social Psychology, 39*, 784–798. doi:10.1037/0022-3514.39.5.784

Krebs, D. (1975). Empathy and altruism. *Journal of Personality and Social Psychology, 32*, 1134–1146. doi:10.1037/0022-3514.32.6.1134

Kyle, D. J., & Mahler, H. I. M. (1996). The effects of hair color and cosmetic use on perceptions of a female's ability. *Psychology of Women Quarterly, 20*, 447–455. doi:10.1111/j.1471-6402.1996.tb00311.x

Ladefoged, P., Draper, M., & Whitterridge, D. (1958). Syllables and stress. *Miscellanea Phonetica, 3*, 1–14.

Lalljee, M. (1981). Attribution theory and the analysis of explanations. In C. Antai (Ed.), *The psychology of ordinary explanations of social behaviour* (pp. 119–138). London, England: Academic Press.

Lalljee, M., & Abelson, R. P. (1983). The organization of explanations. In M. Hewstone (Ed.), *Attribution theory: Social and functional extensions* (pp. 65–80). Oxford, England: Blackwell.

Lalljee, M., Lamb, R., & Abelson, R. P. (1992). The role of event prototypes in categorization and explanation. *European Review of Social Psychology, 3*, 153–182. doi:10.1080/14792779243000050

Lambert, S. (1972). Reactions to a stranger as a function of style of dress. *Perceptual and Motor Skills, 35*, 711–712.

Landauer, T. K., & Freedman, J. L. (1968). Information retrieval from long-term memory: Category size and recognition time. *Journal of Verbal Learning & Verbal Behavior*, 7, 291–295. doi:10.1016/S0022-5371(68)80003-9

Landauer, T. K., & Streeter, L. A. (1973). Structural differences between common and rare words: Failure of equivalence assumptions for theories of word recognition. *Journal of Verbal Learning & Verbal Behavior*, 12, 119–131. doi:10.1016/S0022-5371(73)80001-5

Latané, B., & Darley, J. M. (1970). *The unresponsive bystander: Why doesn't he help?* New York, NY: Appleton-Century-Crofts.

Launer, D., & Schiff, P. (Producers), & Lynn, J. (Director). (1992). *My Cousin Vinny* [Motion picture]. USA: 20th Century Fox.

Lay, C. H., & Burron, B. F. (1968). Perception of the personality of the hesitant speaker. *Perceptual and Motor Skills*, 26, 951–956.

Lay, C. H., & Paivio, A. (1969). The effects of task difficulty and anxiety on hesitations in speech. *Canadian Journal of Behavioural Science/Revue canadienne des sciences du comportement*, 1, 25–37. doi:10.1037/h0082683

Leach, C. W., Snider, N., & Iyer, A. (2002). "Poisoning the consciences of the fortunate": The experience of relative advantage and support for social equality. In I. Walker & H. J. Smith (Eds.), *Relative deprivation: Specification, development, and integration* (pp. 136–163). New York, NY: Cambridge University Press.

Leavitt, C., & Kaigler-Evans, K. (1975). Mere similarity versus information processing: An exploration of source and message interaction. *Communication Research*, 2, 300–306. doi:10.1177/009365027500200310

Lee, C. H. (2001). Absence of syllable effects: multisyllabic [correction of monosyllabic] words are easier than monosyllabic [correction of multisyllabic] words. *Perceptual and Motor Skills*, 93, 73–77. doi:10.2466/PMS.93.5.73-77

Lee, H. (1960). *To kill a mockingbird*. New York, NY: Grand Central.

Lee, K., & Ashton, M. C. (2008). The HEXACO personality factors in the indigenous personality lexicons of English and 11 other languages. *Journal of Personality*, 76, 1001–1053. doi:10.1111/j.1467-6494.2008.00512.x

Lee, Y.-T., & Ottati, V. (1995). Perceived in-group homogeneity as a function of group membership salience and stereotype threat. *Personality and Social Psychology Bulletin*, 21, 610–619. doi:10.1177/0146167295216007

Lefkowitz, M., Blake, R. R., & Mouton, J. S. (1955). Status factors in pedestrian violation of traffic signals. *The Journal of Abnormal and Social Psychology*, 51, 704–706. doi:10.1037/h0042000

Lehiste, I. (1970). *Suprasegmentals*. Cambridge, MA: MIT Press.

Lehnert, W. G. (1981). Plot units and narrative summarization. *Cognitive Science*, 5, 293–331. doi:10.1207/s15516709cog0504_1

Lerner, J., Goldberg, J., & Tetlock, P. E. (1998). Sober second thought: The effects of accountability, anger, and authoritarianism on attributions of responsibility. *Personality and Social Psychology Bulletin, 24,* 563–574. doi:10.1177/0146167298246001

Levin, I. P. (1987). Associative effects of information framing. *Bulletin of the Psychonomic Society, 25,* 85–86.

Levin, I. P., & Gaeth, G. J. (1988). How consumers are affected by framing of attribute information before and after consuming the product. *Journal of Consumer Research, 15,* 374–378. doi:10.1086/209174

Levin, I. P., Johnson, R. D., Russo, C. P., & Deldin, P. J. (1985). Framing effects in judgment tasks with varying amounts of information. *Organizational Behavior and Human Decision Processes, 36,* 362–377. doi:10.1016/0749-5978(85)90005-6

Levy, B. R., & Banaji, M. R. (2002). Implicit Ageism. In T. D. Nelson (Ed.), *Stereotyping and prejudice against older persons* (pp. 49–75). Cambridge, MA: MIT Press.

Leyens, J.-P., Cortes, B., Demoulin, S., Dovidio, J. F., Fiske, S. T., Gaunt, R., . . . Vaes, J. (2003). Emotional prejudice, essentialism, and nationalism. *European Journal of Social Psychology, 33,* 703–717. doi:10.1002/ejsp.170

Leyens, J.-P., Cortes B. P., Rodriguez, A. P., Rodriguez, R. T., Viki, G. T., & Demoulin, S., (2002). Infra-humanization versus stereotyped groups: The case of men and women. Unpublished manuscript. As reported in J.-P. Leyens, B. Cortes, S. Demoulin, J. F. Dovidio, S. T. Fiske, R. Gaunt, . . . J. Vaes. (2003). Emotional prejudice, essentialism, and nationalism. *European Journal of Social Psychology, 33,* 703–717. doi:10.1002/ejsp.170

Lieberman, J. D., & Sales, B. D. (1997). What social science teaches us about the jury instruction process. *Psychology, Public Policy, and Law, 3,* 589–644. doi:10.1037/1076-8971.3.4.589

Lieberman, J. D., & Sales, B. D. (2007). *Scientific jury selection.* Washington, DC: American Psychological Association. doi:10.1037/11498-000

Light, L. L., & Carter-Sobell, L. (1970). Effects of changed semantic context on recognition memory. *Journal of Verbal Learning & Verbal Behavior, 9,* 1–11. doi:10.1016/S0022-5371(70)80002-0

Lind, E. A., Maccoun, R. J., Ebener, P. A., Felstiner, W. L. F., Hensler, D. R., Resnik, J., & Tyler, T. R. (1990). In the eye of the beholder: Tort litigants' evaluations of their experiences in the civil justice system. *Law & Society Review, 24,* 953–996. doi:10.2307/3053616

Lingle, J. H., & Ostrom, T. M. (1981). Principles of memory and cognition in attitude formation. In R. E. Petty, T. M. Ostrom, & T. C. Brock (Eds.), *Cognitive responses in persuasion* (pp. 399–420). Hillsdale, NJ: Erlbaum.

Linn, M. D., & Piche, G. (1982). Black and white adolescent and preadolescent attitudes toward black English. *Research in the Teaching of English, 16,* 53–69.

Linz, D., Penrod, S., & McDonald, E. (1986). Attorney communication and impression making in the courtroom: Views from off the bench. *Law and Human Behavior*, *10*, 281–302. doi:10.1007/BF01047342

Linz, D. G., & Penrod, S. (1984). Increasing attorney persuasiveness in the courtroom. *Law & Psychology Review*, *8*, 1–47.

Lippman, M. Z. (1972). The influence of grammatical transform in a syllogistic reasoning task. *Journal of Verbal Learning & Verbal Behavior*, *11*, 424–430. doi:10.1016/S0022-5371(72)80023-9

Liss, M., Crawford, M., & Popp, D. (2004). Predictors and correlates of collective action. *Sex Roles*, *50*, 771–779. doi:10.1023/B:SERS.0000029096.90835.3f

Littlepage, G. E., & Mueller, A. L. (1997). Recognition and utilization of expertise in problem-solving groups: Expert characteristics and behavior. *Group Dynamics: Theory, Research, and Practice*, *1*, 324–328. doi:10.1037/1089-2699.1.4.324

Littlepage, G. E., Schmidt, G. W., Whisler, E. W., & Frost, A. G. (1995). An input-process-output analysis of influence and performance in problem-solving groups. *Journal of Personality and Social Psychology*, *69*, 877–889. doi:10.1037/0022-3514.69.5.877

Lockhart v. McCree, 476 U.S. 162 (1986).

Loewenstein, G., & Lerner, J. (2003). The role of emotion in decision making. In R. J. Davidson, H. H. Goldsmith, & K. R. Scherer (Eds.), *Handbook of affective science* (pp. 619–642). Oxford, England: Oxford University Press.

Loewenstein, G., & Small, D. A. (2007). The scarecrow and the tin man: The vicissitudes of human sympathy and caring. *Review of General Psychology*, *11*, 112–126. doi:10.1037/1089-2680.11.2.112

Loewenthal, K. (1969). Semantic features and communicability of words of different classes. *Psychonomic Science*, *17*, 79–80.

Loftus, E. F., & Goodman, J. (1985). Questioning witnesses. In S. M. Kassin & L. S. Wrightsman (Eds.), *The psychology of evidence and trial procedure* (pp. 253–279). Beverly Hills, CA: Sage.

Loftus, E. F., & Palmer, J. C. (1974). Reconstruction of automobile destruction: An example of the interaction between language and memory. *Journal of Verbal Learning & Verbal Behavior*, *13*, 585–589. doi:10.1016/S0022-5371(74)80011-3

Loh, W. D. (1984). *Social research in the judicial process*. New York, NY: Springer.

Lott, A. J., & Lott, B. E. (1965). Group cohesiveness as interpersonal attraction: a review of relationships with antecedent and consequent variables. *Psychological Bulletin*, *64*, 259–309. doi:10.1037/h0022386

Lubet, S. (2000). *Modern trial advocacy*. Notre Dame, IN: National Institute for Trial Advocacy.

Lucchesi, G. (Producer) & Hoblit, G. (Director). (1996). *Primal fear* [Motion picture]. USA: Paramount pictures.

Luce, P. A., & Pisoni, D. B. (1998). Recognizing spoken words: The neighborhood activation model. *Ear and Hearing, 19,* 1–36. doi:10.1097/00003446-199802000-00001

Luchins, A. (1957). Primacy-recency in impression formation. In C. I. Hoveland (Ed.), *The order of presentation in persuasion* (pp. 62–75). New Haven, NJ: Yale University Press.

Luchins, A. S. (1958). Definitiveness of impression and primacy-recency in communications. *The Journal of Social Psychology, 48,* 275–290. doi:10.1080/00224545.1958.9919292

Luchok, J. A., & McCroskey, J. C. (1978). The effect of quality of evidence on attitude change and source credibility. *Southern Speech Communication Journal, 43,* 371–383.

Luhman, R. (1990). Appalachian English stereotypes: Language attitudes in Kentucky. *Language in Society, 19,* 331–348. doi:10.1017/S0047404500014548

Lupia, A., & McCubbins, M. (1998). *The democratic dilemma: Can citizens learn what they need to know?* Cambridge, England: Cambridge University Press.

Machotka, P. (1965). Body movement and communication. *Dialogues: Behavioral Science Research, 2,* 33–66.

Mackie, D. M., Devos, T., & Smith, E. R. (2000). Intergroup emotions: Explaining offensive actions in an intergroup context. *Journal of Personality and Social Psychology, 79,* 602–616. doi:10.1037/0022-3514.79.4.602

Mackie, D. M., Gastardo-Conaco, M. C., & Skelly, J. J. (1992). Knowledge of the advocated position and the processing of in-group and out-group persuasive messages. *Personality and Social Psychology Bulletin, 18,* 145–151. doi:10.1177/0146167292182005

Mackie, D. M., & Queller, S. (2000). The impact of group membership on persuasion: Revisiting "who says what to whom with what effect?" In D. J. Terry & M. A. Hogg (Eds.), *Attitudes, behavior, and social context: The role of norms and group membership* (pp. 135–155). Mahwah, NJ: Erlbaum.

Mackie, D. M., Worth, L. T., & Asuncion, A. G. (1990). Processing of persuasive in-group messages. *Journal of Personality and Social Psychology, 58,* 812–822. doi:10.1037/0022-3514.58.5.812

Macnamara, J., O'Cleirigh, A., & Kellaghan, T. (1972). The structure of the English lexicon: Simple hypothesis. *Language and Speech, 15,* 141–148.

Majerus, S., & Van der Linden, M. (2003). Long-term memory effects on verbal short-term memory: A replication study. *British Journal of Developmental Psychology, 21,* 303–310. doi:10.1348/026151003765264101

Mandelbaum, J. (2003). How to "do things" with narrative: A communication perspective on narrative skill. In J. O. Greene & B. Burleson (Eds.), *Handbook of communication and social interaction skills* (pp. 595–633). Mahwah, NJ: Erlbaum.

Mandler, J. M. (1984). *Stories, scripts, and scenes: Aspects of schema theory.* Hillsdale, NJ: Erlbaum.

Mandler, J. M., & DeForest, M. (1979). Is there more than one way to recall a story? *Child Development, 50,* 886–889. doi:10.2307/1128960

Manis, M., Cornell, S. D., Moore, J. C. (1974). Transmission of attitude relevant information through a communication chain. *Journal of Personality and Social Psychology, 30,* 81–94. doi:10.1037/h0036639

Marcel, A. J., & Steel, R. G. (1973). Semantic cueing in recognition and recall. The Quarterly *Journal of Experimental Psychology, 25,* 368–377. doi:10.1080/14640747308400358

Maricchiolo, F., Gnisci, A., Bonaiuto, M., & Ficca, G. (2009). Effects of difference types of hand gestures in persuasive speech on receivers' evaluations. *Language and Cognitive Processes, 24,* 239–266. doi:10.1080/01690960802159929

Markel, N. N. (1965). The reliability of coding paralanguage: Pitch, loudness, and tempo. *Journal of Verbal Learning & Verbal Behavior, 4,* 306–308. doi:10.1016/S0022-5371(65)80035-4

Markham, D. (1968). The dimensions of source credibility of television newscasters. *Journal of Communication, 18,* 57–64. doi:10.1111/j.1460-2466.1968.tb00055.x

Markovits, D. (2003). Legal ethics from the lawyer's point of view. *Yale Journal of Law & the Humanities, 15,* 209–293.

Marks, L. E. (1968). Scaling of grammaticalness of self-embedded English sentences. *Journal of Verbal Learning & Verbal Behavior, 7,* 965–967. doi:10.1016/S0022-5371(68)80106-9

Marks, L. E. (1987). On cross-modal similarity: Auditory-visual interactions in speeded discrimination. *Journal of Experimental Psychology: Human Perception and Performance, 13,* 384–394. doi:10.1037/0096-1523.13.3.384

Massaro, D. W. (1998). *Perceiving talking faces: From speech perception to a behavioral principle.* Cambridge, MA: MIT Press.

Matlon, R. J. (1982). Bridging the gap between communication education and legal communication. *Communication Education, 31,* 39–53. doi:10.1080/03634528209384658

Mauet, T. A. (1992). *Fundamentals of trial techniques* (3rd ed.). Boston, MA: Little, Brown & Co.

Mauet, T. A. (2005). *Trials: Strategy, skills, & new powers of persuasion.* New York, NY: Aspen.

Mayberry, R. I., & Jacques, J. (2000). Gesture production during stuttered speech: Insights into the nature of gesture-speech integration. In D. McNeill (Ed.), *Language and gesture* (pp. 199–214). Cambridge, England: Cambridge University Press. doi:10.1017/CBO9780511620850.013

Maynard, D. (1988). Narratives and narrative structure in plea bargaining. *Law & Society Review, 22,* 449–481. doi:10.2307/3053625

McCroskey, J. C. (1966). Scales for the measurement of ethos. *Speech Monographs, 33,* 65–72. doi:10.1080/03637756609375482

McCroskey, J. C. (1967). The effects of evidence in persuasive communication. *Western Speech, 31*, 189–199.

McCroskey, J. C. (1969). A summary of experimental research on the effects of evidence in persuasive communication. *The Quarterly Journal of Speech, 55*, 169–176. doi:10.1080/00335636909382942

McCroskey, J. C. (1970). The effects of evidence as an inhibitor of counter-persuasion. *Speech Monographs, 37*, 188–194. doi:10.1080/03637757009375664

McDonald, S. A., & Shillcock, R. C. (2001). Rethinking the word frequency effect: The neglected role of distributional information in lexical processing. *Language and Speech, 44*, 295–323. doi:10.1177/00238309010440030101

McDonald, T. (2002). *The business of portrait photography*. New York, NY: Amphoto Books.

McGinnies, E. (1973). Initial attitude, source credibility, and involvement as factors in persuasion. *Journal of Experimental Social Psychology, 9*, 285–296. doi:10.1016/0022-1031(73)90066-8

McGinnies, E., Comer, P. B., & Lacey, O. L. (1952). Visual-recognition thresholds as a function of word length and word frequency. *Journal of Experimental Psychology, 44*, 65–69. doi:10.1037/h0063142

McGinnies, E., & Ward, C. D. (1980). Better liked than right: Trustworthiness and expertise as factors in credibility. *Personality and Social Psychology Bulletin, 6*, 467–472. doi:10.1177/014616728063023

McGuire, W. J., & Papageorgis, D. (1962). Effectiveness of forewarning in developing resistance to persuasion. *Public Opinion Quarterly, 26*, 24–34. doi:10.1086/267068

McNeill, D. (1992). *Hand and mind: What gestures reveal about thought*. Chicago, IL: University of Chicago Press.

Mehl, M. R., Pennebaker, J. W., Crow, M. D., Dabbs, J., & Price, J. H. (2001). The Electronically Activated Recorder (EAR): A device for sampling naturalistic daily activities and conversations. *Behavior Research Methods Instruments, & Computers, 33*, 517–523. doi:10.3758/BF03195410

Mehl, M. R., Vazire, S., Holleran, S. E., & Clark, C. S. (2010). Eavesdropping on happiness: Well-being is related to having less small talk and more substantive conversations. *Psychological Science, 21*, 539–541. doi:10.1177/0956797610362675

Mehrabian, A. (1966). Immediacy: an indicator of attitudes in linguistic communication. *Journal of Personality, 34*, 26–34. doi:10.1111/j.1467-6494.1966.tb01696.x

Mehrabian, A. (1967a). Attitudes inferred from non-immediacy of verbal communications. *Journal of Verbal Learning & Verbal Behavior, 6*, 294–295. doi:10.1016/S0022-5371(67)80113-0

Mehrabian, A. (1967b). Orientation behaviors and nonverbal attitude communication. *Journal of Communication, 17*, 324–332. doi:10.1111/j.1460-2466.1967.tb01190.x

Mehrabian, A. (1968a). Inference of attitudes from the posture, orientation, and distance of a communicator. *Journal of Consulting and Clinical Psychology, 32*, 296–308. doi:10.1037/h0025906

Mehrabian, A. (1968b). Relationship of attitude to seated posture, orientation, and distance. *Journal of Personality and Social Psychology, 10*, 26–30. doi:10.1037/h0026384

Mehrabian, A. (1969). Significance of posture and position in the communication of attitude and status relationships. *Psychological Bulletin, 71*, 359–372. doi:10.1037/h0027349

Mehrabian, A. (1970). *Tactics of social influence*. Englewood Cliffs, NJ: Prentice-Hall.

Mehrabian, A. (1971). *Silent messages*. Wadsworth, CA: Belmont.

Mehrabian, A. (1972). *Nonverbal communication*. Chicago, IL: Aldine.

Mehrabian, A. (1976). *Public places and private spaces: The psychology of work, play, and living environments*. New York, NY: Basic Books.

Mehrabian, A., & Ferris, S. R. (1967). Inference of attitudes from nonverbal communication in two channels. *Journal of Consulting Psychology, 31*, 248–252. doi:10.1037/h0024648

Mehrabian, A., & Friar, J. T. (1969). Encoding of attitude by a seated communicator via posture and position cues. *Journal of Consulting and Clinical Psychology, 33*, 330–336. doi:10.1037/h0027576

Mehrabian, A., & Ksionzky, S. (1972). Categories of social behavior. *Comparative Group Studies, 3*, 425–436.

Mehrabian, A., & Williams, M. (1969). Nonverbal concomitants of perceived and intended persuasiveness. *Journal of Personality and Social Psychology, 13*, 37–58. doi:10.1037/h0027993

Melara, R., & O'Brien, T. (1987). Interaction between synesthetically corresponding dimensions. *Journal of Experimental Psychology: General, 116*, 323–336. doi:10.1037/0096-3445.116.4.323

Merriam-Webster's collegiate dictionary (11th ed.). (2009). Springfield, MA: Merriam-Webster. Retrieved from http://www.m-w.com

Milgram, S. (1963). Behavioral study of obedience. *The Journal of Abnormal and Social Psychology, 67*, 371–378. doi:10.1037/h0040525

Milgram, S. (1974). *Obedience to authority*. New York, NY: Harper.

Miller, G. A., & Isard, S. (1964). Free recall of self-embedded English sentences. *Information and Control, 7*, 292–303. doi:10.1016/S0019-9958(64)90310-9

Miller, G. R. (1983). Telling it like it isn't and not telling it like it is: Some thoughts on deceptive communication. In J. I. Sisco (Ed.), *The Jensen lectures: Contemporary communication studies* (pp. 91–116). Tampa: University of South Florida Press.

Miller, G. R., Bauchner, J. E., Hocking, J. E., Fontes, N. E., Kaminski, E. P., & Brandt, D. R. (1981). . . . and nothing but the truth. How well can observers detect deceptive testimony? In B. D. Sales (Ed.), *Perspectives in law and psychology, Vol. II: The trial process* (pp. 145–179). New York, NY: Plenum Press.

Miller, G. R., & Lobe, J. (1967). Opinionated language, open-and-closed-mindedness and response to persuasive communications. *Journal of Communication, 17*, 333–341. doi:10.1111/j.1460-2466.1967.tb01191.x

Miller, G. R., & Stiff, J. B. (1993). *Deceptive communication*. Newbury Park, CA: Sage.

Miller, J. F. (1973). Sentence imitation in preschool children. *Language and Speech, 16*, 1–14.

Miller, L., & Cox, C. (1982). For appearances' sake: Public self-consciousness and makeup use. *Personality and Social Psychology Bulletin, 8*, 748–751. doi:10.1177/0146167282084023

Miller, L. M., & Roodenrys, S. (2009). The interaction of word frequency and concreteness in immediate series recall. *Memory & Cognition, 37*, 850–865.

Miller, N., Campbell, D. T., Twedt, H., & O'Connell, E. J. (1966). Similarity, contrast, and complementary in friendship choice. *Journal of Personality and Social Psychology, 3*, 3–12. doi:10.1037/h0022731

Miller, N., Maruyama, G., Beaber, R. J., & Valone, K. (1976). Speed of speech and persuasion. *Journal of Personality and Social Psychology, 34*, 615–624. doi:10.1037/0022-3514.34.4.615

Mills, J., & Aronson, E. (1965). Opinion change as a function of communicator's attractiveness and desire to influence. *Journal of Personality and Social Psychology, 1*, 173–177. doi:10.1037/h0021646

Mills, J., & Kimble, C. E. (1973). Opinion change as a function of perceived similarity of the communicator and subjectivity of the issue. *Bulletin of the Psychonomic Society, 2*, 35–36.

Minichiello, V., Aroni, R., Timewell, E., & Alexander, L. (1990). *In-depth interviewing: Researching research. A resource for social scientists and practitioner researchers*. Oxford, England: Blackwell.

Mio, J. S. (1996). Metaphor, politics, and persuasion. In J. S. Mio & A. N. Katz (Eds.), *Metaphor: Implications and applications* (pp. 127–146). Mahwah, NJ: Erlbaum.

Mitchell, D. J., Russo, J. E., & Pennington, N. (1989). Back to the future: Temporal perspective in the explanation of events. *Journal of Behavioral Decision Making, 2*, 25–38. doi:10.1002/bdm.3960020103

Mitchell, H. E., & Byrne, D. (1973). The defendant's dilemma: Effects of jurors' attitudes and authoritarianism on judicial decisions. *Journal of Personality and Social Psychology, 25*, 123–129. doi:10.1037/h0034263

Monsen, R. B., & Engebretson, A. M. (1977). Study of variations in the male and female glottal wave. *Journal of the Acoustical Society of America, 62*, 981–993. doi:10.1121/1.381593

Montes, S. D., & Zweig, D. (2009). Do promises Matter? An exploration of the role of promises in psychological contract breach. *Journal of Applied Psychology, 94*, 1243–1260. doi:10.1037/a0015725

Moons, W. G., & Mackie, D. M. (2007). Thinking straight while seeing red: The influence of anger on information processing. *Personality and Social Psychology Bulletin, 33*, 706–720. doi:10.1177/0146167206298566

Moore, D. L., Hausknecht, D., & Thamodaran, K. (1986). Time compression, response opportunity and persuasion. *Journal of Consumer Research, 13*, 85–99. doi:10.1086/209049

Morgan, M., & Hummert, M. (2000). Perceptions of communicative control strategies in mother-daughter dyads across the life span. *Journal of Communication*, *50*, 48–64. doi:10.1111/j.1460-2466.2000.tb02852.x

Morgan, P. S. (1997). Figuring out figure out: Metaphor and the semantics of English verb-particle construction. *Cognitive Linguistics*, *8*, 327–358. doi:10.1515/cogl.1997.8.4.327

Morrill, C., & Facciola, P. C. (1992). The power of language in adjudication and mediation: Institutional contexts as predictors of social evaluation. *Law & Social Inquiry*, *17*, 191–212. doi:10.1111/j.1747-4469.1992.tb00610.x

Morris, D. (1977). *Manwatching. A field guide to human behavior*. Oxford, England: Elsevier International Projects.

Morrison, E. W., & Robinson, S. L. (1997). When employees feel betrayed: A model of how psychological contract violation develops. *The Academy of Management Review*, *22*, 226–256.

Morsbach, H. (1973). Aspects of nonverbal communication in Japan. *Journal of Nervous and Mental Disease*, *157*, 262–277. doi:10.1097/00005053-197310000-00006

Morton, J. (1969). Categories of interference: Verbal mediation and conflict in card sorting. *The British Journal of Psychology*, *60*, 329–346. doi:10.1111/j.2044-8295.1969.tb01204.x

Morton, J., & Jassem, W. (1965). Acoustic correlates of stress. *Language and Speech*, *8*, 159–181.

Motley, M. T. (1993). Facial affect and verbal context in conversation. *Human Communication Research*, *20*, 3–40. doi:10.1111/j.1468-2958.1993.tb00314.x

Motley, M. T., & Camden, C. T. (1988). Facial expression of emotion: A comparison of posed expressions versus spontaneous expressions in an interpersonal communication setting. *Western Journal of Speech Communication*, *52*, 1–22. doi:10.1080/10570318809389622

Munn, W. C., & Gruner, C. R. (1981). "Sick" jokes, speaker sex, and informative speech. *Southern Speech Communication Journal*, *45*, 411–418.

Murray, I. R., & Arnott, J. L. (1993). Toward the simulation of emotion in synthetic speech: A review of the literature on human vocal emotion. *Journal of the Acoustical Society of America*, *93*, 1097–1108. doi:10.1121/1.405558

Murray, P. (1995). *Basic trial advocacy*. Boston, MA: Little, Brown & Co.

Muscarella, F., & Cunningham, M. R. (1996). The evolutionary significance and social perception of male pattern baldness and facial hair. *Ethology & Sociobiology*, *17*, 99–117. doi:10.1016/0162-3095(95)00130-1

Nabi, R. L. (1999). Cognitive-functional model for the effects of discrete negative emotions on information processing, attitude change, and recall. *Communication Theory*, *9*, 292–320. doi:10.1111/j.1468-2885.1999.tb00172.x

Nabi, R. L. (2002). Discrete emotions and persuasion. In J. P. Dillard & M. Pfau (Eds.), *The persuasion handbook: Developments in theory and practice* (pp. 289–308). Thousand Oaks, CA: Sage.

Nairne, J. S. (2002). Remembering over the short-term: The case against the standard model. *Annual Review of Psychology, 53,* 53–81. doi:10.1146/annurev.psych.53. 100901.135131

Namy, L. L., Nygaard, L. C., & Sauerteig, D. (2002). Gender differences in vocal accommodation: The role of perception. *Journal of Language and Social Psychology, 21,* 422–432. doi:10.1177/026192702237958

Narvaez, D. (1998). The effects of moral schemas on the reconstruction of moral narratives in 8th grade and college students. *Journal of Educational Psychology, 90,* 13–24. doi:10.1037/0022-0663.90.1.13

Neath, I., & Nairne, J. S. (1995). Word-length effects in immediate memory: Overwriting trace decay theory. *Psychonomic Bulletin & Review, 2,* 429–441. doi:10.3758/BF03210981

Newman, H. M. (1982). The sounds of silence in communicative encounters. *Communication Quarterly, 30,* 142–149. doi:10.1080/01463378209369441

Nippold, M. A. (1998). *Later language development: The school-age and adolescent years* (2nd ed.). Austin, TX: Pro-Ed.

Nippold, M. A. (2000). Language development during the adolescent years: Aspects of pragmatics, syntax, and semantics. *Topics in Language Disorders, 20,* 15–28. doi:10.1097/00011363-200020020-00004

Nippold, M. A. (2006). Language development in school-age children, adolescents, and adults. In K. Brown (Ed.), *Encyclopedia of language & linguistics* (pp. 368–373). Amsterdam, The Netherlands: Elsevier.

Nippold M. A., Hesketh L. J., Duthie J. K., & Mansfield T. C. (2005). Conversational versus expository discourse: a study of syntactic development in children, adolescents, and adults. *Journal of Speech, Language & Hearing Research, 48,* 1048–1064. doi:10.1044/1092-4388(2005/073)

Nisbett, R., & Ross, L. (1980). *Human inference: strategies and shortcomings of social judgment.* Englewood Cliffs, NJ: Prentice-Hall.

Noble, C. E. (1954). The familiarity–frequency relationship. *Journal of Experimental Psychology, 47,* 13–16. doi:10.1037/h0060025

Noller, P. (1980). Gaze in married couples. *Journal of Nonverbal Behavior, 5,* 115–129. doi:10.1007/BF00986514

Norman, R. (1976). When what is said is important: A comparison of expert and attractive sources. *Journal of Experimental Social Psychology, 12,* 294–300. doi:10.1016/0022-1031(76)90059-7

Norton, R. W. (1983). *Communicator style: Theory, application, and measures.* Beverly Hills, CA: Sage.

Nourse, V. (1997). Passion's progress: Modern law reform and the provocation defense. *Yale Law Journal, 106,* 1331–1448. doi:10.2307/797186

Nygaard, L. C. (2005). Linguistic and paralinguistic factors in speech perception. In D. B. Pisoni & R. E. Remez (Eds.), *Handbook of speech perception* (pp. 390–413). Oxford, England: Blackwell. doi:10.1002/9780470757024.ch16

Nygaard, L. C., & Lunders, E. R. (2002). Resolution of lexical ambiguity by emotional tone of voice. *Memory & Cognition, 30*, 583–593. doi:10.3758/BF03194959

O'Barr, W. M. (1982). *Linguistic evidence: Language, power, and strategy in the courtroom.* New York, NY: Academic Press.

O'Barr, W. M., & Conley, J. M. (1985). Litigant satisfaction versus legal adequacy in small claims court narratives. *Law & Society Review, 19*, 661–701. doi:10.2307/3053424

O'Brien, S., Pheterson, S., Wright, M., & Hostica, C. (1977). The criminal lawyer: The defendant's perspective. *American Journal of Criminal Law, 5*, 283–312.

O'Donnell, R. C. (1974). Syntactic differences between speech and writing. *American Speech. A Quarterly of Linguistic Usage, 49*, 102–110.

O'Donnell, R. C., Griffin, W. J., & Norris, R. C. (1967). A transformational analysis of oral and written grammatical structures in the language of children in grades three, five, and seven. *The Journal of Educational Research, 61*, 36–39.

O'Hara, B. S., Netemeyer, R. G., & Burton, S. (1991). An examination of the relative effects of source expertise, trustworthiness, and likability. *Social Behavior and Personality, 19*, 305–314. doi:10.2224/sbp.1991.19.4.305

Ohbuchi, K., Kameda, M., & Agarie, N. (1989). Apology as aggression control: Its role in mediating appraisal of and response to harm. *Journal of Personality and Social Psychology, 56*, 219–227. doi:10.1037/0022-3514.56.2.219

Okamoto, S., & Robinson, W. P. (1997). Determinants of gratitude expressions in England. *Journal of Language and Social Psychology, 16*, 411–433. doi:10.1177/0261927X970164003

O'Keefe, D. J. (1998). Justification explicitness and persuasive effect: A meta-analytic review of the effects of varying support articulation in persuasive messages. *Argumentation and Advocacy, 35*, 61–75.

O'Keefe, D. J. (1999). How to handle opposing arguments in persuasive messages: A meta-analytic review of the effects of one-sided and two-sided messages. *Communication Yearbook, 22*, 209–249.

O'Keefe, D. J. (2002). *Persuasion: Theory and research* (2nd ed.). Thousand Oaks, CA: Sage.

Olson, D. R., & Filby, N. (1972). On the comprehension of active and passive sentences. *Cognitive Psychology, 3*, 361–381. doi:10.1016/0010-0285(72)90013-8

Olson, J. C., Toy, D. R., & Dover, P. A. (1978). Mediating effects of cognitive responses to advertising on cognitive structure. *Advances in Consumer Research, 5*, 72–78.

Olson, J. C., Toy, D. R., & Dover, P. A. (1982). Do cognitive responses mediate the effects of advertising content on cognitive structure? *Journal of Consumer Research, 9*, 245–262. doi:10.1086/208921

O'Neill, B. J. (1972). Definability as an index of word meaning. *Journal of Psycholinguistic Research, 1*, 287. doi:10.1007/BF01067784

Oprah free speech rocks. (1998, February 26). *CNN*. Retrieved from http://www. cnn.com

Opotow, S. (1990). Moral exclusion and injustice: An introduction. *Journal of Social Issues, 46*, 173–182. doi:10.1111/j.1540-4560.1990.tb00280.x

O'Quinn, J. M. (2001, July). Use of pathos and effective persuasion skills to win substantial verdicts. In Association of Trial Lawyers of America, *ATLA annual convention reference materials: Volume 1: Stalwarts* (pp. 1–7). Author.

Ortony, A., Clore, G. L., & Collins, A. (1988). *The cognitive structure of emotions*. New York, NY: Cambridge University Press.

Osborn, D. R. (1996). Beauty is as beauty does? Makeup and posture effects on physical attractiveness judgments. *Journal of Applied Social Psychology, 26*, 31–51. doi:10.1111/j.1559-1816.1996.tb01837.x

Ostermeier, T. H. (1967). Effects of type and frequency of reference upon perceived source credibility and attitude change. *Speech Monographs, 34*, 137–144. doi:10.1080/03637756709375533

Ottati, V., Terkildsen, N., & Hubbard, C. (1997). Happy faces elicit heuristic processing in a televised impression formation task: A cognitive tuning account. *Personality and Social Psychology Bulletin, 23*, 1144–1156. doi:10.1177/01461672972311003

Packel, L., & Spina, D. B. (1984). *Trial advocacy: A systematic approach*. Philadelphia, PA: ALI-ABA.

Packwood, W. T. (1974). Loudness as a variable in persuasion. *Journal of Counseling Psychology, 21*, 1–2. doi:10.1037/h0036065

Paivio, A. (1971). *Imagery and verbal processes*. New York, NY: Holt, Rinehart & Winston.

Paivio, A., & O'Neill, B. J. (1970). Visual recognition thresholds and dimensions of word meaning. *Perception & Psychophysics, 8*, 273–275. doi:10.3758/BF03212591

Pallak, S. R. (1983). Salience of a communicator's physical attractiveness and persuasion: A heuristic versus systematic processing interpretation. *Social Cognition, 2*, 158–170. doi:10.1521/soco.1983.2.2.158

Pallak, S. R., Murroni, E., & Koch, J. (1983). Communicator attractiveness and expertise, emotional versus rational appeals, and persuasion: A heuristic versus systematic processing interpretation. *Social Cognition, 2*, 122–141. doi:10.1521/soco.1983.2.2.122

Palmer, M. T., & Simmons, K. B. (1995). Communicating intentions through nonverbal behaviors: Conscious and nonconscious encoding of liking. *Human Communication Research, 22*, 128–160. doi:10.1111/j.1468-2958.1995.tb00364.x

Patzer, G. L. (1983). Source credibility as a function of communicator physical attractiveness. *Journal of Business Research, 11*, 229–241. doi:10.1016/0148-2963(83)90030-9

Pearce, W. B., & Brommel, B. J. (1972). Vocalic communication in persuasion. *Quarterly Journal of Speech, 58*, 298–306. doi:10.1080/00335637209383126

Pechmann, C. (1992). Predicting when two-sided ads will be more effective than one-sided ads: The role of correlational and correspondent inferences. *Journal of Marketing Research, 29*, 441–453. doi:10.2307/3172710

Pellegrini, R. J. (1973). Impressions of the male personality as a function of beardedness. *Psychology: A Journal of Human Behavior, 10*, 29–33.

Pennington, N., & Hastie, R. (1986). Evidence evaluation in complex decision making. *Journal of Personality and Social Psychology, 51*, 242–258. doi:10.1037/0022-3514.51.2.242

Pennington, N., & Hastie, R. (1987). Explanation-based decision making. *Proceedings of the Ninth Annual Cognitive Science Society Meeting* (Vol. 9, pp. 682–690). Hillsdale, NJ: Erlbaum.

Pennington, N., & Hastie, R. (1988). Explanation-based decision making: Effects of memory structure on judgment. *Journal of Experimental Psychology: Learning, Memory, and Cognition, 14*, 521–533. doi:10.1037/0278-7393.14.3.521

Pennington, N., & Hastie, R. (1991). A cognitive theory of juror decision making: The story model. *Cardozo Law Review, 13*, 519–557.

Pennington, N., & Hastie, R. (1992). Explaining the evidence: Tests of the story model for juror decision making. *Journal of Personality and Social Psychology, 62*, 189–206. doi:10.1037/0022-3514.62.2.189

Pennington, N., & Hastie, R. (1993). Reasoning in explanation-based decision making. *Cognition, 49*, 123–163. doi:10.1016/0010-0277(93)90038-W

Pennycook, A. (1985). Actions speak louder than words: Paralanguage, communication, and education. *TESOL Quarterly, 19*, 259–281. doi:10.2307/3586829

Penrod, S., & Cutler, B. (1995). Witness confidence and witness accuracy: Assessing their forensic relation. *Psychology, Public Policy, and Law, 1*, 817–845. doi:10.1037/1076-8971.1.4.817

Perlman, P. (1986). Jury selection. In D. L. Rumsey (Ed.), *Master advocates' handbook* (pp. 47–60). St. Paul, MN: National Institute for Trial Advocacy.

Perlman, P. (1994). *Opening Statements*. Washington, DC: ATLA Press.

Perrin, L. T., Caldwell, H. M., & Chase, C. A. (2003). *The art & science of trial advocacy*. Cincinnati, OH: Anderson.

Perrin, P. G. (1965). *Writer's guide and index to English*. Glenview, CA: Scott, Foresman and Co.

Petty, R. E., & Cacioppo, J. T. (1977). Forewarning, cognitive responding, and resistance to persuasion. *Journal of Personality and Social Psychology, 35*, 645–655. doi:10.1037/0022-3514.35.9.645

Petty, R. E., & Cacioppo, J. T. (1979). Issue involvement can increase or decrease persuasion by enhancing message-relevant cognitive processes. *Journal of Personality and Social Psychology, 37*, 1915–1926. doi:10.1037/0022-3514.37.10.1915

Petty, R. E., & Cacioppo, J. T. (1986). *Communication and persuasion: Central and peripheral routes to attitude change*. New York, NY: Springer-Verlag.

Petty, R. E., Cacioppo, J. T., & Goldman, R. (1981). Personal involvement as a determinant of argument-based persuasion. *Journal of Personality and Social Psychology, 41,* 847–855. doi:10.1037/0022-3514.41.5.847

Petty, R. E., Cacioppo, J. T., & Kasmer, J. (1988). The role of affect in the elaboration likelihood model of persuasion. In L. Donohew, H. E. Sypher, & E. T. Higgins (Eds.), *Communication, social cognition, and affect* (pp. 117–146). Hillsdale, NJ: Erlbaum.

Petty, R. E., Cacioppo, J. T., & Schumann, D. (1983). Central and peripheral routes to advertising effectiveness: The moderating role of involvement. *Journal of Consumer Research, 10,* 135–146. doi:10.1086/208954

Petty, R. E., Cacioppo, J. T., Sedikedes, C., & Strathman, A. (1988). Affect and persuasion: A contemporary perspective. *Advances in Consumer Research. Association for Consumer Research, 15,* 209–212.

Petty, R. E., Cacioppo, J. T., Strathman, A. J., & Priester, J. R. (2005). To think or not to think: Exploring two routes to persuasion. In T. C. Brock & M. C. Green (Eds.), *Persuasion: Psychological insights and perspectives* (pp. 81–116). Thousand Oaks, CA: Sage.

Petty, R. E., Fleming, M. A., & White, P. H. (1999). Stigmatized sources and persuasion: Prejudice as determinant of argument scrutiny. *Journal of Personality and Social Psychology, 76,* 19–34. doi:10.1037/0022-3514.76.1.19

Petty, R. E., Gleicher, F., & Baker, S. M. (1991). Multiple roles of affect in persuasion. In J. Forgas (Ed.), *Emotion and social judgments* (pp. 181–200). Oxford, England: Pergamon.

Petty, R. E., Schumann, D. W., Richman, S. A., & Strathman, A. J. (1993). Positive mood and persuasion: Different roles for affect under high and low elaboration conditions. *Journal of Personality and Social Psychology, 64,* 5–20. doi:10.1037/0022-3514.64.1.5

Picheny, M. A., Durlach, N. I., & Braida, L. D. (1986). Speaking clearly for the hard of hearing II: Acoustic characteristics of clear and conversational speech. *Journal of Speech & Hearing Research, 29,* 434–446.

Picheny, M. A., Durlach, N. I., & Braida, L. D. (1989). Speaking clearly for the hard of hearing III: An attempt to determine the contribution of speaking rate to differences in intelligibility between clear and conversational speech. *Journal of Speech & Hearing Research, 32,* 600–603.

Pisoni, D. B., & Luce, P. A. (1987). Acoustic-phonetic representations in word recognition. *Cognition, 25,* 21–52. doi:10.1016/0010-0277(87)90003-5

Pitt, M. A., & Samuel, A. G. (2006). Word length and lexical activation: Longer is better. *Journal of Experimental Psychology: Human Perception and Performance, 32,* 1120–1135. doi:10.1037/0096-1523.32.5.1120

Planalp, S., DeFrancisco, V. L., & Rutherford, D. (1996). Varieties of cues to emotion in naturally occurring situations. *Cognition and Emotion, 10,* 137–154. doi:10.1080/026999396380303

Pople, H. E., Jr. (1982). Heuristic methods for imposing structure on ill-structured problems: The structuring of medical diagnostics. In P. Szolovits (Ed.), *Artificial intelligence in medicine* (pp. 119–190). Boulder, CO: Westview Press.

Posavac, E. J., Kattapong, K. R., & Dew, D. E., Jr. (1999). Peer-based interventions to influence health-related behaviors and attitudes: A meta-analysis. *Psychological Reports, 85,* 1179–1194. doi:10.2466/PR0.85.7.1179-1194

Postman, L. (1970). Effects of word frequency on acquisition and retention under conditions of free-recall learning. *The Quarterly Journal of Experimental Psychology, 22,* 185–195. doi:10.1080/00335557043000113

Powell v. Alabama, 287 U.S. 45 (1932).

Poythress, N. G., Bonnie, R. J., Hoge, S. K., Monahan, J., & Oberlander, L. B. (1994). Client abilities to assist counsel and make decisions in criminal cases: Findings from three studies. *Law and Human Behavior, 18,* 437–452. doi:10.1007/BF01499049

Preston, D. R. (1989). *Perceptual dialectology: Nonlinguists' views of areal linguistics.* Providence, RI: Foris.

Pryor, B., & Buchanan, R. W. (1984). The effects of a defendant's demeanor on juror perceptions of credibility and guilt. *Journal of Communication, 34,* 92–99. doi:10.1111/j.1460-2466.1984.tb02176.x

Putnam, U. B., & Street, R. L. (1984). The conception and perception of non-content speech performance: Implications for speech-accomodation theory. *International Journal of the Sociology of Language, 46,* 97–114.

Pyszczynski, T. A., & Wrightsman, L. S. (1981). The effects of opening statements on mock juror's verdicts in a simulated criminal trial. *Journal of Applied Social Psychology, 11,* 301–313. doi:10.1111/j.1559-1816.1981.tb00826.x

Ramsey, S. (1981). The kinesics of femininity in Japanese women. *Language Sciences, 3,* 104–123. doi:10.1016/S0388-0001(81)80016-2

Ratneshwar, S., & Chaiken, S. (1991). Comprehension's role in persuasion: The case of its moderating effect on the persuasive impact of source cues. *Journal of Consumer Research, 18,* 52–62. doi:10.1086/209240

Read, S. J. (1987). Constructing causal scenarios: A knowledge structure approach to causal reasoning. *Journal of Personality and Social Psychology, 52,* 288–302. doi:10.1037/0022-3514.52.2.288

Reskin, B. F., & Visher, C. A. (1986). The impacts of evidence and extralegal factors in jurors' decisions. *Law & Society Review, 20,* 423–438. doi:10.2307/3053582

Reyes, R. M., Thompson, W. C., & Bower, G. H. (1980). Judgmental biases resulting from differing availabilities of arguments. *Journal of Personality and Social Psychology, 39,* 2–12. doi:10.1037/0022-3514.39.1.2

Reynolds, A., & Paivio, A. (1968). Cognitive and emotional determinants of speech. *Canadian Journal of Psychology/Revue canadienne de psychologie, 22,* 164–175. doi:10.1037/h0082757

Reynolds, D. J., Jr., & Gifford, R. (2001). The sounds and sights of intelligence: A lens model channel analysis. *Personality and Social Psychology Bulletin, 27,* 187–200. doi:10.1177/0146167201272005

Rice, G. P. (1961). The meets and bounds of speech and law. *Communication Studies, 13,* 7–10.

Rich, J. (1975). Effects of children's physical attractiveness on teacher's evaluations. *Journal of Educational Psychology, 67,* 599–609. doi:10.1037/0022-0663.67.5.599

Richard, L. (1993). The lawyer types. *ABA Journal, 79,* 74–78.

Robinson, J., & McArthur, L. Z. (1982). Impact of salient vocal qualities on casual attributions for a speaker's behavior. *Journal of Personality and Social Psychology, 43,* 236–247. doi:10.1037/0022-3514.43.2.236

Robinson, S. L. (1996). Trust and breach of the psychological contract. *Administrative Science Quarterly, 41,* 574–599. doi:10.2307/2393868

Robinson, S. L., & Rousseau, D. M. (1994). Violating the psychological contract: Not the exception but the norm. *Journal of Organizational Behavior, 15,* 245–259. doi:10.1002/job.4030150306

Roelofs, A. (2002). Syllable structure effects turn out to be word length effects: Comment on Santiago et al. (2000). *Language and Cognitive Processes, 17,* 1–13. doi:10.1080/01690960042000139

Rogers, W. (2007). *Persuasion: Messages, receivers, and contexts.* New York, NY: Rowman & Littlefield.

Roggeveen, A. L., & Johar, G. V. (2002). Perceived source variability versus familiarity: Testing competing explanations for the truth effect. *Journal of Consumer Psychology, 12,* 81–91.

Rook, K. S. (1986). Encouraging preventive behavior for distant and proximal health threats: effects of vivid versus abstract information. *Journal of Gerontology, 41,* 526–534.

Rosenberg, S. W., Kahn, S., & Tran, T. (1991). Creating a political image: Shaping appearance and manipulating the vote. *Political Behavior, 13,* 345–367. doi:10.1007/BF00992868

Rosenthal, H. F., & Cochran, M. (1977, November 20). [Associated Press report]. Retrieved from http://www.lexisnexis.com/

Roskos-Ewoldsen, D. R., & Fazio, R. H. (1992). The accessibility of source likeability as a determinant of persuasion. *Personality and Social Psychology Bulletin, 18,* 19–25. doi:10.1177/0146167292181004

Rosnow, R. L. (1966). Whatever happened to the "Law of Primacy." *Journal of Communication, 16,* 10–31. doi:10.1111/j.1460-2466.1966.tb00013.x

Rosnow, R. L., & Robinson, E. (1967). *Experiments in persuasion.* New York, NY: Academic Press.

Ross, B. (1987). This is like that: The use of earlier problems and the separation of similarity effects. *Journal of Experimental Psychology: Learning, Memory, and Cognition, 13,* 629–639. doi:10.1037/0278-7393.13.4.629

Ross, L. (1977). The intuitive psychologist and his shortcomings: Distortions in the attribution process. In L. Berkowitz (Ed.), *Advances in experimental social psychology* (Vol. 10, pp. 173–240). Orlando, FL: Academic Press.

Ross, R. S. (1986). *Speech communication: Fundamentals and practice*. Englewood Cliffs, NJ: Prentice-Hall.

Rossiter, J. R., & Percy, L. (1978). Visual imaging ability as a mediator of advertising response. In K. H. Hunt (Ed.), *Advances in consumer research* (pp. 621–629). Ann Arbor, MI: Association for Consumer Research.

Rousseau, D. M. (1995). *Psychological contracts in organizations: Understanding written and unwritten agreements*. Thousand Oaks, CA: Sage.

Rousseau, D. M. (1998). The "problem" of the psychological contract considered. *Journal of Organizational Behavior, 19*, 665–671. doi:10.1002/(SICI)1099-1379 (1998)19:1+<665::AID-JOB972>3.0.CO;2-X

Rousseau, D. M. (2001). Schema, promise and mutuality: The building blocks of the psychological contract. *Journal of Occupational and Organizational Psychology, 74*, 511–541. doi:10.1348/096317901167505

Rubenstein, H., Garfield, L., & Millikan, J. A. (1970). Homographic entries in the internal lexicon. *Journal of Verbal Learning & Verbal Behavior, 9*, 487–494. doi:10.1016/S0022-5371(70)80091-3

Rubin, J. Z., & Brown, B. R. (1975). *The social psychology of bargaining and negotiation*. New York, NY: Academic Press.

Rubin, Z. (1970). Measurement of romantic love. *Journal of Personality and Social Psychology, 16*, 265–273. doi:10.1037/h0029841

Rucker, M., Taber, D., & Harrison, A. (1981). The effect of clothing variation on first impression of female job applicants: What to wear when. *Social Behavior and Personality, 9*, 53–64. doi:10.2224/sbp.1981.9.1.53

Rumelhart, D. E. (1975). Notes on a schema for stories. In D. G. Bobrow and A. Collins (Eds.), *Representation and understanding* (pp. 211–236). New York, NY: Academic Press.

Rumelhart, D. E. (1977). Understanding and summarizing brief stories. In D. LaBerge & S. J. Samuels (Eds.), *Basic processes in reading: Perception and comprehension* (pp. 265–303). Hillsdale, NJ: Erlbaum.

Rumelhart, D. E., & Siple, P. (1974). Process of recognizing tachistoscopically presented words. *Psychological Review, 81*, 99–118. doi:10.1037/h0036117

Rumsey, D. L. (1986). Selecting, preparing, and presenting the direct testimony of lay witnesses. In D. L. Rumsey (Ed.), *Master advocates' handbook* (pp. 73–103). St. Paul, MN: National Institute for Trial Advocacy.

Russo, R., & Grammatopoulou, N. (2003). Word length and articulatory suppression affect short-term and long-term recall tasks. *Memory & Cognition, 31*, 728–737. doi:10.3758/BF03196111

Ryan, E. B. (1979). Why do low-prestige language varieties persist? In H. Giles & R. N. St. Clair (Eds.), *Language and social psychology* (pp. 145–157). Oxford, England: Blackwell.

Ryan, E. B., Anas, A., & Gruneir, A. J. S. (2006). Evaluations of overhelping and underhelping Communication. *Journal of Language and Social Psychology, 25*, 97–107. doi:10.1177/0261927X05284485

Ryan, E. B., Hummert, M. L., & Boich, L. H. (1995). Communication predicaments of aging. *Journal of Language and Social Psychology, 14*, 144–166. doi:10.1177/0261927X95141008

Ryan, E. B., Kennaley, D. E., Pratt, M. W., & Shumovich, M. A. (2000). Evaluations by staff, residents, and community seniors of patronizing speech: Impact of passive, assertive, or humorous responses. *Psychology and Aging, 15*, 272–285. doi:10.1037/0882-7974.15.2.272

Sales, B. D., Elwork, A., & Alfini, J. J. (1977). Improving comprehension for jury instructions. In B. D. Sales (ed.), *Perspectives in law and psychology: The criminal justice system* (Vol. 1, pp. 23–90). New York, NY: Plenum Press.

Sales, B. D., & Krauss, D. A. (2011). *Psychology of law: Moving from 'is' to 'ought'.* Washington, DC: American Psychological Association. Manuscript in preparation.

Salter, D., & Haycock, V. (1972). Two studies on the process of negative modification. *Journal of Psycholinguistic Research, 1*, 337–348. doi:10.1007/BF01067787

Sampson, E. E., & Insko, C. A. (1964). Cognitive consistency and performance in the autokinetic situation. *The Journal of Abnormal and Social Psychology, 68*, 184–192. doi:10.1037/h0041242

Samuel, A. G. (1981). Phonemic restoration: Insights from a new methodology. *Journal of Experimental Psychology: General, 110*, 474–494. doi:10.1037/0096-3445.110.4.474

Samuel, A. G. (1996). Does lexical information influence the perceptual restoration of phonemes? *Journal of Experimental Psychology: General, 125*, 28–51. doi:10.1037/0096-3445.125.1.28

Sandys, M., & Dillehay, R. C. (1995). First-ballot votes, predeliberation dispositions, and final verdicts in jury trials. *Law and Human Behavior, 19*, 175–195. doi:10.1007/BF01499324

Santiago, J., McKay, D. G., Palma, A., & Rho, C. (2000). Sequential activation processes in producing words and syllables: Evidence from picture naming. *Language and Cognitive Processes, 15*, 1–44. doi:10.1080/016909600386101

Savin, H. B. (1963). Word-frequency effect and errors in the perception of speech. *Journal of the Acoustical Society of America, 35*, 200–206. doi:10.1121/1.1918432

Savitsky, J.C., & Sim, M.E. (1974). Trading emotions: Equity theory of reward and punishment. *Journal of Communication, 24*, 140–146. doi:10.1111/j.1460-2466.1974.tb00400.x

Sawusch, J. R., & Ganon, D. A. (1995). Auditory coding, cues, and coherence in phonetic perception. *Journal of Experimental Psychology: Human Perception and Performance, 21*, 635–652. doi:10.1037/0096-1523.21.3.635

Scarborough, D. L., Cortese, C., & Scarborough, H. S. (1977). Frequency and repetition effects in lexical memory. *Journal of Experimental Psychology: Human Perception and Performance, 3*, 1–17. doi:10.1037/0096-1523.3.1.1

Schachter, S., & Singer, J. E. (1962). Cognitive, social, and physiological determinants of emotional states. *Psychological Review, 69*, 379–399. doi:10.1037/h0046234

Schank, R. C. (1975). The structure of episodes in memory. In D. G. Bobrow & A. M. Collins (Eds.), *Representation and understanding: Studies in cognitive science* (pp. 237–272). New York, NY: Academic Press.

Schank, R. C. (1982). *Dynamic memory: A theory of learning in computers and people*. Cambridge, England: Cambridge University Press.

Schank, R. C. (1990). *Tell me a story: A new look at real and artificial memory*. New York, NY: Scribner.

Schank, R. C., & Abelson, R. P. (1977). *Scripts, plans, goals and understanding*. Hillsdale, NJ: Erlbaum.

Schank, R. C., & Berman, T. R. (2002). The pervasive role of stories in knowledge and action. In M. C. Green, J. J. Strange, & T. C. Brock (Eds.), *Narrative impact: Social and cognitive foundations* (pp. 287–313). Mahwah, NJ: Erlbaum.

Scheflen, A. E. (1964). The significance of posture in communication systems. *Psychiatry, 27*, 316–331.

Schenck-Hamun, W. J. (1978). The effects of dialectical similarity, stereotyping, and message agreement on interpersonal perception. *Human Communication Research, 5*, 15–26. doi:10.1111/j.1468-2958.1978.tb00619.x

Scherer, K. R. (1978). Personality inference from voice quality. *European Journal of Social Psychology, 8*, 467–487. doi:10.1002/ejsp.2420080405

Scherer, K. R. (1979a). Non-linguistic indicators of emotion and psychopathology. In C. E. Izard (Ed.), *Emotions in personality and psychopathology* (pp. 495–529). New York, NY: Plenum Press.

Scherer, K. R. (1979b). Personality markers in speech. In K. R. Scherer & H. Giles (Eds.), *Social markers in speech* (pp. 147–209). Cambridge, England: Cambridge University Press.

Scherer, K. R. (1981). Speech and emotional states. In J. Darbey (Ed.), *Speech evaluation in psychiatry* (pp. 189–220). New York, NY: Gruen & Stratton.

Scherer, K. R., Banse, R., Wallbott, H. G., & Goldbeck, T. (1991). Vocal cues in emotion encoding and decoding. *Motivation and Emotion, 15*, 123–148. doi:10.1007/BF00995674

Scherer, K. R., London, H., & Wolf, J. J. (1973). The voice of confidence: Paralinguistic cues and audience evaluation. *Journal of Research in Personality, 7*, 31–44. doi:10.1016/0092-6566(73)90030-5

Schlenker, B. R., Weigold, M. F., & Hallam, J. R. (1990). Self-serving attributions in social context: Effects of self-esteem and social pressure. *Journal of Personality and Social Psychology, 58*, 855–863. doi:10.1037/0022-3514.58.5.855

Schrager, S. (1999). *The trial lawyer's art*. Philadelphia, PA: Temple University Press.

Schreier, M., Groeben, N., & Blickle, G. (1995). The effects of (un-)fairness and (im-)politeness on the evaluations of argumentative communication. *Journal of Language and Social Psychology, 14*, 260–288. doi:10.1177/0261927X95143002

Schütz, A., & Tice, D. M. (1997). Associative and competitive indirect self-enhancement in close relationships moderated by trait self-esteem. *European Journal of Social Psychology, 27,* 257–273. doi:10.1002/(SICI)1099-0992(199705)27:3<257::AID-EJSP820>3.0.CO;2-1

Schwanenflugel, P. J., Harnishfeger, K. K., & Stowe, R. W. (1988). Context availability and lexical decisions for abstract and concrete words. *Journal of Memory and Language, 27,* 499–520. doi:10.1016/0749-596X(88)90022-8

Schwanenflugel, P. J., & Shoben, E. J. (1983). Differential context effects in the comprehension of abstract and concrete verbal materials. *Journal of Experimental Psychology: Learning, Memory, and Cognition, 9,* 82–102. doi:10.1037/0278-7393.9.1.82

Schweitzer, D., & Ginsburg, G. P. (1966). Factors of communicator credibility. In C. W. Backman & P. F. Secord (Eds.), *Problems in social psychology* (pp. 94–102). New York, NY: McGraw-Hill.

Seger, C. R., Smith, E. R., & Mackie, D. M. (2009). Subtle activation of a social categorization triggers group-level emotions. *Journal of Experimental Social Psychology, 45,* 460–467. doi:10.1016/j.jesp.2008.12.004

Segrin, C. (1993). The effects of nonverbal behavior on outcomes of compliance gaining attempts. *Communication Studies, 44,* 169–187.

Segrin, C. (1998). Interpersonal communication problems associated with depression and loneliness. In P. A. Anderson & I. K. Guerrero (Eds.), *Handbook of communication and emotion: Research, theory, applications, and contexts* (pp. 215–242). San Diego, CA: Academic Press.

Seifert, C. M., McKoon, G., Abelson, R. P., & Ratcliff, R. (1986). Memory connections between thematically similar episodes. *Journal of Experimental Psychology: Learning, Memory, and Cognition, 12,* 220–231. doi:10.1037/0278-7393.12.2.220

Semin, G. R., & Fiedler, K. (1988). The cognitive functions of linguistic categories in describing persons: Social cognition and language. *Journal of Personality and Social Psychology, 54,* 558–568. doi:10.1037/0022-3514.54.4.558

Semin, G. R., & Fiedler, K. (1989). Relocating attributional phenomena within a language-cognition interface: The case of actors' and observers' perspectives. *European Journal of Social Psychology, 19,* 491–508. doi:10.1002/ejsp.2420190602

Settle, R. B., & Gorden, L. L. (1974). Attribution theory and advertiser credibility. *Journal of Marketing Research, 11,* 181–185. doi:10.2307/3150556

Severance, L. J., Greene, E., & Loftus, E. (1984). Toward criminal jury instructions that jurors can understand. *Journal of Criminal Law & Criminology, 75,* 198–233. doi:10.2307/1143210

Severance, L. J., & Loftus, E. (1982). Improving the ability of jurors to comprehend and apply criminal jury instructions. *Law & Society Review, 17,* 153–197.

Shepard, C. A., Giles, H., & Le Poire, B. (2001). Communication accommodation theory. In W. P. Robinson & H. Giles (Eds.), *The new handbook of language and social psychology* (pp. 33–56). Chichester, UK: John Wiley & Sons.

Sherman, D. K., & Kim, H. S. (2002). Affective perseverance: The resistance of affect to cognitive invalidation. *Personality and Social Psychology Bulletin, 28*, 224–237. doi:10.1177/0146167202282008

Sherman, M. A. (1973). Bound to be easier: The negative prefix and sentence comprehension. *Journal of Verbal Learning & Verbal Behavior, 12*, 76–84. doi:10.1016/S0022-5371(73)80062-3

Shih, M., Pittinsky, T. L., & Ambady, N. (1999). Stereotype susceptibility: Identity salience and shifts in quantitative performance. *Psychological Science, 10*, 80–83. doi:10.1111/1467-9280.00111

Shintel, H., & Nusbaum, H. C. (2007). The sound of motion in spoken language: Visual information conveyed by acoustic properties of speech. *Cognition, 105*, 681–690. doi:10.1016/j.cognition.2006.11.005

Shintel, H., Nusbaum, H. C., & Okrent, A. (2006). Analog acoustic expression in speech communication. *Journal of Memory and Language, 55*, 167–177. doi:10.1016/j.jml.2006.03.002

Shore, L. M., & Tetrick, L. E. (1994). The psychological contract as an explanatory framework in the employment relationship. In C. Cooper & D. Rousseau (Eds.), *Trends in organizational behavior* (Vol. 1, pp. 91–109). New York, NY: Wiley.

Shuter, R. (1977). A field study of non-verbal communication in Germany, Italy and the United States. *Communication Monographs, 44*, 298–305. doi:10.1080/03637757709390141

Sia, T. L., Lord, C. G., Blessum, K. A., Thomas, J. C., & Lepper, M. R. (1999). Activation of exemplars in the process of assessing social category attitudes. *Journal of Personality and Social Psychology, 76*, 517–532. doi:10.1037/0022-3514.76.4.517

Siegman, A. W. (1978). The telltale voice: Nonverbal messages of verbal communication. In A. W. Siegman & S. Feldstein (Eds.), *Nonverbal behaviors and communication* (pp. 329–378). Hillsdale, NJ: Erlbaum.

Siegman, A. W. (1987). The telltale voice: Nonverbal messages of verbal communication. In A. W. Siegman & S. Feldstein (Eds.), *Nonverbal behaviors and communication* (2nd ed., pp. 351–433). Hillsdale, NJ: Erlbaum.

Siegman, A. W., & Pope, B. (1966). Ambiguity and verbal fluency in the TAT. *Journal of Consulting Psychology, 30*, 239–245. doi:10.1037/h0023374

Siegman, A. W., & Reynolds, M. (1982). Interviewer–interviewee non-verbal communications: An interactional approach. In M. Davis (Ed.), *Interaction rhythms: Periodicity in communicative behavior* (pp. 249–289). New York, NY: Human Sciences Press.

Simons, H. W. (2001). *Persuasion in society*. Thousand Oaks, CA: Sage.

Simons, H. W., Berkowitz, N. N., & Moyer, R. J. (1970). Similarity, credibility, and attitude change: A review and a theory. *Psychological Bulletin, 73*, 1–16. doi:10.1037/h0028429

Singer, A. (2000). 10 Common mistakes attorneys make with jurors. *Trial, 35*, 76–81.

Slobin, D. I. (1971). *Psycholinguistics*. Glenview, IL: Scott Foresman.

Small, D. A., Loewenstein, G., & Slovic, P. (2007). Sympathy and callousness: The impact of deliberative thought on donations to identifiable and statistical victims. *Organizational Behavior and Human Decision Processes, 102,*143–153. doi:10.1016/j.obhdp.2006.01.005

Small, D. A., & Simonsohn, U. (2007). Friends of victims: Personal experience and prosocial behavior. *Journal of Consumer Research, 35,* 532–542. doi:10.1086/527268

Smith, E. R. (1993). Social identity and social emotions: Toward new conceptualizations of prejudice. In D. M. Mackie & D. L. Hamilton (Eds.), *Affect, cognition, and stereotyping: Interactive processes in group perception* (pp. 297–315). San Diego, CA: Academic Press.

Smith, E. R., Seger, C. R., & Mackie, D. M. (2007). Can emotions be truly group level? Evidence regarding four conceptual criteria. *Journal of Personality and Social Psychology, 93,* 431–446. doi:10.1037/0022-3514.93.3.431

Smith, G. H., & Engel, R. (1968). Influence of a female model on perceived characteristics of an automobile. *Proceedings of the 76th Annual Convention of the American Psychological Association, 3,* 681–682.

Smith, R. C., & Dixon, T. R. (1971a). Effects of exposure: Does frequency determine the evaluative connotations of words? *Journal of Experimental Research in Personality, 5,* 124–126.

Smith, R. C., & Dixon, T. R. (1971b). Frequency and judged familiarity of meaningful words. *Journal of Experimental Psychology, 88,* 279–281.

Smith, V. L. (1991). Prototypes in the courtroom: Lay representations of legal concepts. *Journal of Personality and Social Psychology, 61,* 857–872. doi:10.1037/0022-3514.61.6.857

Snow, C. E., & Ferguson, C. A. (1977). *Talking to children: Language input and acquisition.* New York, NY: Cambridge University Press.

Snow, R. E. (1977). Individual differences and instructional theory. *Educational Researcher, 6,* 11–15.

Snyder, M., Grether, J., & Keller, K. (1974). Staring and compliance: A field experiment on hitch-hiking. *Journal of Applied Social Psychology, 4,* 165–170. doi:10.1111/j.1559-1816.1974.tb00666.x

Snyder, M., & Rothbart, M. (1971). Communicator attractiveness and opinion change. *Canadian Journal of Behavioural Science/Revue canadienne des sciences du comportement, 3,* 377–387. doi:10.1037/h0082280

Solomon, R. L., & Postman, L. (1952). Frequency of usage as a determinant of recognition thresholds for words. *Journal of Experimental Psychology, 43,* 195–201. doi:10.1037/h0054636

Sopory, P., & Dillard, J. P. (2002a). Figurative language and persuasion. In J. P. Dillard & M. Pfau (Eds.), *The persuasion handbook: Developments in theory and practice* (pp. 407–426). Thousand Oaks, CA: Sage.

Sopory, P., & Dillard, J. P. (2002b). Persuasive effects of metaphor: A meta-analysis. *Human Communication Research, 28,* 382–419. doi:10.1111/j.1468-2958.2002. tb00813.x

Spencer, S. J., Steele, C. M., & Quinn, D. M. (1999). Stereotype threat and women's math performance. *Journal of Experimental Social Psychology, 35,* 4–28. doi:10.1006/jesp.1998.1373

Spiecker, S. C., & Worthington, D. L. (2003). The influence of opening statement/closing argument organizational strategy in juror verdict and damage awards. *Law and Human Behavior, 27,* 437–456. doi:10.1023/A:1024041201605

Spoehr, K. T., & Smith, E. E. (1975). The role of orthographic and phonotactic rules in perceiving letter patterns. *Journal of Experimental Psychology: Human Perception and Performance, 104,* 21–34.

Sporer, S. L., Penrod, S., Read, D., & Cutler, B. (1995). Choosing, confidence, and accuracy: A meta-analysis of the confidence–accuracy relation in eyewitness identification studies. *Psychological Bulletin, 118,* 315–327. doi:10.1037/0033-2909. 118.3.315

Spray-Rite Services Corp. v. Monsanto Co., 684 F.2d 1226 (1982).

Stalans, L. J. (1993). Citizens' crime stereotypes, biased recall, and punishment preferences in abstract cases: The educative role of interpersonal sources. *Law and Human Behavior, 17,* 451–470. doi:10.1007/BF01044378

Stanfield, R. A., & Zwaan, R. A. (2001). The effect of implied orientation derived from verbal context on picture recognition. *Psychological Science, 12,* 153–156. doi:10.1111/1467-9280.00326

Stanners, R. F., Jastrzembski, J. E., & Westbrook, A. (1975). Frequency and visual quality in a word–nonword classification task. *Journal of Verbal Learning & Verbal Behavior, 14,* 259–264. doi:10.1016/S0022-5371(75)80069-7

Stark, K. (1972). Synonym responses to 100 free association stimuli. *Psychonomic Monograph Supplements, 4,* 269–274.

Steele, C. M., & Aronson, J. (1995). Stereotype threat and the intellectual test performance of African Americans. *Journal of Personality and Social Psychology, 69,* 797–811. doi:10.1037/0022-3514.69.5.797

Steele, R. with Kasindorf, M. (1977, April 4). CRIME: Texas Gothic. *Newsweek, 30.*

Steffen, V. J., & Eagly, A. H. (1985). Implicit theories about influence style: The effects of status and sex. *Personality and Social Psychology Bulletin, 11,* 191–205. doi:10.1177/0146167285112007

Stenneken, P., Conrad, M., & Jacobs, A. M. (2007). Processing of syllables in production and recognition tasks. *Journal of Psycholinguistic Research, 36,* 65–78. doi:10.1007/s10936-006-9033-8

Sternthal, B., Dholakia, R., & Leavitt, C. (1978). The persuasive effect of source credibility: Tests of cognitive response. *Journal of Consumer Research, 4,* 252–260. doi:10.1086/208704

Stiff, J. B. (1994). *Persuasive communication*. New York, NY: Guilford.

Stiff, J. B., Kim, H. J., & Ramesh, C. (1992). Truth biases and aroused suspicion in relational deception. *Communication Research, 19,* 326–345. doi:10.1177/009365092019003002

Stiff, J. B., & Miller, G. R. (1986). "Come to think of it . . . ": Interrogative probes, deceptive communication, and deception detection. *Human Communication Research, 12,* 339–357. doi:10.1111/j.1468-2958.1986.tb00081.x

Stiff, J. B., Miller, G. R., Sleight, C., Mongeau, P. A., Garlick, R., & Rogan, R. (1989). Explanations for visual cue primacy in judgments of honesty and deceit. *Journal of Personality and Social Psychology, 56,* 555–564. doi:10.1037/0022-3514.56.4.555

Stolz, W. S. (1967). A study of the ability to decode grammatically novel sentences. *Journal of Verbal Learning & Verbal Behavior, 6,* 867–873. doi:10.1016/S0022-5371(67)80151-8

Stotland, E., & Patchen, M. (1961). Identification and change in prejudice and authoritarianism. *The Journal of Abnormal and Social Psychology, 62,* 250–256. doi:10.1037/h0041445

Strawn, D. U., & Buchanan, R. W. (1976). Jury confusion: A threat to justice. *Judicature, 59,* 478–483.

Street, R. L., Jr. (1982). Evaluation of noncontent speech accommodation. *Language & Communication, 2,* 13–31. doi:10.1016/0271-5309(82)90032-5

Street, R. L., Jr. (1984). Speech convergence and speech evaluation in fact-finding interviews. *Human Communication Research, 11,* 139–169. doi:10.1111/j.1468-2958.1984.tb00043.x

Street, R. L., Jr., & Brady, R. M. (1982). Speech rate acceptance ranges as a function of evaluative domain, listener speech rate, and communication context. *Communication Monographs, 49,* 290–308. doi:10.1080/03637758209376091

Street, R. L., Jr., Brady, R. M., & Putman, W. B. (1983). The influence of speech rate stereotypes and rate similarity on listeners' evaluations of speakers. *Journal of Language and Social Psychology, 2,* 37–56. doi:10.1177/0261927X8300200103

Suedfeld, P., Bochner, S., & Matas, C. (1971). Petitioner's attire and petition signing by peace demonstrators: A field experiment. *Journal of Applied Social Psychology, 1,* 278–283. doi:10.1111/j.1559-1816.1971.tb00366.x

Suggs, D., & Sales, B. D. (1978). Using communication cues to evaluate prospective jurors during the voir dire. *Arizona Law Review, 20,* 629–642.

Swartz, T. (1984). Relationship between source expertise and source similarity in an advertising context. *Journal of Advertising, 13,* 49–55.

Swenson, R. A., Nash, D. L., & Roos, D. C. (1984). Source credibility and perceived expertness of testimony in a simulated child-custody case. *Professional Psychology: Research and Practice, 15,* 891–898. doi:10.1037/0735-7028.15.6.891

Swidler, A. (1986). Culture in action. *American Sociological Review, 51*, 273–286. doi:10.2307/2095521

Tajfel, H. (1981). *Human groups and social categories*. London, England: Cambridge University Press.

Tajfel, H., Billig, M. G., Bundy, R. P., & Flament, C. (1971). Social categorization and intergroup behavior. *European Journal of Social Psychology, 1*, 149–178. doi:10.1002/ejsp.2420010202

Tamborini, R., & Zillman, D. (1981). College students' perceptions of lecturers using humor. *Perceptual and Motor Skills, 52*, 427–432.

Tannen, D. (1987). Repetition in conversation: Towards a poetics of talk. *Language, 63*, 574–605. doi:10.2307/415006

Tannen, D. (1989). *Talking voices: Repetition, dialogue, and imagery in conversational discourse*. New York, NY: Cambridge University Press.

Tannenbaum, P. H., & Williams, F. (1968). Generation of active and passive sentences as a function of subject or object focus. *Journal of Verbal Learning & Verbal Behavior, 7*, 246–250. doi:10.1016/S0022-5371(68)80197-5

Tavris, C., & Aronson, E. (2007). *Mistakes were made (but not by me): Why we justify foolish beliefs, bad decisions, and hurtful acts*. Orlando, FL: Harcourt.

Taylor, D. W., Berry, P. C., & Block, C. H. (1958). Does group participation when using brainstorming facilitate or inhibit creativity? *Administrative Science Quarterly, 6*, 22–47.

Taylor, P. M. (1974). An experimental study of humor and ethos. *Southern Speech Communication Journal, 39*, 359–366.

Taylor, S. E. (1991). Asymmetrical effects of positive and negative events: The mobilization-minimization hypothesis. *Psychological Bulletin, 110*, 67–85. doi:10.1037/0033-2909.110.1.67

Taylor, S. E., & Thompson, S. C. (1982). Stalking the elusive "vividness" effect. *Psychological Review, 89*, 155–181. doi:10.1037/0033-295X.89.2.155

Tehan, G., & Tolan, G. A. (2007). Word length effects in long-term memory. *Journal of Memory and Language, 56*, 35–48. doi:10.1016/j.jml.2006.08.015

Teven, J. J., & Comadena, M. E. (1996). The effects of office aesthetic quality of students' perceptions of teacher crediblity and communicator style. *Communication Research Reports, 13*, 101–108. doi:10.1080/08824099609362076

The law: Murder in Texas. (1977, November). *Time*. Retrieved from http://www.time.com/time/magazine/article/0,9171,912041,00.html

Thorndyke, P. (1977). Cognitive structures in comprehension and memory of narrative discourse. *Cognitive Psychology, 9*, 77–110. doi:10.1016/0010-0285(77)90005-6

Thorndyke, P. W., & Yekovich, F. R. (1980). A critique of schema-based theories of human story memory. *Poetics, 9*, 23–49. doi:10.1016/0304-422X(80)90011-X

Tiersma, P. M. (1995). Dictionaries and death: Do capital jurors understand mitigation? *Utah Law Review, 1*, 20–21.

Tiersma, P. M. (1999). *Legal language*. Chicago, IL: University of Chicago Press.

Tiersma, P. M. (2001). A message in a bottle: Text, autonomy, and statutory interpretation. *Tulane Law Review, 76*, 431–482.

Tiersma, P. M. (2006). Some myths about legal language. *Law, Culture and the Humanities, 2*, 29–50. doi:10.1191/1743872106lw035oa

Toch, H. (1961). *Legal and criminal psychology*. New York, NY: Holt, Rinehart & Winston.

Trabasso, T., & van den Broek, P. (1985). Causal thinking and the representation of narrative events. *Journal of Memory and Language, 24*, 612–630. doi:10.1016/0749-596X(85)90049-X

Tracy, J. L., & Robins, R. W. (2007a). Emerging insights into the nature and function of pride. *Current Directions in Psychological Science, 16*, 147–150. doi:10.1111/j.1467-8721.2007.00493.x

Tracy, J. L., & Robins, R. W. (2007b). The prototypical pride expression: Development of a nonverbal behavior coding system. *Emotion, 7*, 789–801. doi:10.1037/1528-3542.7.4.789

Tracy, J. L., & Robins, R. W. (2007c). The psychological structure of pride: A tale of two facets. *Journal of Personality and Social Psychology, 92*, 506–525. doi:10.1037/0022-3514.92.3.506

Trafimow, D., & Finlay, K. A. (2001). Evidence for improved sensitivity of within-participants analyses in tests of the theory of reasoned action. *The Social Science Journal, 38*, 629–635. doi:10.1016/S0362-3319(01)00156-2

Treffner, P. J., Peter, M., & Kleidon, M. (2008). Gestures and phases: The dynamics of speech–hand communication. *Ecological Psychology, 20*, 32–64. doi:10.1080/10407410701766643

Tse, C.-S., & Altarriba, J. (2007). Testing the associative-link hypothesis in immediate serial recall: Evidence from word frequency and word imageability effects. *Memory, 15*, 675–690. doi:10.1080/09658210701467186

Tuppen, C. J. S. (1974). Dimension of communicator credibility: An oblique solution. *Speech Monographs, 41*, 253–260. doi:10.1080/03637757409375844

Turbak, N. J. (1998). Effective direct examination. *Trial, 34*, 68–73.

Turner, E. A., & Rommetveit, R. (1968). Focus of attention in recall of active and passive sentences. *Journal of Verbal Learning & Verbal Behavior, 7*, 543–548. doi:10.1016/S0022-5371(68)80047-7

Tversky, A., & Kahneman, D. (1974). Judgment under uncertainty: Heuristics and biases. *Science, 185*, 1124–1131. doi:10.1126/science.185.4157.1124

Uchanski, R. M. (2005). Clear speech. In D. B. Pisoni & R. E. Remez (Eds.), *The handbook of speech perception* (pp. 207–235). Malden, MA: Blackwell. doi:10.1002/9780470757024.ch9

Uchanski, R. M., Choi, S. S., Braida, L. D., Reed, C. M., & Durlach, N. I. (1996). Speaking clearly for the hard of hearing IV: Further studies of the role of speaking rate. *Journal of Speech & Hearing Research, 39*, 494–509.

Uphoff, R. J., & Wood, P. B. (1998). The allocation of decisionmaking between defense counsel and criminal defendant: An empirical study of attorney–client decisionmaking. *University of Kansas Law Review, 47*, 1–60.

Vaissière, J. (2005). Perception of intonation. In D. B. Pisoni & R. E. Remex (Eds.), *The handbook of speech perception* (pp. 236–263). Malden, MA: Blackwell. doi:10.1002/9780470757024.ch10

Vaes, J., Paladino, M. P., Castelli, L., Leyens, J.-P., & Giovanazzi, A. (2003). On the behavioral consequences of infra-humanization: The implicit role of uniquely human emotions in intergroup relations. *Journal of Personality and Social Psychology, 85*, 1016–1034. doi:10.1037/0022-3514.85.6.1016

Vaes, J., Paladino, M. P., & Leyens, J.-P. (2002). The lost e-mail: Prosocial reactions induced by uniquely human emotions. *British Journal of Social Psychology, 41*, 521–534. doi:10.1348/014466602321149867

Vaes, J., Paladino, M. P., & Leyens, J.-P. (2006). Priming uniquely human emotions and the in-group (but not the out-group) activates humanity concepts. *European Journal of Social Psychology, 36*, 169–181. doi:10.1002/ejsp.279

Vakoch, D. A., & Wurm, L. H. (1997). Emotional connotation in speech perception: Semantic associations in the general lexicon. *Cognition and Emotion, 11*, 337–349. doi:10.1080/026999397379827

Valentine, M. E., & Ehrlichman, H. (1979). Interpersonal gaze and helping behaviour. *The Journal of Social Psychology, 107*, 193–198. doi:10.1080/00224545.1979.9922698

Visher, C. A. (1987). Juror decision making: The importance of evidence. *Law and Human Behavior, 11*, 1–17. doi:10.1007/BF01044835

Vitevitch, M. S. (2002). Naturalistic and experimental analyses of word frequency and neighborhood density effects in slips of the ear. *Language and Speech, 45*, 407–434. doi:10.1177/00238309020450040501

Vitevitch, M. S., Stamer, M. K., & Sereno, J. A. (2008). Word length and lexical competition: Longer is the same as shorter. *Language and Speech, 51*, 361–383. doi:10.1177/0023830908099070

Vohs, K. D., & Heatherton, T. F. (2001). Self-esteem and threats to self: Implications for self-construals and interpersonal perceptions. *Journal of Personality and Social Psychology, 81*, 1102–1118. doi:10.1037/0022-3514.81.6.1103

Wachtler, J., & Counselman, E. (1981). When increased liking for a communicator decreases opinion change: An attribution analysis of attractiveness. *Journal of Experimental Social Psychology, 17*, 386–395. doi:10.1016/0022-1031(81)90045-7

Wagner, W. (1984). Social comparison of opinions: Similarity, ability, and the value-fact distinction. *Journal of Psychology: Interdisciplinary and Applied, 117*, 197–202. doi:10.1080/00223980.1984.9923677

Walker, I., & Hulme, C. (1999). Concrete words are easier to recall than abstract words: Evidence for a semantic contribution to short-term serial recall. *Journal of Experimental Psychology: Learning, Memory, and Cognition, 25,* 1256–1271. doi:10.1037/0278-7393.25.5.1256

Walster, E., Aronson, E., & Abrahams, D. (1966). On increasing the persuasiveness of a low prestige communicator. *Journal of Experimental Social Psychology, 2,* 325–342. doi:10.1016/0022-1031(66)90026-6

Wang, M. D. (1970). The role of syntactic complexity as a determiner of comprehensibility. *Journal of Verbal Learning & Verbal Behavior, 9,* 398–404. doi:10.1016/S0022-5371(70)80079-2

Warren, I. D. (1969). The effect of credibility in sources of testimony on audience attitudes toward speaker and message. *Speech Monographs, 36,* 456–458. doi:10.1080/03637756909375639

Washburn, P. V., & Hakel, M. D. (1973). Visual cues and verbal content as influences on impressions formed after simulated employment interviews. *Journal of Applied Psychology, 58,* 137–141. doi:10.1037/h0035410

Wason, P. C. (1965). The contents of plausible denial. *Journal of Verbal Learning & Verbal Behavior, 4,* 7–11. doi:10.1016/S0022-5371(65)80060-3

Wearing, A. J. (1973). The recall of sentences of varying length. *Australian Journal of Psychology, 25,* 155–161. doi:10.1080/00049537308255842

Weisfeld, G. E., & Linkey, H. E. (1985). Dominance displays as indicators of social success motive. In J. F. Dovidio & S. L. Ellyson (Eds.), *Power, dominance, and nonverbal behavior* (pp. 109–128). New York, NY: Springer-Verlag.

Weiss, F. R. (1959). How the lawyer uses rhetoric. *Communication Quarterly, 7,* 6–15. doi:10.1080/01463375909389515

Weiss, W., & Fine, B. J. (1956). The effect of induced aggressiveness on opinion change. *Journal of Abnormal and Social Psychology, 52,* 109–114. doi:10.1037/h0043948

Weitz, S. (1976). Sex differences in nonverbal communication. *Sex Roles, 2,* 175–184. doi:10.1007/BF00287250

Weld, H. P., & Danzig, E. R. (1940). A study of the way in which a verdict is reached by a jury. *The American Journal of Psychology, 53,* 518–536. doi:10.2307/1417631

Weld, H. P., & Roff, M. (1938). A study in the formation of opinion based upon legal evidence. *The American Journal of Psychology, 51,* 609–628. doi:10.2307/1415696

Wells, R. V. (1988). *Successful trial techniques of expert practitioners.* Colorado Springs, CO: Shepard's/McGraw-Hill.

Werner, C. M., Peterson-Lewis, S., & Brown, B. B. (1989). Inferences about homeowners' sociability: Impact of Christmas decorations and other cues. *Journal of Environmental Psychology, 9,* 279–296. doi:10.1016/S0272-4944(89)80010-6

Whaley, B. B. (1997). Perceptions of rebuttal analogy: Politeness and implications for persuasion. *Argumentation and Advocacy, 33,* 161–169.

Whaley, B. B. (1998). Evaluations of rebuttal analogy users: Ethical and competence considerations. *Argumentation, 12,* 351–365. doi:10.1023/A:1007783009424

Whaley, B. B., & Smith, L. (2000). Rebuttal analogy in persuasive messages: Communicator likeability and cognitive responses. *Journal of Language and Social Psychology, 19,* 66–84. doi:10.1177/0261927X00019001004

Whaley, C. P. (1978). Word–nonword classification time. *Journal of Verbal Learning & Verbal Behavior, 17,* 143–154. doi:10.1016/S0022-5371(78)90110-X

Whitehead, J. L., Jr. (1968). Factors of source credibility. *The Quarterly Journal of Speech, 54,* 59–63. doi:10.1080/00335636809382870

Whitehead, J. L., Jr. (1971). Effects of authority-based assertion on attitude and credibility. *Speech Monographs, 38,* 311–315. doi:10.1080/03637757109375723

Widgery, R. N. (1974). Sex of receiver and physical attractiveness of source as determinants of initial credibility perception. *Western Speech Communication Journal, 38,* 13–17.

Wiener, F. M., & Miller, G. A. (1946). *Some characteristics of human speech.* In Office of Scientific Research and Development Washington DC (Ed.), Transmission and reception of sounds under combat conditions. Summary Technical Report of Division 17, NDRC, pp. 58–68. Washington, DC: NDRC. As reported in Vitevitch, M. S., Stamer, M. K., & Sereno, J. A. (2008). Word length and lexical competition: Longer is the same as shorter. *Language and Speech, 51,* 361–383.

Wilder, D. A., & Simon, A. F. (1996). Incidental and integral affect as triggers of stereotyping. In R. M. Sorrentino & E. T. Higgins (Eds.) *Handbook of motivation and cognition: The interpersonal context* (Vol. 3, pp. 397–419). New York, NY: Guilford.

Wilensky, R. (1983). Story grammars versus story points. *Behavioral and Brain Sciences, 6,* 579–623. doi:10.1017/S0140525X00017520

Williams, J. P. (1993). Comprehension of students with and without learning disabilities: identification of narrative themes and idiosyncratic text representations. *Journal of Educational Psychology, 85,* 631–641. doi:10.1037/0022-0663.85.4.631

Williams, K. D., Bourgeois, M. J., & Croylet, R. T. (1993). The effects of stealing thunder in criminal and civil trials. *Law and Human Behavior, 17,* 597–609. doi:10.1007/BF01044684

Wilson, E. J., & Sherrell, D. L. (1993). Source effects in communication and persuasion research: A meta-analysis of effect size. *Journal of the Academy of Marketing Science, 21,* 101–112. doi:10.1007/BF02894421

Wilson, J. (2007). Scientific laws, hypotheses, and theories [Web log post]. Retreived from http://wilstar.com/theories.htm

Winograd, E., & Geis, N. F. (1974). Semantic encoding and recognition memory— a test of encoding variability theory. *Journal of Experimental Psychology, 102,* 1061–1068. doi:10.1037/h0036386

Wood, W., & Kallgren, C. A. (1988). Communicator attributes and persuasion: Recipients' access to attitude-relevant information in memory. *Personality and Social Psychology Bulletin, 14,* 172–182. doi:10.1177/0146167288141017

Wood, W., Kallgren, C. A., & Priesler, R. M. (1985). Access to attitude-relevant information in memory as a determinant of persuasion: The role of message attributes. *Journal of Experimental Social Psychology, 21*, 73–85. doi:10.1016/0022-1031(85)90007-1

Woodall, W. G., & Burgoon, J. K. (1981). The effects of nonverbal synchrony on message comprehension and persuasiveness. *Journal of Nonverbal Behavior, 5*, 207–223. doi:10.1007/BF00987460

Woodall, W. G., & Burgoon, J. K. (1983). Talking fast and changing attitudes: A critique and clarification. *Journal of Nonverbal Behavior, 8*, 126–142. doi:10.1007/BF00986999

Woodside, A. G., & Davenport, J. W., Jr. (1974). The effect of salesman similarity and expertise on consumer purchasing behavior. *Journal of Marketing Research, 11*, 198–202. doi:10.2307/3150562

Workman, J. E., Johnson, K. K., & Hadeler, B. (1993). The influence of clothing on students' interpretative and extended inferences about a teaching assistant. *College Student Journal, 27*, 119–128.

Wright, P. (1975). Factors affecting cognitive resistance to advertising. *Journal of Consumer Research, 2*, 1–9. doi:10.1086/208610

Wurm, L. H., & Vakoch, D. A. (2000). The adaptive value of lexical connotation in speech perception. *Cognition and Emotion, 14*, 177–191. doi:10.1080/026999300378923

Wyer, R. S., & Adaval, R. (2003). Message reception skills in social communication. In J. O. Greene & B. R. Burleson (Eds.), *Handbook of communication and social interaction skills* (pp. 291–355). Mahwah, NJ: Erlbaum.

Yzerbyt, V. Y., & Leyens, J. P. (1991). Requesting information to form an impression: The influence of valence and confirmatory status. *Journal of Experimental Social Psychology, 27*, 337–356. doi:10.1016/0022-1031(91)90030-A

Zadny, J., & Gerard, H. B. (1974). Attributed intentions and informational selectivity. *Journal of Experimental Social Psychology, 10*, 34–52. doi:10.1016/0022-1031(74)90055-9

Zaidel, S. F., & Mehrabian, A. (1969). The ability to communicate and infer positive and negative attitudes facially and vocally. *Journal of Experimental Research in Personality, 3*, 233–241.

Zajonc, R. B. (1968). The attitudinal effects of mere exposure. *Journal of Personality and Social Psychology, 9*(2 pt. 2), 1–27. doi:10.1037/h0025848

Zajonc, R. B. (1980). Feeling and thinking. Preferences need no inferences. *American Psychologist, 35*, 151–175. doi:10.1037/0003-066X.35.2.151

Zanuck, R. D., Brown, D., & Alves, J. (Producers), & Szwarc, J. & Alves, J. (Directors). (1978). *Jaws 2* [Motion Picture]. Okaloosa County, FL: Universal Pictures.

Zebrowitz, L. A., & McDonald, S. M. (1991). The impact of litigants' baby-facedness and attractiveness on adjudications in small claims courts. *Law and Human Behavior, 15*, 603–623. doi:10.1007/BF01065855

Zhao, H., Wayne, S. J., Glibkowski, B. C., & Bravo, J. (2007). The impact of psychological contract break on work-related outcomes: A meta-analysis. *Personnel Psychology, 60*, 647–680. doi:10.1111/j.1744-6570.2007.00087.x

Zimbardo, P. G., Weisenberg, M., Firestone, I., & Levy, B. (1965). Communicator effectiveness in producing public conformity and private attitude change. *Journal of Personality, 33*, 233–255. doi:10.1111/j.1467-6494.1965.tb01384.x

INDEX

ELM. *See* Elaboration likelihood model
Embedded sentences, 56
Emblems, 117
Emotion(s)
    appropriate for courtroom, 149
    and attitude, 83
    attorney communication of client's, 138
    in case theme, 191–192
    and changes in tone, 97
    in decision making, 196–199
    in facial expression, 150
    juror perceptions of, 149–150
    secondary, 154
Emotional homophones, 96
Emotional insincerity, 37
Emotional intensity, 77
Emotional prosody, 89, 95–96
Emotional responses, 132, 169–170
Emotional tone, 94–95
Emphasis
    on eyes, 130–131
    pauses in speech for, 102
    purposeful movement for, 110, 116
    repetition for, 190–191
    of syllables, 93
    vocal volume for, 93
Empirical studies, 171
Environment, 132. *See also* Courtroom environment
Environmental factors, 55
Episodes
    hierarchy of, 172, 173
    in story structure, 183
Ethical code, 18
Ethical guidelines, 6
Evidence
    decision making about, 180
    emotionally laden, 197
    narrative organization of, 165–166
    presented in story form, 174
    promises about, 33–34
    recognition of, 179–180
    source of, 43
    and story connections, 161–162
    and story coverage, 177–178
    in story model, 176–177
    in trial strategy, 205–206
    use of subterfuge to present, 35
Exemplars, 173

Exhaustion principle, 187–188
Exhibits, 195
Expectancies, 35–36, 186
Expectancy model of communication, 124
Expectations
    about eye gaze, 123–124
    and framing, 153
    normative, 149
Expertise
    and likability, 25
    in persuasiveness, 41–43
    of scientific testimony, 211
Explanation-based model, 176–180, 182–183
Expository discourse, 57–58
External plausibility, 163, 164
External validity, 40, 207–210
Eye contact
    as kinesic communication, 111
    makeup to emphasize, 130–131
    strategies for, 122–124
Eye gaze, 123–124, 147
Eyeglasses, 112

Face
    clear view of, 112, 129–131
    touching of, 121–122
Facial expression
    in communication, 129
    drawing attention to, 128–129
    emotion in, 150
Facial hair, 112, 130
Factor analysis scales, 208
Facts, 162, 167
Fairness, 18
Fair trial, right to, 5–6, 206–207
Familiar language, 65–67
Farr, Stan, 3, 4
Fast speech, 98–103
Feldman, M. S., 175–176
Female voices, 98
Femininity, 131
Fidgeting, 115–116, 130
Fiedler, K., 72
Field data, 208–209
Figurative speech
    ability to grasp, 54
    effects of, 51–52
    persuasiveness of, 79–80

and trust, 25
and vulnerability, 15
Linear sentences, 59–61
Linguistic specificity, 77
Liska, J., 208
Literal-mindedness, 80
Literary perspective, 170
Literary references, 166
Logic, 164–165
Long hair, 130
Long-term memory, 65
Longwindedness, 55–56
Long words, 61–63
Loudness, 92–94
Low self-esteem, 31
Low voices, 98

Makeup, 130–131
Mandelbaum, J., 170
Manipulation, 37
Manners, 14–15
Matched-guise methodology, 103
McDonald, S. M., 40
Measurement, 213
Mechanistic dehumanization, 153
Mehrabian, A., 132
Memory
    and likability, 22
    long-term, 65
    scripts in, 175
    short-term, 64, 65
    and storytelling, 161
    and themes, 190–191
    of words, 64–65
Men, 114, 144
Mental states, 183
Message relevance, 27–28
Metaphors, 79–80
Methodology(-ies)
    limitations of, 206–210, 214
    matched-guise, 103
    in mock jury research, 188–189,
        207–209
    phonemic restoration, 63
Milgram, S., 46
Minitheories, 35–36
Mock jury research
    limitations of, 40, 125–126
    methodologies for, 188–189
    realism in, 208–209
    validity problems in, 40, 207–209

Model Rules of Professional
    Conduct, 143
Monotone, 96–97
Monotone voice, 96–97
Mood, 150–151
Moral code, 18, 192
Mortality salience, 197
Motion information, 100–101
Moustaches, 112, 130
Movement. *See* Body movement
Multiple themes, 168, 192–193
Murray, I. R., 50

Narrative format, 174–175
Narratives, 184, 194. *See also*
    Storytelling
Negative behaviors, 29–30
Negative descriptions, 52, 81–84
Negative emotional messages, 198
Negative feelings, 138
Negative sentences, 60–61
Negative stereotypes, 83–84
Neighborhood density, 63
Nervousness, 115–116
Nonimmediacy, 142–143
Nonopinionated statements, 143
Nonverbal communications
    to convey liking, 143
    dress as, 127–128
    of pride, 147
    purposeful, 116–117
Nonverbal cues
    as deception indicators, 32–33
    in likability, 39–40
    operationalization of, 210
Normative expectations, 149
Notetaking, 124

Objectivity, 32
One-sided arguments, 198–199
Opening statements, 201
Operationalization
    in future research, 210
    in storytelling, 170–171
    of word length, 61–62
Opinionated statements, 143
Organizational structure, 174–175,
    177–178
Outgroups, 151–156
Overconfidence, 45–46
Overstatement, 33

Syllables
emphasis of, 93
inflection of, 95–96
number of, 61–65
in verbal strategies, 50, 86
Symbols, 166
Sympathies, 38
Sympathy, 148
Synonyms, 74–75
Syntactic development, 54
Syntax, causal, 185–186
Systematic model of persuasion,
24–25, 212

Taglines, 165–166
Taking notes, 124
Taylor, S. E., 77
Technical language, 67–68. *See also*
Legal language
Teleology, 165
Temporal organization, 174–175, 188
10-year-old level of language, 54–55
Tension, 115
Terminable unit (T-unit), 58
Terror management theory, 197
Testimony, expert, 211
Tests, 211
Thematic frameworks, 189–190
Theme of case
allegorical, 166
in causal reasoning model, 185
and comprehension, 190
emotions in, 191–192
interpersonal, 185
in jury decision making, 189–190
and memory, 190–191
multiple, 168, 192–193
role, 185
sources for, 191
subthemes, 168
Theory-driven studies, 212–213
Theory of case
attorney construction of, 182–189
benefits of, to jurors, 175–189
key points of case in, 174
organization of case with, 174–175
relationship of, to story, 160–161
in relation to the story, 171–175
and storytelling, 171–175

strategies for development of,
162–165
Thesaurus use, 74–76
Thompson, S. C., 77
Thorndyke, P. W., 174
Tiersma, P. M., 56–57, 104
Time, 64, 174–175
Timelines, 188
To Kill a Mockingbird (H. Lee), 7
Tone
changes in, 96–97
emotional, 94–95
in paralinguistics, 90
in speechifying, 102
Transfer-of-affect, 22
Transportation, 193–194
Transportation-imagery model
in future research, 212
overview of, 193–197
storytelling in, 192
strategies with, 198–202
Trial advocacy, 3–8, 205–215
case study, 3–5
future directions for research on,
210–215
importance of, 5–8
methodological problems with
research on, 206–210
Trial commentators, 9
Trust
in attorney-client relationship,
138–145
and likability, 14, 25
and promise breaking, 34
Trustworthiness
and credibility, 41, 43, 208
dimensions of, 31–32
and facial hair, 130
and humor, 47
and likability, 25
strategies of, 32–36
Truth bias heuristic, 38
Truth effect, 191
Truthfulness strategies, 17–18,
32–33
T-unit (terminable unit), 58
TV dramas, 205
Tversky, A., 152
Two-sided arguments, 198–199

ABOUT THE AUTHORS

Jessica D. Findley, JD, PhD, is law clerk to the Honorable Christopher Staring, Pima County, Arizona Juvenile Court. Her scholarly interests focus on the use of social science research and theory to understand and improve civil and criminal law.

Bruce D. Sales, PhD, JD, is the Virginia L. Roberts Professor of Criminal Justice and director of graduate studies in the department of criminal justice at Indiana University, Bloomington. His recent books include *Courtroom Modifications for Child Witnesses: Law and Science in Forensic Evaluations* (with S. R. Hall, 2008); *Sex Offending: Causal Theories to Inform Research, Prevention, and Treatment* (with J. D. Stinson & J. D. Becker, 2008); *Scientific Jury Selection* (with J. D. Lieberman, 2007); *Criminal Profiling: Developing an Effective Science and Practice* (with S. J. Hicks, 2006; Italian translation, 2009); and *Experts in Court: Reconciling Law, Science, and Professional Knowledge* (with D. W. Shuman, 2005; Korean translation, 2009). He is the first editor of the journals *Law and Human Behavior* and *Psychology, Public Policy, and Law*, as well as a fellow of the American Psychological Association (APA) and the Association for Psychological Science. He is an elected member of the American Law Institute and twice served as president of the American Psychology-Law Society (Division 41 of APA). He received the Award for Distinguished Contributions to Psychology and Law from the American Psychology-Law Society, the Award for Distinguished Professional Contributions to Public Service from APA, and an honorary doctor of science degree from the City University of New York for being the "founding father of forensic psychology as an academic discipline."